ARGENTINA NOIR

SUNY series in Latin American and Iberian Thought and Culture
JORGE J. E. GRACIA AND ROSEMARY G. FEAL, EDITORS

# ARGENTINA NOIR

## NEW MILLENNIUM CRIME NOVELS IN BUENOS AIRES

CYNTHIA SCHMIDT-CRUZ

Cover image: Photograph #175 of the Obelisk in Buenos Aires. Used with permission by Silvina Frydlewsky

Published by State University of New York Press, Albany

© 2019 State University of New York

All rights reserved

No part of this book may be used or reproduced in any manner whatsoever without written permission. No part of this book may be stored in a retrieval system or transmitted in any form or by any means including electronic, electrostatic, magnetic tape, mechanical, photocopying, recording, or otherwise without the prior permission in writing of the publisher.

For information, contact State University of New York Press, Albany, NY
www.sunypress.edu

**Library of Congress Cataloging-in-Publication Data**

Names: Schmidt-Cruz, Cynthia, author
Title: Argentina noir : new millennium crime novels in Buenos Aires
Description: Albany : State University of New York Press, [2019] | Series: SUNY series in Latin American and Iberian thought and culture | Includes bibliographical references and index.
Identifiers: ISBN 9781438473031 (hardcover) | ISBN 9781438473048 | ISBN 9781438473055 (e-book)
Further information is available at the Library of Congress.

10 9 8 7 6 5 4 3 2 1

# CONTENTS

ACKNOWLEDGMENTS, vii

INTRODUCTION. ARGENTINA NOIR, ix

    From the Whodunit to the *Novela Negra*: The Poetics of Crime Fiction, xiv

    Development of the Genre in Argentina, xviii

    An Overview of Current Practitioners in Argentina, xxviii

    Toward a Characterization of and Approach to the Genre in Argentina, xxxix

1. COMBATTING ORGANIZED CRIME AND INSTITUTIONAL COMPLICITY, WITH A SENTIMENTAL SUBTEXT, 1

    Trafficking Enabled by Institutional Corruption, 2

    A Sentimental Cop Goes Up against Human Traffickers: *Los hombres te han hecho mal* by Ernesto Mallo, 6

    The Foul Breezes of Buenos Aires: *Ciudad Santa* by Guillermo Orsi, 26

2. THE PRESIDENT AND ALL HIS MEN: WATCHDOG JOURNALISTS TACKLE CORRUPTION DURING THE MENEM PRESIDENCY, 51

    The Menem Presidency and the Neoliberal Era, 52

    "Novelas menemistas": *El vuelo de la reina* by Tomás Eloy Martínez and *El muerto indiscreto* by Rubén Correa, 55

3. TERRORIST ATTACKS ON JEWISH BUENOS AIRES AND THE MYSTERIOUS DEATH OF ALBERTO NISMAN, 85

    The Hapless Investigation of the Attack on the AMIA, 86

    A Sexy Journalist Cracks an Anti-Semitic Plot: *Asalto al paraíso* by Marcos Aguinis, 91

    The Rogue Spy and the Demise of the Special Prosecutor: *El fiscal* by R. S. Pratt, 108

4. TROUBLE IN THE COUNTRY CLUB, OR "LOS NUEVOS RICOS TAMBIÉN LLORAN", 121

    The Gated Community as Emblematic of the Neoliberal Era, 123

    Disintegration of Family Ties: *Retrato de familia con muerta* by Raúl Argemí, 127

The High Cost of Keeping Up Appearances: *Las viudas de los jueves* by Claudia Piñeiro,   142

Regendering the Genre: *Betibú* by Claudia Piñeiro,   156

The Gated Community: A Disturbing Message,   172

5. THE "OTHER SIDE": THE URBAN POOR AND THE CRIME NOVEL,   175

No Longer a Middle-Class Society,   175

Collateral Damage of Consumer Society: *Puerto Apache* by Juan Martini,   179

Fatal Attraction: *La fragilidad de los cuerpos* by Sergio Olguín,   197

CONCLUSION. SOCIAL COLLAPSE AND HUMAN CONNECTIONS,   221

Territorialization and Transformation,   223

The Sentimental Subtext,   233

NOTES,   237

WORKS CITED,   255

INDEX,   281

# ACKNOWLEDGMENTS

WHEN I WAS FINISHING MY BOOK ABOUT FEMALE CHARACTERS IN THE SHORT stories of Julio Cortázar, I thought that it would be impossible to find another research topic that intrigued me as much as that one. Fortunately, I was wrong. I turned my attention to Argentine crime fiction and never looked back! It has taken me well over a decade to complete this book, but I have enjoyed every minute (well, almost every minute) of this voyage of discovery. I loved dedicating time to reading novel after novel—my primary sources. My background work on the development and theory of the genre as well as my attention to sociological studies about issues that the novels engage proved to be fascinating. Especially rewarding and exciting were my trips to Argentina to meet and talk with authors and familiarize myself with the rich and varied contemporary scene of the *novela negra* along with the reality that inspires it. Particularly memorable were my interactions with writers Ernesto Mallo, María Inés Krimer, Mercedes Rosende, Miguel Ángel Molfino, Guillermo Orsi, Osvaldo Aguirre, Claudia Piñeiro, Mempo Giardinelli, Leopoldo Brizuela, Mercedes Giuffré, Carlos Salem, Leonardo Oyola, Carlos Balmaceda, Juan Carrá, and Javier Chiabrando. I was also fortunate to correspond with Raúl Correa and to meet Tomás Eloy Martínez before his death.

Heartfelt thanks go to the friends and colleagues at the University of Delaware who have supported me in many ways. First, a huge debt of gratitude goes to my dear friend Laura Salsini, who read the entire first version of my manuscript and provided many helpful suggestions to improve it. I also thank Susan McKenna and Annette Giesecke for their support and friendship, and Deborah Steinberger and Gladys Ilarregui for their help with translations. A special thanks to Persephone Braham for her encouragement and belief in this project. Persephone's groundbreaking book on the *neopolicial* with a focus on its manifestations in Mexico and Cuba served as an example and inspiration. A big thank you to Lisa Schulz for her invaluable assistance with the index and word processing challenges as well her friendship and good nature. Turning to colleagues outside of UD, I am very grateful to David Sheinin, who read an early version of chapter 3 and gave me excellent editing advice. My gratitude goes out to Osvaldo di

Paolo Harrison, who expressed faith in my project at a difficult moment, and whose study of the *policial palimpséstico* provided an important model for approaching novels that incorporate real-life news stories. I am also grateful to Glen Close and Shelley Godsland, whose studies of Hispanic crime fiction provided fundamental directions for various aspects of this project. Thanks are also due to the anonymous readers contracted by SUNY, whose reports contained valuable advice that led to significant improvements in my text.

SUNY has been a great press to work with. I thank the acquisitions editors, Beth Bouloukos, who recognized the value of my project and invited me to submit my manuscript, and Rebecca Colesworthy, who saw the acquisition process to completion. I am grateful to Rebecca for helping me craft the abstract and reframe my introductory chapter, as well as for shepherding my project through the final acquisition stages. My thanks also go to the production editor, Jenn Bennett-Genthner, for her excellent work overseeing the many tasks related to this book's production.

For the cover art, I am thrilled to have a photograph by the highly skilled photojournalist Silvina Frydlewsky. I had the good luck to get to know Silvina when we collaborated on a project featuring photography and poetry addressing the 2001 crisis in Argentina, and it is a privilege to feature her striking photo of the Obelisk at nightfall on this book's cover.

I feel fortunate to work at a university that provides generous support for research, and I would like to express my gratitude to the units in the University of Delaware that have extended financial support for my research and conference-participation travel. These include the College of Arts and Sciences; the Department of Languages, Literatures, and Cultures; the Center for Global and Area Studies; the Institute for Global Studies; and the General University Research Program.

I thank the journal publishers that granted me permission to republish revised versions of two articles. An earlier version of chapter 2 was published as "The Argentine *Novela Negra* Critiques the 1990s in *El vuelo de la reina* by Tomás Eloy Martínez and *El muerto indiscreto* by Rubén Correa," in *Chasqui: Revista de Literatura Latinoamericana* 39, no. 2 (2010): 171–91. The analysis of *Retrato de familia con muerta*, the first novel studied in chapter 4, appeared in an earlier version as "Murder in the Country Club: Trouble in Neoliberal Paradise in *Retrato de familia con muerta* by Raúl Argemí," in *Polifonía* 3, no. 1 (2013): 52–67.

Finally, a huge thanks to my husband and daughter, Jesús and Cristina Cruz, who put up with the many years it took me to complete this project. This book is for them.

# Introduction
## ARGENTINA NOIR

> En este lío en el que estamos, tengo la sensación de que hoy
> es mejor no hacer periodismo, y ponerse a escribir ficción.
> —Claudia Piñeiro, quoted in Aguirre,
> "Los temas están en el aire y uno los baja"

CRIME FICTION IS A WORLDWIDE PHENOMENON THAT IS EXPLODING IN POPularity. Acclaimed crime novels hail from the frigid climes of Scandinavia to Shanghai's dark alleys, from Cape Town to Hamburg. French and Italian novelists continue their countries' well-established traditions of detective and crime fiction, and Latin America and Spain have many first-rate practitioners of the genre. Crime fiction has proven to be infinitely adaptable to diverse cultural milieu as authors use this global genre for local expression. Praising its vivid and persuasive engagement with social reality, Jakob Stougaard-Nielsen describes crime fiction as a mode of writing that is "well suited for capturing societies undergoing dramatic change, for representing and responding directly to an age of social conflicts, risks and inequalities," in particular the crises and conflicts of the end of the twentieth and the beginning of the twenty-first centuries (7). Whether these works depict systemic violence and corruption or discrete crimes viewed as symptoms of deeper and wider social processes (Stougaard-Nielsen 5), what varies from society to society is the explanation for the genesis of crime. Reporter Alexandra Alter, in her assessment of the international crime fiction publishing industry, notes that crime writers around the globe blend "classic suspense story telling techniques with regional themes and literary styles" (2). For example, Japanese novels depict exceedingly polite interrogation techniques; South African crime fiction often includes nods to the lingering effects of apartheid; in Italian novels, Albanian, Serbian, and Asian immigrants replace home-grown mafiosos as crime lords; and Latin American crime fiction frequently centers on drug trafficking and police corruption. Accompanying its expanded output and readership, crime fiction is enjoying a renewed critical interest. At a recent convention of the Modern Language Association, six sessions included one or more presentations dedicated to crime fiction, with papers discussing works and authors from Germany, Mexico, Brazil, Argentina, the United States, Asia (specifically Japan and Korea), and Africa (Kenya and Nigeria). Repeated topics in these presentations included crime fiction's hybridization and globalization, its critique of neoliberalism, and the presence of female detectives.

Argentina's literary scene is an important participant in the worldwide surge in the production of works of crime fiction, many of which are regarded as serious literary endeavors, as opposed to a form of mass entertainment. While crime and detective fiction in Argentina have traditionally enjoyed a steady following and a certain academic prestige, recent decades have seen a significant uptick in the publication and consumption of crime novels, or *novelas negras*. Numerous Argentine writers have spoken to the vital role of this genre within their national cultural patrimony as well as its burgeoning popularity. Sergio Olguín has declared crime fiction to be the genre that best represents Argentine literature, and Pablo De Santis has gone as far as to say, "Crime fiction has totally invaded literature.... The idea of telling a story that connects to another hidden story is something that is in our narrative unconscious."[1] Olguín stresses crime fiction's crucial function in representing political and social reality in Argentina: "Today it is almost impossible to think about the political novel: the only way to think about politics is through crime fiction, because crime and politics have been closely linked in recent years. Crime fiction is also the social novel.... Political and social themes have been absorbed by crime fiction, and in turn have transformed it: it is the easiest vehicle to bring these aspects into literature without falling into pamphletism or a didactic register." Thus among Argentine writers, crime fiction is the "go-to genre" for political and social critique.

*Argentina Noir* proposes to serve as a guide to Argentine crime fiction, with a focus on works published in the new millennium. While this introductory chapter traces the history of the genre and provides an overview of the contemporary scene, chapters 1 through 5 concentrate on selected works published since the year 2000. Each chapter centers on a major theme in contemporary Argentine crime fiction, presenting a close and original reading of two or three representative novels preceded by sociopolitical background information to clarify the issues that the works engage. The organizing principles of this book are formal, thematic, and sociohistorical, and I incorporate literary theory selectively to elucidate how these texts present particular subject matter and dialogue with literary traditions. At the beginning of this chapter I cite Alter's observation that drug trafficking and police corruption are repeated themes in Latin American crime fiction, and the Argentine case is no exception. Indeed, the Argentine *novela negra*'s critique of organized crime—specifically drug and human trafficking—enabled by institutional corruption is the first topic I address, in chapter 1. The subsequent chapter deals with the local iteration of a regional concern: it features novels that employ investigative journalists as detectives to ferret out corruption during the presidency of Carlos Menem in Argentina. In chapter 3, I focus on a problem that plagues countries around the world but has been unique to Argentina within a Latin American context: fundamentalist terror attacks that are an outgrowth of the Middle Eastern conflict. The final chapters—4 and 5—return to Argentine versions of regional and global concerns: the exacerbation of class difference, brought about, in large part, by the wholesale adoption of market-based economic policy. My analysis of these texts also explores how they adapt major motifs and figures in Hispanic crime fiction, including city mapping, the absence of a detective, the failure of justice, gender relations, the female detective, the allure of consumer culture, national identity, and the role of the media. Furthermore, I analyze the configuration and the significance of literary tendencies and techniques such as generic hybridity, intertextuality, and metafictional strategies.

While there exists a large body of criticism dealing with Hispanic crime fiction, this book is the first to present an overview of the production of Argentine crime fiction with a focus on works with a sociopolitical orientation and, in particular, works produced since 2000. Its reading of selected novels addresses how these works expose and denounce some fundamental issues that Argentine society faces or has faced in recent decades, and its incorporation of sociological studies provides empirically based background information that helps us understand the situations that the novels engage. My goal in writing this book is to provide an authoritative, historically rich guide to this body of literature, its conventions, and the social ills it works to redress.

A repeated argument of this book is that crime fiction is employed by many Argentine authors to critique changes brought about by the adoption of neoliberal policies, a widespread use of the genre acknowledged by numerous critics.[2] This theme is especially relevant to Argentine literature and cultural criticism due to Argentina's heavy-handed adoption of neoliberal policies. Argentina was considered the star pupil among the Latin American countries that pursued economic globalization and adopted market-oriented economic policies in the 1990s. While this process was initiated in the 1970s under the military dictatorship, the implementation reached a frenetic pace in the last decade of the twentieth century due to President Carlos Menem's ardent embrace of policies advocated by the Washington Consensus.[3] His presidency, which lasted from 1989 to 1999, ushered in a drastic transformation of Argentina's economic structure. The old model of state intervention and protectionism had left a legacy of "chronic 'stagflation' (stagnant production and persistent inflation)," and the debt crisis of 1982 resulted in the so-called lost decade of the 1980s, during which hyperinflation climbed to mind-boggling levels and per capita income sank (Lewis xii). A key aspect of Menem's neoliberal economic program called for the privatization of utilities and nationalized industries, and the hasty and haphazard way in which this was carried out made it possible for government officials to enrich themselves via influence-peddling and kickbacks. Wealth became increasingly concentrated among those who benefited from the structural changes, while import deregulation eroded domestic industry and, along with privatization, led to unprecedented levels of unemployment and poverty. At the same time, austerity policies compromised public security and dismantled the safety net of state welfare programs. In order to restore economic stability, Menem's economic minister, Domingo Cavallo, implemented convertibility, pegging the Argentine peso to the US dollar. While this measure succeeded in halting hyperinflation, it resulted in a lack of policy flexibility, preventing Argentina from devaluating the peso to balance the budget once the wave of financial crises hit emerging-market countries in 1997–98 (Reid 132). The fiscal strategy of the Menem administration produced an initial burst of prosperity, but the manner in which it was implemented, along with other factors, eventually led to the economic, political, and social crisis of 2001.

The arrival to power in 2003 of the left-wing populist Néstor Kirchner drastically changed the course of Argentine economic policies, shifting from neoliberal to neo-Keynesian solutions. Kirchner's plans focused on the rebuilding of Argentina's industrial base, the establishment of public works and services, and the renegotiation of the operation of privatized public services. While the economy experienced a period of significant growth between 2003 and 2009, 30 percent of Argentines still lived under the poverty line. Succeeding her husband for a two-term mandate from 2007 to 2015, Cristina Fernández de Kirchner's policies did not substantially alter economic trends, nor have they improved Argentina's social inequalities.

Decades of failed economic policies, along with pervasive political corruption, have had a lasting effect on Argentine society. The fear of crime has driven the affluent to gated communities while impoverished Argentines and immigrants live in ever-proliferating *villas misera* (shantytowns). Sociologists speak of the "Latin Americanization" of Argentina—a crisis in the self-image of a society that had prided itself as being different from the rest of Latin America—and declare that Argentina can no longer claim to be a middle-class society. The notion of Buenos Aires as the "Paris of South America" has come to be the stuff of nostalgia or illusion. The perpetrators of high-profile crimes during the 1990s—most notably the bombing of the Israeli embassy and a Jewish community center in Buenos Aires—were never brought to justice and authorities were suspected of mishandling the investigations. The Argentine populace lost confidence in its political class as well as the forces of law and order.

The economic and social insecurity of the 1990s and beyond coincided with the rise in the popularity and production of *novelas negras* in Argentina. This "boomlet" has been consecrated by newly minted festivals celebrating the *novela negra*: the Festival Azabache, Buenos Aires Negra! (BAN!), and Córdoba Mata. To what can we attribute the flourishing of the *novela negra* in Argentina? Critics often seek connections between sociological phenomena and literary trends—a case in point is Jonathan Auerbach's study of film noir, which ventures the hypothesis that there could be no American film noir without the FBI (24). An explanation proffered for the recent surge of the crime novel in Argentina is that it is well suited to registering the social malaise brought about by changes linked to neoliberalism and globalization. Could there be a contemporary Argentine *novela negra* without the heavy-handed and irresponsible implementation of market-driven economic policies accompanied by widespread political corruption? Certainly, the reply is yes, but the conditions generated by the repressive dictatorship of 1976–83 and by failed economic policies and corruption have helped define its parameters and contribute to its popularity and its status as the favored genre for many writers. "Since about 1990," observes critic Misha Kokotovic, "most of the [Latin American] continent has experienced something of a boom in narratives that use elements of detective or crime fiction to criticize the effects of neoliberal, free market capitalism imposed on Latin American societies over the past two decades" (15). He refers to this literary phenomenon as "neoliberal noir," a term that characterizes many of the novels featured in this study. An important tendency in cultural studies is to understand literature as a response to larger social and political processes, and this book will look at how crime novels—at the same time that they captivate and thrill us—tell a tale of Argentine society against a backdrop of social change, dysfunctional economics, and endemic corruption.

The subsequent chapters of this book will examine selected Argentine crime novels, all published since the turn of the century, to explore how they engage and critique determined aspects of Argentine society. Hayden White's essay "The Historical Text as Literary Artifact" informs my reading of the "historical" content of some of the novels that are based on or inspired by real events. He argues that histories make stories out of chronicles by an operation he calls "emplotment": the encodation of facts "as components of specific *kinds* of plot structures," such as romances, comedies, or tragedies (83–84). By means of their emplotment, White contends, "the historical narrative does not *reproduce* the events it describes; it tells us in what direction to think about the events and charges our thought about the events with different emotional valences" (91). Following White's line of thought, we can observe that authors who use elements of the crime fiction genre to "emplot" actual events, or simply to portray contemporary society, are shaping our disposition toward these events or toward the society they depict. Seeing society through the lens of crime, with officialdom as the main criminal or in cahoots with the criminals, communicates a pointed criticism, conveying a scenario of widespread and intractable corruption and social disorder.

## FROM THE WHODUNIT TO THE *NOVELA NEGRA*: THE POETICS OF CRIME FICTION

In large part, Argentine detective and crime fiction shares a common history with the rest of Hispanic letters. In the Hispanic world, detective literature originated as an imitation or parody of the classic British-style mystery—also called whodunit, enigma, puzzle-based, analytic, and ratiocinative—practiced by Arthur Conan Doyle and Agatha Christie and popularized in Argentina by Jorge Luis Borges and Adolfo Bioy Casares. In recent decades, however, cultivation of the genre has undergone a transition toward the *novela negra*, which derives from the North American hard-boiled subgenre initiated in the 1920s (known as *novela dura* in Spanish) with Dashiell Hammett and Raymond Chandler as its foremost practitioners. No longer an intellectual game, hard-boiled crime fiction instead emphasizes social critique, depicting a world in crisis and casting a critical eye on the sources of corruption and economic exploitation. The subgenre flourished in the US in the atmosphere spawned by Prohibition and the stock market crash of 1929, as the country struggled with issues such as the rise of organized crime and wars between mafias, strikes and violent strike-breaking, unemployment, and traffic of firearms and drugs. Reflecting a pessimistic view of society, this subgenre offers no resolution to the criminality it depicts. Stylistic characteristics include dizzying action, suspense and intrigue, irony and tough dialogue, and corrosive social criticism. There is also a basic difference in the temporal structure of the classic British mystery and hard-boiled fiction. A characteristic of the whodunit, as Tzvetan Todorov points out, is its duality. All detective fiction, states Todorov, contains two stories—the story of the crime and the story of its investigation—that are consecutive, the first ending before the second begins. He distinguishes this from the "*série noire*" or thriller, which fuses the two stories, suppressing the first and vitalizing the second. While in the whodunit, the detective and his partner are immunized from the danger, in the thriller the detective's health and even his life are at risk (139–41). This sleuth is invariably a professional detective who maintains his personal sense of ethics while dealing with ruthless corporations, greedy families, and corrupt government officials. A stock character is the femme fatale—seen as an indication of male insecurity due to changing sex roles in the postwar period (Rzepka 185). Ricardo Piglia, whose contribution to the genre I will discuss in the next section of this chapter, notes that a basic difference between the enigma-based and hard-boiled crime fiction is a materialist approach to reality. In the latter, the representatives of the law are motivated by self-interest, the detective is a professional who receives a salary as opposed to an amateur motived by curiosity, and the causal chain of the crime is always economic (*Crítica y ficción* 69). Unlike the whodunnit, the hard-boiled subgenre survived World War II and authors have found it suitable "for gender, ethnic, and cultural appropriation" (Scaggs 30).[4]

While there is not universal agreement about what constitutes a "novela negra," I use the term here to refer to what Glen S. Close calls "the predominant understanding of the *novela negra* as a broad generic category encompassing both detective-centered and criminal-centered subgenres" (*Contemporary Hispanic Crime Fiction* 62).[5] Considered a variant or development of detective fiction (called *ficción policial, policiaca,* or *policiáca* in Spanish), the term "novela negra" comes from the French *roman noir*, and the closest English-language equivalent is "crime fiction."[6] A succinct and apt definition of the *novela negra* is rendered by Mexican writer Paco Ignacio Taibo II: "A *novela negra* is one that has a criminal act at its heart and that generates an investigation. What happens is that a good crime novel investigates something more than who killed or who committed the crime, it investigates the society in which the events occur. It begins by telling about a crime, and ends by telling how that society is" (Saldo). Additionally, Genaro J. Pérez points out an aspect I find highly relevant to this book: the *novela negra* "utilizes the vehicle of crime to emphasize a particular moral problem that the author denounces" (15). A central tenet of this book is that the *género negro* has become a favored genre to address social and political reality, reflecting on or critiquing systems of power. In the Latin American variety, there is a focus on situations where the state is involved in criminality, corruption is rampant, and wrongdoers escape with impunity.

José F. Colmeiro provides a cogent discussion of the change in ideology between the classic formula of detective fiction and the *novela negra*. In the classic version, the final solution leads to a restoration of justice. The criminal is discovered and punished, implicitly defending the established social order; the happy ending is thus based on an unambiguous solution to the crime and an optimistic social vision. The ideological charge implies maintenance of the status quo and an unquestioned trust in the law and the bourgeois order. The *novela negra* inverts these ethical and aesthetic principles as it questions the established order, portraying an unjust and immoral society based on the domination of the powerful over the weak and the rich over the poor through exploitation and violence. There is no happy ending in its vision of pessimism and hopelessness, as the true social dimension of crime and the impossibility of regeneration is revealed, with complicit and unethical politicians, business magnates, and agents of order (Colmeiro 61–63). This describes the Argentine *novela negra*—it rarely offers a clean solution to the crime; to the contrary, the criminal behavior will persist, conveying the authors' pessimistic vision of society. The articulation of an ethical problem is a takeaway message of these novels.

While traditional detective fiction is highly formulaic, its basic structure and conventions lend themselves to endless and sometimes playful variations, conveying a radically different message from the original formula. As Persephone Braham points out, "Latin American detective writers naturally test generic boundaries as they try to write stories that reflect their reality, and many use detective formulas simply as a point of departure for other kinds of literary experimentation" (xiv). In *Juegos de seducción y traición* (Games of seduction and betrayal), Ana María Amar Sánchez examines "high" literature that incorporates popular models (21). She explains how popular literary forms seduce the reader with their reproduction of formulas: the reader experiences pleasure upon rediscovering the anticipated, and is consoled with repetition, the return to the same (30). When certain texts employ these codes and transform them in a key point, they betray the reader's expectations. This space, between the reader's seduction and betrayal, opens to the possibility of a political reading (33, 36). Amar Sánchez notes that the detective genre has modified the canonical components of the genre—crime, truth, and justice—as it carries out a progressive politicization of crime (47).

The Argentine *novelas negras* I analyze in this book reproduce and transform formulas of the classic and hard-boiled genre, often including features of film noir and thrillers and making cordial nods to their hard-boiled forerunners and film noir icons. I will consider how the novels repeat and modify patterns as they reflect and critique the values and anxieties of contemporary Argentine society.

Josefina Ludmer's *Corpus Delicti* demonstrates how crime can be a tool to articulate culture. She points out that crime serves as a "conceptual instrument [that] is not abstract, but rather visible, representable, quantifiable, personalizable, subjectivizable" (4). Since crimes change over time, their variation serves to differentiate cultural moments or historical periods (5). What is more, crimes are a story; they are literary. A crime generates a constellation of cultural scenarios, conjuring up the following questions: What is the crime, who are the criminals, and who are the victims? Where does the crime take place and what is the relationship between the scene of the crime and the nature of the crime? What is the motive of the crime—is it power, passion, money, or a combination of these drivers? Is there an investigation of the crime, and if so, who are the investigators, what are their motives, and what is their relationship with the state and with the criminals? Are the criminals brought to justice, and if not, why not? What are the roles of gender and social class in relation to the crime and its investigation? What paths do the criminals and the investigators trace? These questions point to crime fiction's exceptional capacity to produce an incisive portrait of society, and working through the answers traces a reading informed by cultural studies.

## DEVELOPMENT OF THE GENRE IN ARGENTINA

It is not within the scope, nor is it the purpose, of this book to provide a detailed history of detective/crime fiction in Argentina. Such an endeavor is another book in itself, and excellent accounts have been published by Jorge Lafforgue and Jorge Rivera, Glen S. Close, and Román Setton. For these reasons, I will limit this discussion to a synopsis of the high points in the development of the genre in Argentina with a focus on its innovation of the classical style as well as its socially orientated vein. I will also provide an overview of the current state of the *novela negra* in Argentina and its practitioners.

Both the classical enigma formula and the hard-boiled variety of the genre have been cultivated in Argentina. As Close points out, despite the fact that Argentina has the longest tradition of detective writing in the Hispanic world with the publication of two detective novels by Luis V. Varela in 1887 (*La huella del crimen* and *Clemencia*), the hard-boiled subgenre, or *novela negra*, was slow to take root there. While there was considerable interest in translations and imitations of foreign "autores duros" beginning in the 1940s, the *novela negra* did not become the dominant tendency in Argentina until the 1970s (Close, *Contemporary Hispanic Crime Fiction* 93–96). The development of the genre was gradual and problematic due to its lack of prestige as well as the fact that Argentine reality did not adapt to the conventions of the classical genre. For this reason, we see a reformulation and problematization of the norms of the genre in Argentine literature (Lafforgue and Rivera 96). As José Pablo Feinmann explains it, "Argentine detective fiction, in its best manifestations, has worked in the *edges* of the genre, not *within* the genre.... Not writing *within* the genre is not submitting to its rules.... It remains for us as the infinite possibility of experimentation" ("Estado policial" 152). Additionally, few Argentine writers committed themselves exclusively to the genre, a fact that still holds true today. Perhaps evidence of its appeal to Argentine writers is the fact that those who cultivate other narrative forms often try their hand at a *novela negra*.

Key figures in the development and innovation of detective fiction are Jorge Luis Borges and Rodolfo Walsh. Borges and Bioy Casares founded the series El Séptimo Círculo, which published translations of the classic Anglo-American enigma novel as well as River Plate writers but eschewed hard-boiled fiction—"a sadistic or bloody form of the novel of adventure," according to Borges (Lafforgue and Rivera 126)—and berated its detectives for being not intellectuals but simply criminals who are on the side of the law. Together Borges and Bioy Casares wrote *Seis problemas para don Isidro Parodi* (1942), in which an amateur detective solves cases from his prison cell. This parodic text problematizes the viability of a national appropriation of the genre. The parody creates ironic distance from classical texts, which is a constant recourse in Argentine detective fiction. Borges's short stories "El jardín de senderos que se bifurcan" and "La muerte y la brújula," published in the mid-1940s, mark a high point in detective fiction. Both stories, prime examples of metadetective fiction, illustrate the failure of reason and justice as the detective is caught by his own obsession with ratiocination. Piglia calls "La muerte y la brújula" the *Ulysses* of the detective story, the moment when "the form reaches its culminating point and disintegrates" (*Crítica y ficción* 68).

Walsh is credited with the fusion of the detective genre with investigative journalism. He began working with the enigma formula in Borges's footsteps, publishing in 1953 the collection *Diez cuentos policiales argentinos*, which Lafforgue and Rivera consider a fundamental text: "the 'officialization' of the genre from within its own dynamics" (142). Walsh also wrote acclaimed detective stories, the most well known of which is "Cuento para tahúres," in the classical enigma style. Beginning in 1962 until his death at the hands of the military dictatorship in 1977, Walsh expressed a growing political commitment. His *Operación masacre* (1957), the account of the illegal detention and execution of Peronist militants in the aftermath of the 1955 anti-Peronist military coup, created a model for investigative journalism by using techniques of the detective genre to reconstruct and expose a true crime. In this case, since the police and judges were working to cover up the clandestine executions, the investigator's struggle consisted of uncovering and disseminating the truth about criminal activity of the state, thus initiating a key tendency in Latin American crime fiction. While Truman Capote's *In Cold Blood*, published in 1966, is considered a pioneering work of true crime, Walsh's text anticipated it by nearly a decade. Along with Borges, Walsh is a major referent for contemporary crime fiction writers, in particular those who are also journalists or who place an investigative reporter in the detective function to uncover institutional corruption.

Returning to the chronological overview, 1973 is the year signaled by Close that the *novela negra* came into its own as "a new dominant" in Argentine crime fiction with the publication of novels by Manuel Puig, Osvaldo Soriano, Juan Carlos Martelli, and Juan Carlos Martini (*Contemporary Hispanic Crime Fiction* 96). Many of these novels portrayed menacing social violence as young authors realized the *novela negra* could include social thematics and portray a society in crisis. Puig's *Buenos Aires Affair: Novela policial* uses the subtitle to signal its turn to popular culture. While far from conventional crime or detective fiction, the novel depicts a climate of escalating political tension (Close, *Contemporary Hispanic Crime Fiction* 99). *Triste, solitario y final* by Soriano pays homage to Raymond Chandler's detective, Philip Marlowe, and can be considered a parody of North American hard-boiled fiction. Martelli's *Los tigres de la memoria* represents a degraded society in crisis with a corrupt and criminal system, anticipating the terror that will take hold of Argentina. Martini's first detective novel, *El agua en los pulmones*, also parodying North American models, deals with a hired investigator who is tricked by his employer and finds himself involved in a series of murders. Two noteworthy crime novels were published in 1975: *Noches sin lunas ni soles* by Rubén Tizziani and *Ni un dólar partido por la mitad* by Sergio Sinay. These novels incorporate typical hard-boiled motifs such as ambition, corruption, sex, and violence, and have in common indirect social criticism and a sense of frustration and impotence in the face of injustice and impunity.

The installation of an authoritarian dictatorship in Argentina in 1976 altered all aspects of national culture, bringing about a break in literary production. Writers who did publish often used allegory and metaphor to evade the censors as they indirectly depicted the criminality of the state. José Pablo Feinmann's *Últimos días de la víctima* (1979), a compelling novel from this period, portrays a hired hit man stalking a target. Its evocation of a terrorized society is, according to Close, "one of the most enduring fables of a society in which violence had replaced politics as the dominant language of power" (*Contemporary Hispanic Crime Fiction* 114). Speaking to the power of evading censorship, Feinmann declares, "The novel was not at all innocent for those times, but the military did not notice, that is why I am here" (Friera, "Yo no rechazo escribir").

The most prominent example of writing *en clave* during this period is *Respiración artificial* (1980) by Ricardo Piglia. The novel opens in 1976 with an interchange of letters between Marcelo Maggi, a history professor with leftist sympathies, and his nephew, Emilio Renzi. When Maggi mysteriously disappears, the narration turns to an investigation, and the epistolary novel becomes a detective novel (Maristany 68). Maggi had been researching the life of a controversial nineteenth-century Argentine intellectual, which may have shed too much light on the abuses of the current police state.

Since Argentina's return to democracy in 1983, many writers have used the *novela negra* to denounce atrocities of the period and advocate in defense of human rights. Fiction dealing with the military regime depicts the criminality of the state as military personnel kidnapped, tortured, and murdered citizens whom they perceived as enemies of their reactionary and paranoiac conception of the nation. David William Foster notes that many of these novels about the dictatorship reveal a hidden reality (22), and this can be exposed by detective work. To this end, Philip Swanson remarks, in his discussion of the postmodern detective in Latin American literature, that the motive of the investigation "alludes to the need to bring to light the truth and to reveal the hidden realities of societies traumatized by corrupt and deceitful systems" ("Don Quijote" 267).

Novels set in the period often project a climate of fear and paranoia. *Luna caliente* (1983) by Mempo Giardinelli has as protagonist a young lawyer named Ramiro who has returned from his studies in France to Argentina during the dictatorship. Believing that he has suffocated a young "Lolita" and that her father will seek revenge, Ramiro kills the father. Once the police catch up with Ramiro, they offer to let him off lightly for his crimes if he collaborates in their fight against "subversives." The novel envelops the reader in an atmosphere of paranoia as we accompany Ramiro's frantic flight from the authorities—he has to flee not because of his "common" crimes but because he refuses to collaborate with state crimes.[7] Another haunting and paranoiac novel is *77* (2008) by Guillermo Saccomanno, which deals with the terror experienced by an average citizen who carries out a humanitarian act: a schoolteacher who risks his life by giving shelter to a hunted militant. *Arena en los zapatos* (1989) by Juan Sasturain and *Un crimen argentino* (2002) by Reynaldo Sietecase employ common crime as a metaphor for state crime.

Other writers situate their plots in the postdictatorial period, addressing the problematic of memory as the protagonists struggle to understand events that occurred during the time of repression. Many of these novels use the thriller as an approach to a troubled past with powerful secrets. A prime example is *El secreto de sus ojos* by Eduardo Sacheri, which deals with the recovery of memory to make sense of the present. Set in 1999, it follows the efforts of a retired judicial investigator to reconstruct a case that still haunts him: the 1974 rape and murder of a young woman. The murderer received a life sentence but was set free because he was useful to the military regime. For the investigator, 1974 also marked the beginning of a frustrated love affair. With its return to the past, the novel engages the politics of memory as both unresolved situations challenge the characters to decide between moving on and forgetting or repairing the past. *La pesquisa* (1994) by Juan José Saer uses innuendo to critique the dictatorship. While the initial plotline of *La pesquisa* involves the investigation of gruesome serial murders in Paris, we discover that this story is being narrated in Argentina by an individual whose twin brother mysteriously disappeared at the time of the Proceso.[8] Gail González suggests that uncovering, examining, and analyzing the memory of the period of the dictatorship form the nucleus of Saer's text (258).[9]

Some postdictatorial crime novels that reflect on the period focus on individuals who were neither victimizers nor victims but who, through their passivity, compliance, or cowardice, were complicit with the dictatorship. Prominent examples of this register are *Lo que nosotras sabíamos* (2009) by María Inés Krimer, *El secreto y las voces* (2002) by Carlos Gamerro, and *Una misma noche* (2012) by Leopoldo Brizuela. All three feature protagonists who struggle to re-create events that transpired during the dictatorship in an attempt to understand obscure and ominous occurrences. In *El secreto y las voces*, the son of a disappeared man conceals his identity to investigate his father's fate and in the process exposes the complicity of a village with the execution of an innocent man. In *Una misma noche*, on the other hand, the protagonist recalls his own cowardice in face of the persecution of a neighbor. *Lo que nosotras sabíamos* offers a unique perspective through the voices of frivolous and self-serving housewives whose version of events tends to legitimize the dictatorship.[10] In these novels, seemingly innocent incidents take on a new, much more sinister, meaning as the years pass and individuals reflect on their significance.

Incorporating winks and homages to North American hard-boiled classics, *La capital del olvido* (2004) by Horacio Vázquez-Rial moves between the present and the past, and between Spain and Argentina, depicting yet another form of complicity: willful forgetfulness on the part of both victimizers and victims when economic gain comes into play. A victim of imprisonment and torture during the dictatorship who has given herself a new identity in Spain returns to Argentina to seek her son, who was born in captivity, and take revenge on her captors. There she discovers private enterprises that exploited personal tragedy, selling the children of "the disappeared" for profit, a network of which her own protector and rescuer formed part. *Sucesos argentinos* (1995) by Vicente Battista also treats corruption of values from a transatlantic perspective. An Argentine exiled in Spain during the dictatorship is sent back to his homeland by a Spanish company in order to serve as straw man to obtain a bid for the construction of a highway. Lured by easy money, he gets tangled in the shady deal.

Both *Papel picado* (2003) by Rolo Diez and *Qué solos se quedan los muertos* (1983) by Mempo Giardinelli use the *género negro* to reflect on the situation of Argentine exiles in Mexico during the Proceso. The exiles find themselves in danger, in Diez's novel because they meet up with an old enemy, and in Giardinelli's because the protagonist becomes involved in protecting an old friend from a violent network of drug traffickers. Elsa Drucaroff's action-packed novel *El último caso de Rodolfo Walsh* (2010) is based on an actual event—the death of Walsh's daughter Vicki when she and four fellow Montoneros were confronted by a group of 150 soldiers. Was Vicki killed in combat or taken prisoner and murdered in captivity? Drucaroff imagines the investigation that Walsh could have carried out to discover the truth behind her death.

Works published since 2005 that deal with the "Dirty War" include novels and *testimonios* written by children of militants: for example, *La casa operativa* (2006) by Cristina Feijóo, *La casa de los conejos* (2008) by Laura Alcoba, and *A veinte años, Luz* (2008) by Elsa Osorio. In her recent novel, *Doble fondo* (2018), Osorio once again deals with memories and repercussions of the dictatorship. While not all of these are *novelas negras* per se, they include generic elements to tell their tale, such as suspense and an investigation of the past. Other *novelas negras* set in the period of the dictatorship are *Penúltimo nombre de guerra* (2004) and *Siempre la misma música* (2006) by Raúl Argemí, *Nadie ama a un policía* (2007) by Guillermo Orsi, *La aguja en el pajar* (20060) by Ernesto Mallo, *Dos veces Junio* (2005) and *Ciencias morales* (2007) by Martín Kohan, and *Hay unos tipos abajo* (2008) by Antonio Dal Masetto.

Two major Argentine authors, theorists, and promoters of the *novela negra* are the late Ricardo Piglia and Mempo Giardinelli. Piglia played a key role in the promotion, dissemination, theorization, and innovation of the genre. In 1969 he founded the collection Serie Negra, which published hard-boiled stories and contributed to the expansion and variety of reading circuits (Lafforgue and Rivera 88), and edited an anthology titled *Cuentos de la serie negra*, which included US writers such as Chandler and Hammett. In his introduction to the Serie Negra, reprinted in *Crítica y ficción*, Piglia set forth basic observations regarding the hard-boiled genre. Especially resonant is his remark about the role of money in the logic of the genre.

> There is a way of narrating in the *serie negra* that is linked to a handling of reality that I would call materialistic.... The crime, the misdeed, is always sustained by money: murder, robbery, fraud, extortion, kidnapping, the chain is always economic.... The only enigma that these novels propose—and never solve—is that of capitalist relations: the money that legislates morality and upholds the law is the only "reason" of these stories where everything is paid. In this sense, I would say that they are capitalist novels in the most literal sense of the word. (69–70)

While Piglia claimed, "I do not write crime novels"[11] (Kohan), many of his plots include some form of investigation by a person who takes on the role of detective, usually Piglia's alter ego, Emilio Renzi. Joanna Page describes Piglia's narrative projects as "a kind of practical experiment that performs the themes discussed on a more explicit level elsewhere" (28). Piglia has spoken to his use of the genre to explore other issues: "If I have done something with the genre, it has been to work with the model of investigation outside the scheme of crime: to use the form of the investigation in relation to objects that were not necessarily criminal in a direct sense" (*Crítica y ficción* 197).

Some of the themes Piglia develops in his novels are the cross between the critic and the detective; the constant presence of an enigmatic code to be deciphered; the politics of storytelling; and the complex relationship between crime, capitalist society, and the media. Another crucial concept set forth in his theoretical and fictional writing is "paranoiac fiction"; as he explains, "Literature has increasingly taken over the development of a vision of the threat of endangered everyday life" ("La ficción paranoica"). Renzi muses in Piglia's *Blanco nocturno* (2010), "We need to invent a new crime fiction genre, paranoid fiction. Everyone is suspicious, everyone feels pursued" (284). In his study of this novel, Juan Caballero links Piglia's notion of contemporary paranoid crime fiction to "the invisible and almost unthinkable totalities of neoliberal economic power" (120). Piglia further connects this paranoia to the notion of conspiracy: "the subject does not perceive a private crime but rather he confronts a massive assembly of enemies" (Figueiras). Moving beyond the realm of crime fiction, Piglia associates this concept with the individual's view of society, perceived "in the form of a scheme designed to destroy him, or in other words: the conspiracy, the paranoia are linked to the perception that an individual designs around social relations" (Figueiras). This outlook based on conspiracy theory replaces the notion of tragic destiny.

While detection and crime can be identified in all of Piglia's works, key texts in this regard are "La loca y el relato del crimen" (1975), *Respiración artificial* (discussed earlier in this section), and *Plata quemada* (1997), made into a successful movie in 2000. More recent novels involving crime and paranoid fiction are the aforementioned *Blanco nocturno* and *El camino de Ida* (2013). In "La loca y el relato del crimen," a pimp named Almada kills a prostitute, and the only witness is "la loca," a psychotic gypsy woman named Angélica Echevarne. Emilio Renzi, the repeated character in Piglia's fiction who takes on the detective function, is able to solve the crime by deciphering what appears to be the incoherent babbling of the "loca," but her discourse actually communicates in code the facts of the crime. However, Almada is being protected by higher-ups and the only form in which the truth is published will be Renzi's story; thus literature voices what the official history silences (Girona Fibla 529). Piglia's concept of literature as the conveyer of repressed truths will be repeated in subsequent *novelas negras*, for instance *Betibú* by Claudia Piñeiro.

*Blanco nocturno*, a novel exhibiting a complexity comparable to that of *Respiración artificial*, combines two stories: the tragic tale of Tony Durán, a Puerto Rican who is murdered shortly after arriving in the Argentine countryside with a suitcase containing $100,000, and the saga of the powerful Belladona family, whose patriarch founded an automobile factory in the pampa. Emilio Renzi, who is the interlocutor for both tales, serves as the connective element. Caballero proposes that the novel be read as a prehistory of neoliberalism in Argentina, citing the "massive international movements of capital, clearly the root of all the 'crimes' being investigated" (126). In *El camino de Ida*, Renzi is a visiting professor at a prestigious university on the East Coast of the United States. Ida Brown, a brilliant literature professor with whom he had a brief affair, turns up dead and Renzi becomes involved in the case. Was her death accidental or a case of terrorism? When an FBI agent bearing a conspiracy theory turns up to investigate, paranoia ensues.

I have broken the chronological order of my discussion of Piglia's contributions to the *novela negra*, saving *Plata quemada* for the end due to its multiple implications for the present book. This novel is based on an actual incident: the 1965 robbery of five million Argentine pesos from a transport vehicle in Buenos Aires and the subsequent flight of the robbers to Montevideo, where they holed up in an apartment and resisted for more than fifteen hours the siege of three hundred armed policemen. A crowd gathered on the street, the media arrived, and the incident was broadcasted. Finally, surrounded by the police and with no possible escape, the robbers set fire to the bills and, before everyone's eyes, threw the burning money out the window. While *Plata quemada* pretends to be a nonfictional version of an actual event—a documentary thriller—this register is broken in several ways, as the novel delivers a commentary on social ills at the same time that it models Piglia's use of fiction to explore theoretical issues related to writing. Numerous excellent critical readings have explicated how *Plata quemada* delivers its social and theoretical messages.[12] In my discussion, I will focus on three issues I find particularly compelling: the tension between the "true" story and its fictionalized version, the double story or secret story that conveys the social critique, and the possibility of storytelling.

While the epilogue states that "this novel tells a true story," the text problematizes the boundary between truth and fiction, or between truth and its interpretative reconstruction (Clayton 45). As Edgardo H. Berg remarks, "It could be said that the most troublesome aspect of the story that *Plata quemada* tells is its fictionalization" (44). The factual register of the story is undermined via the multiple and sometimes conflicting or incompatible voices or registers that tell the story—the reporters, the police, the public, psychiatric reports, the media, the robbers themselves—and the intervention of a fictional character in the role of crime reporter: Emilio Renzi, Piglia's transparent double. Renzi's fictionalized version of events lends the story mythological overtones when he compares the outlaws to heroes of a Greek tragedy and brings in the ideological charge, implicitly posing questions such as "who is the real delinquent?"

Several critics have pointed out that Piglia's texts contain double stories; in *Plata quemada* the ostensible story is that of the pursuit and capture of a band of criminals, while the inner story transmits a critique of capitalist society and its corrupted values. Page contends that Piglia sees the hard-boiled genre as a possibility for left-wing, politically committed writing, explaining, "What is under investigation [in *Plata quemada*] is not the motive or the identity of the criminal but the complex relations between criminality, capitalist society, and the mass media" (29). The authorities seek to conceal their complicity with the crime, thus the story breaks down the binary between the criminals and the representatives of the law. There is also an implicit critique of the mass media, which sensationalizes crime and violence for public consumption. The scene in which the desperate criminals set fire to the bills delivers a fierce critique of the value system of capitalist society. The public becomes furious with them for burning the money, expressing moral indignation and accusing them of being "cretinos," "malvados," and "bestias" (cretins, evil people, beasts) (172–73), and the reporter calls the ashes of the bills "una pila funeraria de los valores de la sociedad" (a funerary pile of society's values) (174). Michelle Clayton points to the irony that "this indignation, this sudden moral sense, is aroused not by proliferating murder, but by the destruction of money," thus exposing "the warped moral fabric" of a society that values money over human life (51). In the end, the secret story is society's inner workings.

All in all, Piglia's novel is about the possibility and the power of storytelling. Julio Premat points out that the epilogue, in which the author describes his discovery of a preexisting story that he deemed to be "una historia narrable," dramatizes the possibility of fiction (128, 134). Finally, *Plata quemada* is a preeminent model of what I intend to examine in this book: the convergence of crime, storytelling, and popular culture to deliver a powerful critique of the modern state as well as the impact of capitalism and neoliberal values on society and the individual.

The works of Mempo Giardinelli, another prominent Argentine writer and critic, frequently explore ethical questions and cast a critical perspective on culture and social consciousness. Giardinelli has played an important role in the dissemination and reception of the *novela negra* and is outspoken and influential in describing its predominant role in the portrayal of Latin American reality, calling it a good medium "to understand first and then to interrogate the world in which we live" (Kohut 173). His book *El género negro: Ensayo sobre la novela policial* (first published in 1984 and revised in 1996) is a fundamental reference for the antecedents and the development of the genre in North America, Europe, and Latin America. He discusses the genre's hybrid nature, identifying its borrowings from diverse literary traditions: the gothic and horror, adventure, and the North American cowboy or Wild West literature.

Giardinelli's extensive literary production includes four *novelas negras*. Earlier in this section I discussed the two that are set in the period of the dictatorship, *Luna caliente* and *Qué solos se quedan los muertos*. Giardinelli calls his novellete *El décimo infierno* (1999) "una novela menemista" (a Menemist novel). A violent tale about lovers who go on a wild killing spree, it reflects what the author considers the dissoluteness of the period. His subsequent novelette, *Cuestiones interiores* (2003), opens with a man who kills a stranger for no apparent reason. Trying to seek an explanation for his behavior, the text becomes a vision of an anguished and tortured conscience, the product of a history of social and family violence. Similar to *El décimo inferno*, it can be read as a parable for the country at a time of crisis.

## AN OVERVIEW OF CURRENT PRACTITIONERS IN ARGENTINA

The contemporary scene of Argentine *novela negra* writers is rich and varied. Many of these writers convene at the aforementioned festivals celebrating the *novela negra*: the Festival Azabache, inaugurated in 2011 in Mar del Plata by Carlos Balmaceda and taken over by Javier Chiabrando in 2013; Buenos Aires Negra! (BAN!), organized by Ernesto Mallo and held at the Centro Cultural San Martín in Buenos Aires, beginning in 2012; and Córdoba Mata, launched in 2014 by writer Fernando López. Since, to my knowledge, there exists no published overview of Argentina's current practitioners of the *novela negra*, the following pages attempt to provide such a synopsis.

While I discussed several women writers in the previous section, it is important to recognize as an assemblage the sizeable and diverse group of *autoras* who work in the genre. "The presence of women writers in Argentine crime fiction clearly took off in the 21st century," declares Argentine writer and journalist Horacio Convertini (Gigena). Undisputedly, the most prominent is Claudia Piñeiro, whose fiction achieved best-seller status with *Las viudas de los jueves* (2005). This and two other Piñeiro novels, *Tuya* (2005) and *Betibú* (2011), have been made into successful films. Piñeiro's work will be discussed in chapter 4.

Another accomplished writer who has made a mark in the field of the *novela negra* is María Inés Krimer, whose novels have garnered several awards, including the Premio Emecé, the Premio del Fondo Nacional de las Artes, and the Premio Internacional de Novela Letra Sur. Krimer masterfully develops her plots in meticulous detail, revealing keen insight into human behavior and a particular interest, as she notes, in issues that directly affect women's lives ("Sangre y cirugías"). In addition to *Lo que nosotras sabíamos* (discussed in the previous section), she has published several other *novelas negras* that explore women's experience. *La inauguración* (2011) treats the problem of human trafficking and has a rural setting with the conflict between the government and the agricultural sector in the background. Invited by Juan Sasturain to participate in the Negro Absoluto collection, Krimer penned a trilogy featuring a middle-aged Jewish detective named Ruth Epelbaum. In the first novel of the series, *Sangre kosher* (2010), Ruth investigates the disappearance of the daughter of a Jewish jewel merchant. Since the young woman's personal trainer is implicated in her disappearance, Ruth's probe takes her to the fitness world. Ruth continues her detective work in two more scenarios connected to the female image: in *Siliconas express* (2013) and *Sangre fashion* (2015) she investigates wrongdoing in the cosmetic surgery industry and in the garment industry, respectively. Krimer's most recent novel, *Noxa* (2016), once again takes on systemic violence, this time the human toll of toxic fumigation on the countryside. Also publishing in the Negro Absoluto collection is Elisa Bellmann, whose first novel, *Asfixia* (2011), is a psychological thriller with an enigma connected to the years of repression of the dictatorship.

Novels written by Elsa Osorio, Cristina Feijóo, and Elsa Drucaroff, discussed in the previous section, also deal with the period of the dictatorship. Additionally, in 2011 Feijóo published *Los puntos ciegos de Emilia*. This novel uses the background of the 2004 fire in the Cromañón nightclub in Buenos Aires, which resulted in the deaths of 194 people, to explore tensions within an upper-middle-class family. Emilia's discovery of her husband's infidelity forces her to confront ghosts in her past, and her introspection uncovers a web of ugly secrets, lies, and betrayals beneath a façade of respectability.

Natalia Moret's first novel, *Un publicista en apuros* (2012), through its portrait of a racist and corrupt *porteño* yuppie who works in the cutthroat world of publicity, delivers a critique of a certain sector of middle-class Argentine society. Despite the protagonist's cynicism, Moret manages to humanize him, eliciting a degree of reader identification. *¿Quién mató a la cantante de jazz?* (2008) by Tataina Goransky is a thriller that also explores a sub world, that of the *porteño* jazz scene. With a structure inspired by the board game Clue, the plot seeks to solve the mystery surrounding the tragic death of a singer. Goransky later published *Los impecables*, a volume containing two novelettes connected by their common theme of the obsessive, even psychotic, search for perfection by the protagonist. Other new female voices in the genre include those of Solange Camauër, Eugenia Almeida, Selva Almada, and Florencia Etcheves. Camauër's *Sabiduría elemental* was praised by Spanish novelist Lorenzo Silva, one of the judges who awarded it the 2014 Premio de Novela Negra "Ciudad de Getafe," for its rigorous style and the moral ambiguity of its characters ("Solange Camauër"). Opening with the mysterious stabbing death of an internationally acclaimed writer and relating the investigation of events leading up to the murder, the novel reconstructs a circle of envy and distrust within the literary world. Almeida's first detective novel, *La tensión del umbral* (2015), employs multiple voices to develop a political intrigue that reflects on the shadowy power relations between the political class and the media. In *Ladrilleros* (2013) by Almada, old quarrels between two men lead to a tragic destiny. While the novel features scenes of violence and explicit sex, for the author it is a love story (Núñez Jaime). Almada addresses the issue of machistic violence in rural Argentina in *Chicas muertas* (2014), based on true stories—the unresolved cases of three murdered or missing girls. Etcheves, who worked for fifteen years as a reporter on the crime beat, has penned a trilogy featuring a female police detective: *La Virgen en tus ojos* (2012), *La hija del campeón* (2014), and *Cornelia* (2016). The denunciatory tone of her novels conveys the author's stated intent to combat sexual exploitation of women.

Alicia Plante's trilogy of crime novels explores the inner lives of ordinary people confronted with a moral dilemma, and her dense and carefully developed plots follow the rules of the deductive mystery. *Una mancha más* (2011) portrays individuals possessing secrets from the past that involve the destiny of babies born in captivity during the military regime. It is followed by *Fuera de temporada* (2013), which takes place during the off-season in the posh seaside resort of Pinamar; the locals lead a humdrum existence until a homicide shakes things up, revealing hidden scandals. Finally, in *Verde oscuro* (2014) the investigation into a homicide in the Ecological Reserve of Buenos Aires uncovers unscrupulous real estate speculators who are out to exploit the city's nature reserve.

Gabriela Cabezón Cámara's first novel, *La Virgen Cabeza* (2009), was a finalist for the Premio Silverio Cañada of the Semana Negra de Gijón. In this novel, Cabezón Cámara, a regular contributor to the cultural section of *Clarín*, narrates a love story between a lesbian journalist and a transvestite who, inspired by conversations with the Virgin Mary, organizes a welfare state of sorts in a shantytown. With a heady, lyrical style that can flip from tragedy to comedy, the novel denounces conditions that plague shantytown dwellers, such as forced prostitution, drug dealing, police abuse, AIDS, and thievery, at the same time that its unconventional couple challenges heteronormativity. Her subsequent novel, *Le viste la cara a Dios* (2011), submerges the reader into the violent and delirious world of Beya, a victim of human trafficking, as it decries human cruelty and the victimization of women. *Romance de la negra rubia* (2014), the final novel of what Cabezón Cámara calls her *trilogía oscura*, once again encapsulates a political message of pain and resistance through the story of a woman who sets herself on fire to resist eviction and becomes a popular hero thanks to social media.

Also trying to understand Argentina's troubled present, in this case from a historical angle, are Mercedes Giuffré's detective novels: *Deuda de sangre* (2008), *El peso de la verdad* (2010), and *El carro de la muerte* (2011. Set in Buenos Aires' colonial past, specifically the British invasion and the May Revolution, moments that Giuffré believes were key in the formation of Argentine identity, her stories impeccably re-create the period, as her protagonist, medical doctor Samuel Redhead, finds himself in the position of investigating mysterious deaths and seeking justice.

A vibrant presence at the *novela negra* festivals in Buenos Aires and Mar del Plata is that of Uruguayan Mercedes Rosende, winner of the Buenos Aires Negra micro-fiction contest in 2015. In Rosende's *La muerte tendrá tus ojos* (2008), reportedly the first detective novel written by a Uruguayan woman, her protagonist, a government functionary, takes on a detective role when she discovers a dangerous and fraudulent business behind an urban renewal project. *Mujer equivocada* (2011) uses humor and sensitivity to explore the life of Úrsula, an insecure and voyeuristic woman who is plagued by feelings of inadequacy due to her obsession with eating and her excess weight. Mistaken for the ex-wife of a kidnapped millionaire and contacted to pay the ransom, Úrsula's morbid curiosity leads her to play along. As the foregoing discussion demonstrates, women writers of the River Plate are making noteworthy contributions to *novela negra* production.

Turning to other writers, I will comment on some of the more prominent Argentine crime novelists on the contemporary scene. Authors whose works are featured in this book—Guillermo Orsi, Ernesto Mallo, Raúl Argemí, and Sergio Olguín—will be discussed in subsequent chapters. Three acclaimed veterans who remain very active in the crime fiction circuit are Juan Sasturain, Vicente Battista, and José Pablo Feinmann. Sasturain makes an important contribution to the genre in his role as editor of Negro Absoluto, a collection of crime novels set in Buenos Aires. In addition to his work in publishing, journalism, and a variety of popular genres, Sasturain is the author of several crime novels: *Manual de perdedores I* and *II* (1985 and 1987), *Los sentidos del agua* (1992), *Arena en los zapatos* (1989), and *Pagaría por no verte* (2008). The protagonist of these novels is private detective Etchenique, whom Close has dubbed "the most distinctive Buenos Aires detective to have appeared in print since Isidro Parodi" (*Contemporary Hispanic Crime Fiction* 117). Sasturain self-consciously appropriates a foreign model—for instance, Etchenique makes frequent reference to iconic detectives such as Georges Simenon's Inspector Magrit and Humphrey Bogart in his role as Chandler's Philip Marlowe—and transposes it to an Argentine context, using that model to map local realities and confront social ills (Close, *Contemporary Hispanic Crime Fiction* 120). With a serious dose of humor and picaresque wanderings, Etchenique wages an invariably losing battle against political and corporate corruption.

Writer and journalist Vicente Battista has published novels, plays, film scripts, essays, and short story collections. An expert in and enthusiast of crime fiction, he has been called "one of the most original voices of the current Latin American *novela negra*" (Valle). His works within the genre include the novels *Siroco* (1985), *Sucesos argentinos* (discussed in the previous section), *Cuaderno del ausente* (2009), and *Ojos que no ven* (2012), and stories in *La huella del crimen* (2007). Developing an intrigue within a determined historical, geographic, and sociopolitical context, his novels demonstrate "a very clear interest in delineating the extent to which the influence of the corruption of society has reached within the 'Argentine soul'" (Valle). For example, in *Ojos que no ven*, a journalist who is investigating the seemingly accidental death of a teenager in an aristocratic Buenos Aires social club discovers that it involves scandalous dealings and must decide whether he will follow his personal ethics or pursue journalistic fame.

José Pablo Feinmann is a public intellectual who has worked in fiction, journalism, politics, philosophy, film, and classical music. According to a critic, "Basically Feinmann is a professor of philosophy with political and aesthetic concerns who—suffering on a personal and generational level the misfortunes of recent contemporary history—has continued to engage in multiple tasks, such as expressing (in a creative, non-pamphletary manner) pain for the failures of Argentine society" (Porretti). Feinmann found in the crime novel genre an effective way to critique social and political reality. His novel *Últimos días de la víctima*, discussed in the previous section, constitutes a major contribution to detective fiction. His other incursions into the genre include *Ni el tiro del final* (1982), *El cadáver imposible* (1992), and *Los crímenes de Van Gogh* (1994).

For the majority of contemporary Argentine writers of the *novela negra*, the genre functions as an avenue of social critique. "Small town, big hell" is an expression Guillermo Saccomanno uses to describe his novel *Cámara Gessell* (2012), citing *Peyton Place* and *Twin Peaks* among the many works that marked it (Bogado). Winner of the Premio Dashiell Hammett of the Semana Negra de Gijón, the novel is set in a seaside resort during the off-season and, in a series of chronicles, presents a biting critique of the evils that lie beneath a surface of seeming small-town tranquility. On a much more humorous note, *Fernández mata a Fernández* (2011) by Federico Jeanmaire uses black comedy and the absurd to deliver a critique of contemporary Argentine culture. All in dialogue form, it initiates as casual street corner conversation in Buenos Aires between two men, both named Fernández, about an incident in which a Fernández runs over and kills another Fernández. As the conversation continues, broaching urban problems and politics, others join in—all named Fernández, of course—and the initial amiability of the neighborhood encounter deteriorates into insults and threats of violence. *Que de lejos parecen moscas* (2011) by Kike Ferrari presents an unscrupulous businessman who has attained a life of luxury and scorns all who surround him; he considers them insignificant individuals whom he has no problem crushing like flies. One day, however, he discovers a cadaver in the trunk of his customized BMW, surely planted by one of his many enemies. While the action of this fast-paced novel spans only several hours, as the protagonist drives around the city frantically trying to get rid of the corpse, we are introduced through flashbacks to a corrupt society populated by selfish and base social climbers.

Reynaldo Sietecase's *A cuántos hay que matar* (2010) borrows from an actual crime—the 2004 kidnapping and murder of twenty-three-year-old Alex Blumberg, son of a wealthy textile engineer. In the real-life case, cell phone conversations suggested that the kidnappers were protected by police who expected to receive a share of the ransom (Eaton 6). Sietecase, who asserts that he used the Blumberg incident as a model to tell a good story and lend verisimilitude, focuses not on police corruption in his novel but rather on the fictional father's perverse arrangement to eliminate the killers of his son when he learns that they will be released from jail after a mere three-year sentence. In this tale of revenge and vigilantism, one of the targets of critique is the unscrupulous journalist who interviews one of the assassins, à la Truman Capote, and agrees to poison the prisoner in exchange for a sum of money. Sietecase also published a chilling collection of short stories, *Pendejos* (2007), about youths who commit violent crimes. Similarly, the novels of Matías Néspolo, *Siete maneras de matar a un gato* (2009) and *Con el sol en la boca* (2015), delve into the situation of youth caught in a world of urban deprivation, crime, and violence. Also dealing with dark and troubling youth culture is Javier Sinay's *Sangre joven: Matar y morir antes de la adultez* (2009), with the sobering difference that the six stories Sinay relates are nonfiction.

Several recent *novelas negras* employ the genre as a vehicle to explore or convey actual political scandals. Jorge Fernández Díaz affirms the power of fiction to tell a truth that journalism cannot deliver in his novel *El puñal* (2014), a thriller that delves into the world of "narcopolítica." Deputy director and columnist of the Argentine daily *La Nación*, Fernández Díaz has confirmed that the bizarre episodes in his novel occurred in Argentina but cannot be put in print because proof is lacking. "We journalists can publish only 10% of what we know.... Many times the paradox occurs that only fiction can portray reality," he insists (Peregil). Depicting the "glamourous" side of the narcotrade, the novel dramatizes the fact that this crime circuit could not exist without the participation of judges, police, politicians, and government functionaries. Fernández Díaz's protagonist, Remil, a spy who is a Malvinas veteran, continues his involvement in the dark underside of political espionage in a second novel, *La herida* (2017).

Fabio Nahuel Lezcano's *Crímenes apropiados* (2015), winner of Spain's Cosecha Roja prize, is a suspenseful roman à clef depicting the violence of the last thirty years of Argentine history. The plot revolves around the corrupt machinations of the ruthless director of the newspaper *Diario*, whose two sons discover they were stolen babies, born to *desaparecidas* during the dictatorship. This is clearly an allusion to the publisher of Argentine daily *Clarín*, whose adopted children were suspected to be taken from mothers in captivity. A critique of journalistic practices, the novel depicts the press's complicity with government corruption during the dictatorship as well as during the fledgling democracy.

Another political thriller, *La mafia política: Renacerás de tus cenizas* (2013) by Diego Grillo Trubba, deals with the period of 1983–89, the years of the transition to democracy in Argentina, through the story of el Cabeza, a provincial political boss who became vice president in 1989. The plot advances year by year, employing an omniscient narrator and ample use of dialogue to narrate the intricate and sinister ties between party politics and organized crime. Indeed, in the "Author's Note" at the end of the novel, Grillo Trubba writes, "The objective was to portray Argentine politics from the economic bases that sustain it, that is, crime," and he further clarifies the concept behind the book title with the following statement: "In Argentina, there are no political parties or movements, only illicit associations" (377).

Grillo Trubba—who in 2010 published *Crímenes coloniales*, a historical novel that develops around the resolution of an enigma—explains that *La mafia política* is the first in a cycle of novels that will take on the contemporary political scene in Argentina.

Writers whose novels relate the experience of the immigrant communities and *villas miseria* of Buenos Aires (in addition to Cabezón Cámara, discussed earlier in this section, and Sergio Olguín and Juan Martini, whose texts I analyze in chapter 5) are Leonardo Oyola and Federico Levín. Oyola's contributions to the Negro Absoluto series, *Santería* (2008) and *Sacrificio* (2010), are set in the world of the *villa miseria* and narrated by their protagonist, Fátima Sánchez, known as the Víbora Blanca for her ability to read the future. The Víbora Blanca is aided by popular saints as she confronts her powerful nemesis, La Marabunta, a femme fatale who pressures the Víbora to use her magic for questionable ends. In the parallel universe of the phantasmagoric *villa* created by Oyola, the ambience of marginality and social violence is infused with spirituality, fantasy, and pop culture. Oyola's other novels include *Siete & el tigre harapiento* (2005), *Chamamé* (2007, winner of Semana Negra de Gijón's Dashiell Hammett prize), *Gólgota* (2008), *Hacé que la noche venga* (2008), and *Kryptonita* (winner of Eterna Cadencia Libro del Año 2011).

Levín's trilogy—*Ceviche* (2009), *Bolsillo de cerdo* (2011), and *La lengua estofada* (2013)—has been referred to as "novelas gastronómicocriminales" (Clavé). In his "saga of hunger," Levín develops realistic and compelling plots typical of detective fiction while experimenting with language—his prose incorporates digressions, grotesque stereotypes, and the absurd and fantastic. The lead character is el Sapo Vizcarra, an obese food writer with gourmand tendencies, and the setting is Buenos Aires' Abasto neighborhood. Famous for its former wholesale fruit and vegetable market (now a shopping mall) and for being the home of Carlos Gardel, Abasto is also known for its ethnic diversity, having received an influx of immigrants. In his crawl through ethnic restaurants—Peruvian and Russian eateries are featured—el Sapo finds himself investigating strange cases involving mysterious deaths, disputes between criminal gangs, and individuals who hide a shadowy past.

The coordinator of the Negro Absoluto series is Ricardo Romero, whose novel *El síndrome de Rasputín* (2008) portrays a group of friends who are affected by Tourette's syndrome and find themselves enmeshed in a gang of assassins and pornographers in a dystopic Buenos Aires of the future. Their condition affords them a heightened sensibility that helps them survive the chaos. Romero continues the saga of the three friends with Tourette's in postapocalyptic Buenos Aires in *Los bailarines del fin del mundo* (2009) and *El spleen de los muertos* (2011). Fernando López, whose works include the Philip Lecoq detective series, written with humor, irreverence, and suspense, directs another series of detective novels by Latin American writers, Tinta Roja. Frequent participants in *novela negra* festivals are brothers José María and Carlos Marcos, coauthors of an epistolary novel of *realismo delirante*, *Muerde Muertos* (2012), named after their publishing house, which is dedicated to literature of the fantastic, erotic, and terror.

In contrast to the urban environment of many *novelas negras*, the tranquil rural setting of Miguel Ángel Molfino's *Monstruos perfectos* (2010) brings to mind Truman Capote's *In Cold Blood*, as does the seemingly senseless and brutally violent way in which an elderly couple is killed. Their terrified son buries them and takes off, falling in with a swindler who schools him in crime. Written in straightforward yet poetic prose, the novel contains a strong dose of social criticism at the same time that it conveys a sense of affection, or at least understanding, for the marginal individuals who establish a bond of solidarity. Another novel set outside Buenos Aires, specifically in Tucumán, is *El secreto de La Quebradita* (2017) by Juan Ángel Cabaleiro. Winner of the Premio García Pavón, it is a macabre story about regional political power.

Several writers use elements of the genre to explore moments in Argentine and world history, albeit with very different styles and approaches. An important figure in the Argentine crime fiction scene is journalist, poet, critic, and novelist Osvaldo Aguirre. His trilogy for the Negro Absoluto series—*Los indeseables* (2008), *Todos mienten* (2009), and *El novato* (2011)—is set in Buenos Aires of the 1930s, a period dubbed the "Década infame" (infamous decade). Initiated with the military coup led by General José Félix Uriburu, this period was characterized by economic crisis, unemployment, labor unrest, and electoral fraud. It is a moment in history that Aguirre knows well, having investigated it for his chronicles *Historias de la mafia en la Argentina* and *Enemigos públicos* (both 2003). Aguirre's trilogy has as protagonist legendary crime reporter Gustavo Germán González, celebrated for his creative and sometimes unscrupulous methods for scooping a story, and creates a parallel world that intersects with historic people and events.

Federico Andahazi is a prolific writer known for his historical novels, which frequently explore sexuality and religion. His *El libro de los placeres prohibidos* (2012), a crime thriller that impeccably re-creates scenarios in medieval Germany, involves a series of grisly murders in a brothel and incorporates the secret story of Gutenberg and the creation of the printing press. Another novelist and essayist, Juan Terranova, is a provocateur whose essay "El pálido género negro" (The pale noir genre) critiqued the terminology used to refer to the genre as well as some of Argentina's most well-known practitioners. Terranova's crime novels, *Lejos de Berlín* (2009) and *El vampiro argentino* (2011), are situated in an intrigue-ridden Buenos Aires and have as protagonist an elite German soldier who must unravel an enigma.

A genial and memorable figure in the *novela negra* circuit is Carlos Salem, who lives in Spain. Many of his novels, which use humor and farce to explore the human condition, are set in Europe, although Salem pays tribute to his Argentine roots in *Camino de ida* (2007), in which an aged Carlos Gardel—who, contrary to popular belief, survived the 1935 plane crash—reappears to seek revenge against Julio Iglesias, who has ruined his songs. Another Argentine writer who lives in Spain is Marcelo Luján. His novel *Subsuelo*, which won the 2016 Dashiell Hammett prize conferred by the Semana Negra de Gijón, evolves around turbid dealings among adolescents during their summer vacation. Convertini characterizes Luján's work as "a profound look at the dark side of the human mind" (Gigena). Two of Convertini's *novelas negras*—*La soledad del mal* (2012) and *El último milagro* (2013)—have won prizes: that of the Festival Azabache and BAN!'s Extremo Negro, respectively. The first, narrated from the perspective of a serial murderer, explores the inner lives of his chosen victims—people with failed and empty existences—while the second delves into the world of soccer fans whose fanaticism leads to crime and conspiracy.

While the socially oriented *novela negra* dominates the scene, the enigma subgenre is alive and thriving in the works of Guillermo Martínez and Pablo De Santis, whose novels spin plots based on deductive reasoning at the same time they explore abstract themes. Guillermo Martínez's *Crímenes imperceptibles*, winner of the Premio Planeta in 2003, was published in Spain as *Los crímenes de Oxford* and made into a movie in 2008 titled *The Oxford Murders*. The novel reveals Martínez's dual passion for Borges and mathematics, as its plot revolves around a series of crimes whose solution involves a mathematical equation, to be deciphered by a brilliant Oxford mathematician and his Argentine graduate student, who serves as narrator. Martínez's subsequent mystery novel is *La muerte lenta de Luciana B.*

(2007), an unsettling and precisely constructed thriller about mysterious deaths in the intimate circle of a woman referred to as Luciana B. No longer in remote and proper Oxford, this novel is set in a Buenos Aires consumed by unrest and invaded by *cartoneros*. Luciana suspects that the deaths are the work of Kloster, a famous writer and her former employer, but Kloster dismisses the allegations, calling Luciana delusional. The novel's fragmented vision leaves the reader uncertain as to whether the diabolical and brilliant Kloster set up the murders, making them appear to be random incidents, or whether this idea is merely the product of Luciana's disturbed mind.

Pablo De Santis, one of Argentina's most well-known and respected writers, began his writing career as a journalist and scriptwriter for comic books. His crime novels include *La traducción* (1998), *Filosofía y letras* (2002), *El enigma de París* (2007), and *Crímenes y jardines* (2013). A professed fan of Agatha Christie, De Santis says that he tries to re-create the rarefied and suffocating ambient of Christie's novels and likes working with an enigma, which he believes lends tension and structure to the text (Abdala; "Pablo De Santis"). The solution to the enigma is invariably an intellectual one involving the deciphering of a key text and ultimately reflecting on the nature of language and writing: for instance, the puzzle may implicate authorship or translation. Another element that De Santis's mysteries have in common is that they involve a sect or brotherhood, individuals who engage in the same pursuit—literary critics, translators, philosopher-detectives, philosophers of gardens—and who meet up in congresses or gatherings and pit their overinflated and brittle egos against each other. When their corpses start appearing, a member of the group becomes the detective. Frequently incorporating the fantastic or melancholic, the setting sometimes evokes a world that is deteriorating or on the verge of extinction, permitting an allegorical reading. For instance, in *La traducción* the translators gather in a half-finished, abandoned hotel in a desolate city on the Argentine coast. Close interprets the ruined, unfinished hotel in the novel as a withdrawn promise of modernity, allowing the novel to be read "not only as a theoretical reflection on abstract themes … but also as a striking parable of the Argentinian predicament in the neoliberal, post-authoritarian period" ("Translators Slain at Seaside" 14).

Another practitioner of the enigma-based novel is Diego Paszkowski, who made his mark in the genre with his novel *Tesis sobre un homicidio*, winner of the prize "Novela del diario *La Nación*" in 1998 and later adapted into a successful movie with the same name. A taut psychological thriller, it enters the brilliant but monstrous mind of a young law student who kills a woman and leaves her body behind the law school, solely for the purpose of demonstrating his thesis to his law professors: that he can commit murder and get away with it. Gabriel Rolón, a well-known Argentine psychoanalyst with best-selling nonfictional books, has also penned a psychoanalytic crime thriller, *Los padecientes* (2010). The protagonist, a psychoanalyst named Pablo Rouviot, is sought out to testify regarding the state of mind of a disturbed young man who is thought to have killed his father, a high-powered industrialist. Suspense builds as Rouviot becomes involved in a complicated and dangerous case involving dark family secrets and corrupt lawyers, businessmen, and police.

While new writers are continually entering the scene, this overview has attempted to include the most well known of the current practitioners of crime fiction in Argentina.

## TOWARD A CHARACTERIZATION OF AND APPROACH TO THE GENRE IN ARGENTINA

Argentine crime fiction displays characteristics that are a response to specific social and political conditions. To open this discussion of tendencies of the genre in Argentina, once again I turn to Sergio Olguín's remarks: "When one wants to talk about political issues, they use crime fiction, and there is a reason for this. The two things are closely linked.... In Argentina there is a certain resistance to traditional realism ... and crime fiction is then, in some way, an excuse to develop traditional realism from a more acceptable, more illustrious place" (Soto). While realism is fundamental to the social critique of the *novela negra*, this is not the naïve realism that assumes there is "an unproblematic fit between the world, language, and the structures of the human mind" (Ryan 166). Germane to this issue is the genre's highly codified nature, which precludes any pretense of overall transparent representation. In addition, some crime writers attenuate their gritty realistic scenarios by incorporating aspects such as a "fairy tale" ending or magical or supernatural elements.

Other writers also speak to the genre's social role: "today the *novela negra* is becoming the social novel of the century; the mirror in which to look at our daily life and, perhaps, understand it," posits Raúl Argemí ("Fantasía, ficción y espías"). Carlos Salem echoes that sentiment, noting that the majority of writers use the genre "as a springboard to narrate society and its changes, or the problems of the individual, alienated by a system that exhausts itself without apparent regeneration" ("Fantasía, ficción y espías").

Repeated thematic and structural elements include the legacy of the dictatorship and the absence of honest police detectives, aspects that Argentine writers have highlighted in their commentary. Guillermo Orsi, at the conference Medellín Negro 2012, discussed the omnipresence of references to the dictatorship in the *género negro*. He remarked that this dark period had a huge impact on the writers of his generation, saying that even though he does not intend to write about it, "the dictatorship invades me because it has produced such disaster, such excess, such damage, so irreparable, that it is impossible to escape that climate, that destruction, those spoils." Orsi also pointed out that although younger writers may say that it does not make sense to continue writing about the dictatorship, the issues that they incorporate—"social marginalization, the breakdown of the values of solidarity, in short, the enormous marginality that exists in Argentine society"—are consequences of neoliberal policies initiated during the dictatorial regime.[13]

The lack of police detectives as heroes is another trait of the national *novela negra* that Argentine writers underscore. Reynaldo Sietecase attributes this to the legacy of the dictatorship, emphasizing the point with a rhetorical question: "How can the good guy be in a uniform?" (Álvarez Plá). Convertini reiterates that sentiment in reference to Latin American writers in general: "Latin American authors ... resort less to the archetype of the policeman who solves everything because in our countries that is not credible" (Álvarez Plá). Carlos Gamerro's statement, also addressing the issue of widespread police corruption, is the most radical. In his "Decálogo del relato policial argentino," the first precept is "The police commit the crime" ("Notas para una redefinición" 64). The absent police detective is often replaced by investigative journalists in the detective function. Other frequent themes include endemic corruption, the widened gap between social classes, and the impact of privatization and globalization.

Many of the novels that have been published since the demise of the dictatorship in 1982 fall into two large groupings: those that deal with the criminality of the state during the "Dirty War" and those that critique the impact of neoliberalism and globalization as well as the corruption and illegality during the 1990s under the Menem presidency and beyond. This book will address the second group. While the focus of my book is the manner in which the novels critique the impact of failed economic policies and endemic corruption, I will also consider other aspects of their sociopolitical context, including the depiction of the city of Buenos Aires, Argentine identity, social class, gender roles, consumerism, and the media.

Buenos Aires is the setting for most of the examined novels, and the way in which it is represented is an integral element of the social and political critique. As Close remarks, the *novela negra* carries out an enterprise of cognitive mapping (*Contemporary Hispanic Crime Fiction* 44), and the concept of mapping the city points to the synthesis of geographic and historical space into a form that produces schemes about their meaning and guides to the search for identity (Gorelik, *Miradas* 21). Maps provide a means to order the chaos, giving us a sense of orientation and control over our surroundings. In a literary text, the interaction between fictional characters and geographic spaces in the city creates an urban imaginary, "both a real and a made-up projection" (Biron 8). The notion of "writing the city" has been disseminated by Ángel Rama in *Ciudad letrada*, and Beatriz Sarlo discusses the production of the "ciudad escrita": "Discourses produce ideas of cities, critiques, analyses, figurations, hypotheses, instructions for use, prohibitions, orders, fictions of all kinds. The written city is always symbolization and displacement, image, metonymy" (*La ciudad vista* 145). Sarlo refers to the power of revelation of "la ciudad escrita" (147), thus the role of the critic consists of teasing out those symbolic meanings in the text.

An analysis of the cityscape depicted in the novels must consider not only the literary techniques that Sarlo enumerates but also in which areas of the cities the writers choose to situate the action. In addition to scenes set in the center city, several novels under study focus on peripheral areas, specifically the luxurious gated communities, known as "countries," on the outskirts of Buenos Aires as well as the *villas de emergencia* and impoverished areas to the south of the city. Different authors ascribe different schemes of meaning to the same neighborhood. For example, in one novel a character calls herself a "chica de Recoleta," meaning an upper-middle-class girl with a privileged upbringing; in another Recoleta is home to the decadent rich; in a third novel it is a place for terrorist plotting; and in a fourth, Recoleta is becoming seedy due to the invasion of beggars, pickpockets, and prostitutes. The spaces chosen as well as how they are depicted invariably speak to the transformation of Buenos Aires due to globalization, privatization, and other market-oriented policies, critiquing the increased fragmentation, gaping contrasts, and deterioration of the city.

Another role of the "urban imaginary" has to do with the search for identity. Adrián Gorelik discusses Buenos Aires' fragile sense of self, as it is forever preoccupied with where and to whom it belongs, seeking models and embodiments ("Buenos Aires" 62). According to Gorelik, the successive "northamericanization" and "latinamericanization" of Buenos Aires beginning in the 1970s have rendered the supposed European character of Buenos Aires a nostalgic illusion (*Miradas* 73). Several novels under study depict a transformed Buenos Aires whose inhabitants must confront an unflattering image reflected back to them.

Social class is also intrinsically linked to urban space. The studies of Argentine sociologist Maristella Svampa provide insight into the novels' depiction of an increasingly polarized society as the wealthy take refuge in gated communities with privatized security while the newly impoverished—"collateral damage" in Zygmunt Bauman's terms—end up in shantytowns. The trajectory of the detective, or the individual(s) carrying out the detective function, may serve to connect diverse neighborhoods within the metropolitan area. Fredric Jameson points to the unifying role of the detective in the fragmented city in which classes are separated into their own geographical space: "Since there is no longer any privileged experience in which the whole of the social structure can be grasped, a figure must be invented who can be superimposed on the society as a whole, whose routine and life pattern serve somehow to tie its separate and isolated parts together" (127).[14] Following this scheme, in some of the novels the character carrying out the detective function travels between the enclaves of the wealthy and the humble sections of Buenos Aires, enabling the reader to see a wide swath of society.

The press and the media often play a key role. Many of the featured novels showcase investigative journalists in the role of the detective—a tribute to Rodolfo Walsh and a reflection of the importance of watchdog journalism in exposing scandals during the 1990s.[15] Other images of the press are less flattering—in some novels it is seen as lacking ethical standards, following market rules by publishing what will sell best. Still another depiction of the press shows it to be manacled and managed by corporate and governmental interests.

Literary noir of recent decades, Lee Horsley argues, has been "concerned with exposing the nature of contemporary consumer society" (*The Noir Thriller* 190). Sarlo's studies of urban culture in *La ciudad vista* help us understand how the daily experience of urban dwellers—elites as well as marginal individuals—is permeated by images and interpretations produced by the market. Reflecting this phenomenon, one novel I discuss transmits the role of mass media and global marketing in creating the desire for consumption and structuring what individuals perceive as "reality."

Gender roles, sexual politics, and strained relations between the sexes are prominent issues in crime stories. The detective genre has traditionally been associated with the masculine due to its focus on science and logic, considered masculine domains. Indeed, Maureen T. Reddy points to the "intense masculinity of the hardboiled" as one of its defining traits (193). In classic crime fiction, women take on clichéd versions of the victim or the catalyst or cause of crime. As Marty Roth puts it, "Detective fiction claims that women are generically useless" (116). The only female character allowed agency is the dangerous femme fatale, who uses her charms to deceive men and lure them to their destruction. Agency, whether it be in the form of the detective or the criminal, is granted to male characters. P. D. James's *An Unsuitable Job for a Woman* (1972), featuring female detective Cordelia Gray and a title ironically negating detective work as appropriate for the "gentler sex," breaks out the gender question. Contemporary crime fiction has spawned many shrewd and empowered female sleuths who are just as capable as their male counterparts at performing what hard-boiled fiction considered a man's job. As several critics have pointed out, feminism has used crime fiction to appropriate a "male" discourse and portray tough and rational-thinking female detectives.[16] In the novels under study, there is a gamut of female roles, from the traditional victims and femmes fatales to savvy investigators. While both male and female authors write women into the detective function in the novels in question, the male authors depict their female investigators as sexually active and the object of sexual fantasies and the female author I study does not. The sexually aggressive woman, still deviant and transgressive according to traditional norms, serves to represent cultural anxieties about gender and sexuality (Worthington 46, 48).

The portrayal of the investigator—whether male or female—provides a distinctive character to the text. Chandler's Philip Marlowe is the iconic model of the hard-boiled detective, and his ethics and brand of masculinity have left an indelible mark on crime fiction. In "The Simple Art of Murder," Chandler defines his detective. He is an idealized figure, a questing knight seeking truth and justice transplanted onto the mean city streets. Unafraid, he courts violence and death in the hostile urban environment. In his quest to restore justice, he sticks to his own personal code of honor, often flouting laws and regulations. A tough-guy figure, he also has a sentimental side. The crime fiction texts I study here are inevitably impacted by the figure of

Marlowe, be his characteristics imitated, altered, or rejected. Among the Chandleresque traits that are carried over, several novels infuse their investigator with a heightened affective dimension.

Curiously, sentimentalism has staked a place in the *novela negra*. This is the thesis of Leonard Cassuto's book *Hard-Boiled Sentimentality*. "Inside every crime story is a sentimental narrative that's trying to come out," he states, defining sentimentalism as "a worldview that emphasizes family and other institutions that connect people." It celebrates "nourishing social ties that result when people extend their sympathy to others around them" (7). The affective dimension of these novels can also be seen as evidence of the "new sentimentalism" that Aníbal González identifies and discusses in *Love and Politics in the Contemporary Spanish American Novel*. Several of the novels in the present book function in two registers—the story of crime and the story of the heart—and these dual stories are connected by the sentimental detective. It seems that sentimentalism has crept into the *novela negra*, and this book explores the relationship between crime fiction and sentimentalism in relevant texts.

Having read well over one hundred Argentine *novelas negras* published since 1990, I have chosen eleven to analyze in depth—all published since 2000—in order to discuss how they portray various aspects of contemporary Argentine society through the lens of crime. In my decision of which novels and novelists to feature, I have tried to balance the selection of representative writers with a choice of novels that highlight key social and political issues of contemporary Argentina. Most of the novelists whose work I analyze are major figures in the Argentine *novela negra* scene: Claudia Piñeiro, Ernesto Mallo, Sergio Olguín, Guillermo Orsi, Raúl Argemí, and Juan Martini. Critics have observed that Argentina has not produced a writer who has penned a series with a repeating detective figure such as Vázquez Montalbán in Spain and Taibo in Mexico,[17] and many Argentine writers make a one-time foray into the genre. This is the case of two novelists I study: Tomás Eloy Martínez and Marcos Aguinis. Finally, I examine the first novel of Rubén Correa, a journalist turned novelist, as well as a novel written by an unnamed Argentine writer using the pseudonym R. S. Pratt.

I address specific thematic concerns in each chapter. Chapter 1 considers novels that depict organized crime rings of human and drug traffickers and the collusion of government authorities: *Ciudad Santa (Holy City)* by Guillermo Orsi and *Los hombres te han hecho mal* (Men have done you wrong) by Ernesto Mallo. The novels studied in chapter 2, *El vuelo de la reina* (The flight of the queen) by Tomás Eloy Martínez and *El muerto indiscreto* (The indiscreet dead man) by Rubén Correa, feature investigative journalists practicing watchdog journalism to expose wrongdoing during the Menem presidency. From an overall critique of the Menem government, in my third chapter I move to the representation of tragic incidents that highlighted corruption during his presidency and beyond: the terrorist bombings of Jewish institutions in Buenos Aires and the mysterious death of Alberto Nisman, the special prosecutor charged with investigating the second attack. *Asalto al paraíso* (Attack on paradise) by Marcos Aguinis draws attention to the institutional corruption surrounding these attacks, while *El fiscal* (The prosecutor) by R. S. Pratt (a pseudonym) sets forth a partisan interpretation of the circumstances surrounding the prosecutor's death. Chapter 4 considers three novels—*Retrato de familia con muerta* (Family portrait with a dead woman) by Raúl Argemí and *Las viudas de los jueves* (*Thursday Night Widows*) and *Betibú* (*Betty Boo*) by Claudia Piñeiro—set in exclusive gated communities, known as country clubs or simply "countries," on the outskirts of Buenos Aires. Finally, chapter 5 turns to the other side, the representation of the urban poor, in the novels *Puerto Apache* by Juan Martini and *La fragilidad de los cuerpos* (The fragility of bodies) by Sergio Olguín.

Chapter One

# COMBATTING ORGANIZED CRIME AND INSTITUTIONAL COMPLICITY, WITH A SENTIMENTAL SUBTEXT

Velasco Oliaga: "En su novela la policía no sale muy bien tratada. ¿En realidad es tal como usted la describe?"
Guillermo Orsi: "Peor."

—Javier Velasco Oliaga, "Tal vez me mude, solo para estar más cerca de Gijón"

A RETIRED COP CONFRONTS A BRUTAL WHITE SLAVE RING, WHILE ANOTHER police detective interjects himself into a violent war between domestic and Colombian drug cartels. The novels by Ernesto Mallo and Guillermo Orsi analyzed in this chapter—*Los hombres te han hecho mal* (2012) and *Ciudad Santa* (2009)—set the scene for the rest of this book as they present wide-ranging portraits of common criminals and mafiosos; corrupt politicians, police, military, and government officials; and the intricate and convoluted relationship between them. For these authors, the *novela negra*—besides being a suspenseful read—functions as a vehicle for interrogating and denouncing the complicity of government officials with organized crime, along with other causes of social disorder. In this first pair of novels chosen for in-depth examination, I consider Argentine versions of arguably the most frequent themes in Latin American crime fiction: illicit trafficking and police corruption.

The novels are replete with elements that characterize the *novela negra*: the depiction of widespread violence and corruption, investigation into wrongdoing, a maddeningly complex plot with a wide array of characters whose paths eventually cross, wiseacre dialogue, sex, strained and predatory gender relations, and gothic undertones.[1] Each combines grisly realism with nonrealistic features such as a fairy-tale ending and a character with a touch of the supernatural. A leitmotiv of Orsi's novel is the image of Buenos Aires as a chaotic, violent, and unholy metropolis. In the introduction, I stated that the lack of a detective, and especially honest police investigators, defines the Argentine *novela negra*. However, this chapter presents notable exceptions with these novels that feature well-intentioned policemen. And, perhaps surprisingly, they also include a sentimental love story. Incongruous as it may seem, for all their monstrous criminal deeds and violent and sadistic thugs, the novels of Mallo and Orsi are deeply invested in sentimentality.

Mallo and Orsi are well-known figures in the Hispanic crime fiction circuit. Mallo created and organizes Buenos Aires Negra! (BAN!). Both have participated in Mar del Plata's Festival Azabache and the Semana Negra in Gijón, Spain, and Orsi participated in Medellín Negro. Besides the novels discussed in this chapter, Mallo has published a novel about the Menem presidency, *Me verás caer* (2013), linking Menem's ostentatious social life to criminal frivolity. A prolific writer with over a dozen novels to his name, Guillermo Orsi is a master of the *novela negra*. His narratives employ abundant sarcasm and humor to deliver a biting critique of Argentine society and its institutions. Two of his earlier novels, *Tripulantes de un viejo bolero* (1995) and *Sueños de perro* (2004), follow the typical Argentine tradition of eschewing the private eye or police detective, employing instead a disc jockey and a taxi driver, respectively, in the investigative role. But in *Nadie ama a un policía* (2007) we meet Gotán, an ex-federal policeman who heeds a friend's call for help and becomes entangled in police and government corruption in the chaos of the 2001 economic meltdown. *Fantasmas del desierto* (2014) brings Gotán back for a round of farfetched adventures when he is hired by a reclusive millionaire to solve a murder, while *Segunda vida* (2011) deals with down-on-their-luck Malvinas War veterans who are recruited by crooked cops to help them rob banks. Finally, *Siempre hay alguien a quien matar* (2015) fuses the crime genre with a love story as the protagonist, a solitary writer, springs into action upon the death of the woman he loves. Like *Ciudad Santa*, these stories present a caustic commentary on a wide range of social ills.

## TRAFFICKING ENABLED BY INSTITUTIONAL CORRUPTION

*Los hombres te han hecho mal* and *Ciudad Santa* depict the inner workings of human and drug trafficking in Argentina; this section discusses their real-life context. Human trafficking is a worldwide scourge, and while Argentina is not considered a major human trafficking center on a global scale, it is a place of origin, transit, and destination for human victims, and analysts report a worrisome increase.[2] According to analysts, human trafficking rings in Argentina remain small and informal—often family-run—and depend on state protection and support, in particular police and security forces that encourage this activity ("Nuevos métodos"). This collusion is central to the plot of Mallo's novel. In regard to narcotraffic, Argentina is a country of transit and manufacture and a marketplace for illegal drugs. Recently, Colombian and Mexican drug cartels have encroached in Argentine territory, and the novels of Orsi and Mallo highlight this phenomenon.

What makes Argentina attractive to foreign drug cartels? A variety of factors—mainly stepped-up enforcement in Mexico and Colombia coupled with lax or nonexistent enforcement in Argentina—has resulted in an intensification of narcotics activity in Argentina. "Mexico's drug war is turning Argentina into the new Wild West of the global narcotics trade," declares an analyst (Cohen). Authorities report that Colombian traffickers have made Argentina an important route to transport cocaine into Europe because they have found it to be a perfect place for smuggling, money laundering, investing, and enjoying themselves. Virginia Messi's and Juan Manuel Bordón's book, *Narcolandia: Por qué la Argentina se convirtió en el paraíso de los narcos colombianos*, details other factors, citing the common language, Argentina's tradition of opening its doors to immigrants, and the ease with which citizens of Mercosur countries can obtain permanent residency in Argentina. Another reason is Argentina's geopolitical position—it is close to three major drug-producing countries (Paraguay, Peru, and Bolivia) and has strong maritime links with Europe, an important market.

The problem is aggravated by the lack of investment in border surveillance and the poor track record of the country's security forces in their battle against drug trafficking. Serious failings in inspections at Argentina's ports and airports—for instance, scanners that are not designed to detect drugs—facilitate the flow of illegal drugs (Cawley; Gallo). The Argentine inspector general claims that these failings are intentional: "There is a general situation of a lack of control concerning the issue of drugs.... There is a deliberate absence: the State refused to exercise control" ("Despouy").

Organized crime would not be possible without institutional complicity, and this situation is integral to the yarns spun by Mallo and Orsi, which depict corruption among politicians, judges, and especially the police. Argentine police official Hugo Antolín Almirón reported in 2003 that while corruption in Argentina "has not reached the dangerous stage as in some other countries," it "has penetrated deep within the public offices and has affected every stratum of the society" (320). The two police forces that operate in Buenos Aires—the federal police and the Bonaerense—are subject to scathing critique in the novels under study. Argentina's federal police force, PFA (Policía Federal Argentina), which has jurisdiction in the capital and in all federal crimes in the nation, is headquartered in Buenos Aires and reports to the Ministry of the Interior. Each province has its own security police with jurisdiction within its territory, and the Bonaerense, the force of Buenos Aires province, is the largest in the country. While the PFA is considered to be more professional and more respected than the Bonaerense, according to numerous analysts both forces have a similar history of corruption and abuse of power. Titles of studies immediately communicate the authors' messages: Carlos Dutil and Ricardo Ragendorfer's book, *La Bonaerense: Historia criminal de la policía de la provincia de Buenos Aires* (The criminal history of the police of the province of Buenos Aires), illustrates with abundant documentation "the saga of corruption and death that the Bonaerense sowed" (307). Krystin Krause's paper "From *Guerra Sucia* [Dirty War] to *Gatillo Fácil* [trigger happy]: Violence and the Argentine Federal Police" analyzes violent behavior of the federal police during and after the dictatorship.[3]

The Argentine police were originally created by state leaders "to defend the state from political threats, not to protect individual citizens." This early militarization is reflected in the police's excessive use of force in the repression of civic unrest (Eaton 9). During the dictatorship, both the federal and provincial police were deeply involved in the notorious human rights abuses of the period. Police were used by the military for the "dirty work": they participated in the capturing, interrogating, torturing, and killing of citizens. Although the top leadership of the police who had been involved in the Proceso was removed under Alfonsín's government in 1987, a considerable number of police personnel were carried over to present-day forces and many repressive methods survived (Hinton 8; McSherry 9).

During the Menem presidency, the shift to a market-driven economy, with its accompanying reduction in state spending in areas such as welfare, education, and security, contributed to a sharp rise in poverty, inequality, and crime. This coincided with frequent media coverage of police abuse and corruption, heightening public panic. Kent Eaton considers "police criminality" as "one of the most pressing and intractable political problems in

Argentina's post-authoritarian period" (6). A form of corruption alluded to in *Ciudad Santa* are extrajudicial killings, when trigger-happy police take "justice" into their own hands. A Ministry of Justice official said, "In Argentina, either you punish criminals by using illegal force, or there will be impunity for the crimes they commit," voicing a sentiment shared by certain sectors of Argentine society (Hinton 33).

Protection schemes for criminal activities are repeatedly depicted in the *novela negra*. Corrupt police take money from rackets in exchange for protection, and distribute it throughout the police departments as well as to civilian officials, forming a network that makes it all but impossible for any person to call another to account. Studies by academics and NGOs have posited that the PFA was at its most efficient when it was geared toward generating illicit revenue. "In this well-organized system of petty corruption, even the price to turn a blind eye to certain activities was pre-established," reports Mercedes S. Hinton (41).

These problems become further entrenched due to the virtual impunity of police, which extends to every sort of crime, including torture and extrajudicial killings. Any legal action, criminal or civil, against the police takes place in an atmosphere of intimidation (Krause). What is more, the police possess a secretive esprit de corps: "Since personal loyalty and obedience to superior officers are sine qua non qualifications for promotion, it is extremely rare for a policeman to denounce corruption or negligence in a precinct" (Hinton 3, 32). Based on all these factors, it comes as no surprise that there is a low level of trust on the part of the Argentine people in the police. Several analysts maintain that the fear of crime and the general sense of insecurity have been artificially inflated—in part by the presence of police violence itself—to allow the police to secure greater control and avoid accountability, especially for crimes related to corruption. This leads to the paradoxical situation in which police are seen as the cause of heightened insecurity while, at the same time, their presence and authority is required more than ever. Attempts at police reform have been largely ineffective due to sabotage by officials at other levels of government, the dependence of politicians on police kickbacks for campaign financing, and the attitude of a conservative sector of civil society who demand a heavy-handed response to Argentina's perceived crime wave. According to Hinton, "dismantling networks of corruption might easily unleash the ire not only of police hierarchies but of the powerful vested interests across the government that thrive in obscurity" (193).

As the failure to achieve reform implies, police corruption is but a cog in an extensive network of state corruption. Dutil and Ragendorfer point out that police corruption is condoned by powerful social and state sectors because they all benefit from it: "The subordinate position of the Police within the powers of the State makes it impossible to believe in their criminal autonomy.... Local power brokers, councilors, deputies, governors, are their constituents or protectors, depending on duties and ability to act" (10). "Detrás de todo gran policía corrupto hay siempre un gran político" (Behind every great corrupt policeman there is always a great politician), conclude Dutil and Ragendorfer, borrowing from a popular riff (10). Politicians protect corrupt police officers in exchange for a cut of the funds that the police collect from protection rackets, using this money to finance their political campaigns (Eaton 19–20). Hinton explains that "the PFA's vast holdings, some of which are believed to derive from involvement in gambling, prostitution, and car theft rings, have enabled the institution to exert considerable influence over politics." What is more, she points out, "some politicians have turned a blind eye to these illegal activities because they benefit handsomely from *pactos mafiosos*—unholy alliances with rogue police elements—or because they consider tolerance for some level of corruption as a reasonable trade-off for keeping control of the streets" (68).

Finally, both Mallo's and Orsi's novels illustrate the failure of the judiciary, an institution that plays a key role in the Argentine system, to effectively prosecute crime. Criminal cases in Argentina are investigated by a magistrate appointed for life who has complete power to look into all the facts (Chevigny 195). Heavy reliance on the judiciary presents another set of problems: not only is the judiciary regarded as one of the most corrupt of all Argentine institutions; it is also perceived to be thoroughly politicized and susceptible to executive manipulation and vulnerable to bribery (Hinton 193). The state of affairs detailed in this background is fodder for critique in the novels under study.

## A SENTIMENTAL COP GOES UP AGAINST HUMAN TRAFFICKERS: *LOS HOMBRES TE HAN HECHO MAL* BY ERNESTO MALLO

The body of María Esther Amaro was found by a highway in the vicinity of Mar del Plata, a popular resort city nine hundred kilometers south of Buenos Aires, in November 1996. On her back the assassin had carved the word "puta" (whore). This killing was part of a series of at least thirteen, and possibly more than fifty, deaths and disappearances of women in the region. All except one of the thirteen were known prostitutes. Many of them had been tortured and dismembered. A journalist speculated that this was the work of a serial killer, whom he dubbed "el Loco de la Ruta." The police and the office of the district attorney also promoted the image of a psychopathic monster who was responsible for the horrific crimes. But people in Mar del Plata whispered that the police were involved in the killings and that the cause was the failure of the girls to "pay their dues." According to vox populi, in one of the red light districts of Mar del Plata, 40 percent of the earnings went to the women and 60 percent to the police (Islas and Míguez 15). It was also suspected that a white slavery ring was involved. Finally, in 2001, the investigation of Judge Pedro Hooft, using data from telephone conversations, identified the existence of a crime network made up of police, judiciary employees, and provincial politicians. The following year charges were filed against ten policemen, a madam, a hoodlum, and a district attorney. The charges included extortion, illegitimate privation of liberty, illicit association, false testimony, and related offenses. Thus "el Loco de la Ruta" was reconfigured into officials responsible for security and social control. In their study of urban violence, Alejandro Islas and Daniel Míguez use this case to illustrate the entanglement of sectors of the state with delinquents in the execution of crimes. For writer Ernesto Mallo, this saga of violent crime and corruption serves as a model for the crime scene of his novel *Los hombres te han hecho mal*.

*Los hombres te han hecho mal* is the final novel of a trilogy that has as protagonist federal policeman "el Perro" Lascano. Set in successive decades, the novels illustrate changes in common crime and institutional violence in Argentina since the 1970s. Mallo's social critique is presented through the exploits of Lascano, a rare honest policeman amid a sea of corruption who is in touch with his "softer side." As I will discuss later in this chapter, Lascano fits the model of what Leonard Cassuto has termed the "sentimental action hero" (15), and the novels gesture toward sentimental values that stand in counterpoint to the self-centered greed of the cast of criminal types. The novels are succinct—two hundred pages or less—and highlight Mallo's skill as a storyteller, maintaining suspense as Lascano overcomes a series of challenges in his perilous investigation of a crime. As is typical of hard-boiled fiction, the stories are narrated in third person, sometimes from the perspective of different characters. The plots advance through changing registers and tones, as lyrical and philosophical passages alternate with rapid action and graphic violence. Abundant use of dialogue, presented in italicized typeface without quotation marks or signals indicating a change of speaker, obligates the reader to figure out who is speaking and lends a sense of immediacy.

In each of the novels of the trilogy, Lascano investigates a "common crime"—a murder, a bank heist, a missing person—but they all turn out to be bound up with institutional crime. The first novel of the series, *La aguja en el pajar* (2006), takes place during the dictatorship; the second, *Delincuente argentino* (2007), deals with the transition period during the Alfonsín presidency; and the third, *Los hombres te han hecho mal* (2012), is situated in the 1990s to the present.[4] This looked like the end of the series, but in 2015 a prequel appeared and in 2017 yet another adventure for Lascano. *La conspiración de los mediocres*, the prequel, is set in the years leading up to the dictatorship and relates Lascano's brief but intense relationship with his wife, Marisa, and her untimely death. In the (possibly) final episode, *El hilo de sangre*, the retired and wealthy Lascano, unable to adjust to a life of tranquility, stumbles upon the opportunity to avenge his parents' murder and embarks on a persecution that takes him to Barcelona.[5]

When we first meet Lascano in *La aguja en el pajar*, he has been recently widowed and is mourning his loss. As if he did not have enough reason for feeling gloomy, there are constant reminders of the brutal military regime—for instance, he witnesses a young couple being taken away by soldiers. The backdrop of the dark and disturbing scenario of Argentina's repressive military dictatorship will not abate throughout the course of the novel. Lascano is tasked with investigating the death of a Jewish moneylender, Elías Biterman, but it turns out that Major Giribaldi, a corrupt and abusive military man, was an accessory to Biterman's murder. Therefore, the investigation of this crime is "off-limits." In the meantime, Lascano gives shelter to Eva, a hunted militant of the ERP (Ejército Revolucionario del Pueblo) who reminds him of his dead wife. Despite the fact that he is a policeman, Eva comes to trust in him and falls in love.[6] Lascano's stubborn pursuit of justice—he refuses to drop the Biterman case despite pressure to do so from his superiors—lands him in deep trouble. He and Eva make plans to escape to Brazil, but Lascano is surrounded by Giribaldi's men and takes a bullet to his chest in the ensuing shoot-out. Thinking that her beloved Lascano is dead, Eva embarks on her journey to Brazil.

In *Delincuente argentino*, we discover that Lascano did not die in the shoot-out, and he is recovering from a gunshot wound to his lung. Set in the fledgling democracy, the face of crime has changed. The Apóstoles, a faction within the police force that is in cahoots with Colombian drug cartels, assassinate Turcheli, the police chief who represents old-style corruption. Since Lascano was being protected by Turcheli during his recovery, the Apósteles mark him for killing. In a comparative study of the first two novels of Mallo's trilogy, Raúl Caplán and Erich Fisbach remark that institutional violence does not change radically from one novel to the next, despite the fact that the first takes place during the dictatorial regime and the second is set in the restored democracy: "the actors are the same—police, military or ex-police and ex-military" (158). The difference, they point out, is that during the democracy there is no longer institutionalized violence with an ideological justification; now there are mafia connections and the only reason for violence is money. Caplán and Fisbach note that in *Aguja* the assassinations do not need to be covered up, while in *Delincuente*, the killing of the police chief is disguised as a heart attack.

A critique of financial crime is presented in the second novel through a new character, "el Topo" Miranda, an old-style "gentleman thief" who uses his wit to rob banks and eschews violence. Recently released from a four-year prison sentence, he plans to go straight and live peacefully with his wife and son once he pulls off one final bank robbery to set up his finances. However, the heist goes wrong: although Miranda makes off with a suitcase full of money, one of his accomplices kills a policeman and is captured. The Miranda and Lascano story lines connect when the bank hires Lascano to find Miranda and recover the money—since the million dollars that Miranda stole is unreported money, the bankers cannot claim it and thus have to resort to extralegal means to try to get it back. At this point, Lascano's only goal is to seek Eva in Brazil, thus he accepts the shady arrangement to get funds for the trip. The tables turn when Miranda's men save Lascano from execution by the Apósteles, and Miranda gives Lascano money to get out of town. Lascano locates Eva in Brazil, watches her from a distance, and is crushed to discover that Eva seems to be happy with another man. As Lascano turns to leave, who should he run into but Miranda, who, also "on the lam," decided to follow him.

An important theme developed in *Delincuente argentino* is the blurring of the divide between criminals and those who represent the law. Lascano and Miranda, the cop and the bank robber, are established as doubles for each other—both have their own sense of professional ethics and both seek an escape from violence and fulfillment with the woman they love. At the end of the novel, their destinies seem to merge. What is more, Miranda points out to Lascano that the bank from which he stole the money has since folded due to corrupt dealings and the bankers took off with what was left of the clients' money. So who is the bigger thief, he asks, the bank robber or the banker? This evokes Bertolt Brecht's line in *Threepenny Opera* that Piglia quotes to describe the hard-boiled subgenre: "What is robbing a bank compared to founding one?" (*Crítica y ficción* 70). The perspective of the criminal outsider serves to critique the sociopolitical world that indicts him, pointing to the contradiction at the base of the capitalist system.

## Hard-Boiled Realism Meets the Fairy Tale

*Los hombres te han hecho mal* is a powerful denunciation of the alliance of police officials and local politicians with organized crime, newly dominated by international cartels. Through the voice of Lascano's chatty intellectual lover, the novel indicts "el evidente desgobierno de la nación" (the evident misrule of the nation) (39). Also to blame for the chaos and corruption are the frivolous elite who care only for their amusement, a rebuke that can be read as an allusion to the culture spawned during the government of Carlos Menem.[7] Mallo delivers this critique in a yarn that combines fast action and gritty hard-boiled realism with lyrical passages and a fairy-tale ending. The plot advances via a series of vignettes developing subplots that are eventually connected by the detective. At the same time, it is the work of the reader to fill in the ellipses and assemble the mosaic to obtain a full picture.

The central plot is reminiscent of a novel by Raymond Chandler: Lascano, after being involuntarily retired from the police force, accepts a job from an ultrawealthy private client, Sofía Taborda, his estranged cousin. Sofía hires her long-lost cousin to investigate the murder of her daughter, Amalia, and search for her missing granddaughter, Candela. Thus, similar to a Chandler plot, Lascano operates as a private eye and his investigation reveals ugly family secrets. Although he is investigating a personal crime, as opposed to institutional wrongdoing, his search for answers leads to the underworld of human trafficking in Mar del Plata, which is controlled and protected by the local police and a local politician. His inquiries prove to be unwelcome by the mafia, making him a target of their hit man. Thus, although Lascano does not set out to do battle with this mafia, his task lands him in the middle of it, and his conscience will not allow him to look the other way when he witnesses the exploitation of young women.

Mallo's novel incorporates details from the real case of María Esther Amaro: Amalia's body was discovered at the side of a highway near Mar del Plata with the word "puta" carved in her back. For this reason, Lascano's investigation takes him from Buenos Aires to the red light district of Mar del Plata, where a sinister individual nicknamed "la Momia" (the Mummy) oversees the prostitution network.[8] Subplots develop the stories of two rival criminal gangs—one led by a trafficker named Yancar, the other by the violent "el loco" Romero. Romero and his thugs eliminate Yancar's gang, but subsequently an even more savage group led by a foreigner named Camacho guns down Romero and his gang. Another plotline follows the corrupt police commissioner, Lobera, who colludes with government official Rodríguez to supervise and protect the lucrative prostitution industry. The Lascano plotline merges with this one when Lascano discovers that Lobera and other policemen killed Amalia, following orders from a higher-up. They were supposed to eliminate little Candela as well, but Lobera's wife saved the child, only for her to die of heat exhaustion in Lobera's car. Returning to Buenos Aires, Lascano informs Sofía that it was her second husband, Abeledo—revealed to be none other than the abject la Momia—who ordered the killing of her heirs. There is a happy ending for Lascano—he is reunited with Eva, the love of his life, and Sofía succumbs to cancer, leaving her millions to him. But corruption remains unabated. In the final scene, a corrupt local politician and the police commissioner of Mar del Plata are chumming it up with their new partner in crime—Camacho, the kingpin of a Mexican cartel.

## A Rare, Honest Policeman

A central tenet of the three novels is Lascano's uniqueness as an honest policeman with his personal ethical code and a sense of human decency. Acknowledging the rarity of his character, Mallo has gone on the defensive: "Commissioner Lascano is the needle in the haystack, the one who is different from all the others. One. Just one. I think I can be allowed to think that there was one good one" (Berlanga). The dismal reputation of the Argentine police forces explains why Mallo felt the need to justify this characterization.

Besides straining credibility, the use of a police detective as protagonist goes against the tendency of the Argentine *novela negra*, which is characterized by the absence of such. How can we understand this exception? In the first novel of the trilogy, *La aguja en el pajar*, the incorruptibility of Mallo's policeman is central to plot development, providing a point of tension and conflict with the unethical members of the force, and thus highlighting the corruption around him. Lascano's exceptionality as an honest policeman—the titular "needle in the haystack"—is communicated repeatedly. For example, as he begins to emerge from the mourning period following his wife's death, he tells himself that now his mission in life is "trabajar para hacer de este mundo un lugar más justo" (to work to make this world a more just place) (30). He refuses to participate in extortion schemes with his colleagues in the police force or make a deal with Major Giribaldi, even though this puts him in danger. Another indication of his forthrightness is Eva's trust in him. When he tells Eva that he tries to respect the law, she underlines his singularity: "*¿Pero quién te creés que sos, el Llanero Solitario?*" (Who do you think you are, the Lone Ranger?) (84).[9] He expresses to Eva his distaste for the corrupt and abusive military, telling her that if he were her age he would also try to get rid of "*estos hijos de mil puta que nos están reventando a todos*" (these sons of bitches who are crushing us all) (203). Thus in the highly polarized world of the dictatorial regime, the military repressors and the collaborators in the police force represent evil and Lascano's struggle for justice aligns him with the opposition to the dictatorship. In *Delincuente argentino*, set in postdictatorial Argentina, Lascano's ethics have become relativized. Discouraged and cynical, and caring only to find the woman he loves, he consents to working for bankers who are white-collar criminals. In other issues, however, his integrity remains intact; a young district attorney speaks to Lascano's reputation when he tells him, "*Usted es un tipo honesto en medio de la corrupción*" (You are an honest guy in the middle of the corruption) (167). In *Los hombres te han hecho mal*, Lascano's incorruptibility and his fight for justice are crucial to the novel's denunciation of organized crime. He is only hired to find out the fate of Sofía's granddaughter, but, in the mode of Chandler's questing knight, Lascano is deeply disturbed by what he finds out about the human trafficking industry in Mar del Plata and risks his life to try to contain this moral disorder.

## Trafficking in Women's Bodies

An important part of Mallo's fiction is the articulation of a moral problem, and, as mentioned earlier, the subject of his critical focus in the third novel of the trilogy is the exploitation of women and girls to sell their bodies for sex. "Los hombres te han hecho mal" is a stanza from the tango "Milonguita," the story of a prostitute, and Mallo chose this title to emphasize the complicity of clients in the exploitation of women ("Mallo desnuda"). The critique of human trafficking is delivered by means of subplots peopled by archetypical characters—the stories of the victims and of the common criminals and their institutional accomplices—and the spaces associated with them. While iconic characters and settings deliver the story line, key to generating moral outrage on the part of the reader is the use of sensationalism to vilify the traffickers.

Fifteen-year-old Lindaura is the archetypal victim. Her family's precarious economic situation and her physical beauty make her a target of traffickers. The subplot involving Lindaura relates how the girls are procured and subdued into submission and their fate if they are "lucky" enough to obtain their freedom. Lindaura is spotted by a local man who points her out to Yancar, functioning as a "cazador" (hunter). This scene takes place in the impoverished exurban squatter community where she lives with her family, illustrating the fact that procurers prey on the desperately poor. Calling himself "Dr. Corona," Yancar offers her a job in the city that will require relocation, and Lindaura says her good-byes to her family. Once Lindaura is in the grips of the traffickers, we witness the process of "ablande" (softening up) to which the women are subjected.[10] Lindaura is held with other girls who are renamed and kept as prisoners in putrid, filthy conditions; they are abused regularly and the more rebellious girls are beaten and drugged into submission. An indication of how their captors strip them of their basic humanity are the terms they use to refer to them: "un paquete de primera" (a first-class package) and "buena mercadería" (good merchandise). La Pocha, the madam of a brothel, exemplifies the exploitation of women by other women. After Lindaura is freed, her father, Braulio, sees his daughter transformed into "una vieja arruinada" (a ruined old woman) (177). Enraged, he kills the neighborhood man who served as a go-between for the procurer and then turns himself in to the police. An entire family is rent asunder by the criminal greed of human traffickers.

Mallo's portrayal of the hoodlums—the traffickers and their associates—emphasizes their brutality and their violent rivalry as the gangs fight savagely to eliminate each other. This subplot involves the battle for supremacy among three gangs, identified by their leaders—Yancar, Romero, and Camacho. Two other underworld figures are la Momia, the ruthless overseer of the prostitution business in Mar del Plata, and "el Pardo" Rocha, his henchman.

The description of brawls among the criminal gangs employs sensationalism to appeal to the reader's emotions. Stephen Knight describes sensationalism as "a stress on sensations, both in the text and in the reader's response to the text" (232–33). "Sensationalism can be defined in terms of topics, tone, and degree," explain David W. Bulla and David B. Sachsman. They point out that topics such as murder and mayhem are inherently sensational; the type of words, appalling minutiae, hyperbole, and alliteration may contribute to the shock value, and the degree of the rhetoric—the repetition of grotesque detail—exaggerates the sensational effect (xxi). The titillation or perverse appeal of sensationalism is acknowledged by John D. Stevens, who maintains that "most adults realize they are morbidly fascinated by sex and violence and wish they were not" (quoted by Bulla and Sachsman xxiv).

Mallo's scenes involving the human traffickers feature dramatic and blood-soaked action with strong visual imagery and graphic details, characteristic of the traditional hard-boiled genre. In the first of these episodes, the escaped convicts steal bricks of cocaine and firearms from a warehouse in La Boca, and subsequent episodes depict violent gang fights. In the warehouse robbery, one of Romero's men is killed by a Rottweiler and another knifes a guard, his action described by an extradiegetic narrator as follows: "Relampaguea la navaja de Hueso y el guardia pierde toda su sangre por el tajo que le corta en la garganta" (Hueso's knife flashes and the guard loses all his blood through the slash in his throat) (106).[11] Pitting a dog against a human being projects bestiality upon the gang members, while the grisly imagery of copious loss of blood produces nausea and repulsion.

The violent shoot-out between Yancar's and Romero's gangs is narrated in lurid detail by an extradiegetic narrator with Romero's sadistic commentary interjected in italics.

> Las Uzis rocían de balas a los invasores con un sonido fuerte de máquina de coser. Brama la escopeta de Bolita y transforma la cara de Correa en una escupida sanguinolenta sobre la pared. Menfis dispara con las dos manos. Jacinto recibe cuarto impactos de 9 mm en el pecho y cae muerto antes de llegar al suelo. Pelusa patalea su agonía en el suelo a los pies de Yancar, que soltó la pistola, se agarra el estómago con las manos y se derrumba a cámara lenta. Bolita salta por encima de los cadáveres y sale a la vereda. . . . Romero se aproxima a Yancar y lo mira apuntándole con su ametralladora. Ríe. . . . Romero le clave el canon de la Uzi en la mejilla.
>
> *¿Sabés lo que te va a hacer esto cuando apriete el gatillo, Pescadito? Te va a dejar esa linda carita como un colador. Después nos vamos a hacer una raviolada con tus sesos, si es que queda algo.*
>
> Yancar se desvanece y afloja las manos. De su vientre comienza a manar sangre a borbotones. (146–47)

[The Uzis spray the invaders with bullets, making a strong sewing machine–like sound. Bolita's shotgun roars and transforms Correa's face into a bloody spit on the wall. Memphis shoots with both hands. Jacinto receives four bullets to his chest and is dead before he hits the ground. Pelusa writhes in agony at the feet of Yancar, who drops his gun, clutches his stomach with his hands and collapses in slow motion. Bolita jumps over the corpses and goes out to the sidewalk.... Romero approaches Yancar and looks at him pointing his machine gun. He laughs.... Romero sticks the canon of his Uzi in his cheek. *Do you know what this is going to do to you when I squeeze the trigger, Pescadito? It's going to leave that cute little face like a sieve. Then we are going to make a ravioli with your brains, if there is anything left.* Yancar faints and loosens his hands. Blood gushes from his belly.]

These actions are inherently sensational, and the word choice and accumulation of gory detail elicit a strong emotional response. The unexpected, yet apt, comparison of machine-gun fire to the sound of a sewing machine creates an impactful auditory image. Especially gruesome is the graphic description of the transformation of faces into bloody messes, and Romero's promise to make a ravioli dish with Yancar's brains evokes cannibalism. Cinematographic imagery is produced with the description of Pelusa writhing in his agony, the slow-motion collapse of the wounded Yancar, and Bolita jumping over the dead bodies. Finally, Romero's amusement with Yancar's torture communicates his extreme cruelty.

Romero's triumph over Yancar's gang is short-lived because Romero has angered another group of mafiosos. While Romero and his men are celebrating their victory and snuffing coke in the brothel, the peeved owner of the stolen cocaine arrives. "*Soy Gustavo Andrés Camacho Orijuela, muchos me conocen como el Patrón*" (I am Gustavo Andrés Camacho Orijuela, many know me as the Boss) (150), he announces. Demonstrating that he is not a national, Camacho comments that he is amused by how the Argentines talk, and his use of "horita," commonly used in Mexico, suggests that he leads a Mexican (or possibly Colombian) cartel. This confrontation is described in equally visceral terms: "Camacho hunde la navaja en el ojo de Romero y se lo hacer saltar con un movimiento de muñeca" (Camacho sinks his knife into Romero's eye and pops it out with a flick of the wrist) (152). After witnessing Romero's brutality, the reader may experience perverse pleasure upon seeing his disfigurement at the hands of Camacho. Similarly horrific is the description of sustained machine-gun fire, leaving the floor covered with cadavers: "Las ventanas de la casa relampaguean con los destellos de las Uzis.... Romero está muerto, amarrado aun a la silla volteada. Menfis yace a poca distancia.... El local está sembrado con los cadáveres acribillados de las chicas" (The windows of the house are flashing with the explosions of the Uzis.... Romero is dead, still tied to the upturned chair. Memphis lies close by.... The place is covered with the bullet-riddled corpses of the girls) (153). The foreign traffickers occupy the territory once held by nationals, reflecting the encroachment of international mafias in Argentine trafficking rings, and show themselves to be even more vicious than their Argentine counterparts, killing the girls along with the gang members.

Sheer evil is seen in the figure of hired assassin el Pardo Rocha, who shoots a mother and her baby in arms in cold blood, saving on ammunition by using the same bullet to pierce both bodies. Pardo Rocha ends up shooting his boss, Abeledo, because "*Sofía paga mejor*" (Sofía pays better) (176), demonstrating that loyalty has no meaning for this thug; his is a market mentality that sells out to the highest bidder—Abeledo's wife—with no ethical considerations. Abeledo is a truly abject individual. Although he poses as a respectable businessman, he leads a double life as la Momia, the overseer of the prostitution business in Mar del Plata. In this character, we see a prominent noir theme: the hidden connection between criminality and supposed respectability. Lascano's description of la Momia highlights his bestiality and secretiveness: "Todo en él es largo, serpenteante. El cuello de garza remata en una cabeza diminuta.... Su mirada es opaca, como la de un jugador de póquer que ambiciona saberlo todo del otro sin revelar su juego" (Everything in him is long, snake-like. His heron neck ends in a tiny head.... His look is opaque, like that of a poker player who wants to know everything about the other without revealing his game) (53–54). A measure of his cold-bloodedness is that he has his employees killed when he is dissatisfied with them. For Yancar, la Momia is a sinister figure of the night: "Nunca lo vio a la luz del día" (He never saw him in the light of day) (77). When it is revealed that Abeledo and the notorious la Momia are actually the same person and that he is the one who arranged for the murder of Sofía's daughter and granddaughter, Sofía's acknowledgment casts a shadow on her judgment: "*Siempre supe que era un hombre con un secreto. Algo oscuro que reptaba en su interior y que a veces asomaba*" (I always knew that he was a man with a secret. Something dark that crawled inside and that sometimes appeared) (168). This wicked character with a secret double life lends a gothic note to the family intrigue.

Sensationalist graphic imagery is used to describe Abeledo's shooting death by el Pardo Rocha: "Rocha dispara. La cabeza de Abeledo se parte y se baña en sangre" (Rocha shoots. Abeledo's head splits open and is bathed in blood) (176). Like Romero's torture, the image of the malevolent Abeledo reduced to "un ovillo sangriento, envuelto en plástico, en el maletero abierto" (a bloody ball, wrapped in plastic, in the open trunk) (176) is a welcome sight for the reader. Dramatic black humor is produced when the police shoot Rocha, who is sitting in the driver's seat, and his head falls on the steering wheel, sounding the horn. Gory deaths are also in order for accomplices to the traffickers. Marcelo, a procurer, falls and cracks his head open, dying in "un vómito de sangre negra" (a vomit of black blood), and his partner, Corina, stabs herself in the neck, which emits "sucesivos chorros de sangre roja y brillante" (successive spurts of brilliant red blood) (163). Finally, in still another truculent scene, the neighborhood man who fingered Lindaura is clubbed to death with a metal bar by Braulio.

The heartless criminals of the nineties and beyond, who live and die by the sword, make Miranda—the gentleman bank robber of the 1980s featured in *Delincuente*—seem quaint and antiquated. As demonstrated, an important part of Mallo's denunciation is the demonization of the traffickers as depraved and less than human. This is delivered with sensationalized violence, as they engage in savage mass killings in their gang wars and display sadistic pleasure in torturing their enemies. Provocative imagery and an accumulation of grisly details with abundant cadavers, body parts, and gushing blood produce a strong emotional response, inciting the reader's indignation and his or her censorship of the brutality and inhumanity of this practice.

Systemic Corruption

These mafias rely on the complicity of politicians, the judiciary, and the police. Even worse, sometimes government officials play key roles in trafficking networks.[12] As mentioned above, Lascano sets out to investigate common crimes—the murder of Amalia and the disappearance of baby Candela—but these are tied to institutional corruption. The newspaper article about Amalia's slaying mentions "una docena de policía que estarían involucrados en la prostitución según el fiscal del caso" (a dozen police officers who were likely involved in prostitution according to the prosecutor) (55–56), and when he begins his mission, Lascano is warned, "*Este negocio de las putas llega más arriba de lo que creés*" (This business of whores reaches higher up than you think) (71), signaling the complicity of powerful and corrupt actors. Once again, this subplot includes iconic characters: a corrupt police commissioner working with a greedy politician and a judge who is co-opted.

Police chief Lobera of the Bonaerense force represents corruption in law enforcement. When Lascano interviews him about Amalia's death, he echoes the misinformation propagated in the actual case of María Esther Amaro, insisting that Amalia was a prostitute who was killed by "el Loco de la Ruta." Lobera openly admits that his commissary is on the take, reflecting the overt nature of corruption among the force. Telling Lascano that the state does not give him enough money to run his office, he acknowledges that he has to obtain the rest by illegal means, blurring the divide between the police and criminals: "*Vos sabés muy bien de dónde sale la plata.... De la calle, Lascano, de la calle. No somos muy distintos de los delincuentes a los que perseguimos*" (You know very well where the money comes from.... From the street, Lascano, from the street. We are not very different from the criminals we pursue) (70). Lobera gestures to posters of political candidates and explains, "*Al lado de estos tipos somos nenes de pecho. Están metidos en todos los negocios que te puedas imaginar y en muchos con los que ni siquiera podrías soñar*" (Next to these guys we are babies. They are involved in all the businesses that you can imagine and in many that you could not even imagine) (70). He also describes their reciprocal arrangement—if the police do not interfere with the crooked wheeling and dealing of the politicians, whom he calls the "grandes criminales," the politicians will ignore the police's protection racket. These passages, in which a police commissioner admits to his corruption, strain verisimilitude, conveying the author's denunciatory intent.

We meet a politician on the take when Lobera delivers a routine payment to a government official in La Plata named Rodríguez. Lobera reports a problem to Rodríguez—Judge Marraco ordered a raid of the brothels because he heard that they were using underage girls. This judge with scruples is effectively handled by Rodríguez, who frames him for purportedly appropriating seventeen kilos of cocaine and changing them for boric acid. If Marraco eases up on investigating trafficking of underage girls, they will forget about the accusation, but if not, he faces the possibility of being discharged of his position and receiving jail time. Thus a well-intentioned judge is neutralized via deceit and blackmail.

A touch of Mallo's black humor humanizes Lobera, who jokes about his heart disease. Telling Lascano that he has been diagnosed with an enlarged heart, he quips, "*Siempre fui un tipo de gran corazón*" (I was always a guy with a big heart) (69). This information sets the stage for Lobera's dramatic death. Speeding along the highway toward Mar del Plata, he suffers a heart attack, and staccato prose communicates the urgency of the situation: "Una puntada en el pecho, aguda. Mareo. Las manos se le duermen. Visión doble. Se desploma sobre el volante" (A sharp pain in the chest. Dizziness. His hands are falling asleep. Double vision. He collapses on the steering wheel) (104). After hitting the low barrier, the car door opens, his body flies out, and the other motorists gawk at the spectacle of an obese cadaver rolling down the cliff.

Any pleasure we experience upon witnessing the death of this crooked cop does not last because Rodríguez handpicks his replacement, Pedro. Rodríguez's instructions to Pedro detail the terms of their complicity: leave my guys alone and pay me in person the first Tuesday of every month. He gives Pedro a list of the names of people who work with him and tells him to memorize it, promising, "*En tres años te jubilás con una medalla y más parado que Onassis*" (In three years you retire with a medal and richer than Onassis) (126). Rodríguez also introduces Judge Marraco to Pedro, telling the judge that he wants him to collaborate with Pedro, and the subdued Marraco agrees to do so. In this way, Mallo uses the words of his characters to detail the mechanisms of official corruption.

Another indication of the level of corruption is Sofía's total lack of faith in the system. When Lascano informs her that Abeledo ordered Amalia's and Candela's murders, he suggests, "*Podemos denunciarlo a la justicia*" (We can denounce him to the courts), and she replies, "*El momento es demasiado dramático para que te pongas a hacer chistes*" (The moment is too dramatic for you to make jokes) (168). Thus for her, justice is a joke. The corrupt partnership between business and government is represented by Sofía's first husband, Juan Taborda, "el rey de la carne" (the king of meat). Sofía refers to him as "*un canalla [que era] un as para sobornar a funcionarios del gobierno*" (a scoundrel [who was] an ace for bribing government officials) (50).

### The Desperate Poor, the Decadent Rich, and the Menem Allegory

Social class comes into play in Mallo's portrait of organized crime. The desperate and vulnerable poor can easily become victims, while the decadent and irresponsible rich bear at least some of the responsibility for their exploitation. The contrast between rich and poor is developed in the juxtaposition of consecutive scenes of the novel. In chapter 4, the wealthy Sofía is in her chauffeured car, looking out at the people waiting for the bus—she has never taken public transportation. The following chapter sketches the lifestyle of the poor via the family of Braulio, the father of ill-fated Lindaura. His family lives in a working-class neighborhood with asphalted streets just by the "frontera volátil" (volatile border) with the *villa miseria* that has dirt streets. Braulio accepts any job with any conditions just to try to keep on the asphalted side of the neighborhood. Braulio's precarious economic situation makes his young daughter a target of traffickers. When Braulio discovers his daughter's sorry fate, he feels guilty because he was tricked into letting her go with the traffickers, and he understands that "no hay barrote que pueda protegerlo de la pobreza, del desamparo de la miseria, del canibalismo" (there is no bar that can protect him from poverty, from the helplessness of misfortune, from cannibalism) (178). He becomes acutely aware that his attempts to improve the condition of his family are futile. Through the character of Braulio, the novel delivers a commentary regarding the insecurity of the poor.

Sofía's daughter, Amalia, rejected her privileged status when she married a working-class man, and another example of the living conditions of the poor is conveyed when Lascano interviews the widower. Lascano's description of his neighborhood creates graphic imagery that underlines its precarious and unsanitary conditions: "casas [que] tiemblan en el lodazal," "miserable construcción," "penetrante aroma cloacal," "adultos [que] no deben pasar los treinta, pero aparentan cincuenta" (houses [that] tremble in the quagmire, shoddy construction, penetrating gutter smell, adults [who] are probably no older than thirty, but look fifty) (85–86). It is not necessary to go far to see the contrast of this neighborhood with a playground of the leisured class: "Al fondo de las transversales brilla el césped de los links del campo de golf" (Across the street is the magnificent grass of the golf course) (86).

There is another echo of Chandler in the depiction of the wealthy, represented by Sofía. Sean McCann observes that "Chandler's most villainous figures are the decadent elite of the non-producing class" (153). Sofía lives on the Avenida del Libertador, one of the most exclusive addresses in Buenos Aires. "La entrada al edificio se asemeja a la de un castillo" (The entrance to the building resembles that of a castle), Lascano reflects, observing "largas alfombras, muebles de estilo y el inevitable hombre de gris que controla el acceso" (long carpets, stylish furniture and the inevitable man in gray who controls access) (47). The castle-like entrance to her building is a fitting (and Chandleresque) passageway into her gothic world, replete with decadent excess and dark secrets. Lascano's first impression of Sofía emphasizes her frivolity and self-indulgence: "Sofía viste una túnica azafrán, lleva un vaso de whisky, un cigarrillo y carga más joyas que Tiffany's" (Sofia is dressed in a saffron tunic, carries a glass of whiskey, a cigarette and displays more jewelry than Tiffany's) (48).

Since Sofía's second husband arranged for the deaths of her daughter and granddaughter, the source of perversity is the father figure, but he is an illegitimate father, an evil stepfather chosen by the irresponsible rich woman. This portrayal lends itself to an allegorical reading when Abeledo is compared to President Carlos Menem: "*Este Abeledo tiene más guita que Menem*" (This Abeledo has more dough than Menem) (172), says a police officer. The allegory can be read as a denunciation of the Argentine elite who fell under the spell of Menem—an allusion to their "marriage" to a charismatic leader who charmed his followers but whose policies and whose example ultimately proved detrimental for the country and its progeny. (The critique of Menemism in the *novela negra* is the topic of chapter 2 of the present book.) In Mallo's novel, there is a day of reckoning for the irresponsible rich. Sofía blames herself for the deaths of her daughter and granddaughter: "*He sido de una frivolidad criminal*" (I am guilty of a criminal frivolity) (169). The indictment of the mindless frivolity of the decadent elite is clear—they are to blame for harboring criminals, only thinking of themselves and their amusement.

## Generically Useless Women and the Sentimental Family

Female characters play a crucial role in the novel, be they love interests, victims, oppressors, or family members. As a sentimental man, Lascano has love interests, but he also has lust interests. "The function of women in [detective] fiction is to signify sexuality, to flesh out male desire," asserts Marty Roth in his discussion of traditional detective fiction (113), and Lila is a lover who serves to flesh out Lascano's desire. Described through Lascano's gaze, Lila is seen as attractive and sexually arousing, but Lascano grows weary of her tiresome chatter and eventually rejects her.

"Detective fiction," Roth tells us, "claims that women are generically useless, and a given work can only fulfill that claim by proving it on the body of an actual woman; the absent woman becomes present, the outside gets inside to show why it should stay out" (116). To this end, the woman is "often recorded as an absence, a diaphanous or aromatic trail, or a peripheral memory" (118). Women are avoided in the thriller, Roth continues, because in the mentality of the detective, "women have no place in your life while you are on a mission," and sexuality must be deferred at the time of an adventure (127). These observations shed light on the function of the love interest in the Lascano trilogy—the original absent woman is Lascano's late wife, Marisa. She is replaced by her lookalike, Eva, who appears briefly in *Aguja*, long enough for her and Lascano to fall in love and for Eva to become the absent woman in the next two books. In *Los hombres*, Eva is introduced as a photo that Lascano regards with longing; she is a trace, only present via a static image. She remains absent while he is on his missions, which include the hunt for Miranda in *Delincuente* and the job for Sofía in *Los hombres* that involves wrestling with the human trafficking mafia. Thus Lascano's love interest is conveniently put aside for him to be free to do his dangerous detective work and will conveniently reappear only when the final mission is completed.

Lascano's nostalgia for his late wife and his subsequent yearning for Eva are a reflection of his sentimentality. Mallo acknowledges that his novels showcase the importance of sentiment because "[feelings] make us more compassionate. The human being by nature is cruel, and feelings make us a little bit better" ("Ernesto Mallo desea"). In *Los hombres*, Eva describes Lascano as "aquel tipo salvaje y tierno al que balearon los perros de la dictadura cuando trataba de salvarla de ellos y de sí misma" (that savage and tender guy who was shot by the dogs of the dictatorship when he tried to save her from them and from herself) (74). The oxymoronic term "salvaje tierno" (tender savage) points to his tenderness and his toughness, bringing together "hard-boiledness" and sentimentality. Humane and decent, Lascano despises having to kill in self-defense and survives by his wit rather than his brawn. As detailed above, Lascano is portrayed as an honest policeman and attention is constantly drawn to his exceptionality in this regard, establishing him as a foil for his crooked colleagues. However, another reason for his uprightness is that Lascano must be depicted as trustworthy and brave in order to qualify as a "sentimental action hero." Similar to Chandler's Marlowe, he is an ethical man who is unafraid to walk the "mean streets" of Buenos Aires and Mar del Plata, both during and after the dictatorship. In *Los hombres*, his failure to be intimidated is witnessed in the words of a corrupt official who was not able to bribe him: "*Lo encaré, pero ese tipo no le da bola a nadie y no creo que se asuste*" (I confronted him, but that guy does not pay attention to anyone and I do not think you can scare him) (102). And his dedication to justice is highlighted when he refuses to accept the initial dead end to his investigation into Amalia's death: "A Lascano le inquieta la sola idea de darse por vencido" (Lascano is troubled by the mere idea of giving up) (114). We see his compassion and his determination in his anguish over the deaths of captive women and his decision to take on the prostitution business single-handedly. He succeeds in solving the case he was hired for but resolves to bring down a ring of human traffickers before leaving Mar del Plata. The extradiegetic narrator depicts him as a solitary knight battling to make a small difference in the insuppressible evil of society: "Lascano ... está corriendo contra la infamia del mundo, de los hombres, y está decidido a ganarles aunque sea una ínfima batalla" (Lascano ... is up against the infamy of the world, of men, and is determined to beat them even if it is in a very small battle) (161).

The emotional essence of hard-boiled crime fiction, Cassuto states, is a family story. And so it is with Mallo's novels. *Los hombres te han hecho mal* is about damaged families. We never see united happy families; rather, there prevails a critical view of broken and dysfunctional families, be the causes external, such as poverty, or internal, such as discord over poor choices of partners. In this way, the novel conveys a desire for a supportive family unit through representations of failed families, in particular, parents who have failed their children. Lindaura's father is depicted as a hard-working and responsible individual who ends up being duped by criminal predators. Lindaura is sent off by a caring family and suffers a horrible fate due to her family's economic situation and her father's lack of worldliness. The novel also describes the "dura infancia" (hard childhood) of el loco Romero, a manifestation of Mallo's desire to understand the criminal mind and transmit "the humanity of evildoers" (Silver). Romero's ignorant and brutish father threw him out of the home when he was eleven, and he had to join a gang of delinquent youths to survive on the streets. Once in the gang, he was forced to prove himself by shooting the only boy who befriended him. Thus at a young age he learned that he must deny sentimentality in order to survive. In both cases, youth are separated from their families due to poverty and ignorance, one becoming a victim and the other a victimizer, and both destinies are linked to malfunction of the nuclear family.

But it is not only the families of the poor and uncultured that are problematic. The middle-class Argentine families vacationing in Mar del Plata are seen as conflictive: "Por la Rambla circulan las familias, lideradas por el marido argentino [quien carga] estoicamente el balde con la palita y el rastrillo de sus caprichosos borreguitos. Le es indiferente el malhumor de su señora" (Along the Rambla stroll the families, led by the Argentine husband [who carries] stoically the bucket with the shovel and rake of his capricious kids. He is indifferent to the moodiness of his wife) (114). Family tensions are perpetual, even during a vacation at the beach.

Sofía's family is yet another story. A wealthy woman who leads a life of privilege, her family is torn apart by her mindlessness as she makes bad choices in husbands. She becomes estranged from her sister, Lascano's mother, due to her marriage to the crooked Juan Taborda. Later she becomes estranged from her daughter because of her choice of the slippery and duplicitous Abeledo Perret as her second husband. Ultimately, *Los hombres* is based on a complex family plot with gothic resonances involving estrangement, double identity, and an evil stepfather.

Through the illustration of family after family in crisis—damaged families and ignorant and callous destroyers of the sentimental household—the novel projects a longing for a nourishing family. The broken families in this story cannot be mended, but Lascano can start a new family with Eva. Lascano is introduced in *Aguja* as without a family—he grew up an orphan and his first attempt to establish a family was dashed when his wife, Marisa, died in a car accident in the early stage of her pregnancy. He falls in love with Eva, a woman who reciprocates his feelings, but he loses her to another man when she believes he is dead.[13] Lascano's reencounter with his estranged cousin Sofía reestablishes a family connection, and his inheritance of her vast fortune is the archetypal "rich uncle" story of the person who suddenly finds themselves the inheritor of riches from a previously unknown, wealthy relative. His reunion with Eva at the end of the final novel of the trilogy rekindles hope for establishing a family. The coupling also represents a technical solution, as plots with multiplicity resolve by return to primal unity (Jameson 146). When Eva looks at him with "*esa mirada llena de chispas, Lascano se siente bello, joven, inspirado, casi un poeta*" (that glint in her eyes, Lascano feels handsome, young, inspired, almost a poet) (184). Lascano and Eva talk about starting a new life with "*casa, familia, algún viaje, preocuparse por la juventud descarriada, buena comida, un hobby*" (a home, a family, the occasional trip, doing something for wayward youth, good food, a hobby) (184). The projected future of Lascano and Eva represents new hope for a happy bourgeois family—socially conscious and comfortable at the same time—among the broken and dysfunctional families. *Los hombres* is as much a nostalgic and yearning gesture toward family as it is a critique of human trafficking. After all, human trafficking represents a grave threat to the family.

Thus there is a fairy-tale ending for the decent but cynical and beleaguered former policeman: spiritual revitalization, a fresh chance at happiness with the woman he loves, and untold riches. The evil stepfather has been eliminated—here we recall the Menem allegory—the death of the frivolous mother makes way for a new order, and Lascano and Eva are the inheritors who will carry it out. Lascano has remained pure—he only killed in self-defense and he never accepted bribes or hush money. It is not a problem for him, however, that the fortune he has inherited was made by Sofía's first husband in fraudulent business dealings. Eva no longer talks of revolution—she seems more interested in making love with Lascano than making war with anyone—and Lascano is disposed to help wayward youth as long as he can still have trips and good food and practice a hobby. The new order is decidedly bourgeois.

While joy prevails in the personal dimension, the conclusion is grim in regard to justice and an end to exploitation. In the final scene, we witness the survival and regeneration of the Mar del Plata trafficking mafia under the control of the same corrupt government officials but in collaboration with an international cartel. Rodríguez, the shady provincial politician, is preparing a succulent barbeque with prime Argentine beef in his yard. Along comes his collaborator, Pedro, the new police chief, sporting expensive clothes and a gold Rolex wristwatch. Their dialogue celebrates what Rodríguez characterizes as two marks of Argentine national identity: meat and corruption. "*Mirá esta carne. La mejor del mundo, che*" (Look at this meat. The best in the world, man), he boasts. In Europe and North America, he continues, "*hay otra conciencia, las cosas se hacen como Dios manda.... [Acá] la chusma, el caos y la desorganización te permiten un margen de maniobra que en otros países no tenés*" (there is a different mentality, people follow the rules.... [Here] the rabble, the chaos and the disorganization allow you a margin of maneuver that you do not have in other countries). They raise their glasses, cynically toasting the lax regulation that makes trafficking possible: "*Por el caos, entonces*" (To the chaos, then) (186). This exchange reiterates the focus of Mallo's critique, as voiced earlier by the garrulous Lila: "*el evidente desgobierno de la nación*" (39). They are joined by a man in a suit, Gustavo Andrés Camacho Orijuela, the foreign drug lord and the last man standing in the gang wars. Rodríguez makes the introduction between his new associate in crime and the new police chief. "*El comisario es mi hombre de confianza en la fuerza*" (The commissioner is my man of confidence in the force), Rodríguez tells Camacho, indicating that he is in cahoots with the racket. "*Para servir y proteger*" (To serve and protect) (187), vows Pedro, ironically repeating the police motto. Of course he is not talking about serving and protecting the public but rather swearing fealty to the new king of the local underworld. Although Lascano has succeeded in busting up a trafficking ring, like cockroaches, the wrongdoers resurface from the woodwork and the unholy triumvirate—the corrupt politician, the police commissioner on the take, and the mafia boss—will continue to prey on Mar del Plata. Thus the fairy-tale, happily-ever-after ending on a personal level for the sentimental policeman/detective is tempered by a realistic portrayal of intractable corruption on a societal level. Similarly, the true crime reference of the case of María Esther Amaro lends urgency and verisimilitude to the story while the "too-good-to-be-true" ending detracts from it, throwing the story into another register. In this case, the textual hybridity functions as a recourse of popular fiction. It allows the author to provide his readers with a certain sense of satisfaction through the hero's attainment of a comfortable bourgeois lifestyle at the same time that the novel denounces both widespread institutional complicity with heinous crime and the consequences of the mindless frivolity of the Menem era.

## THE FOUL BREEZES OF BUENOS AIRES: *CIUDAD SANTA* BY GUILLERMO ORSI

You will not find it in *Frommer's* or in the *Buenos Aires Top Ten Travel Guide*; you need to go to Quirky Guide for a write-up on the Tierra Santa theme park in Buenos Aires. Inaugurated in 2000, Tierra Santa is the world's first religious theme park. Described as "very tacky" by Lonely Planet and "bizarre" even by Quirky Guide standards, it purports to be a replica of ancient Jerusalem, complete with employees dressed in period costumes and scenarios depicting biblical stories. The highlight of the park is the Resurrection scene where every forty-five minutes a gigantic statue of Jesus, with thirty-six mechanical movements but in need of a paint job, rises from a plaster Mount Calvary. This corny artificial Jerusalem constitutes the central metaphor of Guillermo Orsi's bitingly satirical presentation of Buenos Aires as "Ciudad Santa."

The novel opens with a section called "Orientación para el turista" that contains two newspaper clippings. The first describes the papier-mâché Holy Land theme park and the second reports that due to savage devaluations in 2002, foreign tourists are flocking to Argentina to enjoy world-class glaciers, waterfalls, tango, and meat at bargain prices. These two clippings set the scene for the misadventures of travelers that form the basis of Orsi's acerbic critique of a corrupt, globalized Buenos Aires after the financial meltdown of 2001.

Another real-life Buenos Aires locale in Orsi's novel, which functions as a polar opposite of Tierra Santa, is La Salada market, renamed Feria de Riachuelo in its fictional re-creation. Thought to be South America's largest informal market, La Salada consists of "around 30,000 wire mesh stalls [that] spill out of three warehouses in an unsavory neighborhood in the outskirts of Buenos Aires" ("Stall Stories"). Piracy and knock-offs are rife and the police are considered to be complicit, accepting "bribes in exchange for ignoring the contraband goods." An Argentine journalist calls it "at once a display of Argentine creativity, intelligence, resilience and grit, and an exhibit of Argentine cunning and corruption" (28). Thus these two locations—the biblical theme park and the contraband market—serve as iconic polar images for Buenos Aires, representing the saintly and the infernal, the pure and the impure. But of course the "saintliness" is tainted insofar as the theme park is a commercialized replica of the Holy Land.

*Ciudad Santa*, published in English as *Holy City*, is a sweeping portrait of crime and corruption in Buenos Aires, with a focus on the lucrative and brutal illegal drug trade. The novel features two main plotlines: the kidnapping of wealthy international tourists from the grounded cruise ship *Queen of Storms* and the saga of a Bolivian beauty queen and her "monstrous" secret twin brother, the fruits of an Argentine policeman nicknamed el Escocés (Scotty) and an indigenous woman. Each story involves multiple characters whose paths eventually connect. Set in a globalized Buenos Aires, the Argentine capital is the main character, and the central metaphor to represent Buenos Aires is the concept of the "ciudad santa" (holy city). Of course, this is highly ironic because the metropolis—populated by drug traffickers, corrupt police, depraved military men, unprincipled judges, and crooked politicians—is depicted as distinctly "unholy," and the irony functions to thematicize this difference. Orsi's sardonic vision takes no prisoners, targeting men, women, locals, foreigners, Argentina, and other countries. Gothic horror motifs are present in secret parentage, an abject monster, and serial decapitations. And there is plenty of gore, sex, and gory sex. To quote a reviewer, "This book just screams noir" (NancyO).

My analysis will consider the depiction of the fractious, violent drug trade buttressed by institutional complicity, the image of Buenos Aires as an inverse "ciudad santa," and other concerns such as social class, racism, and the portrayal of women. I will also examine the main characters who populate this world—Walter Carroza, a cynical but honest and sentimental cop; Verónica Berutti, an aging but still sexy lawyer; Pacogoya, a dissolute tour guide resembling Che Guevara cum male prostitute and drug dealer; and Ana Torrente aka Miss Bolivia, a femme fatale with a subnormal beastly twin known as el Jaguar. I will consider how the twins' depiction dramatizes issues resulting from Latin America's colonial heritage, introducing a postcolonial critique. The cast of secondary characters is extensive; those who will figure in my analysis include Oso Berlusconi and el Escocés, corrupt federal policemen; Colombian drug lord Osmar Arredri and his mistress Sirena Mondragón; and an Argentine drug distributor known as "Tío" (Uncle). There is a strong presence of an extradiegetic narrator, who frequently intervenes to give the reader access to the thoughts of the characters as well as the narrator's analysis of the ills of Argentina's capital city along with those of our postmodern world in general.

## Drug Trafficking and Official Complicity

Similar to *Los hombres*, this novel deals with the globalization of organized crime, depicting the arrival of a Colombian drug lord who has set up a branch of his business in Argentina, and the jockeying for position of Argentine federal police and military men, who want a share of the profit. *Ciudad Santa* presents a veritable panorama of police corruption: extrajudicial killings, the continuation of abusive practices from the dictatorship, the existence of protection rackets, impunity of wrongdoing police, and internal police loyalty, which means turning a blind eye toward corruption of fellow officers. An integral part of the critique is the tolerance of politicians for the crimes of the police because they also benefit from them, as well as the corruption of the judiciary, who are vulnerable to bribery and manipulation.

In the opening scene of *Ciudad Santa* we are introduced to the ruthlessness of the drug trade and official involvement in it with the execution of Matías Zamorano by henchmen working at the behest of Alberto Cozumel Banegas aka Councilor Viruela (Councillor Pox), a local municipal official and drug czar of a twenty-block area south of the municipality of Matanza. With the mention of this locale, the mapping begins. Matanza and areas to the south are industrial and working-class neighborhoods, and much of the unsavory action will take place in this region of the city. Zamorano was Viruela's right-hand man but, inveigled by the beautiful and ambitious Miss Bolivia, made the fatal mistake of trying to double-cross and unseat him. Zamorano's execution is meant to serve as an example for anyone else who may try to betray Viruela.

The distribution of illegal drugs to individual consumers is depicted through Pacogoya, tour guide and drug dealer for the international passengers on the stranded cruise ship. In the Buenos Aires port their order totals a half kilo of high-quality cocaine. Pacogoya's supplier, known simply as Tío, does not have that quantity readily available and many of Pacogoya's ill-fated adventures in the course of the novel involve obtaining the cocaine and wandering around with a backpack full of the coveted powder.

The drug trafficking plot, which focuses on the turf war between domestic traffickers and the Colombian drug lord who is expanding his network to Argentina, serves to denounce the complicity of a wide sector of officialdom with the drug trade. Osmar Arredri, czar of the Medellín drug cartel, and Sirena Mondragón, his "bella concubina" (beautiful concubine), arrive in Argentina on the *Queen of Storms* posing as tourists on a leisure trip. Argentina is an appealing country for narcos because they have a free pass, as the narrator's reflections critique the total lack of regulations: "En la Argentina nadie les pone trabas, acá pasan todos, dicen los de Migraciones, diplomáticos con merca para derribar caballos y políticos cargados como burros con mochilas llenas de dólares" (Argentina is not like that, say the immigration officials. They can all get in with no problem—diplomats with enough drugs to kill a horse, politicians loaded down like mules with saddlebags stuffed full of dollars) (98; 2.8).[14] But setting up a distribution ring in Argentina does not prove to be so easy, as the drug lords of the Argentine province of Neuquén are not about to let the Colombian ruin their business, and the key figure in the local group is a powerful government official. A complicated tug of war ensues. The Neuquén ring intends to kill Arredri, but the federal police get to him first and kidnap the Colombian couple, supposedly in order to protect them. In reality, they want a piece of the action.

"Oso" Berlusconi, a federal policeman who relished his role as a torturer during the dictatorship, masterminds the original kidnapping. The operation is carried out via an uneasy alliance with Air Force officials who help guard the hostages. Through Oso's associate in the Air Force, Captain Castro, we receive evidence of the military's role in facilitating the entry of drugs into Argentina. The narrator reveals that Castro's military comrades have excluded him from their shady business in the airports, and he is cooperating with the federal police in this kidnapping so that they retain him on the operation called "el jumbo de los narcos," flights that carry more cocaine than passengers and are exempt from entry control (109). Apparently, members of the Air Force are always on the take, resentful of their meager salaries now that Argentina has returned to democratic rule. The kidnapped couple is seized a second time when individuals dressed in military uniforms overpower the guards. Oso is determined to find out who has taken the Colombians and where they are being held. After all, millions of dollars are at stake.

Three other couples from the stranded cruise ship—ultrawealthy CEOs from Italy, France, and Germany—are also kidnapped and held for ransom. The government organizes a rescue mission headed up by none other than Oso Berlusconi, which is curious because he was also behind these kidnappings. But that does not seem to matter because the rescue operation is merely a show on the part of the government, "uno de los habituales simulacros de recuperar la legalidad, espectáculos mediáticos para mostrar cómo las autoridades la emprenden contra la corrupción … en los que nadie cree pero que todos aplauden" (one of those habitual pretences of restoring law and order, a spectacle put on for the media to show how the authorities are fighting corruption … [that] no-one believes in but everyone applauds) (180; 3.9). Thus the narrator takes a jibe at the government's exploitation of the media to project a façade of legality. Oso orders his men to shoot at everyone—the kidnappers have to die so they cannot implicate him in the hostage taking and the hostages have to die so they cannot testify that their guards were shot despite the fact that they surrendered.

The hostage debacle is an international scandal, and Oso is called to account by the cacique, the drug lord of the region, who turns out to be Pacogoya's "Tío." Previously, Tío was a government official—the private secretary of the vice president of the senate—and he could bring drugs directly from Colombia using the diplomatic pouch. Instead of killing Oso himself, the cacique/Tío sends him on a "suicide mission": to execute the government minister who will blame the slaughter of the hostages and their captors on the federal police. Oso carries out the mission and is killed by a rain of bullets. The story of Tío connects to that of the Colombian drug czar and his mistress when we discover they are being held at his ranch. Arredri, who made the mistake of thinking he could depose Tío, is shot trying to escape. In sum, this plotline depicts the violent turf battles occasioned by encroachment of international trafficking cartels in Argentina, and the convoluted involvement of police and military and government officials.

A virtual encyclopedia of corruption, the novel illustrates other forms of institutional wrongdoing. The police are the most frequent target of the narrator's satire, and this is carried out principally through the figure of Oso Berlusconi. Pacogoya, the tour guide, calls Oso a "policía corrupto y asesino" (corrupt, murdering policeman) (3.12), a characterization that is deconstructed ironically by the extradiegetic narrator in a later passage: "Él es policía. Corrupto y asesino, pero policía, o por eso" (He is a cop. Corrupt and a murderer, but a cop—or perhaps because of that) (228; 3.17). The same mordant satire is operative in the narrator's description of his depravity.

> A Oso Berlusconi, en cambio, le gusta la velocidad, echarse sobre pacíficos automovilistas a toda sirena y obligarlos a derrapar o acabar en las banquinas apuntando en dirección contraria a la que llevaban. Para eso se hizo policía, y para hundir el puño con manopla de hierro en los estómagos blandengues de los judíos del Once o de la calle Libertad, buscando reducidores de oro y piedras preciosas, cada vez que se asaltan joyerías o cajas de seguridad de los bancos. (131)
>
> [Oso Berlusconi enjoys speed. He likes to push his way past unsuspecting motorists, siren blazing, forcing them to skid or to end up on the verges facing the wrong way. That is why he became a cop, as well as to sink an iron fist into the flabby stomachs of the Jews of Once or calle Libertad whenever he is searching for the fences of gold and precious stones after a jewellers' or bank security boxes have been raided.] (3.7)

The perverse and anti-Semitic Oso takes delight in roughing up the hostages—"qué memorias" (what memories), says the narrator, who can read Oso's thoughts. Irony is the intentional transmission of both information and attitude other than what is explicitly presented. Irony functions in the space between what is said—the literal meaning—and what is not said, or the implied meaning (Hutcheon, *Irony's Edge* 11, 15). In this terse ironic aside—"qué memorias"—the said is that Oso enjoys the recollection; the unsaid is that he carried out torture during the dictatorship and is a sadist because his recollection of inflicting pain gives him pleasure.

The novel also alludes to extrajudicial killings carried out by the police. For instance, Verónica remarks that her bodyguard, Chuco, is on a better path than those youth who rob taxi drivers and kiosk owners. Verónica uses her legal finesse to get these juvenile delinquents released from police custody only for them to be shot down by police patrols in their own neighborhoods. Federal policeman el Escocés also reflects on how he is rewarded for extrajudicial killings because these disguised murders are a way of getting rid of criminals.

> Le pagan por cazar criminales, por matarlos si es posible, antes que un juez les permita seguir robando y asesinando bajo palabra. Le pagan por eso, por barrer la basura aunque tenga que esconderla bajo la alfombra de los expedientes, si hasta lo alientan a quedarse con los vueltos de las requisas, recompensas bajo cuerda que todos aceptan porque el sueldo nunca alcanza.... Los jueces, agradecidos. (243)
>
> [He is paid to hunt down criminals, to kill them if possible before a judge releases them to go on robbing and killing on parole. That is what he is paid for, to sweep up the rubbish even if he has to hide it under the carpet of police files. He is even encouraged to keep the change from his investigations, backhanders everyone accepts because their salaries are never enough to live on.... The magistrate are all grateful.] (4.2)

While the main actors in the corruption plot are members of the federal police, the narrator also takes stabs at the Bonaerense, who are depicted as being racist and barbaric brutes. They insult and threaten the owner of a gas station simply because he is Bolivian: "*Negrito, boliviano de mierda, cuídate porque a todos los de tu raza los tenemos marcados*" (Asshole Bolivian, be careful because we've got our eye out on all your lot) (224; 3.16). When they take Pacogoya, the Che Guevara look-alike, into custody, a heavy-set policeman takes a shine to him and wants to sodomize him in front of the other police in the station. His colleagues think that this is hilarious, and a lot of joking and good filthy fun is had by all. Oso's commentary on the corrupted values of the Bonaerense—"Esos matan por monedas pero delatan a sus camaradas solo contra divisas fuertes" (They'll kill people for a few bucks, but want paying in foreign currency to betray [their comrades])[15] (204; 3.13)—is a sardonic allusion to their notorious esprit de corps.

Another target of critique is police impunity for their participation in crimes during the dictatorship. This concern is illustrated via the fate of Verónica's first husband, a policeman who acted as a whistleblower for fellow cops who were frantically cleaning up their records when the democracy came. He appeared before a judge and denounced what was going on among the federal police: the burning of files and threats made in order to maintain silence. Apparently, the judge was complicit with the corrupt cops and informed on him, as Verónica explains: "El tiro con el que un mes después le volaron los sesos ya se lo había pegado él mismo, el día nefasto que habló con el juez" (He'd already fired the bullet that blew his brains out the day he went to see the magistrate a month later) (71; 2.2). Oso Berlusconi is a remnant from that nefarious period who remained unpunished because he was useful to corrupt politicians; he is labeled "basura dictatorial que sin embargo protegen los políticos.... Un carnicero eficiente" (garbage left over from the dictatorship who for some reason all the politicians are protecting.... An effective butcher) (179; 3.9). The narrator's cynical commentary—speaking from the politicians' perspective—compares the police favorably to the military during the dictatorship who came with ideological baggage and hawkish ambitions. These useful "ladrones sin madres" (motherless thieves) are cheaper than the military and do not spew grandiose discourse about Argentina's lofty destiny or attempt to go to war with Chile or England.

Still another example of corruption is official tolerance for the existence of the Feria de Riachuelo, the market that specializes in illegal merchandize. Several layers of corruption maintain it: the judge who hires Verónica as inspector of the market to construct a façade of legality; Verónica, who agrees to be inspector in her capacity as a lawyer; and Rosales, the accountant who is paid to produce accounts that show all is above board. Verónica's thoughts about the judge communicate the absence of any semblance of justice.

> Estaba solo, el tipo. Él en una orilla y la justicia en la otra, y en el medio, nada, putrefacción pura, Riachuelo. Era titular de un juzgado tan vacío como su ordenador, tan inútil como el acondicionador de aire o los empleados que archivan expedientes en estanterías arqueadas por el sobrepeso. (28)

> [The guy was on his own. He was on one bank of the river, with justice on the other and in between them, nothing, a putrefying mess, the Rio Riachuelo. He was in charge of a jurisdiction as empty as his computer, as useless as the air conditioning or the employees who stacked case files on shelves already bowing under the weight of them.] (1.4)

Verónica became a lawyer after the dictatorship because she wanted to defend just causes, but, having lost the idealism of her youth along the way, has accepted the job because she needs the money. The accountant, an upright fellow, is shocked when he realizes that he is expected to "cook the books." However, when Verónica declares that they are state employees and the state does not really care about anything, we witness a shift in his disposition toward the job: "Tocado por la varita mágica de una hada boba, Rosales confiesa que tenía pensado viajar a Disneyworld" (Touched by the magic wand of a witless fairy, Rosales confesses he had thought of visiting Disneyworld) (77; 2.3). In this highly satirical passage, Rosales has realized that Verónica is right—state corruption is endemic—and compromises his ethical standards in exchange for the chance to take his grandchildren to see the delights of First World capitalism chez Uncle Sam.

"Gobernar es recaudar" (To govern is to bring in money), Verónica pronounces, cynically rephrasing Sarmiento's historic proclamation "Gobernar es poblar" (To govern is to bring in people) (34; 1.5) in reference to the corrupt local authorities who benefit from the revenue generated by the market specializing in fraudulent and illegal goods. Another manifestation of unethical officialdom are the functionaries who became rich by looking the other way when millionaires bought national park land in Patagonia. The businessmen are also mafiosos: Tío says that the kidnapped foreign CEOs are *traficantes* like him but defended by international diplomacy. Finally, federal policeman el Escocés is cynical about everyone: the capitalists whose businesses are a murky mix of legal and mafia dealings, the revolutionaries who have the same taste for the good life at the cost of others as everyone else, and the police who are "la misma mierda" (the lowest of the low) (244; 4.2).

### The (Relatively) Honest Policeman

Among this array of shady individuals, there is a character who is trying to maintain a scrap of decency, and it is Walter Carroza. "Un policía honesto, no me haga reír" (An honest cop, don't make me laugh), retorts the cacique to Walter Carroza's statement "Sólo mato cuando me paga el estado" (I only kill when the state pays) (266; 4.6). This exchange inscribes Carroza's unique status as a (relatively) honest, if deeply cynical, police officer. Similar to Mallo's narratives, Orsi incorporates an investigator who maintains a Marlowe-like code of ethics in a tainted world. "In his literature a certain sense of duty predominates, a code of honor that leads the characters to put themselves into the mouth of the wolf," a critic writes of Orsi's novels (Zina). In *Ciudad Santa* it will be the lonely role of Carroza to represent this code of honor.

Deputy inspector Carroza, originally from Uruguay, is a detective in the department of "Delitos Complejos" in the federal force. When the wealthy tourists are taken hostage, he is assigned to the case. What makes him furious is his certainty that some of the kidnappers work beside him in the department. He also participates in the rescue mission that is intentionally botched by the unscrupulous Oso. The portrait of Carroza, conveyed mainly through his thoughts and actions as well as Verónica's opinions, is that of a wizened and eccentric loner who lives a Spartan existence. At the same time, he is a decent individual who carries out his duties in a (mostly) ethical manner while swimming amid a sea of corruption. A highly competent professional, he solves cases but never gets much recognition for his work. His job is to hunt down assassins, and he has gone after so many that he is constantly on the defensive, always moving and covering his tracks. He is wise—"lo consultan como a un oráculo" (they consult him like an oracle) (225; 3.16)—and trustworthy, the only policeman Verónica trusts. Most importantly, he is principled. Like Verónica, when he was studying law in Montevideo he had ideals—"soñaba con defender las leyes de otro modo" (he ... dreamed of defending the law some other way) (92; 2.6)—and he did not participate in torturing during the dictatorship and is disgusted by those who did. Verónica suspects that he has suffered a tragedy in the past—he has died spiritually but continues to operate in the world of the living.

Like "el Perro" Lascano in Mallo's trilogy, Walter Carroza is a sentimental action hero. He misses terribly his late wife, Carolina, and we learn that her murder was the reason for his spiritual death. Walter is not chaste, occasionally sleeping with women he hardly knows. When Ana Torrente, Miss Bolivia, throws herself into his arms, he initially resists but gives in when she turns twenty-one. He tells Ana, "*Estoy demasiado flaco ... vas a abrazar a un esqueleto, no sé si te va a gustar*" (I'm too skinny ... it'll be like embracing a skeleton, I don't think you'll like it) (101; 2.8), to which she replies that she finds him full of wisdom and tenderness. Thus this young woman has found his gentle side. But Walter is not in love with Ana—his longtime secret passion is Verónica. His valor and fast action come into play when someone takes aim at Verónica; he acts quickly, pushing her to the floor and saving her life. Carroza expresses his frustration and sense of responsibility vis-à-vis the women in his life to fellow federal officer el Escocés: "¡Me están tiroteando las mujeres, Escocés!" (All my women are getting shot at, Scotty!) (101; 2.8). Carroza's use of the indirect object pronoun—"me"—in this exclamation conveys his sense of personal involvement in the protection of the women he cares about. Verónica represents for Carroza "la débil llama que lo mantiene a salvo de la absoluta tiniebla sentimental" (the weak flame that is saving him from complete emotional darkness) (257; 4.4). This tiny spark of affection will set up the happy ending.

### Noir Dames

The female characters in *Ciudad Santa* assume classic roles sanctified by hard-boiled dames. Just as Walter Carroza represents the male lead, the gallant Chandleresque figure who braves the mean streets to solve his cases, so Verónica Berutti is the female lead, Carroza's love interest with a bit of "Girl Friday." A criminal defense lawyer, Verónica is sought by the Bolivian beauty queen for help when Matías Zamorano is killed and Ana realizes she is also in danger. When an informer at the Feria de Riachuelo tells Verónica that the kidnapped tourists are being held nearby, Verónica contacts Walter Carroza because she has seen him on TV making declarations about the case. Verónica once had the illusion of using her law degree to fight for justice, but, like many who have walked the mean streets, she has acquired a generous dose of cynicism. When discussing with the accountant their role in fabricating a façade of respectability for the dirty business, the narrator reflects: "Si ella [Verónica] en definitiva quiere lo mismo que el contador, vivir tranquila, cobrar lo suyo, seguir viaje, estar lejos cuando empiecen los tiros" (What she wants is the same as the accountant: to live a quiet life, get paid what is owed her, then head off so that she can be a long way away when the shooting starts) (76; 2.3). But her humanity remains intact—"No defiendo leyes, defiendo gente" (I don't defend laws, I defend people) (136; 3.2), she insists to Carroza.

The supporting female role is played by Ana Torrente, blonde-haired Bolivian beauty queen and ambitious femme fatale par excellence, as described by the narrator: "Carita de querubín flotando en una nube y agallas suficientes para regentear ella sola el garito y los prostíbulos de Zamorano.... Las mujeres, si son jóvenes y hermosas, son ambiciosas, y si son ambiciosas no se conforman con nada" (The face of a cherub floating on a cloud, but guts enough to manage the gambling dens and whorehouses run by Zamorano.... Women, especially if they are young and beautiful, are ambitious. And if they are ambitious, nothing satisfies them) (10; 1.1). In Buenos Aires she finds her protectors in two policemen: Carroza and Oso, whom she dubs her *padrino* and her *papito*, respectively. Carroza perceives her lethal power: "la belleza de Ana era un arma química, de destrucción masiva, un arsenal encerrado en un cuerpo perfecto, una dosis de genocidio en esos ojos claros y en esa mirada" (her beauty was like a chemical weapon of mass destruction, an arsenal concealed in her perfect body, a dose of genocide in her blue eyes and gaze) (101; 2.8). While bedding the two policemen, she sought men in power and seduced Matías Zamorano, thinking he was a kingpin.

Besides her role as femme fatale, this character serves to dramatize and explore deep cultural contradictions. The fact that she is known as Miss Bolivia problematizes her identity. Her title indicates she represents her country, but her fair hair makes her an outlier in a country where 62 percent of the population is of indigenous ancestry, and we may suspect she was chosen due to racial bias on the part of the beauty contest judges. While her birth mother was indigenous, her European genetics have prevailed, and, seeming to be in denial of this portion of her heritage, she has only scorn for her indigenous country people. When she was crowned Miss Bolivia, she thought she really was a queen until she found out her world tour was around miserable indigenous villages in Ecuador and Peru, where she was booed and raped. She detests her "país de indios," and she took a bus to Buenos Aires, thinking it really was European as she had been told. Ana represents conflictive identity—a blonde mestiza known as "Miss Bolivia" who disdains her indigenous heritage.

Ultimately, Miss Bolivia is revealed to be a dangerous serial murderer. She comes with a secret twin brother, Ovidio Ladislao Torrente Morelos, aka el Jaguar. Their mother bore el Jaguar in the mountains and he suffered from brain damage. Ill and in need of medical assistance, the mother left him there and went to the city, where she gave birth to Ana. The mother died and thus was unable to recover el Jaguar, but Ana was adopted by a family of German descent. Somehow, el Jaguar found out about his blonde sister; he has always hovered nearby to protect her and has followed her to Buenos Aires. When headless corpses begin to appear, they are thought to be the work of the "subhuman" el Jaguar. But Ana eventually confesses that she is the killer and el Jaguar only beheads her defunct victims.

There appears another, more benign, beauty in Sirena Mondragón, the companion of the Colombian drug czar whose name is usually accompanied by the tagline "la bella concubina." Although she has paired herself with an older, powerful man, this is a woman who knows how to take care of herself. When Arredri is killed, she uses quick thinking to save her own life by shouting out that she knows where the money is. She negotiates with Tío to ensure she will retain a handsome share, and calls in Colombian storm troopers to extricate her from the lair of the Argentine drug kingpin.

Such beautiful and clever women call for counterparts and, along with the stereotypical femmes fatales, the novel reflects the misogyny so characteristic of the classic hard-boiled genre: we meet the god-ugly policewoman Rosamonte, whose physical appearance the narrator likens to a rat, and the wife of an Air Force official, so frightful in her face cream and hair rollers that she would scare Frankenstein's creature. Once again, it is the opinionated extradiegetic narrator who cannot resist offering these insulting descriptions.

We recall Marty Roth's insight into the role of women in traditional detective fiction: they function "to signify sexuality, to flesh out male desire and shadow male sexual fear" (113). Much of Western literature, he explains, consists of a game women cannot play, but when they do enter the game, "they play so badly that a lot of time is taken up helping them to their feet" (113). This sheds light on the function of Verónica and Ana vis-à-vis Walter Carroza. Ana signifies his libido, and his secret desire for Verónica indicates that he has not given up hope of rekindling true love. At the same time, these women represent a problem for him. Verónica has gotten in over her head by accepting the job as market inspector and is targeted for murder, and Walter takes it upon himself to protect her, saving her life. She continues to create problems for him when he allows her to take refuge in his apartment: "No acostumbra, el purohueso, llevar mujeres a su escondrijo. Hizo una excepción con Verónica y ahí estaba el resultado: una noche mucho más complicada de lo que él había temido" (The skeleton man was not in the habit of taking women to his hideout. He made an exception with Verónica and look what happened: an even more complicated night than he had feared) (249; 4.2). When Ana's murderous tendency is revealed, Walter has two goals: to control Ana and to protect Verónica. The objectives of catching the criminals and rescuing the hostages become secondary.

Further elaborating on the function of women in detective fiction, Roth points out that women are often recorded as an absence, and such is the case with Carolina, Carroza's late wife. Finally, Roth notes that "women have two important roles: victim and villainess. The terms exchange themselves: she is exposed as a mad, evil creature, turned over to the police, because she is too attractive to be allowed to roam free in the male imagination" (119). This reflection illuminates the role of Ana—she is first presented as a victim, fleeing from Viruela's henchmen, but when the veil falls, she is exposed as a murderer. As Scaggs and other critics have noted, misreading the femme fatale is the classic error of the hard-boiled detective (77).

## The Che Guevara Parody

In this highly satirical vision of Buenos Aires and its residents, along with most of Western civilization, Pacogoya—the drug-dealing tour guide and "amante delivery de las insatisfechas" (the delivery lover of women who were never satisfied) (163; 3.6)—becomes a focus of satire and the butt of jokes. The satire serves to critique a lack of ethical values and is delivered through facetious comparisons of Pacogoya to Che Guevara, which create a running parody of the "text" constituting the received image of Che Guevara.

"Parody is a form of imitation, but imitation characterized by ironic inversion, not always at the expense of the parodied text," according to Linda Hutcheon. "It is repetition with critical distance, which marks difference rather than similarity" (*A Theory of Parody* 6). Pacogoya is similar to Che in physical appearance; for this reason the tourists confuse him with a leftwing militant and thank him for his services by giving him books about Che written in French or Italian. But the ironic distance between the two is marked by the fact that this imitation Che is a cowardly and corrupt capitalist. A drug dealer points out, "Se parece al Che Guevara" (He looks a bit like Che Guevara), to which his companion replies: "Es cierto, pero el Che era un revolucionario y éste es un mierda" (It's true, but Che was a revolutionary and this guy's a heap of shit) (68; 2.1).

The narrator parodies texts that create the Che myth, pointing to ironic similarities between Pacogoya's experiences and Che's biography. For instance, the narrator contrasts Che's "calvario y crucifixión" in Bolivia with Pacogoya's "calvario" in the *villa* Descamisados de América, the shantytown where the hostages are being held. But Pacogoya's "calvary" has nothing to do with the Socialist Revolution; it consists of the fact that Pacogoya is made to serve guard duty over the trusting tourists he has led to their captors. Next, when Pacogoya boards a bus to escape to the south of Argentina where a Swedish girlfriend awaits him, the narrator tells us, "El cheguavarita se marcha a una sierra no palúdica, sin bolivianos ni rangers, con una sueca rica que le espera para cojer y cojer hasta que el mundo acabe" (The Che Guevara lookalike is heading for the mountains where there are no malaria, Bolivians, or Rangers, only a rich Swede with whom he can fuck and fuck until the end of the world) (164; 3.6), thus creating another derisive comparison to Che's jungle march. Subsequently the imitation Che is plucked off the bus and held captive by Oso Berlusconi, but he manages to escape through the woods and is rescued by a Bolivian immigrant who operates a gas station. Once again, Pacogoya's odyssey is compared mockingly to Che's Bolivian campaign: the only thing in common between this forest and that of the real Che are the Bolivians. He is called "revolucionario de alcoba, amante delivery fuera de combate" (this bedroom revolutionary, this empty-handed delivery lover) (224; 3.16). The humorous incongruity between the original Che and his flimsy imitation serves to ridicule Pacogoya. "Parody is a way for modern artists to come to terms with the past—through ironic recoding or 'trans-contextualizing,'" explains Hutcheon (*A Theory of Parody* 101). Thus the Che figure is transported from the context of the Socialist Revolution to hypercapitalist globalized Buenos Aires. The emphasis is on the difference and distance from the original text: Che's bravery, self-sacrifice, and revolutionary idealism are replaced by Pacogoya's cowardice, treachery, promiscuity, and greed. This parody of Che functions to satirize the loss of idealism in the pleasure-seeking hedonistic capitalist society of the twenty-first century.

## Foul Breezes of Buenos Aires

Among all these corrupt and cynical individuals, Buenos Aires figures as the protagonist. *Ciudad Santa* joins the ranks of the "urban collapse" or "urban decay" subgenre that emerged in the 1980s. According to Stephen Knight, the originator of this subgenre was James Ellroy, whose most celebrated novel, *The Black Dahlia* (1987), depicts extreme violence in Los Angeles, opening with the Zoot Suit Riots (Knight 210). In this subgenre, the modern city is seen as a hell whose inhabitants have been undone by a kind of spiritual and emotional death (Scaggs 70). Another critic observes that the city can be used as "the scapegoat for the failings of the state" (Willett 129–40), and this is clearly the case with *Ciudad Santa*. As Close points out, a tendency of the *novela negra* is "its project of a cognitive mapping of the contemporary metropolis in an era in which large-scale migration from the countryside and the uncontrolled growth of cities ... has threatened the very intelligibility of the urban environment, fragmenting and distending the cityscape and subsuming or displacing traditional points of reference and centers of orientation" (*Contemporary Hispanic Crime Fiction* 19).

In Orsi's novel, a portrait unfolds of the chaotic and violent ubermetropolis that has subsumed a city that once prided itself as being stately, dignified, and livable. Various modalities come into play to develop a multifaceted vision of the port city: a parody of tourist brochure descriptions of Buenos Aires, the frequent voicing of the deteriorated international reputation of Buenos Aires and Argentina, the dramatization of schisms caused by social class and racial differences, and, surely the most potent, the presentation of Buenos Aires as an antithetical "ciudad santa." Osvaldo Di Paolo maintains that *Ciudad Santa* presents a posthuman apocalyptic vision of Buenos Aires—posthuman because it has lost rational thought and human solidarity, and apocalyptic because it is portrayed as a corrupt, prostituted city that deserves to be destroyed ("El poshumanismo apocalíptico" 47).

The contrast between the glorious bygone era of Buenos Aires elegance and its reality in the new millennium is conveyed via a parody of propaganda used to sell Buenos Aires to visitors, flowery descriptions that look back to nostalgic imagery that invariably presents it as the Paris of South America. For example, while the tourists from the stranded ship await its repair, they are told they have a grand opportunity to explore "la París de América del Sur, magnífica oportunidad para aprender a bailar tango y comer muchos bifes de chorizo" (the Paris of South America, a magnificent opportunity to learn to dance the tango and eat lots of steaks) (25; 1.4). But this exalted image is soon demystified when they discover the downside of the city, in particular its chaotic traffic and biting poverty.

> Hartos ya de tango y de bifes de chorizo, los turistas del *Queen of Storms* varados en Buenos Aires empiezan a preguntarse unos a otros cuándo zarparán de esta ciudad de tránsito enloquecido, ruidosa y sucia, harapienta en cuanto sale de los circuitos marcados por los guías, con esa pobreza amenazante que los mismos turistas disfrutan en Bombay o Río de Janeiro, pero que no esperaban encontrar en Buenos Aires, tan al sur, tan europea. (137)

> [Sated by now with tango and the best steaks, the tourists from the *Queen of Storms* stranded in Buenos Aires are beginning to ask one another when they are going to leave this crazy port of call, this noisy, dirty city so full of ragged poverty once you step outside the circuits marked by the guides, the threatening sort of poverty that tourists find attractive in Bombay or Rio, but do not expect to find in Buenos Aires, so far away in the south, but so European.] (3.3)

The most incisive statement in reference to the false European image versus the reality of Third World poverty comes via the kidnapped passengers.

> Las tres parejas de secuestrados en las cercanías de Puerto Madero mientras disfrutaban del clima europeo con el que Buenos Aires se vende a sí misma en los catálogos, han sido distribuidas en tres casillas diferentes, aunque vecinas, y descansan, a la manera sudamericana, atados de pies manos sobre el piso de tierra y amordazados al límite de la asfixia. Vaharadas del putrefacto y tibio olor del Riachuelo contribuyen a sus vigilas. (131)
>
> [The three couples snatched near Puerto Madero as they were enjoying the European climate with which Buenos Aires sells itself in travel brochures have been split up in three separate but neighbouring shacks. They are resting, in a South-American way, bound hand and foot on earth floors, gagged to the point of suffocation. They are kept awake by wafts of the warm, rotten stench from the Riachuelo.] (3.1)

Highlighted in this passage is the contrast between the European lux (or lux associated with Europe) of glossy Puerto Madero—the high-end reclaimed port area of Buenos Aires—and the "South American" barbarism manifested in the captivity of the hapless tourists whose ordeal is punctuated by the stench of the hyperpolluted Riachuelo River.[16] Once again, irony rules as the heavy-handed extradiegetic narrator mocks stereotypical conceptions of Europe and South America.

In addition, Ana Torrente's experiences serve to demystify the falsehoods she heard about Buenos Aires. She fled Bolivia, dreaming of her arrival in Buenos Aires, the Paris of South America, a city without Indians where even the taxi drivers speak to you in French: "Te mintieron [Ana says to herself]. Buenos Aires está tan llena de negros como cualquier ciudad en ruinas de Bolivia o del Perú" (They lied to you. . . . Buenos Aires is overrun by Indians as any ruined city in Bolivia or Peru) (38; 1.6). Thus the European image that Buenos Aires has traditionally touted—an urbane and sophisticated city populated by people of European descent—is repeatedly deflated by the visitors' experience of a violent, chaotic metropolis with pockets of grinding Third World poverty and many immigrants of indigenous extraction.

As if to confirm the collapse of Argentina's image, we see the view from across the Atlantic in the European reaction to the hostage crisis: "Todas las miradas del mundo occidental . . . sobre la policía de una república bananera en el sur del continente, torpe, ineficaz, corrupta, incapaz de proteger a sus ciudadanos en tránsito" (Everyone in the Western world has their eyes on us... on the police in a banana republic in the south of Latin America. Police who are clumsy, inept, corrupt, unable to take of care of their visiting citizens) (236; 4.1). Alternatively, Argentina is called "ese absurdo país de América Latina, conocido apenas por el tango, los bifes de vaca y Maradona" (that absurd Latin-American country known only for tango, beefsteaks and Maradona) (273; 4.8). Mocking the Argentine government as perennially corrupt, the ambassadors' instructions from Europe are to protest energetically whatever corrupt government is in power.

Another running topic of critique is the deterioration of values of the Argentines. For example, when Verónica tells the judge that the accountant is an honest fellow, the judge's response indicates that he belongs to a dying breed: *"Me emociona esa gente, doctora, se les va la vida respetando el sistema. Ya no quedan argentinos así"* (People like him move me, *doctora*. Their lives go by and yet they always respect the system. They don't make Argentines like that anymore) (77; 2.3). Cynicism is evinced in the greed of the hoteliers who delight in the opportunity to take advantage of the stranded tourists, charging them $200 to spend the night in the halls. Lack of professionalism is seen in the maintenance of the port—the cruise ship was grounded because the Rio de la Plata estuary had not been dredged, and this neglect occurred because the personnel were not paid their salary incentives. No one bothered to inform the ship captains of this. Fittingly, rats serve as a symbol for the people: "Es zona portuaria, hay más ratas que gente... hasta en Puerto Madero, donde un departamento cuesta medio millón de dólares, hay ratas... las que bajan de los barcos se cruzan con las nativas.... Buenos Aires, crisol de ratas" (This is the port area. There are more rats than people... even in Puerto Madero, where an apartment can cost a million dollars. Pedigree rats come off the boats and mix with the native ones.... Buenos Aires, a melting pot for rats) (96–97; 2.7).

The area of the city where the decay is most patent are the poverty-ridden southern districts, the vicinity of Lomas de Zamora where the Feria de Riachuelo is located. This is also Viruela's territory: "veinte cuadras... cloaca a cielo abierto habitada por desahuciados del sistema, zombis que roban y matan por la comida, soldados harapientos de un ejército sin otra disciplina que la certeza del hambre, si no obedecen" (twenty blocks... an open sewer inhabited by the rejects of the system, zombies who steal and kill for food, ragged foot-soldiers in an army whose only discipline is the certainty that if they disobey orders they will starve to death) (10–11; 1.1). The description of the *villa* where the hostages are taken emphasizes its noxious contamination and the precarious construction of the dwellings:

"una pústula ... cercana a la ribera del río más contaminado de la Argentina: tumor urbano formado por centenares de casillas armadas, la mayoría, con cartón, madera de cajones de fruta, tablas robadas de las obras en construcción y lata" (a running sore ... close to the bank of Argentina's most polluted river; a tumour made up of hundreds of shacks, most of which are built out of cardboard, wood from fruit crates, planks stolen from construction sites and lot of bits of metal) (82; 2.5).

Another plague of Buenos Aires is racial prejudice toward immigrants from indigenous regions, specifically the Bolivians who frequent the market and represent the changing face of the city. Chuco, Verónica's chauffeur and bodyguard, expresses virulent racism: "Son mugrientos y ladrones.... Nunca se fíe de un *bolita*, doctora. No habría que dejarlos entrar en la Argentina.... Son traicioneros, son indios, qué va a esperar" (They're all filthy thieves.... Never trust a Bolivan, *doctora*. They shouldn't be allowed into Argentina.... They're treacherous. They're indians, so what can you expect?) (80–81; 2.4).[17] And when Pacogoya gives ironic reassurance to his European clients, he voices the *porteños*' generalized bias toward Bolivians, telling them that Argentines are kind to foreigners who do not come from Bolivia.

The most potent exploration of racial prejudice and its depiction as a postcolonial ill comes from the representation of el Escocés and his children. His nickname establishes his European extraction, and his rape of (or affair with) an indigenous woman re-creates the colonial situation, enabling the text to explore its aftermath in Latin America. Their encounter evokes Mary Louise Pratt's concept of "contact zones": "social spaces where disparate cultures meet, clash, and grapple with each other, often in highly asymmetrical relations of domination and subordination" (7). El Escocés's recollection of the incident makes patent his exploitation of the indigenous woman along with his utter disdain for all of her ethnicity:

> Mucho antes me cojí una india, pecado de juventud, qué vas a hacer. Me habían mandado en comisión a Tartagal, en 1984, a investigar a una banda de contrabandistas. Tres meses bajo el sol, levantando temperatura. Las indias se embarazan con nada, son fértiles y prolíficas como las ratas, la perdición de América. (296)

> [A long time ago I fucked an indian woman up in the north of Argentina. The sins of youth, what can you do? That was in 1984. I'd been sent to Tartagal to investigate a gang of smugglers. Three months under that sun, my blood boiling. Those native women get pregnant for nothing, they're as fertile as rats, the scourge of America.] (4.11)

Whether or not the woman participated willingly seems immaterial—the relation of the dominant and subordinate culture and gender is clear. The twins born of this encounter depict the pernicious mentality tainting the aftermath of the colonial situation in Bolivia and Argentina. Ana, a mestiza who is able to pass as being of European heritage due to her fair coloring, rejects her indigenous blood, and this denial is translated into virulent hatred of indigenous people. Her twin brother, el Jaguar, serves to convey the marginalization and rejection of the indigenous "other." His otherness is multiply marked—born brain damaged, his abnormality causes him to be perceived as monstrous by society, and his nickname, el Jaguar, stresses his identification as a savage. The people believe he is a serial murderer, thus his barbarism is overdetermined. The fact that this dread of el Jaguar is exposed as a misconception can be read as a critique of prejudices against the indigenous "other" based on false assumptions. In this sense, the Bolivian twins function to reflect on racism and discrimination as deleterious effects of the colonial legacy.

Calvary and the Christ Figure

The concept of Buenos Aires as a "ciudad santa" is ironic because the metropolis is depicted as crawling with corruption. The novel relentlessly portrays Buenos Aires as violent, mercenary, hedonistic, and corrupt—anything but a holy city. The only "ciudad santa" to be found is the Tierra Santa theme park, the tacky mock-up of ancient Jerusalem that is scorned by the sophisticated *porteños* and international tourists.

The yearning for a holy city, a place of spiritual refuge, is developed through the Bolivian twins. El Jaguar is depicted as abject—the extradiegetic narrator, voicing the perspectives of el Escocés and the German couple who adopted Ana, describes him as a human reject and a humanoid excrescence. He is repeatedly humiliated: Ana's adoptive parents expulse him as if he were a bacteria, and people react to his presence with repulsion and terror. Yet despite, or perhaps because of, his outward appearance, he is a spiritual being and seeks a sanctuary where he and his sister can be pure. When he came across the religious theme park in Buenos Aires, he decided to stay there, proclaiming, *"Ésta es tierra sagrada, estaré limpio"* (I'll stay here, this is sacred ground, it will cleanse me) (261; 4.5).

Paradoxically, the idea of a "ciudad santa" originally came from his beautiful but perverse sister, Ana: "Huiremos juntos, algún día—decía Ana—. Lejos, a una ciudad que no será parecida a ésta ni a ninguna otra, una ciudad sin pecadores, mi jaguar. Ayúdame a encontrarla" (One day we'll run away together, Ana would say. Far away to a city that will be unlike this one or any other one, a city without sinners, my jaguar. Help me find it) (270; 4.7). El Jaguar makes her desire his own, seeking to become a redeemer. Golgota, the place where Christ was crucified, the narrator reminds us, means mountain of the skull, and el Jaguar's project was to construct, using the skulls of Ana's victims, his private altar of resurrection and eternal life.

In this way, the monstrous el Jaguar becomes a Christ figure. As Julia Kristeva points out, Christ, by bearing witness, "confessed" to Pontius Pilate; "the avowal of faith is thus from the very start tied to persecution and suffering" (129). El Jaguar expresses his faith in salvation through the collection of skulls—thus his practice of beheading is for a holy purpose. Since everyone thinks he murders the owners of the heads, they fear him and conceive him as an abject monster. However, the real murderer is Ana, and el Jaguar is tame and gentle—"de peluche" (a fluffy toy) (292; 4.10), according to Verónica's analyst. Identities have broken down and reversed themselves: adorable Ana is actually a serial murderer; the beastly el Jaguar is really a teddy bear. Just as Jesus died for the sins of humankind, el Jaguar will be slain for the sins of his sister. In another biblical parallel, Ana betrays him— she calls him to Carroza's apartment, where she is holding Verónica captive. When el Jaguar arrives, he is surprised to find living people—Verónica and her friend Laucha—because Ana only sends for him when she has killed someone so that he can decapitate them. Laucha, terrified by the appearance of el Jaguar, mortally wounds him with a knife.

Thus el Jaguar becomes a martyr through his persecution and victimization. According to Christian belief, Christ must be killed before he can rise again and return to save the sinful city. Of course, the true sinner is el Jaguar's twin sister and betrayer, the beautiful Ana, who fools everyone with her cherubic appearance. As twins, they represent two parts of a whole: the horror that underlies a surface of beauty, the barbarity hidden beneath the veneer of civilization. Here, the damaged self of the psychopathic twins serves as a metaphor for society's aberrations (Horsley, *Twentieth-Century Crime Fiction* 117). Ana's beautiful and seductive exterior hides a violent reality; el Jaguar's quest represents a misguided search for salvation.

El Jaguar's pursuit of salvation is misguided because the "ciudad santa" where he takes refuge is a paltry commercial mockery of the Holy Land. It is an example of Jean Baudrillard's definition of the simulacra produced by consumer society—a pretend representation that masks the absence of the holy space it purports to represent (1733–36). El Jaguar goes about the search for salvation in a macabre manner: via decapitation, which lends him monstrosity instead of divinity. Also, Calvary, or mountain of the skull, was so named due to its geographic features, which made it resemble a skull. Since the skull is not an intrinsic or enabling feature, he is imitating a superficial detail. The seer and would-be savior is a misguided and monstrous Christ figure. In this gothic morality tale, the truth of contemporary culture resides in the abject subject.

Kristeva explains that literature, along with psychoanalysis, tears away the veil of religion and morality, offering a glimpse of the abyss; it is the privileged signifier of the realm of abjection, the power of horror. As such, literature "represents the ultimate coding of our crises, of our most intimate and most serious apocalypses" (208). The cult of abjection shows the crisis of the symbolic order, and religious, moral, and ideological codes are abjection's purification and repression. Thus the novel's edification of a "ciudad santa," a place of redemption, represents a desire to expel the abject. "But the return of their repressed," Kristeva continues, "make up our 'apocalypse,' and that is why we cannot escape the dramatic convulsions of religious crises." "Religion is sacred horror," she avows; it is a code to repress and cleanse the abject (209–10).

The concept of a holy city implies purity, freedom from sin, redemption, and salvation. And as each term conjures up its opposite, the holy city also evokes the fall and condemnation. In this sense, Buenos Aires is an impure world in need of redemption. Di Paolo discusses the image of Buenos Aires as the corrupted Jerusalem, after the fall.

> Buenos Aires has become the Jerusalem of the past, a prostituted city that deserves to be exterminated. In the text, the narrator says that Pacogoya, the tour guide, wakes up with the image of Buenos Aires as if it were the holy city of Jerusalem (73), and inspector Carroza, talking with another policeman about the decapitated corpses, points out that "Buenos Aires is, today more than ever, a holy city" (152). Both, in an ironic way, are referring to the Jerusalem that deserves to be destroyed. ("El poshumanismo apocalíptico" 47)

Di Paolo points to its meager chance for salvation: "Buenos Aires is a city that has fallen short and is without salvation. Destruction and chaos outstrip any hope of reversing the situation. The possibility of regeneration is scarce" ("El poshumanismo apocalíptico" 57). *Ciudad Santa*, through the portrayal of a corrupt and chaotic metropolis and the disturbed twins' vain search for redemption, delivers a potent message of urban collapse. The twisted twins—the fruit of the European man's plundering of a native woman—bear the marks of a conflictive and violent society that denies its own identity. Ultimately, *Ciudad Santa* portrays a corrupt patriarchal power structure as one of the sources of depravity. This resembles the message of *Los hombres te han hecho mal*, with the difference that Abeledo, the illegitimate patriarch, can be read as analogous to ex-president Menem, and el Escocés can be seen as representative of the colonial European usurper.

At the same time, there is also in *Ciudad Santa* a regeneration of sorts on a personal, emotive level. For this optimistic note, we return to policeman and sentimental action figure Walter Carroza. While fleeing from the cacique's ranch, Carroza is critically injured. After a long recovery in the hospital, he returns to his barren apartment, ready to end it all and rejoin Carolina, his deceased wife. To his surprise, who should show up but Verónica, his secret passion. Thus he will give life and love another chance—the ending is sentimental and hopeful for the world-weary policeman. And there is another sentimental reunion: as Carroza is leaving the hospital, he passes by the room of el Escocés, who was also wounded in the skirmish. From the hallway, he recognizes the figure of Ana Torrente, who has decorated her father's room with flowers and ribbons. Although she may kill him some day, Carroza reflects, at least she has found her father.

Keeping on message vis-à-vis the intractability of urban crime, in the final scenes the drug traffickers remain unpunished. Alberto Cozumel Banegas, aka Viruela, is stripped of his position as councilor Viruela and loses the governor's protection. He declares that he will appear before a judge to denounce the principal drug traffickers in Buenos Aires, but he does not get a chance to do so because he is found hanging from a bridge over the Riachuelo River. Similar to *Los hombres te han hecho mal*, *Ciudad Santa* ends with optimism on the personal, affective level but pessimism on the macro, social level. Although corruption is unabated, the cynical but noble federal policeman is awarded with a new chance at love with the woman he has been yearning for.

In conclusion, both Orsi and Mallo write scripts to bring together hard-boiledness and sentimentality. The honest cops do not restore order but they get the girl, and the domestic detective stands as "the professional embodiment of sympathy in an unsympathetic world" (Cassuto 183). The emotional essence of hard-boiled crime fiction is a family story, and this applies to the novels studied in this chapter. Mallo's trilogy is about damaged families and ends with the establishment of a new one—Lascano and Eva—resurrecting new hope for the family in a difficult age. Like Mallo's novel, Orsi's multistranded plot returns to primal unity, concluding on a sentimental note with the coupling of Carroza and Verónica as well as the tenuous father-daughter reunion of Ana and el Escocés. Ultimately, in the face of societal anomie, these writers envision human bonding as a type of antidote, or at least a healing salve for ravaged souls.[18]

Chapter Two

# THE PRESIDENT AND ALL HIS MEN
## Watchdog Journalists Tackle Corruption during the Menem Presidency

> Es posible concebir la Argentina menemista como una suerte de novela social con una moral particular.... En la frecuentación de la pizza, el champán, Versace, el golf, el dorado, la seda, los encantos de la ostentación, se detectan los vericuetos de una moral trabajada por una libido social, desinteresada de las correcciones de la virtud.
>
> —Luciana Vázquez, *La novela de Menem*

ARGENTINE JOURNALIST MIGUEL BONASSO HAS NOTED THAT RAYMOND Chandler would have been hard pressed to create a fictional plot that could outdo Argentine reality: "In contemporary Argentina, the hard-boiled novelist Raymond Chandler would have died of hunger, because it would have been difficult to find a more noir, perverse, intricate and decadent plot than that provided by the media on a daily basis." Bonasso's observation is slightly off the mark: rather than trying to *compete* with this sinister reality, Argentine writers of fiction have found inspiration in the intricate and brazen manipulations of political operatives. Indeed, the *novela negra* thrives in this milieu.

In *Ficciones verdaderas: Hechos reales que inspiraron grandes obras literarias*, Tomás Eloy Martínez gathers extracts from twelve literary works he calls "rescrituras de hechos de la realidad" (rewritings of real events) (13), preceding each passage with the nonfiction text that served as its source. In the book's prologue, Martínez—known for his novels that engage recent history—describes the circumstances that lead creative writers to choose to "transfigure" certain realities within a fictional narrative: "there must be a prior reality weighing down on him, exerting a force of gravity on the narrator's imagination: a lived experience, a reading, something that excites him, that drives him crazy" (9). He also points out that if "ficciones verdaderas" (true fictions) reflect the mentality of a period, it is because they derive from facts that define that epoch. The *novelas negras* discussed in this chapter—*El vuelo de la reina* (2002) by Martínez and *El muerto indiscreto* (2003) by Rubén Correa—are cases in point.[1] The government and lifestyle of President Carlos Menem were among the defining factors for Argentine society in the 1990s, and these novels appropriate and transpose the figure of Menem along with scandals and chicanery that occurred during his administration. Besides exposing the corruption and excess that characterized the heyday of Argentina's neoliberal experiment, these works feature a procedure common to the Argentine and the Latin American *novela negra*: investigative journalists carrying out the detective function.

## THE MENEM PRESIDENCY AND THE NEOLIBERAL ERA

Menem's presidency is known for its heavy-handed implementation of neoliberal reform; scandals related to weapons smuggling, embezzlement, and other forms of corruption; and the frivolous and ostentatious lifestyle of Menem and his family. While Argentina was not unique in its adoption of neoliberal policy, its consequences there have been deep and lingering. In the 1990s, every country in Latin America, with the exception of Cuba, implemented aspects of the neoliberal model, following a generalized tendency in the Western world. Abandoning decades of Peronist anti-American rhetoric and dismantling labor organizations and protectionist policies, "Argentina adopted neoliberal economic models lock, stock, and barrel" (Sheinin, *Argentina and the United States* 208). In the early 1990s, the Menem government initiated the hasty privatization of public sector enterprises, including telecommunications, the state airlines, oil and energy industries, and the military's industrial enterprises. Argentina eliminated barriers on foreign trade and investment, allowing for freedom of movement for capital, and reduced the fiscal deficit by raising taxes and dismantling costly federal government programs, thus cutting back on the role of the state as a provider of social services. Collective bargaining was abandoned and replaced by decentralized salary negotiations (Grimson and Kessler 70). Perhaps the most dramatic measure of Argentina's economic reforms was the Convertibility Plan launched in 1991 by Domingo Cavallo,

Menem's minister of finance, which pegged the Argentine peso to the US dollar at a one-to-one ratio.

Various historical, political, and economic factors explain why Argentina became such a wholehearted convert to the neoliberal program. When the dictatorship ended in 1983 and Argentina returned to democratic rule with the presidency of Raúl Alfonsín, the military regime had left Argentina with a poor international image and a faltering economy. Although changes in the import-substitution model were introduced by the dictatorship in 1976, the basic rules of the economy remained unaltered between 1975 and 1989. The economic policy of Alfonsín was not successful in fighting inflation, which soared to over 3,000 percent in 1989, and the image of a bloated, inefficient state was promoted by sectors of the media and took hold of public opinion (Grimson and Kessler 61, 69; Norden and Russell 8).

External factors played an important role. The end of the Cold War and the collapse of the Soviet Union "left a world strongly dominated by the principles of economic and political liberalism with the United States occupying the most powerful position in the key liberal international institutions such the International Monetary Fund, the World Bank and the United Nations" (Norden and Russell 3). Seeing alliance with the US as essential for economic growth and leadership, Menem pursued a policy of alignment in the economic and strategic arenas. Cavallo cast the changes in Argentine economic policy as in step with the general neoliberal shift in Latin America and necessary in an age of globalization of trade and finance (Sheinin, *Argentina and the United States* 196–98).

Positive effects of these new economic policies were soon apparent—inflation was arrested and the economy began to grow. However, most of the growth was due to foreign, not domestic, investment and the Argentine economy proved to be highly vulnerable to international swings, seen in the capital flight that occurred during the 1995 Mexican crisis and the 1998 crisis in Asia. While bilateral commerce rose quickly, the cost of labor in Argentina's dollarized economy led to a sharp price increase of Argentine products, resulting in the need to import huge quantities of goods and a subsequent growth of Argentina's trade deficit (Sheinin, *Argentina and the United States* 203). A slowdown in 1996 turned into a full-blown recession in the second half of 1998. The crash came on 19 December 2001 when the government froze bank accounts and massive protests broke out.

Corruption and scandals related to the Menem administration's handling of fiscal matters and criminal justice also served to sour the public's reception of the structural changes along with their regard for the president who championed them. In the early 1990s, Menem's administration "was repeatedly shaken by denunciations of wrongdoing and ensuing scandals" (Waisbord, *Watchdog Journalism in South America* xix). A host of incidents exposed Menem's government as a haven for criminality, and a string of scandals linked it to organized crime. In 1991 a US-based company complained that it was asked for a bribe to facilitate importation of machinery to Argentina, and Menem's brother-in-law was implicated. Later, press exposés revealed that government officials were involved in drug money laundering operations and illegal arms sales (Waisbord, "Reading Scandals" 272–75), and "in each case, there were ties to Argentina's pro-US economic policies and indications of how those policies were implemented recklessly and in many cases criminally" (Sheinin, *Argentina and the United States* 205).

Through the bidding process involved in the privatization of utilities and nationalized industries, government officials enriched themselves via influence peddling and kickbacks.[2] High-level officials, including the president himself, were accused of illicit enrichment. With the implantation of the free market system and cutbacks in social welfare priorities—other mainstays of the new neoliberal economy—those citizens left out of the globalized economic model formed a new group of urban poor. On the other hand, the "winners" in the globalized economy enjoyed new modes of consumption and socialization. Menem's penchant for designer clothes, Rolex watches, Ferraris, and other trappings of luxury and status promoted conspicuous consumption as the nouveau riche who benefited from the new economic program sought to emulate the new hedonism. The private life of Menem, who enjoyed partying with the rich and famous, and his garish, pleasure-seeking family was frequently the subject of tabloid news.[3]

Argentine *novelas negras* set in the 1990s and beyond reflect this environment of political corruption and impunity, and the winners and losers of the neoliberal economy: the high rollers who got rich quickly and those excluded from the system—the topics of chapters 4 and 5, respectively. Reflecting the focus of this chapter, numerous *novelas negras* explore the convoluted world of Argentine political culture. *La mafia política: Renacerás de tus cenizas* by Diego Grillo Trubba, *Crímenes apropiados* by Fabio Nahuel Lezcano, and *El puñal* by Jorge Fernández Díaz, all discussed in the introduction, deal with government corruption, the first focusing on the complicity of the press, the second on the association between party politics and organized crime, and the third on "*narcopolítica*." As mentioned in chapter 1,

Ernesto Mallo's *Me verás caer* renders a fictional version of the Menem decade, re-creating the frivolous party atmosphere in the presidential palace as well as the web of gossip surrounding high-profile deaths that were never clarified but linked by vox populi to political scandals. Other novels excavate the dark side of middle-class lives. *El décimo infierno* (1999) by Mempo Giardinelli tells the hair-raising tale of a businessman and his lover who go on a frenzied killing spree, beginning with the murder of the man's wife. Giardinelli declares it "a Menemist novel.... It express what this government has been: a form of irrational violence, absolute corruption of values ... a vertigo of unreflective action" ("Mi libro refleja la corrupción absoluta del menemismo"). Carlos Balmaceda's *Manual del caníbal* (2005) can be read as an allegory of the society and mentality bred by the Menem presidency. In it, politicians, businessmen, and beautiful models accompanied by tanned millionaires flock to the legendary restaurant Almacén Buenos Aires, unaware that the exquisite dishes that delight their palate are made of human flesh.

## "NOVELAS MENEMISTAS": *EL VUELO DE LA REINA* BY TOMÁS ELOY MARTÍNEZ AND *EL MUERTO INDISCRETO* BY RUBÉN CORREA

The writers under study have turned to the *novela negra* to explore and critique the dealings of the Menem administration and the lifestyle his behavior spawned. Rubén Correa is a journalist who worked for *La Nación* for more than seven years and currently lives in the US, where he works as a news editor for the *Wall Street Journal Americas*. *El muerto indiscreto* is his first novel. It was awarded the Premio de Novela "Ateneo-Ciudad de Valladolid" and distributed widely in Spain but has not been distributed or received critical attention in Argentina. His second literary work, a novella titled *Interrupción del olvido* (2009), is a thriller set in Buenos Aires that explores the violence of the dictatorship and the memories of its victims.

Tomás Eloy Martínez (1934–2010) was one of the most innovative writers of his generation. A journalist, novelist, essayist, and critic as well as a public intellectual, he was forced to flee the Argentine dictatorial regime in 1975 and lived in the US much of his adult life, where he taught at the University of Maryland and at Rutgers. His most renowned novels explore the history and myths of Peronism. *La novela de Perón* (1985), based on a series of interviews carried out by Martínez with the exiled leader in Madrid, blends fact with imagination as it portrays the aging political leader preparing to return to power. *Santa Evita* (1995), his most celebrated novel, deals with the bizarre afterlife of Evita's embalmed corpse. Martínez's two final novels, *El cantor de tango* (2004) and *Purgatorio* (2008), depict people residing in the US who travel to Argentina, whether in actuality or in their mind, in search of an elusive individual: in the first case a legendary tango singer and in the second, a loved one who disappeared during the military regime.

In this chapter, I will examine how *El vuelo de la reina* and *El muerto indiscreto* rework generic conventions to convey a scathing critique of government corruption as well as the spirit of excess and moral abandon that characterized the 1990s in Argentina. Both novels incorporate scandals that surfaced during the Menem presidency and feature the role of the investigative reporter in denouncing official wrongdoing and impunity. Both include fictionalized versions of Menem and highlight the president's greed as well as his skill at flouting the laws and evading justice. They are set in an Argentina that has been infected by the president's shameless transgression of ethical norms. Gender depictions also form part of the social critique.

As mentioned in the introduction, *Juegos de seducción y traición* by Ana María Amar Sánchez explains that certain texts incorporate the codes and formulas of popular literary forms to seduce the reader but alter them in a key point, betraying the reader's expectations. The space between the reader's seduction and betrayal opens to the possibility of a political reading. This chapter will consider how these novels reproduce and transform formulas of the hard-boiled genre as they critique a recent era in Argentine history. Since I will be analyzing and comparing similar issues in both novels, I will discuss them side by side as opposed to consecutively.

### Hard-Boiled Journalists

The investigation of crimes—the basic stuff of detective fiction—is the focus of *El vuelo* and *El muerto*. As may be expected, in the triad of "crime, truth, and justice," the last term is absent. The failure of justice is connected to the alteration of another triad of detective fiction—that of criminal, victim, and detective—as an investigative reporter assumes the role of sleuth. The reporters focus on the president in their investigation into wrongdoing; this manipulation of the formula is a political act, serving to expose systemic state corruption. In "The Journalist as the People's Detective," Horacio González discusses the role that critical journalism in Argentina has played in a political system riddled with corruption (495). González cites Rodolfo Walsh and Raymond Chandler as the basis of modern investigative journalism of the sort practiced by *Página/12*, the Argentine daily credited for having exposed most of the scandals of the early 1990s.[4] Walsh's *Operación masacre*, the nonfictional account of the illegal detention and execution of Peronist militants in the aftermath of the 1956 failed counter-coup against the military that expelled Perón, is considered the first Latin American political *testimonio*. Walsh, who was killed by a special military unit in 1977 the day after he wrote an open letter criticizing the Junta, is seen as the epitome of the lone reporter working tenaciously and at personal risk to expose illegality that goes unpunished. As discussed in the introduction, Chandler's fiction established many of the conventions of the hard-boiled detective subgenre in North America—for instance, the central character of the private eye, the urban setting, and routine police corruption—that would become a model or springboard for Latin American authors of crime fiction. This mix of Walsh and Chandler creates a useful point of departure for the study of these Argentine crime novels as they combine conventions of the hard-boiled detective novel with the story of determined investigative journalists to expose and denounce the atmosphere of corruption that tainted the Menem administration.

Taking a cue from detective fiction, in *El muerto indiscreto*, Correa adopts the classic model of death-detection-explanation. The initial enigma that will set the "detective" in motion has an amusing twist: instead of the typical discovery of a corpse, the first page presents a baffling "resurrection." In the men's room of a Buenos Aires restaurant, reporter Emilio Dargas runs into a man he believes is Luis Kunny, a political figure who reportedly was killed in an automobile accident two years earlier. Dargas will spend the rest of the novel trying to answer the following questions: Is Kunny really alive? If so, how and why did he fake his death and why did he decide to reappear? Another classic formula that Correa incorporates is the use of two stories with a dual logic: the story of the "crime"—the trail of corruption and intrigue in Kunny's political career that led to the staging of his death—and that of Dargas's investigation. When Dargas finally meets up with the revived Kunny a second time, a traditional "detached" investigation turns into a suspenseful thriller as the reporter discovers that he is being pursued by hit men working for powerful interests who wish to silence him.

Incorporating the investigative focus of the classic detective story, the novel describes the three investigative teams—a local police team, the Bonaerense, and private investigators from a US-based firm—that expose several layers of corruption. The Bonaerense, in their reconstruction of the accident that supposedly caused Kunny's death, find a series of inconsistencies that lead them to believe the accident was staged and the body is not Kunny's. Dargas discovers that the local police experts had been pressured by the Ministry of Justice to alter their report. A second investigation into the "accident" is opened when Kunny's "widow," alleging that sloppy road repair work contributed to the fatal crash, sues GAJA, S.A., the company in charge of highway reconstruction. This causes GAJA to hire a North American detective agency, which discovers the reason for flagrant evidence tampering: "detrás del caso se estaban moviendo fuertes intereses vinculados con el poder del gobierno" (behind the case were strong interests linked to the government) (271). This information will be used by GAJA to extort the government and obtain multimillion-dollar contracts for public works. And of course, President Jalil, a character I discuss below, will get his cut of these contracts. This systemic corruption—of top government officials, private enterprise, and independent investigators—is what propels the reporter to the scene to uncover and expose the facts behind Kunny's disappearance.

Characters in *El muerto* draw on detective conventions. Recalling Amar Sánchez's observations about the seduction of the reader with the repetition of formulas, in *El muerto* we reencounter stock characters from Chandler's fiction: a reporter who resembles a private eye and a femme fatale. Dargas has much in common with Chandler's Philip Marlowe: similar to Marlowe, he is a down-and-out character who becomes a solitary crusader in search of truth, continuing to pursue the Kunny story when all odds are against him and the newspapers of Buenos Aires, capitulating to vested interests, decide not to run his investigative report. Sexy, dangerous women working in collusion or at odds with their tough guy counterparts are a standard feature of hard-boiled detective fiction. In *El muerto*, the femme fatale is embodied in the character of Belle Rocco, Kunny's beautiful and manipulative mistress whose know-how, ambition, and taste for luxury are behind his heady accumulation of a vast fortune.

Criminality and suspense are also central features of Martínez's *El vuelo de la reina*, which develops along two interconnected plot lines, each involving a cluster of crimes. The first crime cluster, the story of government wrongdoing, has to do with an arms sale scandal and its spin-offs: bribery, illicit enrichment, and money laundering, as well as the suspicious deaths of several of those involved. The second plotline centers on the sentimental relationship between two journalists—newspaper magnate G. M. Camargo and reporter Reina Remis—who are working to expose government corruption. Reina becomes an obsession for Camargo, and this plotline culminates in a crime of passion: he murders her when she tries to leave him.

The story of official wrongdoing is introduced with the news of the suicide of Valenti, a senator accused of contraband arms sales. He was suspected of receiving a multimillion-dollar bribe, distributed among the complicit parties. A film of him negotiating the transfer of $16 million to a Luxembourg account had been made public, and a judge had ordered his arrest as the organizer of an illicit association. Despite the fact that his widow found him with a gunshot wound to the mouth, the official version will be that Valenti's death was accidental, not a suicide. Camargo, pushing to get to the bottom of the arms sale scandal, finds out from Pimenta Neves, editor of a São Paulo daily, that the son of the Argentine president deposited $6 million in a Brazilian bank account.

The crime of state is inextricably connected to the crime of passion. Camargo, having grown tired of his wife, becomes infatuated with Reina, a cub reporter many years his junior, and they develop an intense personal and professional relationship. When he suspects that Reina is cheating on him with a Colombian journalist, Camargo becomes furious and spies on her obsessively from a window that faces her apartment. In order to humiliate her and revenge her treachery, he secretly arranges her rape by a homeless refugee from the war in Kosovo who is infected with an unnamed disease, possibly HIV,[5] and has her fired from her position at the newspaper. Believing he has humbled her, Camargo begs Reina to marry him. She rejects his advances, and Camargo shoots her dead.

While the story of the state crime is developed chronologically and the narration of the crime of passion begins in medias res with Camargo spying on Reina, both crime stories start on the same date: 1 July 1997. This time reference is established by a historical event—the death of actor Robert Mitchum. Mitchum's death functions as a catalyst for the encounter between Reina and Camargo as their mutual fascination with Mitchum launches the relationship. Later on the same day, the death of the fictional Senator Valenti is reported.

The public crime mirrors or interfaces with the private crime, most notably through the parallels between Camargo and Pimenta Neves, the director of the Brazilian newspaper who provides Camargo with the information that breaks the case in Argentina. Several months after this incident, Neves will murder his lover Sandra Gomes, a crime that prefigures Camargo's copycat crime. The third chapter of the novel, titled "Una pasión brasileña" (A Brazilian passion), establishes the initial parallel between Camargo and Neves, as Camargo reflects that Neves is "alguien de tu misma estatura intelectual y moral" (someone of your same intellectual and moral stature) (57).[6] Camargo's comparison of their moral stature becomes presciently ironic when he repeats Neves's heinous crime. The relationship between the two plotlines in the novel is that of a mise en abyme, as the crime of state and crime of passion infinitely reflect each other.

*El vuelo* incorporates the triangulation of character roles typical of detective fiction—criminal, victim, and detective (in the form of investigative journalists)—but disconcerts the reader when the "detectives" investigating the crime of state become the criminal and the victim in the crime of passion. There is a strong presence of the noir thriller, seducing the reader with passages that bring us close to the twisted thoughts of Camargo as he carries out his revenge against Reina: the use of narrative voices focalized through Camargo enhances our identification with a criminal protagonist. The opening scene—Camargo spying on Reina—is narrated by a disembodied third-person voice that sees through Camargo's eyes. In the third chapter, after Camargo reads about Pimenta Neves's crime of passion, the voice switches to second person, getting even closer to Camargo's mind as speaks to himself while reflecting on whether to publish a report of the murder in his paper. Chapter 4 returns to a third person focalized through Camargo, and chapters 7 and 9 revert to the intimate second person as Camargo contemplates Reina's betrayal, and plans and executes his monstrous scheme to destroy her. Martínez spoke about his use of the second person in an interview: "When I was writing about Camargo, I remember saying ... now I'm going to go down to my own infiernos, because it was a real sensation that I felt ... and that is why there is a moment in the novel when I am not able to capture the full character treating him in the third person, I treat him in the second person, because I could not see him otherwise" (Zambrano).

The thriller atmosphere is heightened by references to classic US noir films. When Camargo meets Reina in the press room at the time of Mitchum's death, he reflects on the actor's starring role in *Night of the Hunter* and its message of good and evil—a prefiguration of Camargo's double persona. Camargo's misogyny, which I discuss in the following section, brings to mind the scene from *Night of the Hunter* in which Mitchum's character, Harry Powell, the conman posing as a preacher, berates women as he talks to the Lord and subsequently focuses his hatred on a scantily clad exotic dancer. Alfred Hitchcock's *The Rear Window* provides the visuals for the passages where Camargo is spying on "la mujer"; Camargo makes a nod to this noir model when he compares his vigil to that of James Stewart in the film. Another evocation of the genre is Camargo's statement that Reina's prose is as insidious as Patricia Highsmith's—arguably the queen of classic American noir. Like Highsmith, Martínez's narrative voices enable us to enter the subjectivity of the criminal who speaks and confesses his crimes. These allusions to iconic noir scenes and figures pay tribute to the novel's noir forerunners while they conjure up visual images and sensations that help create a dark mood of paranoia and suspense.

Gender Trouble

Both novels feature toxic gender relations and an alluring female character—a femme fatale or fatal woman—who can be read as a representation of a society or nation at a time of crisis or change.[7] By definition, the fatal woman and the femme fatale pose a threat to their male counterparts, and Dargas and Camargo, in *El muerto* and *El vuelo*, respectively, respond very differently to their perceived fear of emasculation by these women: while Dargas flees in terror, Camargo stages a vicious multifaceted attack. The two stories also incorporate opposing pairs of women: the savvy and sexy mistress who stands in contrast to the homebody wife, conforming to stereotypical (and misogynistic) conceptions of femininity. But while certain characters in *El muerto* can be seen within the parameters of their hard-boiled forerunners, Martínez's characters do not fit neatly into preordained patterns.

In *El muerto*, Belle Rocco, Kunny's mistress who eventually becomes his second wife, plays a crucial role, both in the story of Kunny's accumulation of a vast fortune and in the story of Dargas's investigation. Her drive to achieve an opulent lifestyle at any cost emblematizes the nouveau riche of the 1990s. Exemplary of the pattern of stereotypical and polarized female figures, Belle is characterized in opposition to Consuelo, Kunny's first wife and mother of his five children. Dargas describes Consuelo as masculine, with short hair "like a boy," emphasizing her unattractiveness, and remarks about "la ley no escrita según la cual una cosa era la esposa y otra la querida" (the unwritten law according to which one thing was the wife and another the mistress) (183). Their names—Consuelo and Belle—serve as shorthand for their roles, as do the titles of the chapters in which Dargas interviews each woman: "El paño de lágimas" (the crying towel) and "La bella," respectively.

Belle is a classic manipulative woman who uses subterfuge to achieve her aims. She begins as one of Kunny's secretaries and strategically plays hard-to-get when Kunny asks her for a date. Belle accompanies Kunny on his first diplomatic mission to Paraguay, and at this point her manipulative nature comes to the fore as she urges him to get on the money train made possible by the privatization process.

> Cada mañana, Belle preparaba para Kunny una carpeta con los recortes de todas las noticias sobre los negocios de los jalilistas y del propio Jalil ... información sobre la firma de tal proyecto, la adjudicación de tal licitación, la venta de tal empresa o la privatización de tales cuales pozos petroleros, para que entre los dos se pusieran a calcular qué comisión dejaba cada operación.... [Kunny] empezaba a dudar de si no fue ella quien le enganchó en su red. (79)
>
> [Every morning, Belle prepared a folder for Kunny with news clippings about the business of the Jalilistas and of Jalil himself ... information about the signing of a project, the awarding of a bid, the sale of a company or the privatization of oil wells, so that between the two of them they could calculate what commission each operation netted.... [Kunny] was beginning to wonder if it was not she who had caught him in her web.]

Perroti, a local politician and Kunny's friend, has no doubt regarding her role in Kunny's dirty dealings: "Esa atorranta tiene la culpa de casi todos los líos en que se metió Luis," he tells Dargas. "Parecía una mosquita muerta, pero resultó una bruja" (That tramp is to blame for almost every mess that Luis got into.... She looked like a babe in the woods, but turned out to be a witch) (157). Belle confirms Perroti's observation when she defends her claim to half of Kunny's worth, insisting that he would not have figured out how to make money out of politics if not for her. During Kunny's subsequent diplomatic mission as ambassador to Chile, their relationship acquires a sadomasochistic component when Belle lures two Chilean businessmen to participate in "fiestas negras" at the ambassador's residence and Kunny secretly films them, using the tape to blackmail and extort the men.

Dargas's description of Belle's appearance and behavior and their effect on him depict an overdetermined femme fatale and a vulnerable "private eye." In his self-appointed role as investigator of Kunny's mysterious death and resurrection, Dargas travels to Miami to interview Belle and experiences her potent allure firsthand. He is taken aback by her altered appearance—a short black bob has replaced her blonde curls, she uses violet eye shadow, and her lips are Ferrari red. As she rises, her panties are visible for a fraction of a second, and Dargas admires her buff body: "se castigaba desde el agotamiento en el gimnasio" (she punished herself to the point of exhaustion in the gym) (217). This masochistic allusion immediately flips to its sadistic counterpart when he describes in an internal monologue the temptation and danger she represents for him: "miel espesa que promete mil delicias ... y hacia la cual la mosca cae en picada.... Me asustó y a la vez me deleitó" (thick honey that promises a thousand pleasures ... and toward which the fly plummets.... She scared me and at the same time she thrilled me) (217).

Belle's aggressive sexuality constitutes a traumatic violation of Dargas's masculinity and he does not measure up to the hard-boiled ethos that calls for male mastery. Far from the ideal of the man who always knows how to handle women, he is berated, belittled, and pushed around by his ex-wife and his female editor. And when a gorgeous and voluptuous woman he is salivating over attempts to seduce him, he experiences visceral fear. The predatory woman is the threatening other to whom the virtuous private eye fears losing control. This fear of feminine seduction is reminiscent of Chandler—various tantalizing women attempt to seduce Marlowe, most famously the Sternwood sisters in *Big Sleep*, but he resists them all. In Chandler's fiction, manipulative women are often "associated with 'the nastiness' of which Marlowe fears he has become a part" (Horsley, *Twentieth-Century Crime Fiction* 81–82). Following in Marlowe's footsteps, Dargas resists the encounter with the dangerous Belle.

The character of Belle can be read as an allegory for the ills of contemporary society. When Dargas visits her sumptuous Miami mansion in search of answers about Kunny, he serves as a foil for Belle's sexual and material excess. Dargas is agog with the exorbitant splendor of her residence, complete with authentic paintings by the best contemporary Latin American artists. Belle's game of seduction and her decadent lifestyle fascinate Dargas but are like a poison that he rejects, retaining his role as the unblemished investigator who clings to his ethical values. Her greed, sexual voracity, and perversion are emblematic of an unbalanced society that is consumed by hedonism and the accumulation of material possessions.

Circling around Camargo like planets around the sun, the female characters' roles in *El vuelo de la reina* are dictated by their relationship with the newspaper magnate, be it that of his employee and lover, Reina; his wife, Brenda; or his mother, who is unnamed. What is more, their portrayal is colored by Camargo's misogyny. Reina's depiction—from Camargo's perspective—is strongly determined by her indomitable, animal-like independence that clashes with Camargo's persistent drive to possess her. This confrontation of iron-willed individuals will have tragic consequences. Other female characters with fleeting appearances in the novel also owe their presence to their relationship with a male character: Sandra Gomides, the unfaithful lover of Pimenta Neves, and the Chilean singer who was the second wife of the president of the nation. While the characters do not conform to predetermined molds of hard-boiled heroes and villainesses, similar to *El muerto* the novel presents polarized female characters and a possible allegorical reading of Reina Remis.

Reina's role as an allegory for Argentina is explored by Shelley Godsland. Godsland points out that the nation is frequently gendered as a woman, particularly at a time of crisis and change, and proceeds to demonstrate that "the abyss into which Argentina has sunk is a premonition of the void that Reina's boss organizes to ultimately engulf her" ("Allegory, Gender and Aggression" 195). Citing scenes in *El vuelo* conveying a sick and crumbling nation, Godsland explains that in this context the male hegemony becomes increasingly precarious, and the aggression directed at a female is a rejoinder to the male's fear of loss of control in other arenas. Imagery in the novel that draws parallels between Reina and the country in crisis underscores the allegorical reading. For instance, Camargo refers to a series of incidents of official corruption as "las pústulas de la pobre patria" (the sores of the poor country) (49), and later Reina will be raped and infected by an indigent immigrant with bleeding sores. In another passage, Reina tells Camargo, "Buenos Aires está mutando. Es una mariposa que vuelve a su estado de larva" (Buenos Aires is mutating. It is a butterfly returning to its larval state) (213), a metaphor that Camargo will repeat in reference to Reina when she strikes out against his possessive behavior: "Era una abeja de luz y ahora es una larva maloliente" (She was a bee of light and now she is a foul-smelling larva) (289). Thus images of contagion and of regression to a more primitive state apply to the civic body as well as to the body of the victimized woman.

Both Reina and Camargo play complex roles; as mentioned above, they shift positions in the crime triangles. In the crime of state, they are the detectives, and in the crime of passion, Camargo is the perpetrator and Reina the victim. These changing positions in the two crimes correspond to

Camargo's and Reina's dual roles. As a newspaper editor, Camargo stands for high ethical values in his unflinching fight to expose official corruption. But in his personal relations, he turns out to be a deranged and cruel aggressor. For her part, Reina is depicted as both a talented professional and as a sensuous sexual partner whose irresistible appeal leads to violent and irrational behavior on the part of her unbalanced lover. Reflecting this doubling, in the narration of the novel, Reina is split into two women: "la mujer" that Camargo spies on from his apartment on Reconquista Street using the telescope he has mounted; and Reina Remis, the young journalist Camargo meets in the newsroom. "La mujer" and Reina are treated as if they were separate individuals until chapter 10, when it is made evident that the two appellations refer to the same woman.

Three of Reina's qualities come to the fore: her intelligence, her sensuality, and her fierce independence. Even as a novice journalist, her arrogant self-confidence is manifest. In their first exchange in the pressroom, when Camargo tells her that she is too young to know who Robert Mitchum was, she lets him know that she is thirty years old, adding, "Sé más de lo que usted cree" (I know more than you think) (22). Reina's esoteric knowledge and her creativity make it possible for *El Diario* to scoop the most recent presidential scandal. Thanks to her familiarity with the gospels, she explains to her superiors at the newspaper why the president's vision of Jesus Christ is a fake. Her skill at improvising is demonstrated when, posing as a relative of the benefactor of the abbey to which the president has retreated, she manages to expose his phony claim. Buoyed by her success, Reina's reflections—conveyed by a third-person narrator focalizing her thoughts—show her belief in her capabilities: "su ambición la llevaría ahora a cualquier parte, ella misma era un viento que subiría a cualquier cielo, pero no de la mano de Camargo sino arrastrada por los ángeles de su propia inteligencia" (now her ambition would take her anywhere, she was a gust of wind that would rise to any sky, not by the hand of Camargo but pulled by the angels of her own intelligence) (173). Her talent and accomplishment are confirmed by Camargo, who promotes her to head up a new unit, "Investigaciones Especiales," and doubles her salary. Later he tells her, "Te estás convirtiendo en una gran periodista, Reina" (You are becoming a great journalist, Reina) (191).

But it is Reina's sensuality, not her intelligence, that initially draws Camargo to her. As noted above, the novel opens with Camargo spying on the woman we later realize is Reina, and he remarks on her sensuality as she undresses, comparing her to a Japanese dancer he once watched. His subsequent observation is of her catlike aura of freedom, indifference, and unattainability. In Camargo's mind, this haughtiness is part of her sexual appeal, as he reflects when they dine together for the first time: "Todo su encanto estaba en la expresión de libertad.... Remis no era linda, volvió a decirse, sólo altanera. Sin embargo, irradiaba una sexualidad primitiva, un irresistible olor animal" (All her charm was in her expression of freedom.... Remis was not beautiful, he told himself again, just haughty. Nevertheless, she radiated a primitive sexuality, an irresistible animal scent) (77). Reina reciprocates his attraction, at least in their first sexual encounter, when she experiences a desire she had never imagined. Camargo is addicted to her, observing as he tries to win her back, "Cogía como una diosa, era verdad, y lograba que Camargo creyera, al acostarse con ella, que su cuerpo se había vuelto joven e insuperable" (She fucked like a goddess, it was true, and she managed to make Camargo believe, when he slept with her, that his body had become young and invincible) (252). Even after she has told him that he means nothing to her and she is in love with another man, he is drawn to her voluptuous movements and feels compelled to retain her by his side.

The arrogance that first drew Camargo to Reina will prove to be the undoing of his drive to possess her. Although she has broken off their relationship, he insists that she cannot leave him, to which she replies: "—Soy una persona, Camargo. No me podés tomar ni dejar. No te pertenezco. Soy de nadie. Solo ahora sé que, por lo menos, me pertenezco a mí" (I am a person, Camargo. You cannot have me or leave me. I do not belong to you. I do not belong to anyone. Only now do I know that, at least, I belong to myself) (215). Camargo responds to Reina's unbending will with cruel cunning and eventually with violence as he seeks to subjugate her. As Myriam Osorio points out, Camargo's obsession to exercise "control over Reina is manifested through his constant surveillance of her" (24), bringing to mind the systemic control of the panoptic structure.[8] Camargo strives to possess her as an object, achieving this by drugging her with a strong sleep-inducing potion and filming her while she sleeps. Once captive in his camera, every fold of her naked body is available for his contemplation. Camargo's denigration of Reina is conveyed in the terms he uses to refer to her: "esa imbécil, esa sombra de la nada, esa cagada de rata" (that imbecile, that shadow of nothingness, that rat crap) (109–10) and "esa mierdita, esa nulidad que tanto te ha costado educar y refinar" (that little shit, that nullity that has cost you so much to educate and refine) (222).

Camargo's misogyny apparently originated in his mother's failure to demonstrate love for him and her eventual abandonment of him and his father. As Horsley points out, citing the character of Norman Bates in Hitchcock's *Psycho* as an example, the mother figure in male crime fiction is often introduced "only to account for the instability of a male transgressor" (*Twentieth-Century Crime Fiction* 254).[9] "¿Nunca me amaste, mamá, nunca me amaste? ¿Nunca querrás abrazarme?" (Did you never love me, mama, did you never love me? Will you never want to hug me?) (65), Camargo implores to the absent woman. The impact of her absence on his psyche is registered by Camargo as a physical lack, like a missing leg or ear that diminishes him in others' minds. Camargo's hatred of women is manifested through his frequent generalizations about them, for instance his explanation to Sicardi for obtaining full medical records for Reina: "Con las mujeres hay que desconfiar, Sicardi" (You have to distrust women, Sicardi) (44).

Reina is depicted as a double for Camargo's unfaithful mother, a doubling that is repeatedly established, in at least six scenes. At first, this parallel is intuitive and not entirely conscious on Camargo's part. He invites Reina to dine in the same tavern where he used to sit waiting futilely for his mother to walk by and experiences palpitations in Reina's presence, because he feels that his mother is close. After they make love for the first time, Camargo regards Reina as if he recognized in her a woman from his past life whom he lost. Finally, when his senile father berates Reina, confusing her with his disloyal wife, Camargo realizes that he is attracted to Reina because she reminds him of his mother. Once he discovers that Reina has another lover, he fuses the identity of the two women. Addressing himself in the second person, he says, "Perra, perra, tu padre tenía razón: era igual a la madre que los había dejado, una reencarnación tal vez, una melliza que regresaba para maldecirte ... abriéndote de nuevo las llagas del abandono" (Bitch, bitch, your father was right: she was just like the mother who had left them, a reincarnation perhaps, a twin who came back to curse you ... opening once again the wounds of abandonment) (210–12). In their final encounter at the riding stables, when he desperately attempts to possess her and she strikes him with her whip, he reflects, "Parece dos mujeres: tu madre y ella misma, amancebadas en un solo cuerpo" (She seems like two women: your mother and herself, cohabiting a single body) (290). In his deranged state, he feels that he has avenged his mother's treachery and regained control by killing the woman he saw as her reincarnation.

Brenda, Camargo's wife, is drawn in opposition to Reina. Camargo reflects that Reina is less refined than Brenda, but Brenda has no interest in ideas or the real world, while Reina has a genuine, savage talent. In contrast to Reina's portrayal as a dedicated and ambitious professional woman, Brenda is invariably depicted as a housekeeper, wife, mother, or daughter, roles she seems to carry out with grace and perfection. Although he once adored Brenda, after their twin daughters are born Camargo suddenly detests everything about her and feels the urge to harm her. Ironically, Brenda will savor sweet revenge on this implacable monster who sought to have total control over others. They reconcile when Camargo is on trial for the slaying of Reina, and Camargo subsequently develops Guillain-Barré syndrome and suffers from immobility in the lower part of his body. Perhaps reveling in a well-concealed hatred of him beneath her smooth façade, Brenda secretly delights in his frail state: "En el fondo ... disfruta llevándolo de un lado a otro y sintiendo su creciente dependencia. Cuando lo ve decaído, va al piano y toca piezas de Alkan y Gabriel Fauré" (Deep down inside ... she enjoys carting him from place to place and perceiving his increasing dependence. When he seems depressed, she goes to the piano and plays pieces by Alkan and Gabriel Fauré) (294). Thwarted in his drive to possess and have control over the women he longs for—his mother and Reina—Camargo lives his final years as the plaything of the wife he despises and who torments him by playing her piano pieces that he detests. This cruel twist of fate for Camargo delivers a degree of satisfying poetic justice.

The portrait of authoritarian masculinity is reinforced by Germán, Reina's Colombian lover, who ultimately displays the same atavistic machista character as Camargo. Days before a planned romantic rendezvous with Germán in Río de Janeiro, Reina is victim to the sexual attack orchestrated by Camargo and begs Germán to come to Buenos Aires instead. His reaction demonstrates that he is just another controlling male chauvinist: "—No, Reina. Tengo cuarenta años, y jamás, ¿oíste?, jamás he permitido que una mujer me manipule" (No, Reina. I'm forty years old, and never, did you hear, I've never allowed a woman to manipulate me) (269). Germán stubbornly adheres to a male code of honor according to which complying with a woman's request is considered being manipulated by her, and this is perceived as a weakness and a violation of cultural expectations (Maxfield 10).

Camargo's violent reaction to abandonment by a woman is echoed in the portrayal of other couples. Sandra Gomide, discussed earlier in this section, wanted to break up with Camargo's double, Brazilian newspaper magnate Neves Pimenta, who proceeded to shoot her. A house rented by Camargo and Brenda in Viña del Mar was the scene of a multiple homicide: in 1976 a Chilean general found his young wife cheating on him, shot her and the lover, poisoned their three children, and then shot himself. Finally, Brenda and Camargo witness the suicide of the ex-president, who crashes his plane into the sea because his second wife, a Chilean singer and actress, has decided to leave him. These incidents highlight the dark reverse side of patriarchal authority fed by an excessive sense of pride and entitlement: the fragile ego behind this posture experiences the loss as intolerable, leading to extreme violence. As Mary Ann Doane points out, the dangerous woman is an embodiment of male fears of loss of control or identity, and the slaying of the defiant woman is "a desperate reassertion of control on the part of the threatened male" (2). Ultimately, *El vuelo de la reina* portrays deeply troubling gender relations, exploring and exposing the poisonous consequences of the attempt of an individual to dominate and subjugate another.[10]

### The Urban Labyrinth

Much of the action of *El muerto indiscreto* occurs in the urban environment of Buenos Aires, depicted as a labyrinth where danger lurks, especially when Dargas begins unraveling hidden circuits of corruption and needs to escape in order to save his life. The images he uses—"telaraña," "laberinto," and "ajedrez" (spiderweb, labyrinth, game of chess)—evoke traditional concepts of entrapment, the chase, and intricate and difficult escape routes. In order to throw his pursuers off his track, he goes into the subway and uses a circuitous route to get to the house of friends who help him cross the Plate River to relative safety in Uruguay. The metro evokes the concept of the city as labyrinth, but this time the labyrinth, rather than signifying entrapment, such as in Borges's "La muerte y la brújula," affords him a way to cast off the men who are chasing him.

The plot action incorporates international venues. In order to question Belle, Dargas travels to Miami, where he is witness to the wealth, artificiality, and ostentation of its inhabitants, and which proves to be a haven for the corrupt, a money-launderer's paradise. The novel's setting also includes countries that border Argentina: Paraguay and Chile, depicted as places where corruption is perpetuated and quantities of dirty money are gained, and Uruguay and Brazil, where the characters escape to take refuge from Argentine mafias.

In *El vuelo*, the streets of Buenos Aires hold a promise of discovery and a rich cultural history, but ultimately their overwhelming imagery is that of poverty and decay. When he first moves to Buenos Aires, Camargo walks the streets of Palermo seeking the mother who abandoned him. The narrator names street after street: "Gorriti, Guatemala, Fitz Roy, Armenia, Soria" (75), tracing a map of hope and hopelessness. The homeless refugees from the Kosovo War who have nested nearby Reina's building with their pieces of cardboard and shabby blankets are emblematic of the dispossessed who landed in Argentina only to find misery and, in this case, exploitation. As if Camargo were impervious or blind to Buenos Aires' deterioration, the images of its chaos and ruin emanate not from his consciousness but from Reina's. Leaving the city en route to Los Toldos, Reina reflects on the streets cut off by the protests of dispossessed groups: poorly paid teachers, impoverished retirees, students without classes. Upon her return to the Buenos Aires bus station (presumably the Retiro area where squatter settlements have sprung up), she finds the streets have been taken over by Peruvian immigrants and other street merchants selling fried food, herbs, and counterfeit items, and she is accosted by a beggar girl. Reina registers the deterioration of Buenos Aires landmarks when she sits down with a cappuccino and copy of *El Diario* at La Perla del Once, a classic bar where Borges gathered with Macedonio Fernández and the Montoneros met. No remnants of this cultural and revolutionary history remain; now there are only vacant-faced unemployed persons and beggars: "Perla del Once se había convertido en la capital de la desdicha ... en un país que se caía a pedazos" (Perla del Once had become the capital of misery ... in a country that was falling apart) (174), muses Reina. Reina's mother also takes note of the change in Buenos Aires, telling her daughter to be careful when she walks alone at night: "ya has visto qué inseguro se ha vuelto Buenos Aires" (you've seen how unsafe Buenos Aires has become) (244). Of course the vicious attack that Reina suffers is a product of Camargo's insane jealousy, not urban perils. Reina's reply to the doctor who advises her to make a police report insinuates police brutality and corruption: "¿Cómo me aconseja que vaya a la policia? ¿Vive en Buenos Aires o en Oslo?" (How can you advise me to go to the police? Do you live in Buenos Aires or in Oslo?) (262). Buenos Aires is depicted as an urban space rendered unsafe by poverty and homelessness, and where crime victims risk double jeopardy if they make the mistake of turning to untrustworthy police for help.

Besides portraying a crumbling and degraded Buenos Aires, like in *El muerto indiscreto* the story moves in a global arena. Brenda, a native of the US, frequently returns to visit her mother, and their daughter's disease is treated in Chicago. Camargo's and Reina's travel for work and leisure takes them afar. In the jungles of Colombia Reina meets the man for whom she attempts to overthrow Camargo. In the happier years of their relationship, Camargo and Reina traverse the globe in style, spending time in Washington, DC, Japan, and European capitals such as Paris, Madrid, and Zurich. Thus in both novels the accumulation of wealth or professional acumen affords certain characters the ability to leave Argentina temporarily or indefinitely and enjoy a cosmopolitan lifestyle.

## Reading over the Edge: *Ficciones Verdaderas*

Through the incorporation of references to real people and events, *El muerto* and *El vuelo* carry out a critique of Argentina in the 1990s. Walsh's *Operación masacre* created a model for investigative journalism by using novelistic techniques to narrate the facts of a crime.[11] *El muerto* and *El vuelo* share the spirit of Walsh's denunciation of official wrongdoing insofar as their plotlines are inspired by actual scandals that have gone unpunished and that will be investigated by individuals who may fancy that they are following in Walsh's footsteps as they expose criminality. A fundamental difference, of course, is that Walsh's *Operación masacre* is nonfiction and the investigator is Walsh himself, while the novels under study make no claim to being true. In these texts, biographical attributes of real people are ascribed to fictional characters who interact with imaginary characters with made-up lives. These "semifictional" characters raise the question of how we read a text that is ostensibly fictional but includes references to historical individuals and events. A related question is the value of these novels as opposed to, for instance, a nonfictional account of the Menem years. I will explore these issues at the end of this section. Daniel W. Lehman uses a topographical metaphor to describe this type of reading: when the audience is lured by their prior knowledge of the real events and people on which the narrative is based, they are reading "over the edge" (3), a reading that I carry out next.

*El muerto indiscreto* incorporates an extensive cast of characters who are thinly disguised versions of individuals associated with the Menem government. Indeed, it can be considered a roman à clef, a genre I discuss in the next chapter. Kunny is introduced as one of the "Doce Apóstoles" of Saud Jalil, the current president. These men were Jalil's closest friends and advisors who orchestrated his successful bid for the presidency and were awarded top-level posts in his administration. While corruption seems to be a way of doing business in the Jalil government, the scandals provoked by Kunny's antics receive constant negative attention from the press. When Jalil uses him in a scheme to steal millions from the Born brothers, powerful businessmen, Jalil suggests that it is time for Kunny to stage his own death. But Kunny double-crosses Jalil, keeping the president's share of the booty for himself, thus doubly determining his fugitive status.

The reader with a basic familiarity of recent Argentine politics will immediately recognize Saud Jalil as a very slightly altered version of Carlos Menem but may think that the outlandish stories of corruption and intrigue are products of the author's fertile imagination. However, those who closely followed events, or, as was my case, were intrigued enough by the novel to research them, will find that much of what seems to be fiction is based on actual individuals and events.

Only superficial details differentiate the man who was president of Argentina in the 1990s from his fictional double in the novel, specifically his name, Saud Jalil (Saud resembles Menem's Arabic middle name Saúl), and ethnicity: Jalil is called "el libanés" (the Lebanese man); his real-life counterpart, who is of Syrian origin, has been called "el turco" (the Turk). The characters often refer to Jalil as "el Jefe"—a nickname associated with Menem, and one that suggests the type of loyalty and obedience that link underlings to a godfather-type figure.[12] Many aspects of Saud Jalil's life, personality, and predilections identify him with Menem, for instance, periodic bouts of depression and insecurity that contrast with delusions of grandeur: his belief that he has been chosen to have a great destiny. Like Menem, the fictional Saud was separated from his wife and his handlers convinced him to reconcile for political ends when he set his stakes on the presidency. Details about the corruption of Saud's extended family—"cuñados, primos y sobrinos de Jalil ... se pusieron a concebir proyectos de ayuda humanitaria en los cuales ellos pudieran ser los intermediarios, negociadores y ejecutores. Todas las comisiones de esos negocios fueron a sus bolsillos" (brothers-in-law, cousins and nephews of Jalil ... began to conceive humanitarian aid projects in which they could be the intermediaries, negotiators and executors. All the commissions of those businesses went to their pockets) (29)—allude to the dealings of the family of first lady Zulema Yoma, as well as Menem's brother Eduardo.[13]

While Jalil's "double" is obvious, the process of identifying the real-life counterparts of Luis Kunny, the eponymous "muerto indiscreto," turns out to be as tortuous as the character himself. Indeed, the reader who allows herself to be drawn into Correa's game and seeks to track down real-life parallels becomes the ultimate detective. I first connected Kunny, "[quien] parecía muy secundario, pero bien que estaba en todas las salsas" (who seemed like a secondary player, but was in all the dealings) (52), to Alberto Kohan, a close Menem collaborator—one of his "twelve apostles," and identified as "the most enigmatic man of the civil service of the '90s who was at the center of all the Menem scandals" (Viau). The fictional Kunny becomes very wealthy through corrupt business dealings, and Kohan had the distinction of being the third Menem functionary to be put on trial for corruption, tried in 2006 for illicit enrichment of more than a million pesos. However, the novel contains many episodes about Kunny that have no bearing to Kohan. As I read biographies and articles about Menem and his administration, bizarre episodes from the novel leapt out at me from the archives of recent history, and I realized that Luis Kunny is a composite character: Correa also incorporates biographical information from Rubén Cardozo, Oscar Spinosa Melo, Alberto Brito Lima, and Juan Carlos Rousselot.[14]

Rubén Cardozo was another of Menem's twelve apostles. Cardozo's resignation from his government post due to his involvement in a voucher scandal, his subsequent tenures as ambassador to Paraguay and consul in Miami, as well as his obituary and his "return from the dead" are part of the life of the fictional Kunny. In his diplomatic destinations, Kunny repeats the misuse of government funds and involvement in drug trafficking in which Cardozo reportedly was involved. Kunny succumbed to the charms of Belle Rocco, his secretary, while the real-life Cardozo fell for his press attaché in Miami, Anabel Lodko.[15] Finally, when Kunny stages his death, his obituary carries the headline "Falleció ayer Luis Kunny" (Luis Kunny died yesterday) and is dated 17 March 1997—the same date and headline as Cardozo's obituary in *La Nación*. What is more, Correa ran into Cardozo in Buenos Aires a year after the publication of his obituary![16]

The episode regarding Kunny's Chilean ambassadorship corresponds to the tenure of Oscar Spinosa Melo. The fictional Kunny filmed sex and drug parties at the ambassador's residence in which Belle Rocco served as the lure. The reader may think that this episode was inserted for the obligatory steamy sex scenes of noir fiction, but it turns out that Correa is not inventing—according to several sources, Spinosa Melo held "fiestas negras" at his residence with the participation of his stunning second wife, María Luisa Sword (Walger 266).[17]

A fourth individual who inhabits Kunny's body is Alberto Brito Lima. And again, fact is stranger than fiction. Kunny's outrageous stall tactics when he was ordered to leave the Miami consulate correspond to the behavior of Brito Lima after his dismissal as ambassador to Honduras in 1993. Kunny's string of puerile excuses for not leaving—that he has to fix up the embassy, that he is experiencing spikes of high blood pressure, that he has remaining protocol functions, that he needs to take leave of the president, that he will wait until the electoral register closes for the Argentine residents who want to vote in the next election—are all attributed to Brito Lima.[18] Finally, the episode in which Kunny is hypnotized by Spanish magician Tony Kamo actually happened to Juan Carlos Rousselot, who served as cultural attaché in Paraguay. In Kunny's televised session with the hypnotist, he denies accusations of illicit enrichment and weeps as he evokes persecution, paralleling Rousselot's protestations of innocence ("Rousselot en trance"; Walger 138). Thus to create his *muerto indiscreto*, Correa pieced together episodes from the lives of some of the shadiest functionaries in Menem's government. This mosaic of capricious, brazen, and corrupt individuals serves to convey the extreme behavior generated by an atmosphere of disregard for the law and the sentiment of impunity.

Secondary characters representing the president's cronies and cabinet members also have historical counterparts: for example, the fictional Hernán Raymonda, who is the powerful personal secretary to the president. His name is a transposition of Ramón Hernández, Menem's personal secretary who enjoyed a close relationship with him.[19] Along with Kohan, Hernández was among the first individuals from the Menem administration to be investigated in Switzerland for money laundering, and the Argentine justice system has investigated a Swiss bank account connected to Hernández.[20] Other reports point to Hernández's involvement in intrigue and corrupt business dealings.[21] The fictional Raymonda, paralleling Hernández, is characterized by his servility and degree of intimacy with the president as well as his greed, corruption, and relentlessness. Among his sources of revenue are the "derechos de peaje" (tolls) he charges individuals to have an audience with the president. Portrayed as being vengeful, Raymonda is involved in the mafia-like plot to eliminate Kunny.

The reference to the money stolen from the Born brothers is another historical wink. Incorporating details of the actual case, the narrator relates that Jorge and Juan Born were kidnapped by the Montoneros and freed after their father, the wealthiest industrialist in Argentina, paid a historic ransom. Continuing to incorporate documented developments, the narrator tells us that millions of the ransom landed in the national bank of Cuba. While the fictional Saud Jalil never gets his hands on this money due to Kunny's decision to double-cross him and keep it all for himself, in reality, Carlos Menem, who issued a pardon for the Montoneros, is said to have obtained a portion of the ransom and to have used it to finance his electoral campaign.[22]

Other mentions of official wrongdoing in the novel cannot be documented: for instance, the amount of money the president has made in undercover deals. Since leaving office, Menem has been under investigation for illicit enrichment—bribery, fraud, kickbacks, and embezzlement. In June 2009, he was indicted for embezzlement and a freeze was imposed on $100 million of his assets. The extent of Menem's fortune is unknown, although in 1995 he reportedly boasted that it had reached $1.5 billion.[23] *El muerto* echoes this misconduct, highlighting president Jalil's illicit dealings. He has received nearly $24 million from Kunny—the 30 percent of each "business deal" that every good jalilista was obligated to render to the president. Kunny knew that Jalil did not keep all his money in Switzerland as legend had it, and speculates that Jalil's fortune may have amounted to $2.5 billion in secret overseas accounts.

Even more disturbing is the fact that Jalil's cronies can murder with impunity, eliminating individuals who have become a political liability, including his own functionaries. Suspicious deaths occur that Dargas links to Jalil. Three people involved in the faked death of Kunny meet "accidental" ends; as Dargas explains, "Los medios de ejecución de algunos de los que sabían demasiado ... eran muertes muy selectivas, avisos para navegantes ... para que el silencio se impusiera" (The means of execution of some of those who knew too much ... were very selective deaths, sailors' warnings ... so that silence could be imposed) (322). The series of suspicious deaths related in *El muerto* resemble real-life events: in the 1990s, more than a dozen potential witnesses in cases involving customs fraud, arms smuggling, and other government scandals met strange ends, fueling conspiracy theories.[24] In sum, many aspects of the characters and events in the novel are taken from reality, although some of the most serious allegations regarding the Menem administration that are re-created in the novel have to date eluded definitive proof. But, of course, fiction does not require documentation, and by incorporating fact and hearsay into a fictional world, *El muerto indiscreto* paints a shocking portrait of pervasive corruption and impunity during a recent era of Argentine history.

An equally unsettling image of Argentina is portrayed in *El vuelo de la reina*. The arms sale scandal and its spins-offs that Camargo and Reina investigate evoke events that unfolded in Argentina between 1995 and 1998.

Argentina sold arms to Ecuador and Croatia, violating international agreements. Government officials stonewalled and lied throughout the investigation, claiming that the arms had been sold to Venezuela and Panama. This scandal begot others to cover up the original crime, including the seemingly unrelated deaths of people who knew too much (part of the previously mentioned series of suspicious deaths). Horacio Estrada, a retired navy captain who was a key witness in the ongoing arms sale investigation, was found dead in his apartment on 25 August 1998, and his death was declared a suicide. However, certain details suggested foul play—for instance, he was right-handed but had been shot in the left temple.[25] In the novel, the event that sets the journalists in motion is the death of Senator Valenti, who appears to be at the center of an illegal arms trafficking and illicit enrichment scheme. Camargo wanted to investigate the circumstances of Valenti's death—was it an accident, as reported, or did he kill himself out of shame?[26] Thus the figure of Valenti and certain details are fictional, but the essence of the official scandal—illegal arms sales, illicit enrichment, and a suspicious death—is the same.

A central element of the historical critique in *El vuelo* is the disparaging portraiture of the unnamed president who resembles Menem, beginning with an unflattering physical description that stresses the falseness of his appearance, a result of his attempt to mask his aging body with a simulacrum of youth. Menem's biographer describes his obsession with maintaining a youthful appearance: "Menem ran his hand across his cheeks and noticed the flaccidity of his flesh. It had been several months since the plastic surgeon Chajchir had come to the country house to apply collagen to lessen the ravages of time. There was nothing he hated more than growing old" (Wornat 308). Correa's novel also depicts the fictional president's vanity and reliance on plastic surgery: "Disimulaba la vejez cultivando la flacura.... La cirugía plástica le daba de lejos un aire de lozanía, pero de cerca parecía un muñeco de torta" (He concealed his old age by cultivating thinness.... The plastic surgery gave him an air of youth from afar, but up close he looked like a doll on a cake) (32). Many of Jalil's other characteristics are taken from Menem, such as his tendency to depression, his frivolity, his reputation as a *mujeriego*, and his taste for "trajes de seda lustrosos que resumían su idea de lo que debía ser la elegancia" (lustrous silk suits that summed up his idea of elegance) (118).

The episode in *El vuelo de reina* about the president's mystic vision and his internment in a monastery are inspired by Menem's life. In *Menem: La vida privada*, Olga Wornat notes Menem's mystic tendencies and observes that he had a special affinity with Jesus Christ, citing his declaration: "I, like everyone else, have a guardian angel.... And mine has always been Jesus Christ" (353). Gabriela Cerruti documents Menem's intent to use a spiritual retreat for political purposes, including his participation in bread-making: "He had conceived it as a publicity scheme: he summoned journalists to the monastery of the Trappist monks in Azul and was photographed kneading the bread with the monks" (368).

The novel mocks the president's spiritual tendencies. Soon after the news of his son's monetary transaction breaks in Camargo's paper, another daily reports that the president had a mystic vision of Jesus Christ—taken as a sign of divine recognition of the president's innocence—and that the president will retire to meditate in a monastery in the pampas. From the monastery, the press transmits images of the president kneading dough with the monks. Of course, this is a diversion tactic to draw public attention away from the scandal, and it is successful insofar as a major newspaper caters to the president and the mystic vision resonates with a superstitious public.

> "El Presidente tiene visiones místicas" era el título de *El Heraldo* en la edición del día siguiente. Camargo estaba seguro de que el diario rival no publicaría una sola palabra sobre los escandalosos depósitos en el banco de San Pablo.... El presidente los había colmado de favores.... Calculó ese silencio, pero no el efecto teatral de un título más llamativo. Visiones místicas. En un país que había sido gobernado por magos y adivinos, esa frase era un imán. (84–85)
>
> ["The President has mystical visions" was the headline of *El Heraldo* in the next day's edition. Camargo was sure that the rival newspaper would not publish a single word about the scandalous deposits in the São Paulo bank.... The president had done them many favors.... He had expected that silence, but not the theatrical effect of a more attention-getting title. Mystical visions. In a country that had been ruled by magicians and fortune tellers, that phrase was a magnet.]

Thus the episode about the fictional president's feigned mystic vision and spiritual retreat serves to parody Menem's mystic bent along with his shameless tactic of preying on the populace's credulity for political gain.

Other episodes relating to the president are largely fictional but contain details that correspond to Menem. A prime example of an episode that blends the author's imagination and elements of reality is the fictional ex-president's suicide in 2003. He plunges his private jet into the sea because his second wife, a Chilean singer and actress, was going to leave him. The suspicion of his hidden wealth is confirmed at the reading of his will when the notary announces that the ex-president's fortune was over $389 million instead of the almost $3 million he had declared as his only capital when he left office. " 'Yo sabía, yo sabía,' se oyó decir a la primera esposa. 'Murió como vivió, engañándonos a todos' " ("I knew it, I knew it," his first wife was heard saying. "He died like he lived, deceiving us all") (170), relates Camargo's account of the event. Of course, Menem did not commit suicide (perhaps the novelist envisioned this as appropriate poetic justice for the corrupt former head of state), but he was married to a Chilean beauty queen. The fictional first wife who is quick to denounce Jalil as a scoundrel resembles Menem's ex-wife Zulema Yoma, whose spats with her husband during his presidency outdid soap operas. For instance, in 1990 the Menem family had a very public row triggered by Zulema's declaration of corruption in her husband's administration (Wornat 81–96).[27] The report of a secret fortune, like in *El muerto*, speaks to his corruption and misbegotten riches.[28]

Significantly, both novels emphasize the breech of justice, as the principle criminal—the president—is never punished for his crimes. In *El muerto*, Dargas, pursued by hired hit men working for Jalil or highly placed members of his administration, ends up fleeing to Montevideo, where Kunny has left him "una bomba": information about Kunny's political career and Jalil's wrongdoing recorded on ten cassettes and four VHS tapes. But because no newspapers will print Dargas's discoveries, he ends up publishing it as the book we are reading. Furthermore, Kunny leaves instructions for Dargas to access additional information safeguarded in Miami. What could be there? Incriminating evidence and documentation of criminal misconduct at the highest levels of Jalil's government? We never know and can only speculate as to what it might contain and whether or not Dargas decides to pursue it. This lack of closure may suggest that the final story about corruption during the Menem years has not yet been told.

The frustration of justice is also underlined in *El vuelo*. The narrator informs us that Reina's investigation came to naught because the president was absolved by corrupt judges and legislators.

> La minuciosa investigación de Remis sobre el contrabando de armas también quedó en la nada, a pesar de las pruebas que ella y Camargo recogieron en los bancos de Zúrich y en los archivos de las cancillerías balcánicas. El presidente penitente fue amenazado con la cárcel por el

gobierno que lo sucedió, pero salvó el pellejo con facilidad. Todos los que debían juzgarlo habían sido nombrados por él, y estaban ansiosos por devolverle el favor. No tardaron en descubrir errores en los sumarios y con esa excusa invalidaron los procesos. También al nuevo gobierno le convenía que estuviera libre, para dividir a los opositores. (179–80)

[Remis's meticulous investigation of the contraband weapons sales also came to naught, despite the evidence that she and Camargo collected in Zurich banks and the archives of Balkan chancelleries. The penitent president was threatened with jail by the administration that succeeded him, but he saved his skin with ease. All those who were to judge him had been appointed by him, and they were anxious to return the favor. It did not take them long to discover errors in the summaries and with that excuse they invalidated the procedures. It was also in the interest of the new administration that he be free in order to divide the opposition.][29]

In sum, both *El muerto* and *El vuelo* portray an extensive network of corruption with the president at its apex, but with slightly different thrusts. *El muerto* fleshes out the crew of power-hungry, greedy, and brash individuals the president brought in with him, depicting an era ruled by the pursuit of money and a life of luxury and the violent and illicit means to which certain individuals resorted in order to obtain it. *El vuelo*, on the other hand, hones in on a despicable and ridiculous chief of state, focusing on lust for power and the consequences when it is abused.

As the above discussion details, both novels fictionalize historical events and characters, and both have in common their highly critical portrait of the administration of a president who is modeled on Menem. Identifying flesh-and-blood characters impacts how we read: in a work of pure fiction, the reader's attention is focused inward, toward the fictional world, while the real-life references cause us to focus outward, toward historical reality, tantalizing the reader who wants to know what is true and what is fiction. But Martínez seems to be attempting to short-circuit that inquiry in the disclaimer he places in his *Nota final*: "Todos los personajes y lugares de esta novela, aun los que parecen tomados de la realidad, corresponden al orden de la ficción. Leerlos de otro modo violentaría su naturaleza" (All the characters and places in this novel, even those that seem to be taken from reality, correspond to the order of fiction. Reading them otherwise would violate their nature) (297).[30] As several critics have pointed out, a valid question in respect to the truth or fictionality of a work is "Who decides?" and those who would reply that the reader decides may object to Martínez's attempt to tell us how we should read his book. But considering his statement from the perspective of the creative writer, Martínez seems to be guiding his readers to immerse themselves in an autonomous fictional world, albeit with a certain degree of overlap with the real world, but a world in which "the place of truth is in the place of the imagination" (Martínez, *Ficciones verdaderas* 10). In *Ficciones verdaderas*, Martínez cogently articulates a crucial distinction between nonfictional works about historical individuals and fictional works inspired by an individual's life: "The Bolívar of Salvador de Madariaga or that of O'Leary are more or less accurate approximations of the historical Bolívar; but the Bolívar of Gabriel García Márquez is not only Bolívar but also García Márquez" (10–11).

To paraphrase the author, the Menems of Correa and Martínez are no longer just Menem but also Correa and Martínez. As Eric Heyne points out, there can be no clear boundary between fiction and nonfiction; rather, where they meet is a "rough terrain." To give Martínez the final word in this discussion, narration is a way of reading reality in another light, transfiguring it and adding other truths that point meaning in other directions, imposing upon it a coherence that does not exist in life (*Ficciones verdaderas* 12).

Portrait of an Era

Both novels show how the example of the freewheeling transgressive president spawns a loosening of moral values in the society as a whole. In *La novela de Menem: Ensayo sobre una década incorregible*, Luciana Vázquez draws a fascinating portrait of what she terms "lo menemista": "the air of the epoch, a social sensibility that during ten years set the tone for an unprecedented way of conceiving reality" (12). Vázquez elaborates: "*Lo menemista* will exalt gratification as an unquestionable right, free the political class from the dictates of virtue and enable the circulation of its desire toward less sacrificial territories" (15). This spirit of excess and transgression operated in the material, sexual, and political realms. The terms frequently used to encapsulate the new sensibility flaunted by Menem and his family were "pizza, champagne, Versace, partying" (Vázquez 13). Indeed, Sylvina Walger's book about the Menem phenomenon is titled *Pizza con champán*. In it she chronicles "the gay, permissive and amoral customs of Argentina at the end of the century" (15). A hedonistic mindset, free of all limits, saw gratification as a right and pursued guiltless indulgence in luxury and life's pleasures, and social climbers indulged in the flashy material possessions that symbolized wealth and power (Vásquez 18). Zulemita, the first daughter, set the tone with her extravagant shopping sprees in Italy.[31] In the political realm, the most evident effect of this moral liberation was corruption—so notorious that the quip of one of Menem's ministers, "Robo para la corona" (I steal for the crown), became emblematic of the era (Vázquez 128–29).[32]

*El muerto indiscreto* and *El vuelo de la reina*, in their portrayal of Argentine society during the Menem era, expose widespread political and social corruption. Key characters in each novel depict cardinal vices of the era—for example, Belle Rocco and Reina Remis can be read as allegories for social ills. *El muerto* emphasizes moral degeneration on a material level: the shameless, hedonistic behavior of government functionaries and unbridled greed and flagrant spending, epitomized by Luis Kunny and Belle Rocco. Belle incarnates excess and transgression. Caught up in the menemista frenzy of hyperconsumerism and the accumulation of status symbols, her overdetermined avarice and sexual aggression symbolize a society that has lost its ethical compass.

*El vuelo* focuses on the corruption of power, as Camargo's abusive behavior mirrors the president in his conviction that he is above the law. In this sense, Camargo's criminality represents a metaphor for and an indictment of the perceived deterioration of moral values in the country. When he refuses to shake the hands of two senators at the funeral of Valenti, the president's assistant tells him: "Sos de terror, Camargo.... Sólo tenés lameculos a tu lado y ni un solo amigo que te diga lo que piensa" (You are a terror, Camargo.... You only have ass-lickers by your side and not a single friend to tell you what he thinks). Camargo replies, "Será que estoy pareciéndome a tu jefe, como el país entero" (It seems that I have come to resemble your boss, like the whole country) (34), thus linking his arrogance to that of the president and the country. Horsley's description of the noir aesthetic is apropos of the portrayal of Camargo: "The noir sensibility may come to the fore at any time of discontent and anxiety.... The damaged self of the psychopath can act as a metaphor for society's aberrations" (*Twentieth-Century Crime Fiction* 116–17).

The rampant corruption among the Argentine political class is described as a disease that infects the country. When Valenti is found dead, presumably by his own hand after he was discovered receiving a bribe, Camargo reflects: "Por fin alguien tenía un gesto de dignidad. La Argentina estaba enferma hasta los huesos" (Finally someone had a gesture of dignity. Argentina was sick to the bone) (30). The disease metaphor also creates a connection between public and private contagion. As mentioned above, Camargo refers to the evidence of government corruption as "las pústulas de la pobre patria" (49), and the destitute man who rapes Reina has sores that bleed and (conceivably) infect Reina. Insofar as the sick man is a tool of Camargo, by extension Camargo is in possession of these "pústulas" and uses them to wreak his twisted revenge on Reina, the fatal woman turned victim—a vision of once-proud Argentina brought to its knees by corruption and social violence.

Walsh and Marlowe: Templates for Dargas and Camargo?

I return to the Walsh–Chandler combination as a point of departure for an analysis of these journalistic sleuths. While Dargas's and Camargo's persistence and dedication to exposing unpunished state crime through their investigative journalism make them fictional continuations of Walsh's tradition, it cannot be said that they reproduce the noble goals and virtues of Chandler's Marlowe. Many critics have noted Marlowe's moral superiority and his characterization as a questing knight who stands in contrast to the depravity that surrounds him, but neither Dargas nor Camargo are immune to the corrupt environment in which they dwell.

In his quest for the truth, Dargas proves to be courageous, refusing to abandon his story even when he realizes he is in danger, and he appears to remain uncorrupted despite the fact that in his investigation he interacts with a social group that is giddily rich from bribes, kickbacks, and extortion. But while Dargas may project the image of a solitary crusader for truth and justice, by informing us that his investigation becomes the novel we are reading, he alludes to the monetary value attached to stories of crime and scandal. Although we never learn if Dargas actually profits from the story, this disclosure serves to transform him from a destitute but determined journalist into the author of a potentially lucrative book-length exposé about the president and his men written in novelistic form. This points to the blurring of the line between entertainment and journalism, a critique that can be found in Piglia's *Plata quemada*.

In *El vuelo*, the detective-reporter is a complex character. The criminality of the state becomes the frame for a story of individual criminality and Camargo is a paradoxical figure, combining the roles of both a respected newspaper magnate who is fighting for justice and a murderous psychopath. In this sense, Camargo embodies the "love" and "hate" tattooed on the fingers of Mitchum's character in *Night of the Hunter*. The novel incorporates a dual explanation for his crimes. On the one hand, Camargo mirrors the president's extreme arrogance. On the other hand, there is a psychological explanation for Camargo's violent behavior: the fact that his mother abandoned him in childhood is blamed for his traumatized masculinity, reflecting a stereotypical misogynistic view of women. Behind his extreme pride, it turns out, is a pathological fear of abandonment and humiliation.[33] Thus with its exploration of human ambitions, passions, and frailties, *El vuelo* goes beyond the circumstantial realm of the hard-boiled detective novel. The duality of the detective who also contains the criminal reflects Borgesian metaphysical speculations about the precarious nature of human identity, recalling Borges's stories in which the boundaries are dissolved between heroes and traitors, between investigators, killers, and victims. As we glimpse inside the disturbed mind of the killer, we find ourselves caught in the amoral universe of the best noir thrillers.

Watchdog Journalism

Both novels incorporate strong accusations aimed specifically at a "fictional" president of the Argentine Republic who is modeled on Menem, and both highlight the watchdog roles of Dargas and Camargo in investigating and exposing stories of corruption. Dargas doggedly continues working the Kunny case even when he is isolated and out of funds and his life is in danger. Camargo is indignant that the president is deceiving the people, and repeatedly insists on the watchdog mission of his paper: "A mi diario no lo puede asustar ni comprar." "Sólo quiero que la gente sepa ... que algo huele a podrido en Buenos Aires." "El presidente ... nos amenazó con un juicio. Le dije que lo haga. Peor para él. Tenemos las pruebas" (My newspaper cannot be scared or bought off./I just want people to know ... that something is rotten in Buenos Aires./The president ... threatened us with a trial. I told him to do it. Too bad for him. We have proof) (34, 40, 78).

Casting journalists as "the people's detectives" reflects the fact that muckraking has moved to the mainstream news media since the return of democracy to Argentina in the early 1980s. In *Watchdog Journalism in South America*, Silvio Waisbord points to the widespread public esteem enjoyed by the Argentine press in the 1990s due to its success in exposing major cases of corruption. In particular, he cites the role of Argentine dailies *Clarín* and *Página/12* in breaking scandals that surfaced during the Menem presidency, such as Swiftgate, Narcogate, Yomagate, and the arms sale scandal (33, 38). However—and in this outcome the novels also reflect reality—press exposure did not mean that wrongdoers were brought to justice. Exploring the impact of watchdog reporting in regard to truth-telling and political accountability, Waisbord reports that journalists interviewed "were highly skeptical about the ability of press disclosures to crystallize in effective change when institutions are largely inattentive to press denunciations" (211). Indeed, he uses the Argentine case as an example of the journalists' sense of failure due to the lack of punishment or resolution for the corruption they expose.[34] Despite the fact that muckraking does not eliminate corruption and many of the wrongdoers never have their day in court, Waisbord says that news stories do make a difference. They function as a symbolic punishment, raising awareness about the existence of corruption and forcing powerholders to give answers for their acts (250). While journalism—the profession of the protagonists of the novels—fulfills a social function, literary works fictionalize historical events, thus providing a different type of knowledge and a different mode of reading. As "ficciones verdaderas," these novels take advantage of the liberty offered by fiction to transfigure reality and impose a determined reading of it. Creating possible worlds that interplay with actual worlds, they turn the Menem era into a fable of corruption and impunity, of greed and self-indulgence.

Chapter Three

# TERRORIST ATTACKS ON JEWISH BUENOS AIRES AND THE MYSTERIOUS DEATH OF ALBERTO NISMAN

> Pocas cosas mueven más pasiones en Argentina que los servicios secretos.
> —Carlos E. Cué, "Nisman, el gran misterio argentino se complica dos años después"

ON 18 JANUARY 2015, PUBLIC PROSECUTOR ALBERTO NISMAN WAS FOUND dead in his Buenos Aires apartment with a gunshot wound to his head. The next day he was slated to testify in the Argentine congress regarding the investigation into the 1994 bombing of the Asociación Mutual Israel-Argentina (AMIA), a Jewish community center in the heart of the city. Four days earlier he had filed a criminal complaint against President Cristina Fernández de Kirchner and her foreign minister Héctor Timerman accusing Fernández de Kirchner's government of taking part in a cover-up to derail the investigation of the presumed Iranian involvement in the bombing. In his appearance before congress he was due to present his findings and explain the charges he recommended be brought against Fernández de Kirchner and Timerman. There was much speculation regarding the cause of Nisman's death—was it suicide? homicide? induced suicide?—and conspiracy theories have abounded.[1] There can be no doubt, however, that the Nisman case is related to an internal fight provoked by different postures concerning Argentina's shifting geopolitics, and his fate was determined by the fact that the AMIA investigation was in the bull's-eye of that global realignment.

This chapter pairs a novel that explores the reasons for the attack on the AMIA with one that focuses on the circumstances leading up to the death of the special prosecutor: *Asalto al paraíso* (2002) by Marcos Aguinis and

*El fiscal* (2015) by R. S. Pratt. While the previous two chapters considered novels that critique Argentine varieties of organized crime and institutional corruption common to many countries in the region, here we turn to the novelistic treatment of tragic events that served to highlight Argentina's singularity within Latin America due, at least in part, to Buenos Aires' sizeable and influential Jewish community. Some issues engaged in Pratt's novel—that we might consider Argentine versions of wider psychological tendencies—are the populace's mistrust of its national intelligence service and its predisposition to believe conspiracy theories.

### THE HAPLESS INVESTIGATION OF THE ATTACK ON THE AMIA

The bombing of the AMIA was the second of two terrorist attacks on Jewish institutions in Buenos Aires. In 1992 an explosion reduced the Israeli embassy in Buenos Aires to rubble, killing 29 people and wounding 242. The attack on the AMIA two years later took a larger toll: 85 deaths and over 300 wounded. These crimes have gone unsolved and government officials have been accused of hampering and sabotaging the investigation. Hezbollah claimed responsibility for the attack on the Israeli Embassy, but no one has been brought to justice for this deed. The leading theory for the AMIA attack, known as the *"pista iraní,"* is that it was also carried out by Hezbollah working at the behest of Iran. Others believe that Syria had a central role—this is the *"pista siria"*—and local connections or criminal groups are implicated in both theories. Both narratives point to Moshen Rabbani, the ex–cultural attaché of the Iranian embassy in Buenos Aires, as the organizer of the attack.

During the administration of President Carlos Menem, politicians, government officials, and judges repeatedly manipulated the handling of the AMIA investigation, using it politically. According to Claudio Grossman, called upon as an observer by the Inter-American Commission of Human Rights, "Every aspect of the case was a disaster, beginning with the initial investigation" (Filkins 40). Many of the investigation's findings were later called into question, rulings were reversed, annulments were annulled, and journalistic reports frequently contradict each other. The initial investigation carried out during the Menem presidency only identified supposed accessories to the attack, and even this investigation of secondary actors came to naught. An Argentine prosecutor accused Carlos Alberto Telleldín, a used car dealer, of selling and delivering the Renault Traffic van that, according to most sources, was used as the car bomb.[2] Telleldín was indicted and jailed. In 1996 he implicated twenty-two people as accessories, mainly Bonaerense police agents. The charges against many of these individuals were eventually dropped due to a lack of evidence, but five were finally put on trial in 2001. The prosecution collapsed in 2003 after a video surfaced of Juan José Galeano, the presiding judge, paying Telleldín a $400,000 bribe to implicate the police. Supposedly, this bribe was endorsed by Menem to embarrass Eduardo Duhalde, his rival and the governor of Buenos Aires. A court dropped all charges in 2004, including those against the police officers. However, in 2009 the Argentine Supreme Court reopened the investigation, revoking Telleldín's absolution and reexamining his role in the case.

In the meantime, a former Iranian agent named Abolghasem Mesbahi, who defected in 1996, began talking about the AMIA attack. He said that Menem was a paid asset of Iran since the 1980s, having received large sums of money from Iran for his political campaigns. He also received money from Libya and Syria. When he became president, however, he did not follow through with the expected payback, halting arms deals with Syria and Libya and annulling a nuclear accord with Iran. Mesbahi claimed that Menem was paid $10 million in a Swiss bank account to declare that there was no evidence pointing to Iran's responsibility in the attack. The said $10 million deposit was never found and Mesbahi was discredited, but suspicions remained.

An early lead and part of the theory known as the *pista siria* was that of Alberto Kanoore Edul, an Argentine citizen of Syrian origin who had a connection to Rabbani and supposedly made a call to Carlos Telleldín eight days before the bombing. Kanoore Edul was detained for a few hours in 1994 and set free. President Menem ordered that Kanoore Edul not be interrogated, and this lead was frozen. In 2001 a federal judge accused Menem, Menem's brother-in-law, ex–federal judge Galeano, the former head of the Secretaría de Inteligencia de Estado (SIDE, Argentine Intelligence Agency), and the retired chief of police of obstruction of justice for concealing information about Kanoore Edul. All were acquitted in 2004, but a new trial for obstruction of justice against Menem and these officials was initiated in August 2015.[3]

In 2003, when Néstor Kirchner became president, he called the handling of the AMIA investigation a national disgrace, and in 2004 he appointed Alberto Nisman to take over the prosecution. Nisman worked closely with Antonio Stiuso, director general of operations of the SIDE, who provided Nisman with intelligence information (Cavanagh, "Antonio Stiuso"). Nisman indicted seven Iranian government officials along with a Hezbollah leader in 2006, and Interpol, the international police organization, issued arrest warrants, known as "red notices," for five Iranians (two had diplomatic immunity). Iran maintained their innocence and refused to turn them over. In 2007, when Cristina Fernández de Kirchner became president, she supported Nisman's work, also denouncing the Iranians. Every year at the United Nations general assembly, she would denounce Iran's presumed role in the AMIA bombing, and the Argentine delegation would exit in protest when the Iranian president spoke. However, in 2010, after Néstor Kirchner's death and Cristina's landslide reelection, her stance toward Iran began to shift. Thanks to Hugo Chávez, the late president of Venezuela, "the Iranian government was a growing force in the region"; Chávez is said to have introduced Iranian president Mahmoud Ahmadinejad to Latin American leaders. As Fernández de Kirchner strengthened her ties with Chávez and his political positions, Argentina also grew closer to Iran (Filkins 45–46). Economics played a central role in the rapprochement, as trade between the countries doubled.

In what the international media characterized as an abrupt about-face in Argentine policy toward Iran and the AMIA case, in 2013 Fernández de Kirchner agreed to the creation of a "truth commission" to break the deadlock with Iran (Sheinin, "The Death of Alberto Nisman" 37). Since Iran refused to allow the five accused men to be tried in Argentina, the agreement allowed prosecutors to interrogate the suspects in Iran and made way for the establishment of a joint committee of inquiry composed of members from other countries. The proposal, formalized in a Memorandum of Understanding negotiated by Foreign Minister Timerman, was controversial. Israel denounced the arrangement, "saying that the recommendations of the joint commitment would not be mandatory and that it would provide Iran with the ability to delay the committee's work indefinitely" (Kershner). Nisman was also dismayed by this seeming concession to Iran as it threatened to unravel almost a decade of his work, and began investigating Fernández de Kirchner and Timerman. Both Stiuso and Nisman were convinced that Iran was the main culprit and wanted to hold it accountable. This was also the position of Israel and the United States, and WikiLeaks exposed Nisman's close connections to US embassy officials in Buenos Aires. While some in the Argentine press declared that Nisman was a puppet of the US and Israel (Filkins 42), the characterization of Nisman as a US stooge is refuted by David Sheinin, who explains that "on Middle East policy the two countries have collaborated extensively and in secret to meet common strategic ends" ("The Death of Alberto Nisman" 36).[4]

In December 2014, Fernández de Kirchner removed Stiuso from his position as the head of the SIDE, and it was speculated that his dismissal was a maneuver to protect herself from investigation when her term ended in 2015 and she no longer had immunity. According to Fernando Oz, "a journalist who spoke with Nisman regularly," Nisman thought he would also be fired, so he believed that he had to make his accusation immediately, before his team was disbanded (Filkins 45).

The thrust of Nisman's accusation against Cristina Fernández de Kirchner and Héctor Timerman was that they were planning to lift the Interpol arrest warrants against the five accused Iranians, offering them impunity in exchange for trade deals with Iran. "Justice for oil" was the accusation: Fernández de Kirchner's secret deal would fabricate Iran's innocence. Nisman believed that his accusation had the power to send Fernández de Kirchner and Timerman to jail. However, a judge voiced serious questions about the strength of Nisman's accusation, saying that "Nisman's case was incoherent and contradictory in his findings" (Fields).[5]

As we know, the day before Nisman was scheduled to present his accusation of the president in Congress, he turned up dead in the bathroom of his apartment. Initially, Fernández de Kirchner said that Nisman committed suicide, but she soon changed her position, claiming that he was murdered by rogue government spies as part of a plot to destabilize her government. Fernández de Kirchner has suggested that Antonio Stiuso gave Nisman false intelligence and then masterminded his death, all part of a plot to take revenge for his ousting as agency head (Cavanagh, "Antonio Stiuso," "One Year Later"). Jorge Asís, a writer and former government official under Menem, declared: "This was from within or against the government," thus keeping options open but highlighting the fact that it was a political murder ("Asís sobre la muerte de Nisman"). Federico Finchelstein, director of Latin American studies at the New School in New York, believes that Nisman's death has " 'suddenly illuminated' ... the crossover between 'politics, the security state and gangsterism' " (Bernas). Many doubted that the truth would ever be known.[6] Nisman's death can be considered a consequence of the changing face of geopolitics—Fernández de Kirchner's shift to the left as part of the so-called Pink Tide in South America—but at the same time, it seems that he was being used as a puppet in a struggle of partisan politics and personal reprisal.

In the preceding pages, I attempted to recapitulate the complex and tortuous investigation and repercussions of the 1994 attack on the AMIA that is the basis of the two novels discussed in this chapter. Both novels blend facts with fiction, incorporating historical details and events with a field of reference that is external to the narrative and that the readers know, or at least can verify, from other sources. In both cases, the nonfictional references are high-profile events reported extensively in international media. Following the thinking and using the terminology of Hayden White, cited in the introduction, I maintain that the novels do not serve merely to chronicle or reproduce situations but rather the authors *emplot* events using familiar forms—specific genres or subgenres—to direct the reader's thinking in a way that supports their political ideology.

Historical events frame the fictional plot of Aguinis's *Asalto al paraíso*: it opens with the bombing of the Israeli embassy and closes with the attack on the AMIA. In between, alternating plotlines tell two stories: that of television personality and reporter Cristina Tíbori, who is trying to find out who is behind the 1992 terrorist attack and prevent a follow-up attack; and that of a Palestinian suicide bomber who has been brought to Buenos Aires to carry out this subsequent strike. Aguinis's emplotment functions to convey his political stance in regard to the attacks while denouncing the apparent complicity of Argentine functionaries with the crimes and the failure to solve them. Published in March 2015, *El fiscal* was hastily written immediately after Nisman's mysterious death by an Argentine writer using the pseudonym R. S. Pratt. It incorporates fictionalized versions of real-life individuals to produce a partisan portrait of the political intrigue that ultimately provoked Nisman's demise.

While the novels present fictional versions of different phases and aspects of the investigation of terrorist strikes in Buenos Aires, they convey different metanarratives and are based on contrasting political ideologies. Aguinis portrays the attack as motivated by a clash of civilizations—an extension of the Arab-Israeli conflict played out on Argentine soil. The author of *El fiscal*, on the other hand, in his speculative re-creation of the events leading up to the death of the special prosecutor, sees his tragic end as the result of political infighting and the desire for personal reprisal. According to this narrative, the internal struggle is triggered by ideological positioning in response to the "left turn" in Latin American politics. Certain government officials perceive the Argentine president as softening her stance toward Iran, thus unleashing the fury of those functionaries who want to maintain a hard line against Iran by pursuing prosecution of the Iranian suspects in the AMIA attack.

Nathaniel Greenberg identifies the two principal theories surrounding the AMIA case, explaining that while they are not mutually exclusive, they reflect what he terms diverse "cultural dispositions" of the Argentine and American sources that back the respective theories. The *pista iraní*, commonly referred to as "the official story," emphasizes the anti-Semitic nature of the attack, alleging that it was sponsored by Iran and carried out by Hezbollah operating out of the Triple Frontera region with help from local officials and police officers. This is the theory on which Aguinis's novel is based, and his cultural disposition is clearly that of a global ideological struggle. The other leading theory, the *pista siria*, is based on the role of local officials and criminal organizations acting in collaboration with the Syrian government and an international crime syndicate from Syria (Greenberg 63). Greenberg posits that "the chroniclers of *la pista siria* convey a distinct cultural temperament . . . less an ideological struggle motivated by religious fanaticism and more as the result of the ongoing violence between political and criminal syndicates motivated by a desire for reprisal, intimidation and profit" (64). Reflecting a deep public distrust of government institutions, it shows cynicism toward aspects of the "official story," such as the designation of Iran as mastermind of the attacks and the existence of a car bomb (Greenberg 71). This is the cultural disposition of R. S. Pratt. My reading of the two novels will consider how the novels rely on generic conventions and other literary devices to emplot their narratives in a way that promotes their respective ideological metanarratives. *Asalto* has features of both the anticonspiracy thriller and the *testimonio* of a stateless subaltern subject, while *El fiscal* is a hybrid combining the roman à clef and the espionage thriller.

## A SEXY JOURNALIST CRACKS AN ANTI-SEMITIC PLOT: *ASALTO AL PARAÍSO* BY MARCOS AGUINIS

Marcos Aguinis, a prolific writer and practicing psychiatrist who served as Argentina's secretary of culture in the Alfonsín government, is best described as a public intellectual.[7] Respected for his defense of political and cultural democratization, Aguinis is lauded by Naomi Lindstrom as "the great diplomat of progressive Jewish social thought in Argentina" (35). While his oeuvre encompasses short stories, biographies, essays, and hundreds of newspaper articles, he is considered a master of the historical novel. With topics ranging from the creation of Israel and the plight of the Palestinians in *Refugiados, crónica de un palestino* (1969) to the Inquisition in colonial Latin America in *La gesta del marrano* (1993) to anti-Semitism in Argentina in the years leading up to World War II in *La matriz del infierno*

(1997), his novels address intolerance, highlighting the injustice suffered by religious and ethnic groups throughout history.

The traumatic effect of the AMIA attack on the Argentine people, and on the Jewish community in particular, cannot be underestimated. Stephen Sadow calls it "*the* turning point in the life of most of Argentina's 220,000 Jews." "The sense of physical and psychological security and the broader participation in national life that had been slowly growing since Argentina's return to democracy in 1983 were suddenly threatened" (150), he explains. Aguinis's novel *Asalto al paraíso* belongs to a body of works written in response to the trauma that "bear witness and demand justice for the crime and equal treatment for Argentina's Jews" (151).[8] With this novel, Aguinis makes his first foray into genre fiction to expose and critique the atmosphere that made the AMIA attack possible.

The story of the two sequential terrorist bombings in Buenos Aires is not a detective or conspiracy story per se, but Aguinis "emplots" the events as such, crafting a fictional plot that takes place between the first and second attacks, and devising fictional characters who embody specific ideological stances to develop the story. To serve as protagonist of the second plotline, Aguinis creates a Palestinian suicide bomber and has him narrate the story of the oppression of his people, a history of suffering that led him to this extreme position. His life story serves to characterize the attack as an extension of the Arab-Israeli conflict. Through the choice of certain literary recourses—the blend of the anti-conspiracy thriller with the *testimonio* and the portrayal of characters with determined ideological positions—the author directs the reader's judgment about the terrorist attacks, underlining their anti-Semitic nature along with the view that they were part of a larger ideological struggle.

The city of Buenos Aires and Argentine society also figure prominently in the novel. As the "detective" attempts to solve the first crime and the perpetrators plan a subsequent attack, their movements map the city and trace a portrait of Argentine society of the 1990s—depicting the media and spheres of power and the corruption that characterized the Menem years. For better or for worse, Buenos Aires is portrayed as a participant in a new globalized society, impacted by the global terror network and global economy, politics, and drug trafficking.

Gender roles are another issue brought to the fore via Aguinis's adoption of a female investigative reporter. The use of a female detective figure, infrequent in Argentine detective fiction, is noteworthy, but does it represent a feminist posture on the part of the author? I will explore how the gender of the investigator impacts the investigation and whether the character of the strong but sexual reporter challenges the "inherent maleness of the genre" (Horsley, *Twentieth-Century Crime Fiction* 245).

## An Anticonspiracy Thriller

Codified genre conventions function to shape the story that the author tells, as it portrays an investigator who seeks to identify those responsible for the destruction of the Israeli embassy and describes a network of influences that create obstacles for her investigation. Basic elements of traditional detective fiction—the investigation of a crime and the character triangle—are at the heart of the novel's structure. The opening passages vividly depict the crime scene—the body-strewn rubble that was once the Israeli embassy—and the action will follow Cristina's attempts to discover who is behind this bombing as well as garner intelligence about a possible repeat attack. The investigator (Cristina), the criminals and conspirators, and the victims of the attack on the Israeli embassy form the character triangle typical of detective fiction.

Cristina's investigation follows the rhythm of the thriller. According to Martin Priestman, the chief aim of the thriller "is suspense: a painful but 'thrilling' state of anticipation rather than mere curiosity about past events" and "the thriller highlights danger within the present rather than (merely) the past action, hence its protagonists must be threatened by powerful forces of some kind" (3, 43). More specifically, *Asalto* integrates the scheme of what Priestman calls the "anti-conspiracy thriller, [in which] the protagonists confront a powerful conspiracy of wrongdoers without the guaranteed support of the forces of law and order" (1–2). John Scaggs points out another central feature of the anticonspiracy thriller: the hero overcomes obstacles and dangers and accomplishes an important moral mission (118).

A television journalist, Cristina Tíbori, is cast as the hero of the anticonspiracy thriller: she confronts a network of antagonists who create obstacles for her efforts to prevent a second attack. Readers are held in suspense as Cristina races against time, putting her career and her life at risk as she attempts to penetrate the murky web of underworld figures and corrupt Argentine officials who have information about the scheme. The local conspiracy that Cristina opposes is formed by corrupt Bonaerense police, neo-Nazis, and recycled henchmen from the dictatorship as well as certain government officials who collude to block the investigation and help the terrorists carry out another strike. The foreign participants consist of Iranian embassy officials who serve as handlers for the members of the Palestinian terrorist cell that arrives in Buenos Aires. A character with a flesh-and-blood counterpart is Hassem Tabbani, depicted as an official from the Iranian embassy. Tabbani is obviously modeled on Moshen Rabbani, the Iranian cultural attaché who is said to have had a central role in the actual attacks. This easily identifiable real-life reference due to the slightly transformed name serves to underscore Rabbani's presumed role in the strikes, emphasizing Iranian involvement in the bombing.

A fictional character who has a central role in the novel's ideological message is Ramón Chávez, Cristina's chief antagonist and an agent of the SIDE who surreptitiously works to thwart the investigation of the attack on the Israeli embassy and plan the second strike. Chávez represents the face of anti-Semitism in Argentina. Schooled in the days of the repressive dictatorship, he has managed to hide his extreme views and rise to a position of power within the intelligence agency. We learn of his background as a neo-Nazi and practitioner of Chrislam, a syncretic religion mixing elements of Christianity and Islam in their common enemy: the Jews. Together with his friend Santiago Branca, he was active in the Triple A, the Alianza Anti-Comunista Argentina,[9] and they pilfered and profaned Jewish graves under the protection of the Bonaerense police. Branca will become Cristina's access to the conspiracy, providing her the tip about the second strike. As I will discuss in the following section, he is the weak link because he is seducible, susceptible to Cristina's steamy come-on.

Another point emphasized in Aguinis's narrative is the failure of Argentine intelligence to solve the bombing of the Israeli embassy and prevent a second strike. The head of the SIDE is depicted as ineffectual—not necessarily part of the terrorist plot but impotent to reign in saboteurs within the ranks. Although he grants Cristina an interview, he is embarrassed to talk to the press due to his agency's lack of progress. Another secondary character, a historian who participates in a talk show hosted by Cristina about the crisis in the Middle East, summarizes her view of why the investigation has not moved forward: "En lo interno existe una red de corrupción vinculada con altos niveles del poder. Ni la SIDE, ni la policía ni la Justicia tienen apuro en sacarlos a la luz porque sacudirían una red de complicidades" (There is an internal network of corruption linked to high levels of power. Neither the SIDE, nor the police nor the judiciary are in a hurry to expose them because it would shake up a network of complicities) (164). This atmosphere of impunity is what motivates the journalist-detective to pursue the investigation, even after her boss at the television network orders her to stop, presciently remarking, "Esclarecer el atentado de la embajada es una utopía" (Clarifying the attack on the embassy is a utopia) (43). Typical of the protagonist of the anticonspiracy thriller, Cristina Tíbori is a maverick fighting the system.

Cristina does have a measure of success—through her sleuthing she learns that a strike is being planned against the Hebraica, the largest Jewish cultural and sports institution in Buenos Aires. She contacts the SIDE head and insists that he post extra security, thus spooking the Iranians, who abort the strike. However, they have a plan B, and bomb the AMIA four days later. "Many Argentine readers would be surprised by the novel's premise that the Sociedad Hebraica had been the intended target," comments Sadow (158–59). Reportedly, an explosion in the Hebraica would have resulted in many, many more casualties than did the bombing of the AMIA; thus this plot twist follows the conventions of the anticonspiracy thriller, allowing Aguinis's heroine to accomplish a victory of sorts.

### When the Investigator Is a Femme Fatale

Similar to the novels discussed in the previous chapter, in *Asalto al paraíso* a journalist assumes the detective function, carrying out the work that government officials fail to perform. Aguinis has spoken to this aspect, noting that the novel represents "a tribute to the press in my country, which in the '90s courageously denounced corruption" ("Los creadores somos aves de rapiña"). At the same time that it praises the press, however, *Asalto* explores the ethics of its methods. Cristina Tíbori's television show, *Palabras cruzadas*, carries out investigations of troublesome themes with hidden cameras, and while Cristina admits that this deception is unethical, she cites the extent of corruption in contemporary Argentina to justify her procedures: "La Argentina necesitaba remedios horribles para combatir la epidemia de corrupción que se había acrecentado hasta niveles de pesadilla en los años 90. 'La mentira no es ética pero a veces ayuda . . .' se decía en el canal" (Argentina needed drastic measures to combat the epidemic of corruption that had risen to nightmarish levels in the '90s. "Lies are not ethical but sometimes they help . . ." they said on the channel) (38). This duplicity will extend to Cristina's use of her body to extract leads from male informants.

Curiously, while Cristina perceives the need to justify her use of hidden cameras, she expresses no compunctions about exploiting her sexuality.

Aguinis has explained that his use of a woman to track down the fundamentalist terrorists was intentional "because religious fundamentalist terrorism does not give women their place ... and what a better slap on the face than using a woman as protagonist" (Campos Hernández). However, as I will discuss in this section, while his use of a female protagonist may fly in the face of fundamentalist Muslim sexism, her portrayal as an indomitable femme fatale sends a mixed message.

Cristina's character is seen from the perspective of multiple viewers who describe her femininity, her tenacity, and her aggressive sexuality. An extradiegetic narrator introduces her in the opening scene of the novel as she conducts a live television broadcast at the site of the Israeli embassy minutes after the bomb has exploded. The very first thing we learn about Cristina is that she breaks one of her high heels walking in the rubble but forges ahead anyway, followed by her camera crew. The narrator relates that she is wearing a pink skirt and silk blouse as she picks her way through the broken glass and debris, pushing past the police cordon to interview those involved and report on the disaster. This scene creates our first impression of Cristina as a gutsy woman who dresses in ultrafeminine attire that seems out of place at a disaster scene yet is determined and professional.

Cristina's tenacity and strength of character is further established in the comments of men with whom she interacts professionally. For instance, her boss suspects that she has continued to investigate the attack on the embassy despite the fact that he ordered her to stop: "No era una mujer que se resignase fácilmente" (She was not a woman who gave in easily), he remarks (229). We also hear of Cristina's reputation at the SIDE, focalized through the agency director as he receives Cristina in his office, "como correspondía a la importancia de su canal y al temor que Cristina Tíbori suscitaba en algunos funcionarios" (as corresponded to the importance of her channel and to the fear that Cristina Tíbori aroused in some officials) (106).[10] He also remarks that she has a reputation as being honest or well intentioned. However, her fierce determination as an interviewer seems to be inseparable from her sexuality, as her male boss comments on her strengths: "no solo tenía un bello rostro de ojos verdes, labios sensuales y templada voz, sino coraje para improvisar comentarios que a los medrosos les causaban taquicardia" (not only did she have a beautiful face with green eyes, sensual lips and a warm voice, but also the pluckiness to improvise comments that gave tachycardia to the skittish) (39).

Sexual politics are central to the plot as Cristina uses her powers of seduction to crack the conspiracy and obtain information. Although some readers, including this one, may take issue with the ethics of her behavior, in the universe of the novel and its extradiegetic narrator, this image of the consummate professional woman apparently is not incompatible with the use of her sexual prowess to achieve her objectives. While the words of the SIDE director characterized her as principled, she is also depicted—from the perspective of her antagonists—as a dangerous and provocative femme fatale. In her character, the femme fatale takes on the detective role, and her exploitation of her sexuality will be her most effective investigative tool. Heather Worthington points out that while in early crime fiction the female criminal used her sexuality in the interest of crime to deceive men, the modern female detective is often actively sexual, thus perpetuating women's depiction as deviant and transgressive, "even while acting on the side of the law" (42, 48). In *Asalto*, the valuation of Cristina's behavior as deviant (or not) is up to the reader since neither the extradiegetic narrator nor Cristina herself seem to view it as such.

Cristina's highly effective use of her body is seen in her interactions with Santiago Branca and Ramón Chávez. As a matter of fact, Cristina views seduction as part of her work: when she discovers that Branca has ties to Chávez, a high-ranking SIDE officer, and decides to seduce Branca in an attempt to extract information, she reflects, "Confiaba en que si Esteban [her boyfriend] la descubría acosando a Branca, no se pusiera demasiado celoso; que pudiera diferenciar la realidad de las exigencias del trabajo" (She trusted that if Esteban found her accosting Branca, he would not be too jealous; that he could differentiate reality from the demands of work) (154). Her tease of Santiago Branca is described in detail. In their first private encounter, Cristina plants a kiss on his cheek, and the sensual movement of her body as she walks away is focalized through the aroused Santiago. The next time they meet, Cristina allows her skirt to gradually slide up, and Santiago, remembering the provocative kiss, has an erection. In their third encounter, Cristina steers him into a dressing room at a shopping center where she opens his fly but suddenly stops at the height of his arousal. Now Cristina plays her card: she tells him tenderly that they can finish what was started, but "antes quiero que me cuentes algunas cosas. No puedo acostarme con un desconocido. Te juro que quedará entre nosotros" (first I want you to tell me some things. I cannot sleep with a stranger. I swear it will stay between us) (160). Thus she uses her body and her wiles to incite Santiago's desire and then leaves him frustrated, promising fulfillment after he provides her with information.

Cristina also has an interaction with Ramón Chávez that is laced with sexual innuendoes. Trying to find out if a second strike is in the works, Cristina pretends to bump into him at the bar he frequents. Ramón invites her to a drink, envisioning her as a sex object for his enjoyment. His gaze dissects her body into sexualized parts: "Ramón la miró de arriba abajo para estudiar sus formas.... Apreció las piernas torneadas y el tajo que le subía por el muslo, el hueco de su talle, los pechos abultados y una cabellera espesa que descendía hasta los hombros. Esta mujer era una inesperada presente de la noche" (Ramón looked her up and down to study her shape.... He appreciated her shapely legs and thighs, the curve of her waist, her full breasts and thick shoulder-length hair. This woman was an unexpected present of the night) (254). However, he soon realizes who she is, and says to himself, "La perra anda buscando carne picada.... Es más peligrosa que nunca" (The bitch is looking for chopped meat.... She is more dangerous than ever) (254). In keeping with Marty Roth's observation regarding hard-boiled detective fiction, this passage verifies the fantasy that the other side of sexual attraction is disappointment and can only script this as betrayal: women want to use men for some end of their own (120). Focusing on her treachery, Ramón perceives Cristina's "paradójica dulzura, lo cual aumentaba el veneno de sus frases" (paradoxical sweetness, which augmented the poison of her words) (255). She accuses him of conspiring to derail the investigation of the embassy bombing by corrupting the evidence and pushes him to tell her what is about to happen. Chávez does not reveal any secrets, but Cristina reads his body language and decides that she is on to something. Although Cristina does not attempt to seduce Ramón, as was the case with Santiago, she is aware of the effect that her sensuality has on him, and uses it to her advantage in order to unnerve him, study his reactions, and get closer to the truth. As an aggressive and sexual woman, she simultaneously attracts and threatens Chávez.

While Chávez keeps mum about the imminent operation, his buddy Santiago Branca has looser lips. Wanting to win Cristina's favor, he informs her that a terrorist strike is planned against the Hebraica. The results of Cristina's successful prevention of the attack are devastating for both men. Ramón is sure that Cristina will come after him; he fears loss of impunity from the SIDE, accusation, conviction, and imprisonment. He will have to flee, get false documents, alter his appearance, and maybe even get plastic surgery.

But that is nothing compared to the horrific revenge that Ramón orders for the loose-lipped Branca. Ramón's thugs tie him up, break some bones, scoop out his eyeballs with a spoon, douse him with gasoline, nail him into a wooden box, and set it on fire. Curiously, the description of his fate echoes the death that Dawud, the would-be suicide bomber, envisioned for himself when he imagined that he had carried out the strike: "un fognazo le hizo creer que saltaría por las nubes" (an explosion made him think that he would jump through the clouds) (320). Thus, the snitch who aborts the terrorist operation is converted into an ironic version of the martyr that Dawud is deprived of becoming thanks to Santiago's lack of discretion. Instead of Dawud being willingly martyred for destroying life, Santiago is unwittingly martyred for saving it. This reversal of destinies is brought about through Cristina's actions, a demonstration of her effectiveness.

Lee Horsley's insight into the function of the femme fatale is relevant for this character. Cristina's seductive behavior with Branca and Chávez corresponds to Horsley's description of the sexually aggressive woman in the noir thriller who appropriates masculine aggression and powers, producing anxiety "in the male protagonist who suffers loss of control and destabilization of identity" (*The Noir Thriller* 130). While Ramón Chávez literally loses his identity thanks to Cristina's exercise of power, Santiago Branca suffers the ultimate price for giving in to the siren call of the femme fatale. The graphic description of Santiago's gruesome torture and death serves to convey dramatically the punishment he apparently deserves—at least according to Chávez's convoluted code of ethics—for betraying a male companion to the temptress. Finally, it was Ramón's and Santiago's own actions that destroyed them. As Horsley notes, women are mere catalysts to men's destruction of self (*The Noir Thriller* 130).

To further mark Cristina as a threatening femme fatale, images of a dangerous "other" are used to describe her. These visions are either articulated directly by the male characters or are focalized through them and voiced by the extradiegetic narrator. Focalizing through Santiago, the narrator says, "Ante su cara rugía una pantera" (Before his face a panther roared) (154). Referring to her teasing advances in the dressing room, Santiago says, "Esa mujer era una loca de novela" (She was a crazy woman) (159), and later calls her "una víbora que le saca datos hasta a las piedras" (a viper who could even extract information from stones) (272). Chávez calls her a "perra" (bitch) (254), "pantera" (257), "demonio" (demon) (259), "serpiente" (snake) (260), and "esa diablesa" (that she-devil) (262). When he fears that she will track him down, he describes her as a crazed bitch and imagines her sinking her fangs in his carotid artery (313). Thus Cristina's appropriation of male powers—of the phallus—converts her into a beast, a demon, and a madwoman in the minds of her male antagonists. Horsley elucidates this depiction, characteristic of the noir femme fatale: "The 'unnaturally' sexual, aggressive, death-dealing woman is also separated from the human norm by her association with images of animality and madness" (*The Noir Thriller* 132).

What can we conclude regarding the role of gender in *Asalto*? Cristina is well intentioned and carries out an effective fight for a vital cause. She is a strong woman who fearlessly carries out her self-appointed mission and is not subjugated, as is often the expectation for clichéd sexually aggressive women in the Hollywood film industry (Horsley, *The Noir Thriller* 98). In this sense, she is admirable. Yet the methods she uses—her merciless toying with Santiago Branca, perceiving sexual aggression as part of her job—seem to be incompatible with the ethics of a professional woman. Significantly, Cristina is not punished for this behavior; rather, she is rewarded by the plot action when she succeeds in thwarting the terrorists' original plan. Furthermore, neither she nor the extradiegetic narrator express any qualms about her modus operandi. While Aguinis sought to confront Fundamentalist sexism via the use of a female protagonist, his portrayal of the reporter as a femme fatale exudes Western sexism, perpetuating the misogyny characteristic of hard-boiled detective fiction and the noir thriller. Far from being a feminist icon, Cristina is turned into a masochistic male fantasy through the perception of Ramón Chávez and Santiago Branca, and this fantasy becomes a reality when their interactions with her result in loss of identity and death, respectively. Cristina's portrayal as a dangerous woman who uses her sexuality to lure and betray men, despite the author's intention to make a progressive statement about women, is an indication of how deeply ingrained are these physic structures.

### Dawud's Story: What Makes a Suicide Bomber?

The depiction of the AMIA bombing as part of a global ideological struggle requires that the enemy's view be presented, and Aguinis does this by inventing the story of the would-be suicide bomber, Dawud Habbif. Dawud's story constitutes a *testimonio*, or more precisely a pseudo-*testimonio* since he is a fictional character. The *testimonio* is defined as "a novel or novella-length narrative, told in the first person by a narrator who is also the actual protagonist or witness of the events she or he recounts. The unit of the narration is usually a life or a significant life episode" (Beverley and

Zimmerman 173). The narrator bears witness in a legal or religious sense as opposed to being a mere participant in the narrative. It is "a story that *needs* to be told—involving a problem of repression, poverty, subalternity, exploitation, or simply struggle for survival, which is implicated in the act of narration itself" (Beverley and Zimmerman 173, citing Vidal and Jara 3). The narrator's situation is representative of a specific group marked by marginalization, oppression, and struggle, and he speaks of the experience of that community as a whole (Beverley and Zimmerman 174–77). In keeping with this function, Dawud's *testimonio* bears witness to the plight of displaced Palestinians at the same time that it explains his own process of radicalization.

The adult Dawud tells his background story in five intercalated chapters in italic typeface, which serves to set these sections apart from the story of Cristina's investigation. Retrospectively narrating his family's oppression, Dawud sets the first episode in Black September 1971 when he was a baby and his family was forced to flee from Jordanian and Syrian bullets across Galilee to Lebanon along with thousands of other Palestinians. Recounting history, Dawud tells of the creation of Israel in 1948, the co-optation of King Abdullah of Jordan, and the disappearance of Palestine. Dawud's family settles in Sabra, the Muslim periphery of Beirut, and his childhood elapses during the gestation of civil war in Lebanon.

The next installment of Dawud's life story begins when he is five years old: his father trains him to handle a Kalashnikov submachine gun and lectures him on the justice of the Palestinian cause. Dawud relates that the Palestinian settlements in Lebanon have become a state within a state; the PLO, now a powerful force, is carrying out attacks on Israel from camps in southern Lebanon with the Israeli army responding by bombing PLO positions. The chapter closes with the 1982 Sabra and Shatila massacre, part of the Lebanese civil war, in which hundreds of Palestinian men, women, and children were killed by Lebanese Phalangist Christian militants, acting at the behest of Israeli commanders (Grenville 916). The young Dawud hid behind bags of flour when the militia charged his home and witnessed in horror first the rape of his mother and sisters and then the murder of his entire family.

The subsequent episode of Dawud's *testimonio* details the horrible aftermath of the Sabra massacre: the devastation etched in the memory of survivors, the cadavers tossed into common graves. Dawud, found unconscious in the rubble that was once his family's home, is rescued by the imam Zacarías Najaf, who places him in a Hezbollah orphanage where the children memorize the Koran as the basis of their education. Subsequently, Dawud is sent to a military training camp and participates in a failed attempt to kill Israelis in a kibbutz in Galilee. Disappointed by this lost opportunity to immolate himself and meet Allah in heaven, and believing that he serves "la justa causa de Islam agredido por las fuerzas de Satán" (the just cause of Islam assaulted by the forces of Satan) (104), Dawud arrives in Buenos Aires anxious to consummate his martyrdom and compensate for the suffering of his people.

By means of Dawud's *testimonio*, the author presents the other side of the Israeli-Palestinian conflict, relating the oppression and struggle of the Palestinian people and the indoctrination of a Palestinian youth. At the same time, the novel presents another view of Islam: that of a peaceful, tolerant culture through the figure of the imam Zacarías Najaf, a founder of Hezbollah and a pacifist. Zacarías has a falling-out with the other Hezbollah leaders when they celebrate the 1983 attack on the US Marine barracks in Beirut. Maintaining that the threats to Islam come not from without but from within, he flees to Argentina after the organization is taken over by fanatics bent on violence. Cristina invites Zacarías to participate in her show's panel discussion, where the imam has a platform to remind viewers of the other Islam—the flourishing and progressive civilizations of Baghdad and Cordoba that coexisted peacefully with Christians for three centuries.

While some readers have taken issue with Aguinis for showing too much tolerance toward the Palestinian position in his writings,[11] I agree with Ignacio López-Calvo, who points out that in *Asalto* Aguinis's pro-Israeli bias causes the Palestinian discourse to undermine itself (173–74). What is more, Zacarías's perspective has planted a doubt that creates an inner conflict for Dawud. In the final episode of the novel, Dawud hears on the radio the news of the bombing of the AMIA and imagines that he was the martyr who blew up the new target. In his vision, however, he ultimately goes to hell instead of paradise as he had anticipated, and he views the victims of the bombing—Jews and non-Jews—going to paradise. We can consider this passage—told in the extradiegetic narrator's voice focalizing through Dawud—to be a type of authorial intrusion because it shows the Hezbollah militant's position to be misguided, thus reflecting what we can presume to be the political position of the author and not his character. Similarly, a pro-Israeli stance can be perceived in the novel's description of the Jewish community in Buenos Aires, as I discuss in the next section.

## Jewish Buenos Aires

Most of the novels discussed in this book feature a particular depiction of Buenos Aires; for instance, several novels portray the city's fragmentation or deterioration due to the Argentine government's fast and loose implementation of market-driven economic practices. *Asalto al paraíso* is distinctive in that it focuses on Buenos Aires' Jewishness.[12] In her essay "The Jew in the City: Buenos Aires in Jewish Fiction," Amy Kaminsky details the diverse definitions and depictions of Jewishness that the city has been taken to symbolize in selected literary texts. She observes, "Jewish identity means marginality, or not quite belonging. In the Argentine symbolic order, the Jew is always inside and outside, marked by his troubled membership in the nation" (179). "Because they cross-cut the nation," she concludes, "Jewish differentiation and globalization both trigger national anxieties" (181).

In *Asalto*, the vision of Buenos Aires' Jewishness is focalized through Iranian embassy officials and Muslim fanatics. The reader is first introduced to Jewish Buenos Aires through the words of Omar Azadegh, an employee of the Iranian embassy. A member of the recently arrived terrorist cell inquires about the Jewish community in the city, to which Azadegh replies: "Son la comunidad más numerosa de América latina, unos doscientos cincuenta mil, pero parecen más" (They are the largest community in Latin America, some two hundred and fifty thousand, but they appear to be more) (48). Continuing to describe the community, the extradiegetic narrator focalizes Azadegh's perception: "No eran solo numerosos, sino muy activos. También se refirió a sus instituciones, las educativas, religiosas y de ayuda solidaria. Daban miedo" (They were not only numerous, but also very active. He also commented on their educational, religious and solidarity aid institutions. They incited fear) (49). While cast as threatening in the eyes of an adversary of the Jewish community bent on their destruction, in objective terms this reference to their activity and solidarity is a favorable valuation. The machinations of anti-Semitic factions of Argentine society that seek to disrupt the community are registered when Tabbani informs Dawud that this neighborhood experiences more frequent blackouts than the rest of the city, carried out by "gente que odia a los judíos tanto como nosotros ... policías, servicios de Inteligencia. Algunos políticos" (people who hate Jews as much as we do ... police, intelligence service personnel. Some politicians) (187–88). His remark points to the existence of aggressive anti-Semitism among powerful actors of Argentine officialdom.

Focalizing the anti-Semitic perception of Tabbani, the extradiegetic narrator delivers a discourse on Jewish immigration to Argentina.

> Los judíos en este país llegaron a conformar la comunidad más numerosa de América latina y eran un auténtico peligro. Aunque vinieron en forma aislada en los siglos previos a la independencia, su aluvión empezó a fines del siglo XIX y siguió hasta mediados del XX. Sucias olas de inmigrantes se derramaron en colonias agrícolas y luego invadieron todos los campos de la actividad nacional. (190)

> [The Jews in this country were the largest community in Latin America and were a real danger. Although they trickled in during the centuries prior to independence, their deluge began in the late nineteenth century and lasted through the mid-twentieth. Dirty waves of immigrants poured into agricultural colonies and then invaded all fields of national activity.]

The informational session continues in Tabbani's voice as he describes the current state of the Jewish community, focusing on their accomplishments. While some Jews get rich with their factories and business, he explains, others join labor unions and leftist political parties. They have invaded universities and become student leaders, teachers, and administrators as well as doctors, engineers, psychologists, and architects. Argentine Jews have also been influential in the realm of music and poetry, seeming to be dozens of millions, not merely a quarter million. Tabbani decries the fact that besides systematically occupying Argentina, they have organized their community life in an enviable manner. Worst of all, they always show solidarity with Israel. "Su objetivo es dominar el mundo, degenerarlo y esclavizarlo" (Their goal is to dominate the world, to debase and enslave it), he concludes (191). This depiction ignites Dawud, who sees them as a legion of criminals that needs to be destroyed immediately, before they can complete their satanic plans. These passages demonstrate why Buenos Aires found itself in the crosshairs of Islamic fundamentalist terrorism at the same time that they cite the accomplishments of the Jewish community in Argentina. Once again, I agree with the critical assessment of López-Calvo, who states that this backhandedly favorable view of the Jewish community seen from the perspective of anti-Semitic Iranians and fundamentalists compromises the novel's verisimilitude (187).

Not unconnected to the depiction of its Jewishness, but perhaps surprising, is the comparison of Buenos Aires to Beirut. In his essay "Buenos Aires Is (Latin) America, Too" Adrián Gorelik comments on Buenos

Aires' constant preoccupation "with where and to whom it belongs, seeking models and embodiments of virtue and progress in other international cities" (62). Referencing the comparisons of parts of Buenos Aires to London, Madrid, Paris, and Genoa, Gorelik says that these comparisons flatter the vanity of Buenosaireans at the same time that they undermine the city's "fragile sense of self" (65). The title of his essay refers to the shantytowns in the center of Buenos Aires, the radical "other" in the heart of the city. In *Asalto al paraíso*, Beirut is an unexpected comparison that can be considered another embodiment of the radical "other." Antagonists Cristina and Dawud both make this comparison, but for different reasons. In a live broadcast, Cristina evokes Beirut as she surveys the rubble of the Israeli embassy.

> —Parece Beirut—dijo Cristina al micrófono—. La Beirut de la larga guerra civil entre libaneses y palestinos, cristianos y musulmanes, palestinos e israelíes. La Beirut donde los edificios se derrumbaban por las bombas como la que hoy ha explotado aquí, en Buenos Aires. Este pedazo de nuestra ciudad es ahora un espejo de Beirut. (12)
>
> [It looks like Beirut, said Cristina into the microphone. The Beirut of the long civil war between Lebanese and Palestinians, Christians and Muslims, Palestinians and Israelis. The Beirut where the buildings were reduced to rubble by bombs like the one that today has exploded here in Buenos Aires. This piece of our city is now a mirror of Beirut.]

In this corner of Buenos Aires, Cristina finds a reflection of the warring ideological factions that destroyed Beirut. In her discussion of Argentina as a place marked by Jewishness, Kaminsky states that, above all, Buenos Aires is a global city due to the literary texts that endow it with symbolic significance. Like Gorelik, Kaminsky speaks to Buenos Aires' "ever-fraught process of identity formation," reiterating the idea that it "has striven to cultivate a narrative of itself that comes from elsewhere," literally consuming places on which it would model itself (167). Cristina's comparison of Buenos Aires to bombed-out Beirut emphasizes a tragic aspect of Buenos Aires' globalization: its new membership in the global terror circuit. Due to its Jewishness, as *Asalto* points out, Buenos Aires became a terrorist target, gaining a spot on the map along with Western cities such as Munich, site of the 1972 Olympic massacre, a group that would soon be joined by New York, which experienced its first terror attack in the basement of the World Trade Towers in 1993.[13] Thus Buenos Aires' Jewishness gives it a unique and tragic distinction among Latin American cities, and the attacks served to underscore its otherness.

The comparison of Buenos Aires to Beirut is echoed by Dawud—his relatives told him that Buenos Aires reminds them of Beirut, but the beautiful Beirut before the war, not the war-torn Beirut that Cristina evokes. Dawud confirms this comparison in his first glimpse of the city. Upon seeing the elegant and imposing buildings along stately Avenida del Libertador, he exclaims, "¡Maldición! ... ¡Cómo se parecen Beirut y Buenos Aires!" (Damn! ... How Beirut and Buenos Aires resemble each other!) (50). The passages narrating Dawud's initial impressions bask in the grandeur of Buenos Aires. Ironically, both the journalist and the terrorist make the Buenos Aires–Beirut comparison but for opposite reasons—rubble versus beauty. Dawud, who is bent on destruction, compares it to Beirut seen as the jewel of the Orient, while Cristina, who is bent on preservation, compares it to the devastated war-torn Beirut.

At the same time that the novel situates Buenos Aires within a network of global cities, its characters trace a map within the city. The streets and neighborhoods of Buenos Aires are named continually as we follow their trajectory. Many scenes are set in the upscale neighborhood of the Recoleta, an area synonymous with traditional wealth and power. This is where much of the advance work for the terrorist strike takes place and where the terrorist cell initially stays. Recoleta is also where Cristina will carry out the bulk of her investigative work. Her treacherous seduction of Santiago Branca begins in his antiques dealership—which serves as a front for drug trafficking—on Avenida Alvear, the most exclusive address in Buenos Aires, and culminates in the posh Patio Bullrich mall. Cristina's boyfriend, Esteban, disguised as a rich Arab, meets with Santiago Branca in the ultraluxurious Hotel Alvear in an attempt to extract information. In these depictions, all located in Recoleta, this enclave of wealth and privilege is also associated with deception and corruption.

The terrorists will trace a path from their hotel in Recoleta to Once, the heart of the Jewish community. On the day of the thwarted attack, Dawud's route is charted as he makes his way through the city toward his target. However, before he turns onto Avenida Sarmiento, where the Hebraica is located, he receives orders to abort the operation. The path of destruction is mapped but truncated before the terrorist can complete his mission.

While much of the action takes place in upscale or middle-class Buenos Aires neighborhoods, there are occasional forays into seedier areas. Azadegh shows the visitors the *villas miseria*, which remind Dawud of Palestinian refugee camps. "Son los premios de Satán a la obsecuencia del país con los Estados Unidos" (They are Satan's prizes for the nation's obsequiousness toward to the United States) (48), explains Azadegh, blaming the poverty on Argentina's adoption of the neoliberal agenda and alluding to the fact that it was promoted by the US. After the cell is discovered, the Middle Eastern men are moved to a two-star hotel in the Constitución district. To explain the reason for this move, the multiethnic complexion of Constitución is described in contrast to the European character of Recoleta: "Allí se alojaban inmigrantes provenientes de Perú, Paraguay y Bolivia. Era más fácil pasar inadvertido en el trajín con olor a fritanga latinoamericana que en las zonas de carácter europeo" (Immigrants from Peru, Paraguay and Bolivia lived there. It was easier to pass unnoticed in the hubbub smelling of Latin American fried food than in areas of European character) (311). Thus *Asalto* depicts Buenos Aires in its contrasts of wealth and poverty as well as its ever-fraught search for identity and self-definition.

As described in the preceding section, the novel's overall design features scenes set in Buenos Aires dealing with the terror attack that alternate with episodes set in the Middle East depicting the plight of the Palestinians. This transatlantic mapping, in addition to reflecting the author's desire to explore what makes a suicide bomber, serves to highlight Argentina's new geopolitical position in a globalized political and economic order. Also implied are president Menem's connections to the Middle East, along with his unfulfilled promises to that region. The panelists on Cristina's show say that because Menem was born a Muslim and visited Syria, which has close ties to Iran and the Hezbollah, some people might have hoped that Argentina would become the first Islamic republic of Latin America. Upon seeing that dream frustrated, they might have felt betrayed and taken revenge by bombing the Israeli embassy. All in all, *Asalto al paraíso* presents a tragic upshot of Buenos Aires' status as a global city: the novel points to its Jewishness, along with the perception in certain quarters that Menem turned his back on his Middle Eastern connections, as factors that made it a target in the Palestinian-Israeli conflict.

To conclude, Aguinis's choice of genres functions to emplot the story of the terrorist attacks in a way that directs the reader's thinking toward the author's ideological stance, which supports the *pista iraní* or "official story." The pseudo-*testimonio* of the suicide bomber serves to highlight the conflict between Palestine and Israel as the root of the problem. The anticonspiracy thriller, portraying a maverick journalist persisting against a network of local anti-Semites, underlines official corruption and impunity. My reading brings out the fact that Aguinis's pro-Israeli position at times compromises the verisimilitude of his characterizations while his stated intent to counter fundamentalist sexism by creating a female investigative journalist backfires when her depiction falls into the hard-boiled pattern of the femme fatale. Notwithstanding these inconsistencies, *Asalto al paraíso* is a spellbinding thriller that bears witness to the terrorist strikes in Argentina and denounces the lack of justice for these crimes perpetrated not only against the Jewish community but against all Argentines. With his novel, Aguinis seeks to correct the forgetfulness or ignorance of those who believe that the 9/11 attacks in the US were the first terror attacks on American soil, reminding us that the tragic precedents in Argentina are still unsolved.

### THE ROGUE SPY AND THE DEMISE OF THE SPECIAL PROSECUTOR: *EL FISCAL* BY R. S. PRATT

The bombing of the AMIA, as discussed in the previous section, is presented in *Asalto al paraíso* as part of the global ramifications of the ideological struggle originating in the Arab-Israeli conflict. By 2015, according to the premise of *El fiscal* by the pseudonymous R. S. Pratt, the investigation of the attack degenerated into an instrument for partisan politics, a personal political vendetta. At the same time, according to this narrative, the clash between the special prosecutor and the president can be linked to a geopolitical shift. While Nisman's persistence on the *pista iraní* represented a continuation of Néstor Kirchner's policy of alignment with the US anti-Iranian posture, Cristina Fernández de Kirchner was veering to the left, becoming close to Venezuela's Hugo Chávez, who was aligning with Russia, China, and Iran.

*El fiscal* is narrated by an extradiegetic voice in chronological order with a single-stranded plot: the perfidious spymaster uses the gullible public prosecutor as his pawn in a high-stakes political game with the goal of discrediting the president, steadily deceiving him until the spymaster decides that the prosecutor is most useful dead. While we may not know the identity of the author, his political leanings are no mystery as the plot is consonant with the position of the Fernández de Kirchner government. The characters are flat, drawn to emphasize their negative traits: the spy, pure evil who will stop at nothing to pursue his selfish ends; the prosecutor, pure sucker who falls for the spy's trickery hook, line, and sinker. The publisher tells us that the author—who is "one of the ten best Argentine writers" ("El misterioso autor")—wanted to use a pseudonym in order to "preserve his name for his books, which are very literary [*bien literarios*]" ("Ya salió"). This seems to imply that "Pratt" envisioned literary history would dismiss this hastily written and topical novel as ephemera or, at best, a lesser work. Despite its partisanship and questionable literary quality, this work merits consideration because it presents an intriguing portrait of how Fernández de Kirchner's geopolitical shift, or "left turn," impacted the AMIA investigation and it offers a counterpart to Aguinis's novel due to its tie-in with the *pista siria*. Also of interest is how it crystallizes the paranoia of the populace in its deep mistrust of the state and its intelligence operations, a sentiment that is aptly expressed in Beatriz Sarlo's description of her fellow Argentines' reaction to Nisman's death, calling them "a people who feel that their destiny is controlled by unknown forces" ("Sarlo: 'La muerte'").

Pratt fuses conventions of spy fiction and the roman à clef in *El fiscal* to emplot his version of the forces that led to Nisman's mysterious death. The spy novel is well suited to Pratt's rendering of events. David Seed defines it as "a close but distinct variation on the tale of detection with the difference that there is no discrete crime involved but rather a covert action which ... transgresses conventional, moral, or legal boundaries" (115), and Alan Furst points out that the spy novel is "of necessity political" (x). Its appeal to readers has to do with its promise to give them access to processes taking place behind official history, and it foregrounds information that will confirm suspected conspiracy. The roman à clef, for its part, enables the author to playfully or deviously pair fictional characters with real-life individuals. The "novel with a key," Sean Latham explains, emerged in the eighteenth century and was used to "encode salacious gossip about a particular clique or coterie. To unlock these delicious secrets a key is required, one that matches the names of the characters to the real-life figures upon whom they are based" (7). The key to *El fiscal* is not in the least bit private or enigmatic; the match-up between the main characters and their flesh-and-blood counterparts will be obvious to anyone who follows the news: Trusso represents Antonio Stiuso, Lerman is Alberto Nisman, Cristina Hernández de Larchner is Cristina Fernández de Kirchner, and so on.

Apparently the celebrated spy fiction novelist John le Carré is Pratt's model or inspiration, as the editor reveals that "Pratt" told him "the case (the death) along with the denunciation was a Le Carré novel" ("Ya salió").

While *El fiscal* does not have the complexity or subtly of a story by this author who specializes in Cold War espionage, the words of a le Carré spy about his work ring true for the Argentine novel: "We do not arrest our targets. We develop them and redirect them at bigger targets. When we identify a network, we watch it, we listen to it, we penetrate it and by degrees we control it."[14] This is exactly what Trusso does with Lerman—he penetrates and controls him, directing him at Trusso's big target: the president.

### The Duplicitous Puppet Master and His Stooge

Spanish novelist Miguel Aranguren states that Graham Greene would have been inspired to write about Nisman's death, but in Aranguren's mind, the story would begin twenty years prior with the bombing of the AMIA (Aranguren). The fact that Pratt's novel opens with an incident demonstrating "Trusso's" dirty dealings reveals immediately the direction that the novel will take: it does not deal directly with the attack and the central character is not the special prosecutor but rather the powerful and Machiavellian superspy. Pratt's emplotment of the story with the spy subgenre resonates with newspaper reports that cite Nisman's dependence on Stiuso, and serves to cast the spy as the driver of forces that led to the prosecutor's death.[15]

As befitting a spy story, Trusso's covert actions transgress ethical and legal boundaries, and the first scene effectively establishes him as deeply amoral at the same time that it foreshadows Lerman's end. Trusso is in the dock area of Buenos Aires setting up an assassination to look like a suicide. The massaged murder scene is a work of art, no one doubts that it is suicide, and Trusso proceeds to fabricate connections between the dead man and narcotrafficking rings. Thus Trusso's work consists of cleaning and dirtying: "ensuciar la vida de la víctima y luego limpiar la escena del crimen" (dirty the life of the victim and then clean up the crime scene) (11). A James Bond fanatic, he believes that Bond gives him "license to kill": "Hay cosas que solo se solucionan matando" (There are things that can only be solved by killing), he reflects (83). Described as a shadow prince, Trusso has the key weapon of his anonymity, and he thinks that he has more power than the president because he lasts longer.

In his analysis of the James Bond phenomenon, Umberto Eco discusses how the Bond stories are built on a series of oppositions—opposing characters and opposing values (36). This structure is present in *El fiscal* insofar as we see a relationship of "dominated-dominant" in the interaction between

Lerman and Trusso. Opposing actions that advance the plot are assistance versus treachery. All the while Lerman thinks that Trusso and others are helping him, but it turns out that they are betraying him.

The central action is Trusso's gradual development and penetration of his target: Lerman. Trusso's objective is to use Lerman to weaken the president by convincing him to denounce her alleged plan to give impunity to the Iranian suspects. Trusso has a personal motive for damaging the president: it has been rumored that the powerful spy will be ousted. But Trusso will not go gracefully: "Antes de que yo me vaya se va a ir ella" (Before I go, she will go), he vows, planning to execute a "soft coup" (105). Soon the president follows through with her threat and replaces Trusso as "el señor 5," the nickname for the operational head of the SIDE. Thus Pratt's emplotment shows that Trusso's desire to take revenge on the president is the nefarious hidden force behind the prosecutor's actions.

The cunning spy employs a multipronged approach: he breaks Lerman down psychologically, keeps him under constant secret surveillance, feeds him lies, and puts him in compromised situations. Lerman idolizes Trusso and considers him "una persona superior, dueño de una inteligencia sobrenatural" (a superior person, gifted with a supernatural intelligence) (51). What is more, Lerman is described as a narcissist with a low level of self-esteem, making him highly susceptible to Trusso's control. Although Trusso is a true villain who cares only for himself and will stop at nothing to retain his position, *El fiscal* does not draw a Manichean world made up of good and evil forces in conflict. While Lerman insists that his aim is to bring about justice for the victims of the AMIA attack, the novel's focus on his character flaws along with the portrayal of him as Trusso's dupe scuttles any possibility of making him into a hero.

Trusso has effective techniques for messing with Lerman's nerves and creating a sense of paranoia. He compromises Lerman by coaxing him to try cocaine and by taking him to an upscale house of prostitution and getting him involved with a prostitute. He operates a panopticon-type situation to achieve total vigilance of Lerman. Trusso is obsessed with spying—he finances a global chain of cabarets where he carries out secret filming that is useful for blackmailing powerful people, and he enjoys spending time in his secret spy lab that is equipped with all the latest surveillance gadgetry. The depiction of the systematic control that Trusso maintains over Lerman is consonant with D. A. Miller's observation that the novel (in general) represents a domestic version of Foucault's description of the panopticon in the prisons. Beyond the carceral system, in the private space where the individual believes he is free from vigilance, he is being controlled. *El fiscal*'s portrait of Trusso's fixation with surveillance and strategies of policing exemplifies Miller's perception of the "radical *entanglement* between the nature of the novel and the practice of the police," viewing the novel as "a set of representational techniques—[that] systematically participate in a general economy of policing power" (2).

When Lerman returns home from a trip, he finds that his documents about the AMIA investigation that were locked in his safe are now out on the table with a line highlighted; this is followed by similar intrusions that make him feel invaded and unsafe. All are the work of Trusso. Trusso also enlists others to help him watch and control Lerman. The prostitute that Lerman believes he chose of his own free will is actually Trusso's agent and reports to him. Using a combination of blackmail and monetary incentives, Trusso co-opts Lerman's faithful assistant, Castagnino, to spy on him and to convince him to carry out the denunciation of the president.[16] Trusso gifts Lerman with a huge flat-screen television—little does Lerman know that it is Trusso's watching and listening device, as it is equipped with a camera and microphones. A remark that one of Trusso's SIDE associates makes to him underscores the idea of Lerman as a puppet controlled by Trusso: "Es que Lerman sos vos. ¿O ahora Lerman es alguien?" (The thing is, Lerman is you. Or is Lerman now someone?) (161).[17]

Trusso's most pointed way of getting Lerman to carry out his ends is by means of the information and misinformation that he feeds him: facts mixed with lies. Trusso tells Lerman that there is trouble on the horizon: the president aims to finalize a Memorandum of Understanding with Iran. Because Argentina wants to buy crude oil from Iran, a terrorist state, and since buying oil from such is state is not allowed, Iran will be reclassified. Trusso claims that he has secret information that the government aspires to lift the arrest order against the Iranian suspects in the AMIA case and insists that he has a recording of the president talking to her foreign minister about it. This is the proof Lerman needs to advance his denunciation of the president. He will expose the existence of "un plan delictivo destinado a dotar de impunidad a los imputados de nacionalidad iraní acusados en dicha causa, para que eludan la investigación y se sustraigan de la acción de la justicia argentina" (a criminal plan designed to provide impunity to the defendants of Iranian nationality accused in said case, so that they can evade the investigation and remove themselves from the action of the Argentine justice system) (168). Most importantly, the decision will be traced to the president and her foreign minister.

Trusso ultimately achieves his objective of persuading Lerman to put forward the complaint by telling him that the president is going to dismiss him from the case. As evidence, he doctors a tape, splicing sequences of words uttered by the president to make her say that she wants to remove Lerman. Upon hearing the manipulated tape, Lerman realizes that he must present the denunciation before this happens. Confiding in Trusso's promise to hand over the necessary evidence to back up his claim, Lerman presents the accusation. However, as he prepares to make the presentation before Congress, he begins to despair because Trusso still has not given him the proofs.

A culminating point in the spy story is the revelation of the dominator to the dominated. After Lerman's repeated frantic attempts to get in touch with him, Trusso finally appears and lets Lerman know that he has been controlling him. Paula, the prostitute who became Lerman's companion, works for Trusso; Trusso has filmed him in compromising positions; he has been spying on him in his apartment. "En este piso mando yo" (I am in charge in this apartment), Trusso declares (211). Worst of all, Lerman comes to the realization that Trusso never intended to give him proofs. Treachery and reversal is a standard procedure in the spy novel, as a confidant and helper is revealed as an enemy. This is the case with Trusso—Lerman thought that they were allies in the AMIA investigation, but ultimately all Trusso cared about was to retain his power, and when the president decided that it was time to get rid of him, he used Lerman to retaliate. Trusso's modus operandi is to bring people to the point of personal crisis and leave them hanging.

The subsequent plot events set up the motives to justify the prosecutor's possible suicide. To compound Lerman's anguish, the former secretary of Interpol declares, "'Lo que dice Lerman es falso'" (What Lerman says is false) (221).[18] He says that no Argentine government official ever tried to lift the arrest warrants against the accused Iranians, and what is more, only the judge who ordered the warrants has the authority to request that they be lifted. This is a huge blow for Lerman and he considers not going to testify in Congress. Castagnino tells Lerman that he should have a gun and brings one to him, and then reports to Trusso that Lerman is extremely agitated and anxious.

Having created a scenario that supports the government theory of Nisman's death—that it was the work of a rogue spy—Pratt presents an ending that incorporates two theories of Nisman's death; in this way he is able to float two different explanations as possibilities. A Brazilian and a Chinese man under Trusso's hire are supposed to kill Lerman and make it look like a suicide. But when they enter the apartment, they find that Lerman has already shot himself. Now the novel backtracks in time to narrate how Lerman, realizing that Trusso has been deceiving him and that the principal points of his accusation are based on falsehoods, suffers a crisis in confidence. Feeling empty and exhausted, he walks into the bathroom and shoots himself. In either scenario, murder or suicide, the blame falls squarely on the mastermind behind the prosecutor's death: the rogue spy.

The late Ana Barón, *Clarín* correspondent in the US, wrote about the CIA's theory concerning Nisman's death: "Actually there are two hypotheses on the table. The first is that Cristina expressed her desire to get rid of Nisman because of the denunciation he presented accusing her of covering up the Iranian authors of the AMIA attack. And, consequently, a group within the intelligence services decided to carry out her wishes, be it with or without her consent. The second is that members of the services carried out the operation to weaken Cristina due to the restructuring she had begun to do in the former SIDE." As detailed in this section, Pratt's novel portrays the second theory, which makes the president a political victim of the prosecutor's death, as opposed to the first theory, in which she figures as its instigator, whether intentional or unintentional.[19]

### Uncle Sam's Heavy Hand

Spy fiction portrays the hidden processes behind official history (Seed 117). As a case in point, Horsley remarks that a frequent depiction of the United States in post-9/11 spy novels is that of a global empire that "goes about its business of destabilizing other governments" ("A Life Spent Lying" 175). This feature is borne out in *El fiscal* with the depiction of behind-the-scenes control of the investigation of the AMIA bombing by foreign governments that promote their own national agenda and Argentine agents who cater to them. Thus an important piece of the reading of the crime scenario that Pratt advances is the heavy-handedness of the US and Israel, but especially the US, which wants the Argentines to focus on Iran as the culprit. US government officials see this as an opportunity to show the world that Iran continued to be an outlaw state since the 1983 bombing of the US Marine barracks in Beirut. *El fiscal* goes as far as to depict the CIA's tacit approval of the spy's plan to eliminate the special prosecutor.

We are told that the "Compañía" (the nickname given to the CIA) considers Trusso to be a US agent and he became even more favored after the AMIA attack because he carried out devious measures to comply with the interests of the US and Israeli secret services by planting clues that would point to Iran's culpability. Articulating a tendentious version of the AMIA investigation, the narrator reports that Trusso created false leads and red herrings, bought witnesses, and fabricated the theory that a Renault Traffic van bomb was the cause of the blast, planting car parts brought from a junkyard. Trusso's intimacy with CIA agents and his eagerness to follow their directives is demonstrated in the opening scene of the novel when he and Lerman are reacting to the implications of the geopolitical shift of the current Argentine administration. Trusso receives a call from Lerman, "aturdido por lo que había leído en los diarios sobre el acercamiento del gobierno a Irán" (stunned by what he had read in the newspapers about the government's approach to Iran) (8), and replies that he is traveling to Washington the following week and will ask his CIA contact what to do about this matter. After the president fires Trusso as head of the SIDE, Trusso announces to Lerman that now his work has doubled: he works for both the CIA and Mossad.

Similarly tendentious is *El fiscal*'s depiction of the special prosecutor's relationship with the US. Lerman is pressured by the US and Israel to continue pursuing the *pista iraní*, to the detriment of the *pista siria*, which, according to the narrator, freezes the investigation. He is invited by the US government to a conference about Iranian terrorism, which links the 2001 attack in the US, the 2005 bombing in Madrid, and the 2007 strike in London—and could be considered a bid to influence his thinking about the AMIA attack. Lerman's dependence on the US is exposed by WikiLeaks, which reveal that Lerman reported to the US embassy. "Es nuestro" (He's ours) (15), Trusso informs Cocker, his CIA contact, in reference to Lerman.

Of course the Argentine president's softened stance toward Iran is not met with favor by the US and, according to Trusso, both the US embassy and Tel Aviv approve of the denunciation of her. The novel's most speculative and most damning allegation regarding the unspoken complicity of the US comes shortly before Lerman's death. While lunching in Washington with Cocker, Trusso tells him that Lerman's denunciation did not have teeth and the campaign against the government "estaba dando resultados pero se iba a diluir si no pasaba algo más" (was producing results but was going to fizzle out if something else didn't happen). Like what? Cocker asks. "'Una tragedia personal'" (a personal tragedy), Trusso replies, and illustrates his idea with an example from US politics: "'Imaginate que Monica Lewinsky tiene que ir a declarar contra Clinton y el día antes muere, se suicida, no sé, le pasa algo'" (Imagine that Monica Lewinsky has to testify against Clinton and the day before, she dies, she commits suicide, I don't know, something happens to her) (228). Cocker gets the idea, concluding that Clinton would have a big problem. The what-if scenario makes it clear that Trusso plans for Lerman to die in order to make the president look bad, and Cocker's silence signals that he has no objection to the plan. This passage is the culmination of Pratt's depiction of the US as an evil, meddling empire with Trusso ostensibly working at its behest while in actuality, US interests dovetail with his desire for revenge.

The spy novel emplotment—by presenting nefarious, hidden forces behind recent events—advances Pratt's spin on history, setting forth a partisan view of a highly polemic issue with distinct positions. On one side of the issue are journalists such as Santiago O'Donnell who emphasize that the US embassy controlled the AMIA investigation. Historian David Sheinin contests this view: according to his reading of events, Argentine and US officials worked cooperatively on Iran policy, part of extensive secret collaboration between the two countries in matters of shared strategic interest ("The Death of Alberto Nisman" 36).[20] While not advancing a specific interpretation regarding the authors of the AMIA bombing, *El fiscal* works to discredit the so-called official story—that it was carried out by Hezbollah at the behest of Iran—by presenting basic tenets of the theory as falsehoods manufactured by Trusso in compliance with the political agenda of Washington and Tel Aviv. All in all, it conveys a pro–Fernández de Kirchner stance by clearing her of a direct association with the prosecutor's death, depicting it as the doing of the manipulative rogue spy who wanted revenge for his ousting from the top post of the SIDE. Absolving himself of responsibility by hiding behind a pseudonym, "Pratt" pens a hurried and speculative paperback that can be considered a piece of Kirchnerista propaganda.

### Geographic Spaces and the Media

Similar to the other novels studied in this book, the spaces represented in Buenos Aires are linked to messages and critiques that *El fiscal* delivers. The novel emphasizes the fact that the places Lerman and Trusso frequent are associated with wealth, power, and exclusivity. Lerman lives in an apartment on the thirteenth floor of a Puerto Madero high rise. Thus his splendid view of the river is located in Buenos Aires' upscale urban renewal project considered the showcase of Menem's neoliberal agenda. Lerman likes to read the newspapers in the lobby of the Hilton of Puerto Madero and eat at a sushi restaurant near his apartment. Lerman's trips also demonstrate his wealth and privilege—he vacations in Punta del Este, Uruguay's vacation beach spot for the beautiful people, and he takes his daughters and ex-wife on a tour of European capitals to celebrate the older girl's fifteenth birthday. The meeting places favored by Trusso are luxurious as well—he and Lerman meet in Patio Bullrich, the posh shopping center in Recoleta, or in the coffee shops of art museums. Both men travel frequently to Washington, DC, a signal of their closeness to US shapers of foreign policy. In contrast to these places associated with wealth is the area that will provide a clandestine exit for the men hired to kill Lerman: Trusso's helper sends them to Misiones, where Trusso controls ports, thus signaling his connection with the notoriously porous "Triple Frontera," considered a haven for the criminal and the corrupt.

*El fiscal* also incorporates a critique of the press, implying that it values sensational stories and the bottom line over pursuing the truth and ethical reporting. For instance, in the initial episode, Trusso reflects that his doctored assassination escapes serious scrutiny by the press because it prefers the spectacle over serious investigation. Another observation by Trusso points to the hypocrisy of prominent journalists: "Trusso odiaba a los periodistas más conocidos porque se volvían locos por la plata pero se escudaban en un discurso moralista" (Trusso hated the best-known journalists because they went crazy over money but hid behind a moralistic discourse) (57). Underlining the WikiLeaks fray, another episode shows a successful attempt of the government prosecutor to control the press. A *Página/12* editor, Sebastian O'Farrell (in reality the aforementioned Santiago O'Donnell), published a book with WikiLeaks information he obtained from Julian Assange. The leaks showed that Lerman reported to the US embassy. Lerman called the paper's director to get him to suppress this part in the paper's advance publication of the book, and he complied. Soon, however, another, pro-government paper began publishing news of Lerman's "affair" with the embassy. The anti–Fernández de Kirchner press is seen in the figure of Wachoski, who works for El Gordo Lanari (in reality Jorge Lanata[21]) and urges Lerman to follow through with the denunciation of Cristina.

## Having It Both Ways with the Roman à Clef

The entire space of the *El fiscal* book cover is occupied by a black-and-white photo of Nisman's head, but a big red square in the center covers Nisman's face from above the eyebrows to the bottom lip;[22] in this box are written the (pseudo)name of the author, the title, and the line "Una ficción demasiado parecida a la realidad" (A fiction too similar to reality). The tease here is double-barreled: the partially hidden face and the tagline used to market the book allow the publisher to exploit the slippery slope between fact and fiction that is a trademark of the roman à clef. The roman à clef allows the writer to "have it both ways": blurring the line between truth and invention, he can deliver a partisan version of Nisman's death, inculpating certain individuals without really doing so and without fear of libel or need for proofs because it is fiction. Latham points out that the genre "is distinguished by what Gérard Genette calls 'conditional fictionality,' meaning that the narrative that for some readers is true for others is pure fiction" (15). It occupies an ambiguous space by presenting itself as fiction "while encoding scandalous and often disturbing facts about real people and events." Even those who have a key may not know where to draw the line between fact and fiction (Latham 13).[23]

*El fiscal* depicts scandalous behavior of "fictional" characters, but what is true and what has come from Pratt's imagination? Some details of the fictional Lerman's personal life are based on verifiable facts about Nisman: for instance, that Nisman lived in Le Parc Tower in Puerto Madero, that he had two daughters whom he adored, and that he was divorced from his wife, a judge. But what about the unflattering episodes referencing his personal foibles and his sex life? Was Nisman as vain, narcissistic, and insecure as Lerman? Did he have seven types of antidepressants in his medicine cabinet? Was he addicted to PlayStation and video games? Did he live with a prostitute and "wife-swap" with Trusso/Stiuso? Was he such a sucker for Trusso/Stiuso's purported deception? The character assassination of Trusso is even more damning. He is truly Machiavellian, using everyone for his own selfish, personal ends, and is responsible for numerous political executions. Given the many factual details of the novel, readers wonder how much of its contents are true, and we can believe the worst if we are so inclined. In this way, Pratt can insidiously smear the characters of these individuals.

Shortly after Nisman's death, the yellow press published photos of him partying with prostitutes. Sarlo attributes this character defamation to a government campaign: "It was a decision of the Government ... to dirty Nisman's image by getting into his private life, linking him to yellow journalism. The Government threw that meat onto the grill, to journalism, so that it would leak" (Duchini). If Sarlo's statement is true, the fact that Pratt dirties the fictional figure that represents Nisman is further indication of his novel's alignment with the government position vis-à-vis Alberto Nisman, and is comparable in its irresponsibility.

These issues lead to the question of the ethics of Pratt's narrative. Hiding behind a pseudonym to present defamatory portraits of easily recognizable public figures—including one who met an untimely, unsolved, and highly political death—represents an abdication of responsibility on the part of the writer to readers as well as to the real people affected by his novel. Real-life ethics are linked to narrative ethics and reader empathy: in her analysis of Truman Capote's story "La Côte Basque, 1965," Kelly A. Marsh emphasizes "the close relationship between empathy and ethical judgement in the reading process" (220), and presents a model of how we can understand the role of the narrative configuration in the generation of empathy.[24] The narrator of *El fiscal* presents both characters as unlikable at best, despicable at worst—Trusso for his selfish, evil machinations, and Lerman for his vanity and gullibility that cause him to fall prey to Trusso. But in addition to their characterization via their actions and reactions, the flat tone of the narrator, along with the fact that the narrator never enters their consciousness, blocks our empathy. Thus the reader is unable to empathize with the characters, even with the tragic figure representing Nisman, who, despite his alleged shortcomings, surely seems deserving of our empathy.

Finally, the roman à clef enables this author to set forth a speculative account of the intrigue within Argentina's intelligence agency and the Fernández de Kirchner government, and, with a big wink of the eye (I know that you know), inculpate certain individuals and exonerate others. Emplotting his story as spy fiction and pairing fictional characters with flesh-and-blood people, the author delivers a politicized and partisan version of the death of the special prosecutor while evading responsibility by coyly refusing to sign his real name. Ultimately, the novel resonates with the Argentine public's distrust of officialdom and their inclination to believe that a conspiracy is afoot by depicting skullduggery within the Argentine secret service. At the same time, it illustrates how geopolitical shifts can provoke domestic discord.

In conclusion, both novels explore tensions surrounding Argentina's struggle to define its place in a new global reality as they construct their versions of the tortuous, botched, and sabotaged investigation of the AMIA bombing and its ramifications. They mix fact with imagination and combine spy or conspiracy fiction with another genre to convey their distinct cultural dispositions toward Argentina's global connections. Aguinis's 2002 novel with its pro-Israeli stance takes for granted that the bombing was an extension of an ideological war exported from the Middle East and depicts it as such, reminding us that the US 9/11 was preceded by harrowing terrorist attacks in Buenos Aires that continue to elude justice. *El fiscal* explores the internal clash generated by Argentina's geopolitical shift when Fernández de Kirchner's government took a "left-turn," softening its stance toward suspected Iranian involvement in the AMIA strike. Depicting a tragic spin-off of the AMIA investigation—the mysterious death of special prosecutor Alberto Nisman—the spy novel subgenre and roman à clef function to emplot a pro–Fernández de Kirchner version of the circumstances behind his death. Whereas the emplotment of both novels promotes a specific political stance in respect to Argentine national and international politics, Aguinis takes responsibility for his depiction while "Pratt" evades it. Finally, these novels serve to confirm writer Jorge Fernández Díaz's observation that "la política argentina es una novela negra" (Argentine politics are a *novela negra*),[25] at the same time that they go beyond national politics and foray into thorny and complex international issues, reflecting Argentina's vexed role in a precarious global order.

Chapter Four

# TROUBLE IN THE COUNTRY CLUB, OR "LOS NUEVOS RICOS TAMBIÉN LLORAN"

> La conducta de los seres humanos se vuelve ilimitada cuando se pierden las bases éticas.
> —Mempo Giardinelli, "Mi libro refleja la corrupción absoluta del menemismo"

ON 27 OCTOBER 2002, MARÍA MARTA GARCÍA BELSUNCE MET HER DEATH IN the bathroom of her home in Carmel Country Club, one of the exclusive gated communities known as "countries" in the outskirts of Buenos Aires. García Belsunce's family members and doctor said she had suffered a domestic accident, held a wake, and interred her. But five weeks later a district attorney called for an autopsy: it revealed that she had five bullets in her head. The García Belsunce crime and its elaborate, yet flimsy, cover-up had a huge impact on the public imagination. Sociologist Maristella Svampa calls it "the event that most shook the 'tranquility' of the countries, revealing as few others the unthinkable limits of an elitist lifestyle where the illusion of absolute security tends to be perversely coupled with class impunity" (*La brecha urbana* 91). It immediately turned into a media sensation and became emblematic of things gone terribly wrong in the picture of bucolic bliss touted by promoters of the "countries." As such, it is a "true crime" reference for three *novelas negras* set in fictional "countries" and serves as a point of departure for this chapter.

Writer Raúl Argemí, appalled by the brazen conspiracy to cover up the murder, penned a novel inspired by the actual crime. *Retrato de familia con muerta* (2008) is a searing criticism of a society that has lost its moral compass. With its focus on the crime and its grotesque cover-up, the novel highlights the ironic contrast between the tranquil, paradisiacal lifestyle that the "country" purportedly offers its privileged residents, and the violent and shameless behavior to which they resort to preserve their status. Two of Claudia Piñeiro's novels—*Las viudas de los jueves* (2005) and *Betibú* (2011) (published in English as *Thursday Night Widows* and *Betty Boo*)—offer ironic portraits of crime and hypocrisy in the "countries." *Las viudas*, written before the García Belsunce crime occurred, eerily foreshadows it by portraying a sensational crime committed by insiders of a "country," and *Betibú* references a death with details resembling the García Belsunce crime as the trigger for a series of murders. All three focus on the psychology of the perpetrators of the crimes and take an ethical stance, casting a critical eye on certain aspects of life in the "country" and denouncing the sense of impunity that seems to be pervasive among certain social groups. The "country" or gated community, then, in these works becomes a venue to showcase and question the new modes of class differentiation brought about by the neoliberal economic model. My approach to the novels focuses on how the crime genre and the country club setting work together to present a critical portrait of contemporary society, in particular the new rich.

Both Raúl Argemí and Claudia Piñeiro are major figures in Argentine crime fiction. Argemí was involved in the Ejército Revolucionario del Pueblo (ERP), and during the dictatorship, he was incarcerated for ten years. Upon his release, he lived in Patagonia, the setting for several of his novels, and subsequently moved to Spain, where his literary career blossomed. Since 2013 he has resided in Buenos Aires. In addition to *Retrato de familia con muerta*, his *novelas negras* include *El gordo, el francés y el ratón Pérez* (1996), *Los muertos siempre pierden los zapatos* (2002), *Penúltimo nombre de guerra* (2004), *Siempre la misma música* (2006), and *A tumba abierta* (2015). *Penúltimo* is a psychological intrigue featuring a man who has been in a car accident and awakens from a coma with nearly total amnesia, knowing only his name and that he is a reporter. However, as he begins to recall his past, the reader becomes aware that he may be other than whom he believes himself to be. In *Siempre la misma música*, set in the years of the dictatorship, a small band of traffickers anticipates an easy run to the Chilean border with a shipment of drugs, but their situation is complicated when the military becomes involved. *A tumba abierta* is a thriller that deals with the recent history of Argentina through the story of a former leftist militant who, after years of exile in Spain, returns to his homeland in an effort to recover a large sum of illicit money. In these tales, Argemí paints a dark, unsettling, and sometimes bitter portrait of reality and the human condition.

Finding her work as an accountant boring and meaningless, Claudia Piñeiro asked for vacation time to write a novel for a contest in erotic literature. While her entry did not win, it placed among the ten finalists, and she experienced the power of writing, seeing it as her salvation (Núñez). Piñeiro did eventually land a big prize: *Las viudas de los jueves* won the 2005 Premio Clarín, garnering widespread readership and admiration for her work and bestowing her with best-seller status. Piñeiro's other *novelas negras*, besides *Betibú*, include *Tuya* (2005), *Elena sabe* (2007), *Las grietas de Jara* (2009), *Una suerte pequeña* (2015), and *Las maldiciones* (2017). *Tuya*, considered Piñeiro's debut, is a farce critiquing narrow and hypocritical middle-class bourgeois values. In *Elena sabe*, an elderly woman with Parkinson's disease refuses to accept the ruling that her daughter, who had served as her caretaker, committed suicide and sets out to prove the contrary. *Las grietas de Jara* has a gripping beginning: an architect buries an old man named Jara in the foundation of a building he is constructing. Years later, a young woman's unexpected appearance in his office threatens to expose this secret and shakes up his empty existence. In *Una suerte pequeña*, a mother abandons her son to spare him the opprobrium of living with her terrible mistake and lives in Boston with another identity. When a job assignment takes her back to her old Buenos Aires neighborhood and in contact with her son, she must confront her past. Finally, *Las maldiciones* is a suspenseful drama highlighting the perversity behind political ambitions. The success of Piñeiro's work lies in her precise prose and well-developed characters and her deep sensitivity to human relationships, penetrating and exposing the falsehoods and hypocrisy that sustain superficial lives.

## THE GATED COMMUNITY AS EMBLEMATIC OF THE NEOLIBERAL ERA

The setting of Argemí's and Piñeiro's novels in elite gated communities has both artistic and sociological significance. In *Scene of the Crime*, David Geherin addresses works in which location is woven into the very fabric of the novel, becoming essential to its artistic vision (3). This is clearly the case with the novels in question—their setting is fundamental to their development and their messages. While Geherin discusses novels that reference specific geographical locations—Paris, Edinburgh, Chicago, and so on—these novels are set in fictional gated neighborhoods based on the features of actual communities of this type in greater Buenos Aires.

From a generic viewpoint, the closed community recalls the hermetic environment of the country house mystery, an iconic subgenre of the golden age of detective fiction; from a socioeconomic perspective, the country club is the location of those who benefited from Argentina's recent neoliberal economic transformation. Various critics of detective fiction have studied the use and ideological implications of the country house or country estate mysteries. Scaggs tells us that *The Mysterious Affair at Styles* (1920) by Agatha Christie—a murder mystery set in a large, isolated country manor—"marked the transition from the Holmes story to the whodunit novel" and made the country house subgenre popular in the interwar period (52). "The country-house murder, which may incorporate within it the locked-room mystery, has important structural implications," he explains. "First, and most importantly, it limits the number of suspects to the guests, residents, and staff of the country house, or its substitute.... Secondly, it provides a restricted setting from which the various suspects cannot leave, and into which new suspects cannot enter ... creating the social equivalent of the hermetically sealed environment of the locked-room mystery" (52). He notes that this setting was reassuring for the interwar public, as it reduced the world to "self-contained, enclosed, manageable proportions and dimensions" (52). Priestman observes that a murder in the country house setting with its intertwined characters allows a picture of a single social group "to develop slowly and with satisfying completeness" (19). Critics invariably point to the conservative nature of Christie's plots—the crime is solved, the criminal is punished, and order is restored—as well as her conservative social vision. Horsley, however, comments on the disruptive class implications of this venue, observing that the exclusive setting and insular community "was the source of tensions, deceptions, betrayals, and death" (*Twentieth-Century Crime Fiction* 37). In Horsley's reading of these stories, the "'containment' of crime is double-edged"; she notes that while Christie's plots allow "reassuring closure," at the same time, they involve a class "preying on itself [that] contains the seeds of its own destruction" (40). Worthington adds to this sociological reading, pointing out that *The Mysterious Affair at Styles*, as well as *The Murder of Roger Ackroyd* (Christie, 1926), reveal "anxieties concerning social identity" (163).

In Argemí's and Piñeiro's novels, the gated community indeed functions as the locked room because the comings and goings of residents, visitors, and service providers are closely monitored. It also renders an in-depth portrait of the lifestyles and the anxieties of its residents. Unlike Christie's fiction, the affluent setting fails to be reassuring, and justice is but an illusion. And in both *Retrato* and *Las viudas*, this setting delivers a new twist:

because the privatized internal security is controlled by the residents—they hire, fire, and pay for the guards—it offers a scenario where individuals could conceivably commit crimes with impunity.

Considering the country club setting from a socioeconomic perspective, this venue makes patent material and cultural conflicts brought about by the economic and structural changes that took place during the 1990s in Argentina. A consequence of the implementation of the neoliberal model was to deepen socioeconomic inequalities, widening the gap between the "winners" who benefited from the plan and the "losers" who were excluded from the model. This exacerbation of social contrasts, asserts Svampa, constituted one of the most troubling aspects of Argentina in the 1990s (*La brecha urbana* 12); it was visible in modes of consumption, residential styles, and forms of socialization (*Los que ganaron* 15). According to Svampa, these changing lifestyles were accompanied by new beliefs and values such as personal success, individualism, the "logic of the winner," and the myth that Argentina was part of the First World, used to cement the confidence of the middle classes in ascent. Neoliberal discourse re-created social relations; the base of the " 'buena' sociedad" would not be secondary solidarity but rather free competition between individuals (*Los que ganaron* 15, 38). Argentina traditionally had had a mainstream middle class, Svampa points out, so the widening gap between rich and poor was a disturbing regressive trend, part of a tendency called the "Latin Americanization" of Argentina (*La sociedad excluyente* 23). Increasing poverty and cutbacks in state expenditures on security were linked to a rise in urban crime and violence, creating a sense of insecurity that fed a middle-class flight out of the city and a boom in gated communities and country clubs. Svampa considers the country club lifestyle, with its privatized security and social segregation, emblematic of neoliberal changes, a reflection of the frenetic pace of implantation of the model in Argentina (*Los que ganaron* 183).

These upper-class communities, which required huge areas of land, were constructed on the fringe of metropolitan Buenos Aires where slums and shantytowns are located. This resulted in the paradox "that gated communities create a strange mix of social distances, symbolised by walls and fences, and physical proximity between the richest and the poorest dwellers of the Metropolitan Area of Buenos Aires" (Thuillier 264). Thus the "presence of these islands of wealth amongst a sea of popular neighbourhoods creates frustration and envy and finally generates the insecurity and violence that gated communities were supposed to remove for their residents" (264).

Sarlo's *Instantáneas*—scenes of everyday life that she views from a critical perspective—capture the broken social contract and the loss of a sense of belonging to a society. The highway scene that she describes paints a vivid image of the interaction—or lack of such—of what she terms "the two nations": "At six o'clock in the afternoon, the cars head toward the country clubs in caravans; together they feel more protected from the violence of assaults. Close to the country clubs there are *villas miseria* and poor neighborhoods, which the caravan of cars passes by, almost without touching them. But it is impossible not to see them: pieces of sheet metal and cardboard that look like the material of a Berni painting" (90–91).[1] The only interaction between "the two nations" is mercantile. This is illustrated by a surrealistic scene composed of familiar objects made strange in their unexpected setting: "Under the highway, in the main corners, big yards sell swimming pools of synthetic material: blue and gigantic, they are stacked up against each other" (*Instantáneas* 92).

In her studies of the "countries" in the vicinity of Buenos Aires, Svampa presents two key characteristics: the value the residents give to the concepts of security and a "green" lifestyle, close to nature; and the intensification of the marking of class difference. Some residents whom her team interviewed portrayed the setting in idyllic terms, citing its peace and tranquility and the healthy lifestyle with the opportunity to exercise and play outdoors (*Los que ganaron* 88–89). Residents make an exhibition of security as a symbol of distinction, boasting that they do not lock their houses and can leave bicycles and other expensive paraphernalia unguarded (93–94). However, privatized security can lead to a feeling of impunity. As an example, an individual spoke to the contradiction posed by the fact that residents hire the people who regulate the community: a response to a speeding ticket can be "How can you slap a fine on me if in reality you are my employee?" (185). One of the risks of these self-regulated microcities is that accountability can be shifted to the internal authorities, and, as another resident pointed out: "the manager [of the country] is my slave.... I can fire him" (189).

The social homogeneity within the closed communities can create prejudice toward difference, both internal, in the form of the employees of the "countries," and external, the "poor" people who live outside the walls. Svampa notes that within the "countries" all employees are required to wear uniforms. This makes visible the mercantile character of the social relationship and establishes an explicit hierarchy of roles and positions, controlling the difference and separating equals (the residents) from the "others" (the employees) (*Los que ganaron* 216). The location of "countries" in pockets of poverty increases the visibility of social distances, and residents tend to evoke those who live in the surrounding area as " 'los pobres,' as if they were a different entity, not a human being" (222). "Los pobres" can take on one of two different images: honest, hard-working people and, as such, objects of compassion; or the violent poor. In the second case, the fear of dangerous surroundings generates a mindset of anxiety and insecurity accompanied by a binary code of security within and insecurity without the walls of the "country" (228), and this fear often triumphs over equality in treatment of the other. In sum, Svampa's research serves to highlight problematic and discriminatory aspects of the "utopic" country club lifestyle, and these issues are vividly portrayed in the crime novels under study.

## DISINTEGRATION OF FAMILY TIES: *RETRATO DE FAMILIA CON MUERTA* BY RAÚL ARGEMÍ

*Retrato de familia con muerta*, as it spins a fictional re-creation of a true crime, examines pressing social problems plaguing contemporary Argentina. It critiques the effects of the neoliberal economic reform—the polarization of social classes coupled with a growing sense of insecurity—that fed the boom in popularity of the "countries." In particular, it points to the weakening of traditional values and institutions, indicting the shameless behavior of the nouveau riche who made money through illicit dealings. While continuing to reap benefits from their alliance with the former dictatorship, they are winners in the new social order. Argemí is particularly outraged by the sense of impunity and lack of basic human decency of those involved in the cover-up of the García Belsunce murder.

### The Infamous García Belsunce Case

Revisiting the scene of the crime, it is no surprise that Argemí was inspired by the García Belsunce case to create his novel. When the story of the findings of the autopsy broke on 12 December 2002, the headlines were sensational: "Dijeron que murió en un accidente doméstico, pero la mataron a tiros" (They said that she died in a domestic accident, but they shot her to death), announced *Clarín*, one of Argentina's leading dailies. The victim, María Marta García Belsunce, came from a prominent family and was a sociologist who worked with a foundation for missing children. An element of added prurient curiosity was the fact that the crime showcased the miseries of the rich: the murder took place in an exclusive and highly guarded gated community. The husband claimed that he had been watching a River-Boca soccer match at his brother-in-law's house and returned home to find his wife with her head submerged in a bathtub full of water. Surely she had tripped and hit her head on the tub faucets, family members insisted. Two doctors agreed that she had fractured her skull and had lost brain matter. A wake was held in the home and María Marta was interred the day after her death, on 28 October. However, in early December, upon request of the district attorney, the body was removed from the crypt and autopsied. María Marta had been shot six times with a .32 caliber revolver—five bullets were in her head, and the sixth grazed it ("Dijeron que murió"). An investigation of the house revealed that the victim had been attacked on the first floor and killed in the upstairs bathroom. Blood stains throughout the house had been cleaned. Since security had not been breached, the perpetrator had to have been someone who lived in the country or had access to it ("Cronología de la investigacion").

The investigation into the murder and cover-up was an ongoing media event. Reportedly one of the most intricate cases in the history of Argentine law, it was bogged down in challenges and appeals, and the judges were accused of complicity with the defendants (Barbano, "A dos años," "Carrascosa"). María Marta's husband, Carlos Carrascosa, who initiated the hypothesis of an accidental death, was arrested in March 2003 for homicide and put under house arrest. After a tortuous series of appeals and other legal maneuvers, in June 2009 he was sentenced to life imprisonment for homicide.[2] However, in December 2016 the court absolved Carrascosa of the crime due to a lack of proof to maintain the sentence ("Caso Belsunce: Absolvieron").

Relatives, friends, employees, and first responders were all implicated in the cover-up. The brother-in-law of the victim obtained a false death certificate, and a brother and stepbrother were accused of tampering with the evidence. Two doctors—one who endorsed the theory of accidental death, overlooking the five bullet holes in the victim's skull, and another who signed the death certificate—were charged, along with nine employees of the funeral home. Also named were the victim's masseuse, who cleaned up the blood; a neighbor who instructed the community president to bribe the police to keep them from entering; and a female friend who prevented an autopsy.[3]

Sentences for cover-up were finally handed down in September 2011, eight years and eleven months after the murder had been committed. Ultimately, only five individuals were found guilty and given prison sentences ranging from four and a half to six years for cover-up.⁴ But this was not the end of the case. Two months later the five individuals found guilty of participation in the cover-up were freed on bail and their lawyers initiated appeals for their sentences to be reverted ("Caso Belsunce: Los condenados"). In October 2015, the lower court confirmed the sentences of three of the defendants—who remained at liberty while awaiting the decision of the Bonaerense Supreme Court—revoked the sentence of a fourth, and dropped proceedings against one who died (Carabajal).⁵

Officially, the motive of the crime remains an enigma. A theory reported by the media in 2007 was based on the family's alleged involvement in a drug trafficking ring. A district attorney received an anonymous note connecting the crime to an argument about drug money laundering for the Juárez Cartel, suggesting that they investigate if there was a family pact of silence out of fear of the cartel (Sassone y Messi). Cecilia González, in her study of Mexican narcotrafficking in Argentina, also cites an argument over the handling of money belonging to the Juárez Cartel as the motive for María Marta's death. According to journalistic sources, the money laundering hypothesis was later dropped by investigators due to lack of evidence,⁶ while Cecilia González says that it was not thoroughly investigated by the judge because it involved other federal cases that were underway and because it was not necessary to establish a motive (105). In 2015 a new criminalistic study was released that pointed to two possible suspects/explanations: an unstable former neighbor or a murder-for-hire by the husband ("Caso García Belsunce: Un nuevo informe"). Then May 2018 ushered in a promising new development: thanks to technological advances, new DNA was found at the crime scene and suspects were brought in to extract their blood for analysis (Balonga).⁷ As of this writing no new arrests have been made, but a solution may be imminent for this crime that has captivated the Argentine public for nearly sixteen years.

### "Policial palimpséstico": Framing the Crime Scene

It is important to clarify that while it deals with a real crime, Argemí's novel does not belong to the true crime genre. Rather than reconstructing the crime in a nonfictional novel à la Truman Capote, Argemí created a fiction based on an imaginative reconstruction of selected aspects of the actual event. *Retrato* corresponds, then, to the literary modality termed *"policial palimpséstico"* by Osvaldo Di Paolo, who uses this designation to describe narratives and television series inspired by real-life events. Drawing from Gérard Genette's *Palimpsests*, Di Paolo examines the relationships uniting a text B, what Genette calls the hypertext, with an earlier text A, termed the hypotext. In his insightful study of the *policial palimpséstico* in Argentina, Di Paolo sustains that in the interstice—or the hypertextual process—between the journalistic article and the literary text, "the creative process of the author is developed . . . in which the events are modified, incorporating economic and sociopolitical problems of corruption and violence, as well as crucial historic factors, to produce a literature of social denunciation" (*Cadáveres en el armario* 20–21). This is the process that occurs in Argemí's novel. Of all the novels included in this book, *Retrato* has the strongest reference to a single, preexisting real crime and its spins-offs, thus the hypertextualization—the techniques used to transfigure the hypotext and deliver the hypertext's sociopolitical critique—is a key process. The referentiality is strong even for non-Argentine readers because hundreds of stories about the García Belsunce crime can be found on a myriad of news portals. Employing narrativization and the points of view of various individuals, the novelistic format serves to dramatize these events, crafting a story that conveys a unified impression and is contained within a single volume instead of hundreds or thousands of news stories and judicial transcripts.

To tell the tale of crime and cover-up in the "country," Argemí creates a frame story and a fictional narrator who will tell his own version of events: Juan Manuel Galván, a circuit court judge who becomes obsessed with the dead woman and wants to discover who she was and why she was murdered. Juan Manuel's account of his fixation with the dead woman, his appropriation of confidential information, his speculations, and his writing process comprise this frame story. Thus the story of the crime and cover-up constitutes a story within a story. The first word of the novel's title—*Retrato*—reinforces the framing, offering an image of spatial surround. While the *frame* story is entirely fictive, as we know, the *framed* story, although highly imaginative, derives from actual events. Paradoxically, then, the framed story, while positioned at a greater remove from the reader, is less distanced from reality than its frame.

The novel opens and closes with the frame story, and the intervening chapters alternate unevenly between the story of Juan Manuel's composition of his text and this text itself. The conspicuous framing created by the constant back and forth between Juan Manuel's world and the world of the crime reminds us that this story is a product of his elaboration. Juan Manuel gives his subjective interpretation of judicial transcripts, allowing himself to judge the individuals and speculate when facts are absent. In the frame story, Juan Manuel is a homodiegetic narrator—he speaks in first person and is present in this story as its protagonist. In the framed story, Juan Manuel is a heterodiegetic narrator; using the third person and inventing the characters' thoughts, feelings, and words, he tells a story that he is absent from. However, the boundary between the frame and the framed story is porous, as Juan Manuel's voice, in the first person, occasionally enters the framed sections to comment on the characters' behavior, the social setting, and other matters. The framing procedure helps illustrate how Juan Manuel—as Argemí's alter ego—turns "raw" objective documents into a parable, or a morality story of sorts.

In order to access classified information about the case, Juan Manuel gets in touch with a childhood friend, Jorge Gustavo Ritter Pueyrredón, an ex-military man who uses his connections to provide him with "stolen" records from judicial and police archives. Ritter serves as Juan Manuel's interlocutor and as a second homodiegetic narrator. He too is a character in the frame story and reads Juan Manuel's speculative re-creation of events, becoming alarmed by its increasing fabrication.

For the reader who is unfamiliar with the García Belsunce crime, the novel can be read as entirely fictional. However, at the end of the novel, Argemí provides what he calls an "Aclaración necesaria" (Necessary clarification) in which he explains its genesis: "El origen de esta novela fue un caso real, sucedido en Argentina, que me llamó la atención por la brutalidad y la falta de pudor con que se quiso encubrir un asesinato.... Un par de años después, un 'pajarito' me envió gran cantidad de información de primera mano" (This novel originated in a real case that occurred in Argentina, which caught my attention due to the brutality and brazenness with which they tried to cover up a murder.... A couple of years later, a "little bird" sent me a lot of firsthand information) (201). This "Aclaración necesaria" throws the preceding text into a different register when the real-life author clarifies for readers that this novel originated in a true story. The "Aclaración" creates yet another frame that encompasses Juan Manuel's story, producing a mise en abyme effect: Juan Manuel and his "archivos robados" mirror Raúl Argemí and his material from the "pajarito." At the same time, Juan Manuel's script mediates between Argemí and his material from the "pajarito," transforming the story that is told into Juan Manuel's version, and *not* Argemí's version, of events.

Interestingly, Argemí's denomination "Aclaración *necesaria*" (emphasis added) deems this note is not merely a curious anecdote but rather the author considers it indispensable—his readers *need to know* that there is a real-life reference. In an interview, Argemí elaborates on his reaction to the crime, explaining his motivation for writing the novel.

> I was visiting Argentina when this [the real crime that inspired the novel] came to light, and what was evident was the impunity, and the poker face of those who were involved. They exuded certainty that nothing would happen to them. A couple of years later I was able to access judicial information, and everything they did with that corpse made my stomach turn. Compared to the simple and pure murder, that was a filthy circus. So my priority, my interest was focused on the staging, on the macabre game of concealment. (Stallard)[8]

Thus Argemí, like his detective-narrator, was outraged by the shameless behavior of the defendants. Juan Manuel serves as a construct to express Argemí's consternation with the crime as well as the society that spawned it. It is Juan Manuel's commentary about the case's actors and setting, as well as his ultimate failure to bring about justice, that will deliver the social critique.

Argemí's plot—or Juan Manuel's story—seeks to explore what he considers the fundamental unanswered questions of the case: "¿Por qué su marido, su hermano y todos sus amigos se complotaron para ocultar su asesinato? ¿Por qué todos, absolutamente todos, se comportaron como culpables? ¿A quién estaban protegiendo? ¿Quién era la muerta para merecerse el odio de los 'inocentes'?" (Why did her husband, her brother and all her friends plot to hide her murder? Why did everyone, absolutely everyone, behave like they were guilty? Who were they protecting? Who was the dead woman to deserve the hatred of the "innocent ones"?) (102). Juan Manuel's framed story fills in the blanks to resolve enigmas surrounding the true crime, including the motive and the murderer. In this way, Juan Manuel carries out the detective function. He is described as a misfit of sorts—we learn of his loveless marriage as well as a birth defect that causes intermittent paralysis of his left side and affects his speech. In this sense, he conforms to the classic portrayal of the detective figure as a socially marginal or malcontent outsider. Since Juan Manuel is a judge, we could expect him to treat the material impartially and objectively, but, to the contrary, he is highly subjective and opinionated as he evaluates the individuals based on his gut feelings about them. His intense emotional connection to the scenes he narrates—he decides that he is in love with the dead woman—heightens the drama.

In the framed story, Juan Manuel presents the cast of characters: the victim and those involved in the cover-up, whom he ironically calls "Los inocentes" (The innocent ones). Through his narrativization, these individuals come to life as the characters speak for themselves and we read their thoughts and see events through their eyes. The characters in the framed story are imaginative and renamed versions of real individuals: "Arturo *Oso* Ferrasanes, el marido de la muerta. Abel *Lito* Pérez García, el hermano. Susana Lucrecia *Susy* Hornos, la masajista de la muerta. Graciela *Chiquita* de Cooningan, la amiga. Ernesto Bonanova, amigo del Oso" (Arturo *Oso* Ferrasanes, the husband of the dead woman. Abel *Lito* Pérez García, the brother. Susana Lucrecia *Susy* Hornos, the masseuse of the dead woman. Graciela *Chiquita* de Cooningan, the friend. Ernesto Bonanova, friend of Oso). "Todas las manos en la misma mierda" (Everyone's hands in the same shit) (15), comments Juan Manuel—all are linked by their complicity and collective guilt. First responders and others who stumble onto the scene will also become accomplices to the cover-up—for instance, the family doctor and the undertaker. And we meet the dead woman: "Y la muerta, la mayor de los Pérez García... tirada en el suelo, a medias en el baño" (And the dead woman, the oldest of the Pérez Garcías... lying on the floor, halfway in the bathroom) (15). Juan Manuel never mentions a first name and always refers to her only as "la muerta," even when he references her activities prior to her death. This becomes a source of dark humor and a prefiguration of her imminent death, for instance, when he comments that two neighborhood boys saw the dead woman go by on her bicycle (99).

## A Crime Sparked and Fed by Drug Money

As mentioned above, authorities have failed to clarify publicly the reason for María Marta's murder, but Juan Manuel's fictional re-creation depicts it as the result of an argument over laundered drug money. This motive, corroborated by various sources, serves to develop the critique of a corrupt, newly rich social class. In Juan Manuel's tale, illicit money and lots of it triggers the crime and fuels the cover-up. The centrality of the material motive and the complex relationship between money and the law in *Retrato* and other "neoliberal noir" novels make them clear inheritors of hard-boiled novels such as Dashiell Hammett's *Red Harvest*, which Piglia calls "novelas capitalistas" (*Crítica y ficción* 70). In this case, the "dinero negro" is supplied by international drug trafficking: the Tijuana Cartel is laundering money in Argentina, and one of the neighbors, El Inglés Coonigan, husband of Chiquita, has recruited his friends, including *la muerta* and her brother and husband, to open accounts to move Mexican money. Juan Manuel remarks, "[Había] mucho dinero para quien podía poner la cara y justificar algunas sumas importantes.... El dinero de los mexicanos era inagotable" (There was a lot of money for those who had the nerve and could justify important sums.... The money of the Mexicans was inexhaustible) (132–33).

When an account disappears, the soon-to-be *muerta* is suspected, and the trouble begins. Juan Manuel speculates as to *la muerta*'s "fatal flaw"— apparently she is not a "player": "Abel *Lito* Pérez García siempre lo supo, su hermana los iba a meter en problemas" (Abel *Lito* Pérez García always knew that his sister would get them into trouble), referring to her "veta idiota ... a veces moralista" (idiotic, sometimes moralistic vein) (16). It is indicative of his corrupted value system that in the brother's thinking, "moralista" is equated to "idiota." We learn that the dead woman had founded a charity for poor children and Juan Manuel speculates that she diverted funds from the Tijuana Cartel to this charity: "Tal vez era cierto que estaba un poco loca" (Maybe it was true that she was a little bit crazy) (131). Here, "craziness" in Juan Manuel's mind refers to the fact that she is not mindful of the consequences of stealing money belonging to the drug cartel. Juan Manuel imagines how the murder could have occurred. Trying to make her understand that she cannot mess with these individuals or they will all get killed, her husband, Oso Ferrasanes, fires a gun in her direction, accidently grazing her head. She becomes furious and threatens to go to the police, so he is forced to continue shooting to finish her off.

Juan Manuel stresses the brazenness of the accomplices: despite the fact that *la muerta* has numerous bullet-entry holes in her head and is lying in a huge pool of blood, they maintain that she tripped in the bathroom and hit her head on the tub. Dirty money provides the means of the ensuing crude cover-up. Susy, the masseuse, is the first outsider to arrive on the scene. Oso buys her silence at the same time that he threatens her: "Acá se juega más plata de la que te imaginás. Y los dueños de la plata no joden, ¿me entendés? Vos elegís: o mucha plata o te hacen matar" (Here more dough is in play than you can imagine. And the owners of the dough don't screw around, understand? You choose: either a lot of dough or they get you killed) (17). After Susy insists on payment in cash, Oso calls an associate to get ahold of more money because "hay que untar a mucha gente" (we need to grease many palms) (18). Two other key conspirators who are bribed are the "médico ciego" (blind doctor) who later claimed that he did not notice anything was awry because he was blinded by his concern for the family's pain, and the funeral director. Juan Manuel seethes with disgust for the so-called blind doctor, deciding that the most apt word to describe him is *cretino*: "Me gusta la palabra 'cretino,' señala tanto al idiota congénito como al hijo de puta que actúa con un desconocimiento tal de las normas de la decencia que parece ignorarlas de nacimiento" (I like the word "cretin," because it indicates both the congenital idiot and the son of a bitch who acts with such ignorance of the rules of decency that he seems to be unaware of them since birth) (37). The lack of "decencia" becomes a basic criterion for Juan Manuel's censure of those involved in the cover-up. While the funeral director realizes this was not a natural death, Juan Manuel describes his cooperation in the following terms, underlining the material motivation: "Estoy seguro, cuando el funebrero entra en escenarios como Los Reyunos [the fictional name of the 'country' where the crime took place], un sitio donde el poder del dinero cambia hasta el color del aire, ve menos que nunca" (I'm sure that when the undertaker enters scenarios like Los Reyunos, a place where the power of money can change even the color of the air, he sees less than ever) (150). The corrupted values are echoed when Juan Manuel focalizes the thoughts of Chiquita—a friend of *la muerta* turned conspirator—who represents the epitome of unmitigated greed: "*Chiquita* . . . no está dispuesta a perder nada de lo que ha conseguido. Nada. Y menos por los errores de una idiota muerta" (Chiquita . . . is not willing to lose anything of what she has attained. Nothing. And much less for the mistakes of a dead idiot) (16). The crime is eventually brought to light by two professionals whom Juan Manuel suspects are decent individuals. "Y de golpe apareció un Serpico" (Suddenly a Serpico appeared) (57), he tells us, using the name of the New York City whistle-blowing policeman to describe the district attorney who goes against the family's wishes and calls for an investigation. The other individual who tells the truth is the paramedic, whose declaration before the judge points to a homicide rather than an accident—he states that there is clear evidence of a violent death. The actions of these two individuals in denouncing the crime and cover-up serve as examples of ethical behavior, which is juxtaposed to the behavior of the "indecent" or shameless people that Argemí—through his fictive narrator—indicts.

## Undressing the Dead Woman

"Desnudarse y morir" is the title of an article by Glen Close as well as a paperback he analyzes. In his study, Close critiques misogynistic portrayals of shapely female corpses and then discusses novels that offer a more sensitive treatment of the dead gendered body. Argemí's novel belongs to the second group. The treatment of the dead woman is an example of how the hypertext expands and imaginatively elaborates on selected details, providing a social critique. In this case, it reflects the author's compassion for the female victim, who was treated callously after her death, and for whom there would be no justice. Juan Manuel provides a detailed portrayal of the undignified way in which her corpse is handled as the conspirators attempt to hide the traces of her violent death. He also creates a female chorus to represent the absent woman. Envisioning a group of men devouring a woman's body, Juan Manuel emphasizes gender issues related to the fact that the victim is a woman and the staging of her death is being carried out largely by men. In a section titled "Ella: La vejación" (She: The vexation), he imagines the men removing the bloody clothing from the corpse with a scissors. His description emphasizes the men's clumsy manipulation of the scissors and their discomfort with the entire operation, especially when the removal of the jogging outfit she was wearing reveals her pink underwear and they have to confront her subjectivity in the form of her coquettish sexuality. Shorn of her asexual sporting attire, the woman's body suddenly becomes sexualized, embarrassing the men who knew her as neighbor or sister.[9] El Inglés Coonigan, upon viewing the results of their work, makes a crude attempt at locker-room humor: "—La pusieron en pelotas. No se los puede dejar solos a ustedes, son terribles—" (You got her naked. You guys can't be left alone, you're terrible) (194). His ill-conceived joke is met with silence, another indication of their awkwardness in the presence of the unclothed female corpse.

Reinforcing and critiquing the stereotypical male perspective, Juan Manuel transmits the thoughts of the male stagers as they blame the female victim for putting them in this situation: "De odiar la cosa, ese sucio pedazo de carne sobre la cama, que los obliga a verse como carniceros; a ellos, los inocentes, los que nunca quisieron matar a nadie" (To hate the thing, that dirty piece of meat on the bed, which forces them to see themselves as butchers; they, the innocent ones, who never wanted to kill anyone) (187). The comparison of the woman's cadaver to dead meat effectively dehumanizes her. Chiquita Coonigan's reaction provides a foil to the men's callous transference of their guilt. Called upon to apply makeup to the dead woman, she has a moment of tenderness when she identifies with and sympathizes with her friend: "*Chiquita* Coonigan ve la ropa rota, el ingenuo color de rosa, y siente aún más pena. Se siente manoseada por esa piara de cerdos. Como manosearon a la muerta.... Chiquita se inclina sobre la muerta, tan indefensa, tan vulnerable, como si hubiera sido violada" (*Chiquita* Coonigan sees the torn clothing, the naïve pink, and feels even more sorrow. She feels groped by that herd of pigs. Like they fondled the dead woman.... Chiquita bends over the dead woman, so helpless, so vulnerable, as if she had been raped) (194–95). Thus the revictimization of the dead woman through the crass treatment of her body is perceived by her female friend as a rape. By calling attention to the abusive and insensitive treatment of the corpse, Argemí, through his narrator, constructs a space of resistance to the male control of the female victim.

Acutely aware of *la muerta*'s lack of a voice, Juan Manuel conjures up a set of female voices: the Euménides or Furies, who serve as advocates for the dead woman. In an interview, Argemí comments that he created this chorus to provide a female perspective on the event and the victim: "Suddenly I needed another voice, another register that would tell the tale with a different depth, that would voice their opinion, and the chorus of the Euménides appeared. Fierce, intransigent, these goddesses (women) gave me the thrust of anger that the story needed, and that no other character could give me" (Stallard). The final time that the chorus appears—to witness the disrobing and staging of the body—*la muerta* joins them to express her indignation with the way she is being treated. At the end of the section, the chorus remarks about the rictus on the corpse's face, which they imagine to be a smile as she thinks of her revenge. Thus the creation of the Euménides, as well as the voice given to the silenced woman, provide a heightened sensitivity to gender issues. This female chorus enables the author to articulate female subjectivity that would otherwise be suppressed by stereotypical male control of a female victim.

The corpse plays a symbolic role—it is "written on" with the marks of its manipulation by "los inocentes," conveying the message of their duplicity. As an object, it works to bind these individuals together through their shared sense of guilt, constituting them as a group of suspects and symbolizing a corrupt society.

A False Paradise

Juan Manuel focuses on the setting in the exclusive gated community as a determining factor in the course of events. His emphasis on the "country's" bucolic nature and open-air sports installations that promise a healthy lifestyle stands in stark contrast to the heinous crime and sordid cover-up. Introducing los Reyunos, in a section titled "Vivir al sol (Bucólicos paisajes)" (Living in the sun [Bucolic landscapes]), he highlights its illusion of tranquility and innocence.

> Hay mucho, mucho verde. Verde y silencio. Lo último es una regla de oro. Para eso los chalés están suficientemente separados unos de otros por unos cuantos metros y por barreras de arbustos altos ... que protegen la intimidad, al tiempo que mantienen la ilusión de que no hay nada que ocultar. (12)
>
> [There is lot of green. Green and silence. The latter is a golden rule. For that reason the houses are separated by several meters and by barriers of tall bushes ... that protect privacy, while maintaining the illusion that there is nothing to hide.]

His description also underscores the community's elaborate security system: "una alambrada, alta, con puestos de vigilancia ... como los castillos medievales, un solo pórtico de entrada. Como los castillos: barrera y guardia armada" (a high wire fence with guard posts ... like the medieval castles, a single entrance portico. Like the castles: a barrier and armed guard) (13). Ironically, while this gothic fortress protects them from danger from without, the murderer is among them, in the heart of the family.

Juan Manuel stresses the setting's key role in the initial success of the flimsy cover-up: "El sitio donde se produjo el asesinato puede intimidar a cualquiera, incluyendo a la policía y a los jueces," he notes. "Los Reyunos es un 'barrio cerrado,' y los barrios cerrados, los 'country' o como quieran llamarse, son geografías donde se puede jugar con reglas propias" (The site where the murder took place can intimidate anyone, including the police and the judges.... Los Reyunos is a "gated community," and the gated communities, the "countries" or whatever you want to call them, are places where you can play with your own rules) (32). Once the cover-up is revealed, however, the tables are turned as this setting becomes a liability for the perpetrators—the fortification makes it unfeasible to blame the crime on an outsider, drastically limiting the pool of suspects.

The venue of the crime gives Juan Manuel occasion to make one of several generic winks in his telling of the story. As Hutcheon points out, the detective genre is a highly self-conscious form, and frequently includes intertextual references that create a metatextual level, calling attention to its artifice (*Narcissistic Narrative* 71–76). In reference to the servants cleaning up the blood spilled by *la muerta*, Juan Manuel comments, "En conjunto harían un maravilloso puñado de culpables, si la vida fuera una novela de Agatha Christie. Pero la vida y Agatha Christie nunca tuvieron mucho que ver. Un montón de años de trabajo en el poder judicial me lo han demostrado hasta el aburrimiento" (Together they would make a wonderful bunch of suspects, if life were a novel by Agatha Christie. But life and Agatha Christie never had much to do with each other. Many years of work in the judiciary have shown me that to the point of boredom) (169). The upper-middle-class "country" scenario with its restricted pool of suspects brings to mind the classic works of the grand dame of the golden age of the detective novel. But Juan Manuel's comment highlights the unreality of the golden age puzzle-type plots in which the case is always solved after the detective successfully assembles the puzzle pieces and punishment is vetted out for the guilty parties, serving justice and reestablishing order. Argemí also incorporates a nod to Poe and the closed room mystery in "Aclaración necesaria" where he refers to the crime as "Algo que sucedió entre vallas de seguridad, como si fuera un homenaje a los misterios de 'cuarto cerrado,' que tanto gustaban a Edgar Allan Poe" (Something that happened within secure walls, as if it were a tribute to the "closed room" mysteries that Edgar Allan Poe liked so much) (201). While, as Argemí points out, the crime's setting can be compared to the closed room motif of Poe's "The Murders in the Rue Morgue," one might observe that the novel also has resonance with "The Mystery of Marie Rogêt" insofar as it follows the essence of an actual case and the focal point is a female corpse with marks of violence.[10] Finally, we recall that the honest DA who ordered an autopsy is called "un Serpico," referencing police procedurals. These nods to classic detective stories and the police procedural serve to draw attention to *Retrato*'s intractable dissimilarity with them and its status as a *novela negra*, dramatizing social problems but offering no justice or solution.

Juan Manuel also utilizes the country club setting to illustrate the material and cultural conflicts: the widened gap between rich and poor that has crystallized the polarization of social classes, and the sensation of increased violence and insecurity. Juan Manuel's commentary explicitly connects the boom in popularity of the gated communities to recent economic policies.

> La transformación económica de Argentina ... cerró fuentes de trabajo, y empobreció vertiginosamente a la clase media.... Muy pocos se hicieron ricos, y el resto a lamer el plato vacío. Entonces se multiplicaron los robos y el fantasma de la inseguridad se hizo dueño del imaginario

colectivo.... Los country son un hijo de ese casamiento entre el miedo, el dinero fácil y la corrupción de todas clases. (129)

[The economic transformation of Argentina ... closed sources of work, and drastically impoverished the middle class.... Very few became rich, and the rest were left to lick the empty plate. Then the robberies multiplied and the specter of insecurity took hold of the collective imagination.... The countries are a product of that marriage between fear, easy money and all kinds of corruption.]

The counterpart to the "countries" are the *villas miseria*, which have a complementary relationship with them, providing labor, services, and goods for the dwellers of the gated communities. Juan Manuel describes the resentment that *villeros* feel toward the inhabitants of the country: "Los otros viven fuera de las alambradas, y es fácil saber que se alimentan del country y el rencor" (The others live outside the wire fences and it is obvious that they feed on the country and their rancor) (130). While the privileged lifestyle of the inhabitants of Los Reyunos depends on the *villeros*, they live in fear that one day their impoverished neighbors will take over the "country" by storm. According to Juan Manuel, the social divide is extreme—the workers waiting to enter cast looks of hatred at the privileged country dwellers as they exit: "¿Sabés cómo miran a los que salen en coche? Para tu suerte la lucha de clases se fue al carajo, si no, ahí tenías una revolución con mucha guillotina" (Do you know how they look at those who leave in cars? Lucky for you that the class struggle went to hell, if not, you'd have a revolution with a lot of guillotine) (157). Ironically, in this case, the violence done to a "country" resident will not come from the feared "other" but from the rotten bosom of the community.

An underlying cause of social decay, according to Juan Manuel's rendering of events, is the lingering effect of Argentina's brutal dictatorship, which disseminated a mentality of abuse of authority and impunity. In his portrait, both *la muerta*'s brother and her husband are connected to the former dictatorship, and their shady past provides a network of lucrative ties: "Se dice que [Lito, the dead woman's brother] estuvo íntimamente relacionado con los grupos de tareas de la dictadura de Videla, o con los servicios, los amigos que le dieron puerta a ganar dinero con mucha mugre" (They say that [Lito] was intimately connected with the task forces of the Videla dictatorship, or with the services, friends who gave him access to make a lot of dirty money) (20).[11] Thus the brother's illicit riches have their origins in his role in the sinister death squads.

Concluding his frame story, Juan Manuel, a pathetic detective, admits his failure: "No me queda nada, ni siquiera la arrogancia. Lo único que he conseguido es algo así como un retrato de familia en torno a un muerto" (I have nothing left, not even arrogance. The only thing I have achieved is something like a family portrait around a dead person) (198). His reference to the family portrait around a dead person, reiterating the novel's ironic title, drives home a pithy message. A family portrait conjures up an image of cozy family unity, but this family generates treachery instead of protection when it destroys one of its members and blocks justice.

Thus in the creative interstice between the journalistic accounts of the enigmatic García Belsunce case and the literary work, Argemí fixes on a motive and fleshes out the actions of those involved in the crime.[12] But while the framed story can be considered a moral parable of the grotesque consequences of the lust for money, what about the ethical consideration in regard to fictionalizing an unsolved crime, speculating on it, and assigning guilt? Can we excuse this speculation by considering it a minor concession in behalf of a larger ethical project? In *Betibú*, the third novel I examine in this chapter, Piñeiro's protagonist refuses to speculate on a crime that is unsolved—this very crime!—saying that she considers it unethical because her readers could be confused. Yet this is precisely what Argemí's character does. At the same time, the narrative structure offers mitigating factors; for instance, the creator of the imaginary scenario is not Argemí himself but his fictive narrator. What is more, Ritter voices another hypothesis—that the murderer could have been any of the associates in the money laundering scheme—and proceeds to delete Juan Manuel's entire file, thus figuratively canceling his imaginative reconstruction of the crime. Nevertheless, the trace has been etched in our brains, and the novel's portrayal of the husband as the assassin remains problematic from an ethical standpoint.

Ultimately, Argemí's transformation of a news story into a gripping novel about corrupt rich people and their bold crime in the "country" serves to denounce problems faced by contemporary Argentine society. Juan Manuel provides a running critique of what he perceives as the causes of social decay and corruption of values, circumstances that laid the ground for the crime and cover-up. What seems to concern Argemí's narrator most of all is the weakening of the social fabric, resulting in a breakdown in traditional values: a crisis in the family and a loss of basic human decency. The novel dramatically depicts Sarlo's observation: "The crisis of the legitimacy of all authorities, which affects schools and families, has a particularly intense impact where the social fabric has already weakened" ("Violencia en las ciudades" 210). While not a "true crime" novel in a strict sense, *Retrato* possesses what Laura Browder identifies as a trait of the subgenre insofar as it can be considered "a form of social history" (123). Similar to Truman Capote's *In Cold Blood*, which laid bare the unspoken fears among the members of a community (Browder 121), *Retrato de familia con muerta* reveals the disintegration of ties of family, friendship, and community when they are overpowered by an eagerness to grab fistful after fistful of dirty money.

## THE HIGH COST OF KEEPING UP APPEARANCES: *LAS VIUDAS DE LOS JUEVES* BY CLAUDIA PIÑEIRO

*Las viudas de los jueves* by Claudia Piñeiro, like Argemí's tale, reveals the ugly reality beneath the surface of what appears to be the perfect life in a paradisiacal setting, a fictional "country" with the pretentious name of Los Altos de la Cascada. Set in the 1990s, it reflects the precipitous rise followed by the sharp fall of Argentina's economy, with a focus on the impact of the economic downturn on the members of this elite community—specifically the anxiety they experience about maintaining their lifestyle. By means of running references to political and economic directives, Piñeiro's novel points to the policies of the Menem administration as the driver of the socioeconomic roller coaster that Argentina experienced. In unadorned and concise prose with flashes of dark humor, the novel uses multiple voices and temporal perspectives to depict the ambitions and terrors of the country club residents in the context of the happenings of the 1990s.

While *Las viudas* is not a traditional detective novel—there is no detective figure and no investigation—it clearly is a crime novel as it opens with the unexplained deaths of three men in a swimming pool. In the final chapters we discover that their deaths, made to look like accidental electrocution, were in reality intentional, carried out to enable their families to continue the elite lifestyle with insurance money. The intervening chapters develop a portrait of a society of consumers in which the members' worth is based on their ability to consume, a society that led one of its members to an unimaginable extreme in his attempt to maintain that lifestyle. The swimming pool deaths are the organizational axis of the novel: the fact that we already know that three neighbors will meet an unnatural death lends the story of their lives in the "country" an aura of impending doom.

## Noir as a Reaction to Consumer Culture

In *America Is Elsewhere: The Noir Tradition in the Age of Consumer Culture*, Erik Dussere perceives in the heart of American noir a crisis of national identity and authenticity due to the rise of consumer culture. His study focuses on noir as a response to that phenomenon as it stages a conflict between consumerist society and authentic identity. Noir, then, takes the form of the negation of consumer culture. As a performance of that repudiation, noir is in essence about authenticity as it unmasks the lies "to discover the essential rot that they disguise" (5). Dussere states that this noir tradition of repudiating consumerism "continues and evolves long after the era of the forties and fifties in which it is generally located," as each text "constructs an aesthetic intervention into this problem" in a space appropriate to the era (4, 250). *Las viudas de los jueves* partakes of this conception of noir as a repudiation of consumerism and conceives the gated community as the appropriate space in Argentina of the 1990s to carry out this project.

Sociologist Zygmunt Bauman provides insight into the society portrayed in *Las viudas*. He calls consumerism a type of social arrangement resulting from the recycling of " 'regime-neutral' human wants, desires and longings into the *principal propelling and operating force* of society." This force is central to "the process of individual and group self-identification and the selection and pursuit of individual life policies" (*Consuming Life* 28). Bauman identifies the stigma of not being able to participate in consumer society along with the psychological elixir that lavish consumption provides its members.

> Those who cannot act on the desires so induced [by the enticement to consume] are treated daily to the dazzling spectacle of those who can. Lavish consumption, they are told, is the sign of success, a highway leading straight to public applause and fame. They also learn that possessing and consuming certain objects and practicing certain lifestyles are the necessary condition for happiness; and since "being happy" ... has become the mark of human decency and entitlement to human respect, it tends also to become the necessary condition of human dignity and self-esteem. (*Consuming Life* 130)

Bauman's description of the mentality of those who subscribe wholeheartedly to the lifestyle of the consumer society makes explicit why the characters in *Las viudas* are so addicted to consumption. In a society where consumerism is central not only to group self-identification but also to self-esteem, a portrait is drawn of a family man whose winner's mentality is so deeply ingrained in his psyche that he cannot bear to admit financial defeat. As *Las viudas* seeks to probe the social milieu and mind-set of a man who would kill to retain his social status, we may be reminded of the characters of Patricia Highsmith, an author whom Piñeiro says she admires (Núñez). Surely the most notorious of Highsmith's characters is Tom in *The Talented Mr. Ripley*, who brazenly murders his friend Dickie Greenleaf and assumes his identity, happily sacrificing his integrity and authenticity as he usurps Dickie's privileged bourgeois lifestyle.

### Speaking from the Grave? The Disembodied Choral Voice

The distance between the time of the story and the time of its telling is a key feature of *Las viudas* that creates its ominous mood. The narrating instance is split in three: a homodiegetic first-person narrator named Virginia Guevara speaking from a time subsequent to the events, a homodiegetic choral voice also speaking from a later vantage point, and a heterodiegetic third-person narrator relating events as they took place from a point in the immediate past. Thus a portion of the story is evoked from an unspecified future moment when the narrators already know what is going to happen. They forewarn us of, or hint at, looming future events and situate the course of the characters' lives within a historical context.

The novel opens with the voice of Virginia—a resident (or former resident) of the community—speaking from a time that is after the swimming pool deaths, setting the scene and recalling the minute details of that fateful night. This perspective enables her to reflect on these events as she recalls her thoughts at that moment—what she did not know then and knows now. For instance, in reference to the presentiment by her husband, Ronie, of impending tragedy when he returns early from his weekly gathering with the men who will soon be dead, she says, "Se movía cada tanto en la reposera sin encontrar la posición adecuada, estaba nervioso. Más tarde supe que no eran nervios sino miedo, pero entonces no lo sabía" (He kept moving around on the lounger without finding the right position; he seemed nervous. Later on I discovered that fear was the problem, not nerves—but I didn't know that at the time) (15; 13).[13]

In the first lines of the third chapter, the mysterious choral voice makes its appearance: "Altos de la Cascada es el barrio donde vivimos. Todos nosotros" (Cascade Heights is the neighbourhood where we live. All us lot) (25; 21). The phrase indicates that all of those who are talking are residents (or that they *were* residents per the original version, the morphological particularity of the Spanish verb system lending an equivocal status to the time reference). However, it does not necessarily mean that *all* the residents are part of the group that is narrating. So whom exactly does "Todos nosotros" include? We never know for sure, although at times there are markers that indicate who is *not* in the speaking group. For instance, when they speak *about* Virginia, it excludes her from the voice, and when they speak about their envy of the Scaglias' house, it excludes the members of this family. At one point, it appears to be the dead men speaking from the grave: "Pero la muerte, la nuestra, la cercana, todavía estaba bastante lejos por aquella época" (But at that time death had not yet come closer to us, it had not touched our circle of friends) (62; 54).[14] The fact that one of the dead men is el Tano Scaglia, who obviously would not be included in the group that admits to envying his house, indicates that the group's composition mutates or that it just includes the other two dead men.

Like Virginia, this voice is speaking from a vantage point that is sometime after the deaths, enabling the speakers to take cognizance of their erroneous assumptions regarding the stability of their lifestyle. For instance, they admit, "Si no fuera por ciertos accidentes provocados por elementos de la naturaleza como eso, en La Cascada no corremos demasiados riesgos. *Eso creíamos*" (If it weren't for this sort of accident of nature, life at the Cascade would be almost free of risks. That was what we used to believe) (22, emphasis added; 20–21). Whether it is the voices of the dead or the still living, this enigmatic disembodied choral voice emits an aura of otherworldliness. It functions like the voice-over effect so characteristic of film noir, infusing the tale with an atmosphere of doom.[15] The most legendary voice-over of film noir may be that of Walter Neff, Fred MacMurray's character in *Double Indemnity*, speaking his confession into a Dictaphone in the middle of the night, admitting that he killed a man. This confessional tone is perhaps the most salient characteristic of the disembodied voice in *Las viudas* as the group looks back on the time when they enjoyed the privileged country club lifestyle that they mistakenly thought would be eternal. Their displaced temporal perspective and introspective posture enables them to reflect on the errors of their ways as well as what led them to this misguided assumption. As an examination that takes place *after* the tragedy, it is surely propelled by it, an attempt to understand how it could have happened. Relying on its anonymity, the confessional voice admits to nasty little secrets—their envy of the Scaglias' house, unflattering gossip about the neighbors, behavior that points to their hypocritical and corrupted values—enabling the reader to view the mindset and motivations of the characters.

As disembodied voices, the speakers elude our grasp. Exactly what times and what spaces are these narrators speaking from? How many months or years have elapsed since the events they evoke? If they are alive, are they still in Los Altos or are they someplace else? Is Virginia speaking at the same moment in time as the choral voice? Where is she speaking from? We never know the answers to these questions.

These voices from the future—that of Virginia and that of the mysterious "nosotros"—alternate with yet another narrating instance: a third-person heterodiegetic voice that narrates the lives of a series of characters as they unfold, describing their actions and sometimes revealing their thoughts. Relating these events in the immediate past tense, as if they had recently occurred, this voice only knows about the moment it is relating and does not know the future. These sections describing the lives of residents resemble vignettes, merging to form a mosaic representing a cross-section of life in Los Altos.

The novel's shifts between narrative levels can be considered a type of "metalepsis," a mechanism named and examined by Genette (*Narrative Discourse* 234–37). More specifically defined, metalepsis is the disruption of the border between "the world in which one tells [and] the world of which one tells" (236). Genette explains that this can only be achieved by narrating, by introducing into one situation the knowledge of another situation. This concept helps us understand that while the first-person narrators—Virginia and the choral voice—are homodiegetic because they are participants in the story they tell, they are also metadiegetic because they are temporally removed from it: there is a division between the time they were actants in the story and the time of their narrating act. As they narrate, they stand above and apart from their earlier selves, wiser than they were then, and eager to share what they have learned about the errors of the ways. Their hindsight contaminates, at the same time that it elucidates, the universe of the story.

### The Consuming Lifestyle and the Authenticity Effect

Piñeiro has stated that she is most interested in the "why" of crimes, and, in order to understand the circumstances that culminated in this crime, we are taken back in time to the establishment of the community, seen, in large part, from the perspective of Virginia. One of the early residents who became a real estate broker specializing in Los Altos, she knows the community and its residents well. The choice of the real estate broker as the main voice of the community (or at least the main voice that is connected to a specific, named person) seems fitting in a society in which identity and self-worth are linked to market value. Additionally, as Carolina Rocha points out, Virginia is the only wife who works and thus possesses an insider/outsider perspective that affords her a revealing and critical perspective on her neighbors' lifestyle (125).

Virginia's voice blends seamlessly with the other, unnamed, narrators and together they flesh out the state of affairs that led el Tano to the breaking point. From the alternating narrators we learn of the residents' opulent lifestyles, fueled by the economic prosperity enjoyed by a segment of the Argentine population in the early 1990s, and subsequently of their economic problems as international financial crises cause the breadwinners to be laid off from their lucrative jobs. The narrators provide a detailed portrait of the "consuming life" in Los Altos through the intertwined lives of several families. A tight circle of friends forms among four couples: el Tano and Teresa Scaglia, Virginia and Ronie Guevara, Martin and Lala Urovitch, and Gustavo and Carla Masotta. It is significant that el Tano—the mastermind of the swimming pool suicide scheme—and his wife, Teresa, are the pace setters and the envy of their neighbors. Their house is the paramount symbol of their status: "La casa de los Scaglia ... era la que más llamaba la atención.... Muchos de nosotros la mirábamos con cierta envidia" (The Scaglias' house ... was the one that most caught the eye.... Lots of us were secretly envious of it) (19; 17), admits the choral voice. We are told that it is made of superior materials, boasts six bedrooms, eight bathrooms, and a home theater, and has been featured in decoration magazines. The competition is palpable: "A todos nos gustaría que nuestra casa fuera la más linda. O la más grande" (We would all like our house to be the prettiest. Or the biggest) (28; 24), they confess. We learn of not only the competitive spirit among the neighbors but also the high standards that el Tano has set for himself.

Conspicuous consumption is the name of the game. To get an audience for the display of their latest acquisition, the residents present luxurious gifts to their spouses at dinner parties. For instance, Carmen Insúa chooses such an occasion to unveil a Mercedes Benz van for her husband: the chauffeur-driven van decorated with a white bow appears while the group is dining. When el Tano invites their friends over, Teresa thinks that he will be announcing a trip, one even more spectacular than the vacation in Maui she has suggested. Two neighbors meet on the golf course, and their conversation turns to their wives' excessive spending, of which they are critical but at the same illustrates their family's level of consumption. When Ernesto Andrade's shady business with bond sales takes off, he signals his new status by changing his Ford Mondeo for an Alfa Romeo.[16]

Piñeiro's text functions as a scathing critique of the inauthenticity of this society. Dussere sheds light on how this critique functions, explaining that noir's "confrontation with consumer capitalism inspires noir to produce authenticity effects as a response" (10), or in other words, "staged authenticity" consisting of " 'spurious' structures in an effort to reproduce that which is perceived as genuine" (Dussere 10, citing MacCannell 589). To this effect, *Las viudas* exposes that the touted natural oasis—a safe and healthy sporting life surrounded by nature—is in reality an elaborate construct. The residents boast about their peace of mind in this community, pointing out that they do not need bars nor do they need to lock their doors and they can walk anywhere in the neighborhood at any hour without fear for their safety. However, their tranquility comes at the high price of private security along with strict controls: "Quince vigiladores en los turnos diurnos, y veintidós en el de la noche. Algo más de doscientas hectáreas protegidas a las que sólo pueden entrar personas autorizadas por alguno de nosotros" (Fifteen security guards working shifts during the day, and twenty-two at night. That's more than five hundred acres of land, accessible only to us or to people authorized by one of us) (25; 21). The supposedly natural "ambiente verde" (green environment) is carefully constructed with landscaping norms regulated by the community: fences are not allowed, and the houses are separated by bushes that are meticulously cut to be uneven so that they seem natural. The residents marvel at the natural beauty of the eighteen-hole golf course, but the choral voice admits that it is not so natural. It used to be a swampy area and the pumping system to drain it regularly floods the neighboring low-income municipality.[17] Fertilizers and insecticides are used to keep the course green, and after the stream running through the course was "purified," all the fish died.

The falseness behind this supposed natural paradise is emblematic of the community as a whole. The phony façade is signaled when Virginia finds that the library in the house she has purchased showcases fake books—only gold-embossed covers with nothing inside. The repeating titles allude to the essence of Las Cascadas: *La vida es sueño, Fausto, Crimen y castigo* (34). The narrative repeatedly demonstrates that the idyllic life is but an illusion, and behind the outward appearance of perfection lie racial and religious prejudice; dirty secrets including infidelity, alcoholism, and spousal abuse; illicit business dealings and corruption; class discrimination and isolation. We see an example of racial prejudice in Mariana Andrade's discomfort with the dark skin color of her adopted children, and anti-Semitism is evident in the measures taken to discourage Jewish people from purchasing property in Los Altos.

The residents of Los Altos establish and maintain their sense of superiority and separation by firmly marking class difference, both internally—with their employees—and externally—with the neighboring working-class community. For example, when the Andrade family moves from the city to the gated community, they signal their maid's subservient status by making her wear a uniform, just like all the other domestic employees in Los Altos de la Cascada. Mariana Andrade envisions the maids as a different species, perhaps as a way of justifying her own languid existence: "Evidentemente estas mujeres tienen otro biorritmo, pensó Mariana, son mulas de carga" (These women obviously have a different biorhythm, thought Mariana; they are pack mules) (67; 59). The discriminating treatment of domestic employees is most vividly illustrated in the case of Gabina, the maid of the Insúa family. When Carmen Insúa treats her as an equal, taking her to eat at the community club, a resident complains to the waiter, " 'Che, ¿las domésticas pueden comer acá?' " Look, are domestic servants allowed to eat here?) (203; 174).

Wire fences, walls, and barriers separate and protect the country dwellers from the low-income neighboring community, Los Tigrecitos. The narrator stresses its difference from Los Altos: it consists of simple houses built by the owners, some with dirt floors. Their livelihood depends on work at Los Altos, and the residents are advised to support the community, because this impacts their own security. Thus, their "generosity" is motivated by self-interest, and the potential for the poor to become violent is clearly implied. The well-off residents of Los Altos objectify the "poor" people: for instance, when Teresa organizes a feng shui seminar to benefit a children's home, Carmen asks if it is for the Los Tigrecitos, to which Teresa replies, "No, otros pobres, no los nuestros" (No, some other poor children, not ours) (128; 109).

A dirty secret of this consuming society is the fact that many of the men have made their fortunes by questionable or outright fraudulent means.

Ernesto Andrade passes himself off as a lawyer, but he has not finished high school, and Fernández Luengo's law practice specializes in keeping smugglers out of jail. Then there is the case of the anti-Semite Lila Laforque, whose husband is under suspicion of fraudulent bankruptcy. Another neighbor, Díaz Batán, had an idea that many neighbors considered brilliant: in the early 1990s he registered in Argentina the brand names of major US companies such as Macy's and Starbucks. Then when the moment came that these companies wanted to register in Argentina, it was more economical and expedient for them to buy the rights from him than take him to court. It is noteworthy that the neighbors praised this scheme—in this atmosphere, clever get-rich-quick schemes are valued over honest hard work.

Probably the most pernicious of the schemes is the "viaticación" (a neologism taken from the word "viaticum" or last rights) insurance scam practiced by Alfredo Insúa. He buys the insurance policies of terminally ill individuals in need of cash, in exchange for being named the beneficiary. When they die, he collects the premium instead of the relatives. His choice of victims is a testament to his cynicism: he stopped buying the policies of people with AIDS because now with the new drugs they live too long; he prefers certain cancer patients. He explains that these get-rich-quick schemes are always changing and you have to be quick on your feet to make a killing: " 'Y, el mercado financiero es así, un *flash*, hay que estar buscando todo el tiempo cosas nuevas' " (And the financial markets are like that, things change quick as a flash, you have to be constantly looking out for new ways of doing stuff) (258; 222). These moneymaking tricks, James M. Griesse points out, can be viewed as a reflection of how the nation pursued neoliberal policies (68).

### A Fragile Lifestyle

Although many residents prefer to ignore the world outside their perverse little paradise, their story is situated within the course of history via allusions to current national and international events—for instance, the swimming pool deaths take place on 27 September 2001, when the residents of Los Altos are still reacting to the terrorist attacks of 9/11. Much of the national news has to do with corruption and abuse of power. For example, there is a reference to the second term of President Carlos Menem—the choral voice comments that he can be reelected thanks to the constitutional reform that he promoted. In 1998, we are told, suspicious suicides were linked to high-level corruption.[18] "Ninguno de estos hechos tuvo alguna incidencia ni en nuestras vidas ni en la de los Altos" (None of these events had a direct impact on our lives, or on the life of the Heights) (105; 89), the voice informs us, demonstrating the political apathy and self-centeredness of residents. Apparently, if the news does not affect their income, it is of no concern to them. Néstor García Canclini's explanation of this attitude—that in the neoliberal Latin American nation-states, social participation has shifted from the exercise of citizenship to the practice of consumption (cited by Griesse 61)—echoes Dussere's view of the conflation of consumption with citizenship in American society beginning after World War II.

The voices that speak from the future possess the hindsight to understand how national and international events affected the course of their lives, emphasizing the ephemeral nature of the economic boom that financed their lavish lifestyle. The period of economic euphoria brought on by the dollarization of the Argentine peso in 1991 provides a shot in the arm for the exodus to the country: "Un dólar, un peso. El famoso 'uno a uno' que nos hizo creer que otra vez podíamos, y facilitó el éxodo a lugares como Altos de la Cascada" (One peso would be worth one dollar: the famous "one for one" that restored Argentines' confidence and fueled an exodus to places like Cascade Heights) (35; 31). The prosperity promises to continue indefinitely, as noted in this passage where the choral voice focalizes Virginia's perspective: "El precio de los terrenos subía con la euforia de bienestar de los 90, y Virginia no quería perderse la euforia. Nadie se la quería perder. Todos especulábamos con cuánto aumentaba día a día el precio de nuestras casas y hasta dónde podía llegar" (The price of land was climbing in line with the economic euphoria of the 1990s, and Virginia wanted a piece of that euphoria. Everyone wanted a piece. All of us speculated on how much the value of our houses was rising each day and how much higher it might go) (106; 89–90). This attitude, Virginia now realizes, led the community into problems, and she speaks to the fleeting nature of financial success for the "winners" in Argentina's euphoric '90s: "Es que el error de muchos de nuestros vecinos fue creer que se podía vivir eternamente gastando tanto como se ganaba. Y lo que se ganaba era mucho, y parecía eterno. Pero algún día se corta el chorro, aunque nadie lo hubiera sospechado" (The thing is, many of our neighbours made the mistake of thinking that they could keep spending as much as they earned for ever. And what they earned was a lot, and seemed eternal. But there comes a day when the taps are turned off, although nobody expects it) (269; 231). Ultimately, as Griesse observes, the voices show how neoliberal economy "could not deliver on its promises" (68).

The fragility of the ostentatious country club lifestyle becomes apparent when men in the community are laid off and they struggle to keep up an outward appearance of prosperity. Virginia describes the situation, hinting at what is to come as she speaks from the future: "Veníamos de varios meses de crisis económica, algunos lo disimulaban mejor que otros, pero a todos de una manera u otra nos había cambiado la vida. O nos estaba por cambiar" (We had already weathered a few months of the economic crisis. Some people were putting a better face on it than others, but one way or another all our lives had changed—or were about to change) (12; 10). We see the different ways in which the residents of Los Altos deal with their economic problems. Virginia's husband, Ronie, is the first of the group of friends to lose his job, and the family is able to get by with Virginia's real estate earnings and a cutback in their household staff. When Martín Urovich loses his job, he and his wife eventually face the reality of their dwindling resources and decide they will move to Miami, where others cannot witness their reduced lifestyle. But el Tano Scaglia, the envy of the community, is incapable of accepting that reality.

Foreshadowing the Fall

Through the character of el Tano, a portrait is drawn of the psychological make-up of an individual whose identity comes from his status as a consumer. His attitude illustrates Bauman's explanation of the elixir of lavish consumption and how the ability to participate becomes necessary for human dignity and self-esteem. El Tano clings so tightly to this identity that he is unable to assimilate his new reality when his company lets him go. Only eighteen months later does he admit to his family and neighbors that he is no longer with the company, but he lies, saying that it was voluntary and that he has lots of projects and possibilities. The reaction of his wife to his announcement that he is unemployed shows she is also in denial—she reminds him of their plan to vacation in Maui, clinging to her cherished lifestyle and refusing to acknowledge that the family no longer has an income. El Tano has a self-image as a winner, augmenting his salary and his responsibility with each job change. He believes that he is "programmed to win," identifying himself in opposition to friends such as Martín Urovitch, who is programmed to fail. When el Tano finally faces the fact that his family will eventually run out of money, he contemplates the options, again establishing his superiority over his neighbors who are also out of work. He considers eliminating the school fees or the maid like Martín Urovitch or Ronie Guevara but tells himself he is neither Martin Urovitch nor Ronie Guevara. The Scaglias have become so attached to the material trappings of their country club existence that el Tano cannot accept a lesser lifestyle. He cannot see himself eliminating any of the luxuries that money can buy: "Cine, ropa, música, vinos, todo era necesario si querían seguir manteniendo la vida que llevaban. Y el Tano no se imaginaba llevando otra vida" (Cinema, clothes, music, wine: it was all necessary if they wanted to maintain their lifestyle. And El Tano could not picture himself living any other sort of life) (281; 241). Since el Tano's consumption has become essential to his self-respect, he will choose death over relinquishing his consumer habits. When he tells the others, "Si no podés vivir con dignidad, morí con dignidad" (If you can't live with dignity, die with dignity) (302; 259), he is equating personal dignity to participation in consumer culture. Paradoxically, his lifestyle is worth more than his life. In the end, he is a fraud like everyone else, as Ronie points out when he tries to talk him out of committing suicide: "¿Electrocutarse te va a salvar de ser un fraude?" (Is electrocuting yourself going to save you from being a fraud?) (306; 262).

Piñeiro is a master of suspense, and the final section of the novel builds up to the climax as el Tano arrives at the decision to stage his accidental death. On the golf course, Alfredo Insúa brags about his insurance scams, unknowingly planting an idea in el Tano's head. Subsequently we see el Tano making numbers and coming to the realization that his funds will only support his family's lavish lifestyle for fifteen more months. Finally, we find out that his life insurance policy provided by his former company will expire in three months and is void in the case of suicide. A third-person narrator, focalizing Virginia's thoughts, recounts the details of the "accident" as Ronie told them to her. The men will be listening to cool jazz in the pool when the extension cord for the speaker falls in the water. Believing that the electrocution of a group of four will not raise suspicion of suicide, his intent is to convince his three friends to join him—after all, Ronie and Martín are unemployed losers in his estimation and Gustavo has been humiliated by his wife, who is having an affair. But Ronie will have no part of it. He is offended when el Tano calls him a loser and leaves the gathering early, thinking that el Tano will not carry it out. Ironically, however, el Tano has indeed chosen as his instrument of death one of the prime symbols of a life of leisure and affluence. The image of the swimming pool serves to frame the men's corpses, signaling the lifestyle that was their undoing.

## A Place for Redemption outside the System?

*Las viudas* is all about space—the country club setting, with its private, internal security and restricted access, is central to the initial success of el Tano's scheme. Thanks to an internal justice system, infractions are generally resolved internally, and going to the police is very much frowned upon. The community is virtually self-regulated, as the third-person narrator explains: "La justicia del país, la externa, la que está afuera, en los tribunales, en el Palacio de Justicia, casi nunca llega a intervenir.... La policía tampoco entra, la de verdad, ni la Bonaerense ni la Federal, sólo entran los vigiladores que pagan los socios" (Federal law, as it applies to the world outside, the tribunals and law courts, almost never intervenes here.... The real police never even set foot in here—neither the Buenos Aires force nor the federal police—only the private security guards paid for by members) (241; 206–7). When the bodies are found, the chief of security of Los Altos calls his friend, the police chief, on his private line, and is assured a rapid investigation. The police issue a hasty ruling of the deaths as accidental.

A week after the funerals, however, Ronie tells the truth to the widows—that the deaths by electrocution were planned by el Tano. Soon the unscrupulous Ernesto Andrade and Alfredo Insúa appear at his house, telling him to maintain silence because "'no pudo haber suicidio.... Si hubo suicidio estas mujeres [the widows] se quedan en la calle.... Nosotros les estamos dando una mano.... Ernesto con el tema legal, y yo con el tema de los seguros'" (it can't have been a suicide.... If it was suicide, those women will be left with no roof over their heads.... We're giving the widows a hand.... Ernesto with the legal stuff and me with the insurance) (309; 266–67). Thus these men have a selfish motivation for maintaining the lie as they have found a way to profit from the tragedy.

In this community of corrupted values, it is the youth who provide hope for change. Indeed, Piñeiro has commented: "It's true that in my novels adults are condemned and the only hope is found in adolescent characters" (Gallego-Díaz). Teenagers Romina (adopted daughter of Mariana and Ernesto Andrade) and Juani (the son of Virginia and Ronie) see beyond the façade perpetrated in their community. Both outsiders in a way—Romina for her dark skin, and Juani because he is on the list of "drug addicts" for his marijuana habit—the two become fast friends. These bored teenagers spy on their neighbors at night; they have witnessed and filmed the occurrences that fateful night at the Scaglias' pool. They play for Virginia and Ronie the video that shows that Gustavo did not want to die, but el Tano pulled him into the pool and then grabbed the electrical cord. Ronie voices the awful truth, "'Lo mató'" (He killed him) (316; 272), and Juani is the first to articulate the question of whether they should go to the police, exposing el Tano's scheme and the homicide, as well as breaking the community's taboo in regard to bringing in outside authorities. Ronie hesitates, knowing that there is no return for them, knowing that their neighbors will never forgive them. But Juani convinces his parents to take the evidence of crime to the police. As Rocha puts it, the "disaffected, maladjusted, and marginalized teenagers" serve to reveal "the systemic violence (corruption, coercion, fraud) that has sustained the lifestyle of the community" (127, 129).[19]

When the Guevara family arrives at the gate to the outer world, the guard warns that things have gotten ugly outside; it is late September 2001, three months before Argentina's crash, and economic conditions in the country are rapidly deteriorating. People are looting on the other side of the highway, the family is told, and the guards are armed with rifles in case the mob arrives at Los Altos. Ronie seems afraid, and the novel ends with Virginia's question: "'¿Te da miedo salir?'" (Are you scared to go out?) (318; 274). This last line can be understood on two levels. On the one hand, they may fear for their physical safety as they leave their secure fortress and confront a violent mob; on the other hand, if they go to the police and expose the lies, they will burst the "paradisiacal" bubble based on façades and inauthenticity. Their departure from Los Altos—if they go through with it—would signify redemption of sorts for the characters living false lives. By telling the truth, they would leave the world of lies of Los Altos, facing ostracism from their community and the uncertainty of the outside world.

Using retrospective disembodied voices that forewarn the reader of impending tragedy, contemplate what caused it, and confess their unsavory secrets, Piñeiro narrates a suspenseful noir-tinged tale of a decadent consumer society in neoliberal Argentina in the final decade of the twentieth century. The novel's focus on the demise of an individual "consumed" by his addiction to consumer culture endorses Bauman's observation that in this type of lifestyle, profuse consumption became the necessary condition of human worth. The frequent references to the administration and directives of Carlos Menem along the course of the decade make the novel a critique of his government's adoption of the peso to dollar peg along with the market-driven fiscal policy that left the Argentine economy exposed to the international monetary crises of the 1990s. Piñeiro has constructed an aesthetic intervention appropriate to her era in order to repudiate the rise in consumer culture in Argentine neoliberal society.

## REGENDERING THE GENRE: *BETIBÚ* BY CLAUDIA PIÑEIRO

*Betibú*, published six years after *Las viudas de los jueves*, returns to the country club setting to tell the story of an investigation into a series of murders made to look like accidental deaths or suicides. In contrast to *Las viudas*, which provides a portrait of the "country" using the voices of its residents, *Betibú* depicts it from the perspective of outsiders. And times have changed. While Argentina's crisis of 2001 resonates in Piñeiro's tragic saga of the widows, *Betibú*'s overall tone—despite the murders—is much lighter as it follows the sometimes hilarious and often bizarre adventures of its protagonist, Nurit Iscar, known as "la dama negra de la literatura argentina" (the Dark Lady of Argentine literature) (21; 19). Like *Las viudas*, *Betibú* reveals problematic aspects of the exclusive gated communities, in particular, the prejudice and perverseness of the security routines. At the same time, it comments on lifestyles outside the "country" to treat a broad gamut of contemporary issues, including matters central to women's experience. Indeed, Piñeiro's use of a savvy female investigator, along with her insistence on women's issues, constitute an act of defiance toward the traditionally male-centered and misogynist genre.

This novel is narrated by a third-person extradiegetic voice with limited omniscience—limited because it focalizes through certain characters, primarily the members of the investigative team but not others; for instance, it never enters the thoughts of their antagonists. The story is told mainly in chronological order following the discovery process of the reporters but disturbs the continuity of its telling by inserting lengthy digressions that delay the plot action. Besides putting the story on hold, the narrative voice transgresses diegetic levels—the universe the story and that of its telling—by backtracking to relate what a character was doing during the plot action of the previous section as well as by sharing with the reader what the characters do not know yet but will soon find out. These devices, which foreground the story's artifice, will be discussed in the section titled "Taking Hold of the Telling."

### Turning the Detective Genre on Its Head

The novel opens with the arrival of the housekeeper, Gladys Varela, at the gated community of La Maravillosa. After awaiting her turn to be admitted at the security gate, she arrives at the house of her employer, Pedro

Chazarreta, and finds him dead in his easy chair with his throat slit. Next, we meet Nurit Iscar, a dispirited novelist who agrees to write a series of chronicles for the daily *El Tribuno* about the atmosphere in La Maravillosa in the wake of Chazarreta's death. Despite herself, Nurit will form part of a trio of investigators who attempt to discover the reason behind not only Chazarreta's death but also a string of seemingly connected deaths. The other two individuals are also writers: Jaime Brena, a middle-aged reporter who has recently been reassigned from the crime beat to the social scene; and "el pibe" (the kid), a cub reporter who has been given Brena's former assignment. (We are never told the rookie's name.) The plot follows the footsteps of the investigators, and in the process we are introduced to social issues. For instance, the reporters and other individuals involved in the investigation must go in and out of La Maravillosa, each time suffering the vicissitudes of privatized security, which provides differential treatment depending on the social class of the individual being admitted. The journalists experience or comment on official corruption—from the members of the police force to the president of the nation. They also engage in a running commentary on the practice and ethics of journalism in the twenty-first century. Another issue discussed is the literary scene with its rivalries and pettiness. Piñeiro's stated interest in "la historia cotidiana" (daily life) is evidenced in abundant details of the characters' interpersonal relationships, including among girlfriends, between the sexes, mother-child relationships, and love relationships. Via its female sleuth, the novel explores concerns related to the lives of contemporary women. These issues are treated with wry, self-mocking humor and biting satire.

Critics have called *Betibú* the most *policial*, or detectivesque, of Piñeiro's novels to date, and, indeed, it faithfully incorporates conventions of the deductive mystery, only to turn them on their head. It deals with the investigation of an enigma, or rather, a series of enigmas. Chapter 1 produces the requisite cadaver, and the plot follows the steps of the trio who investigates the death. The "detectives"—once again—are journalists who become investigators by default because law enforcement does not seem to be doing its job. The journalists' curiosity is piqued by the unnatural death of Pedro Chazarreta, and, to their fascinated horror, the body count mounts as their investigation proceeds. In this way, Piñeiro fulfills her promise that this novel will produce "more dead people" (Friera, "La ficción"). The victims are by no means innocent—they are bold and perverse victimizers themselves. The character triangle—criminal-victim-detective—presents interesting twists: similar to *El vuelo de la reina*, there is a shifting of roles between victim and criminal, and ultimately between detective and criminal.

The clue that sets the investigation in motion—an empty picture frame—is subtly introduced in the first chapter, and little by little it leads the investigators to the information that will unravel the mystery. They find out that the missing photo is that of Chazarreta and his circle of high school buddies, six men in all. Several of the men in the photo have died recently, and others will expire during the course of the investigation, leading the trio to suspect serial murder. The investigators solve the mystery using a combination of intuition (Nurit's province) and reasoning or ratiocination (Brena's province). The workings of the serial murderers are based on ingenious concepts: the "sastre de la muerte" (the murders are tailored so that each victim dies in a way that was expected) and the "empresa sicaria" (a company whose service is murder to order). The ending has a surprising twist. We think the murders have been solved once the trio fingers a powerful businessman named Roberto Gandolfini, who is seeking vengeance against the men for their role in an incident of sexual abuse in the past: as a young boy he was forced to witness the gang rape of one man in the photo by the other five. However, Roberto Gandolfini's subsequent murder along with the reporters' sighting of police superintendent Venturini at the crime scene and the fact that Venturini is the "last man standing" point to his role as "el verdadero asesino" (the true assassin).

For the trio of investigators, there is a happy ending that comes in the form of a fresh chance at love. Nurit and Jaime Brena confess their mutual attraction, and *el pibe* ends up in a romantic scene with Karina Vives, a journalist in the culture section. Saccomanno has commented on Piñeiro's use of the happy ending: "And that happy, uplifting ending has been a rule of popular fiction since the time of [Eugène] Sue. Piñeiro, in this sense, is an orthodox of the genre in ideological terms" ("De género y popular").[20] With this resolution, we can read the investigators' reward for solving the mystery and for their ethical stance: they persisted despite the danger in an effort to save the lives of the other men in the photo. The culprit, however, proves to be so powerful that he is untouchable.

Part of the "grammar of the detective novel," as described by José Colmeiro in his detailed study of Spanish detective fiction, are flashbacks or digressions that postpone the resolution. Colmeiro cites Dennis Porter's observation that "it is precisely these digressive effects, and not the progressive sequences of actions, that give character and individuality to a detective novel" (84). Beyond their role in delaying the solution, the digressions help create an "espacio novelesco" as well as develop the characters. The digressive elements can also be appreciated in themselves, apart from their contextual role, for the pleasure they give the reader and for their humor and ingenuity (Colmeiro 84). Colmeiro cites as classic examples of digressions the excessive alcohol consumption of Nora and Nick Charles in Hammett's *The Thin Man*, performed as a ritual of provocation against Prohibition, and Pepe Carvalho's gastronomic flights in the novels of Manuel Vázquez Montalbán (80). Likewise, in *Betibú* it is the flashbacks and digressions about Nurit's past—her friends, her family, and her recent failures both in love and with her sentimental novel—that flesh out the characters and develop important themes in the novel.

While the novel observes certain tenets of detective fiction, at the same time it subverts the masculinist trend of the genre. In her seminal study of women's crime writing in Spain, Shelley Godsland demonstrates that despite those who posit crime or detective fiction as inimical to the feminist project, female-authored texts can reverse the patriarchal ideology of the traditional detective novel. Their female characters, be they criminals or sleuths, asserts Godsland, "are uniquely well placed to comment on a vast range of gendered issues from within the narratives they protagonize" (*Killing Carmens* 204). Subscribing to this mission, *Betibú* brings in issues that are central to the female experience, a conscious decision on the part of the author, who has commented on this aspect of her novel: "What seemed interesting to me was the cross of the detective genre with a woman's life.... One thinks that the genre has nothing to do with the feminine world; or if it comes in, as is the case with Raymond Chandler, it has to do with beautiful women who killed someone and in passing seduce the detective. In my novel women enter with children, who also bring in their friends, and besides they are old; it's a little more real" (Aguirre, "Los temas están en el aire"). What is more, Piñeiro "regenders" violence, using literature to take revenge on unsolved murders of women in Argentina: "I intentionally just killed men, to reinvent reality," she says (Vilalta). Godsland notes that the genre "facilitates *par excellence* the portrayal of the rational, thinking female" (*Killing Carmens* 7) and Nurit indeed is a highly competent, intelligent, and strong-willed woman, although in solving the crimes she is guided more by her intuition than rational deduction. The portrait of Nurit is nuanced and realistic: while she has achieved success with her detective fiction, her self-doubt about her recent literary failure as well as about her aging body highlights her vulnerability. She mentions details that women can relate to: for instance, her menstruation and her messy purse. Our heroine is clearly not a femme fatale, and her insecurities make her character true-to-life and endearing.[21]

The novel depicts other issues that strike a chord with many women. For instance, female bonding and a female support network is played out in Nurit's close friendship with Carmen and Paula, who try to intervene in order to protect her from being hurt again by her former lover. At the same time, the friends are deliciously catty. The portrayal of male characters is balanced—Lorenzo Rinaldi, Nurit's former lover, is slick and charming on the surface but a jerk when it comes to issues that matter, while Jaime Brena is not as smooth as Rinaldi but is sensitive to women's feelings.

Most significantly, Piñeiro deals directly with the issue of violence against women. The figure of Betty Boop, the inspiration for Nurit's Hispanized nickname, provides at once a model of female transgression as well as the victimization of women. Nurit was supposedly nicknamed "Betibú" by Rinaldi. Researching the origin of Betty Boop, Nurit and her friends find that she was the first cartoon version of a flapper, a term originating in the 1920s to describe women who defied conventions by cutting their hair, shortening their skirts, and smoking in public. Olive Thomas, the actress considered the authentic flapper, died an early and suspicious death, possibly at the hands of her husband. The mention of Olive Thomas's tragic fate provides the occasion to bring in actual cases of unsolved murders of women in Argentina, a topic that Brena will also raise in a discussion with *el pibe*. Finally, Piñeiro intentionally regenders violence in her fiction. All the physical violence in the plot, including murder and gang rape, is directed against men. In this way, Piñeiro calls attention to the paradoxes and ambiguities that characterize the experience of contemporary women as well as the lack of justice for criminal cases involving women. At the same time, she uses her fiction to subvert the sexist tendencies of the genre.

Another way in which Piñeiro interrogates the crime genre is through self-reference and parody, creating a metafictional level. The writings of Linda Hutcheon help us understand how parody functions in *Betibú*. Parody, Hutcheon explains, is repetition with ironic inversion and "critical distance, which marks difference rather than similarity" (*A Theory of Parody* 6). It is a mode of coming to terms with the rich legacy of the past as well as an inscription of literary-historical continuity (4, 35). To this end, it revisits, replays, inverts, and "trans-contextualizes" previous works of art (11). Not necessarily an act of ridicule, parody can be a playful, genial mockery of codifiable forms (15).

Two targets of Piñeiro's parody are the legacy of detective fiction and her own career as a writer of crime fiction. The plot incorporates a formula from Chandler: in his stories, "the underlying crime is always old, lying half forgotten in the pasts of the characters before the book begins" (Jameson 147). This is the case with the crime triggering the serial murders. And *Betibú* has intertexual moments with parodic replays of two well-known works of fiction. First, Chazarreta's death in a green velvet armchair imitates the short story "Continuidad de los parques" by beloved Argentine author Julio Cortázar. While Cortázar's story ends just as a knife-wielding intruder enters the room where a man is reading in a green armchair, Piñeiro's tale continues where Cortázar's story leaves off, beginning after Chazarreta's throat has been slit. And while Cortázar's microrelato is a metadiscourse on the act of reading, we might consider *Betibú* a metadiscourse about the creative process, as I will explain in the next section. Another target of playful spoof is Stephen King's gothic thriller *Carrie*, made into a horror classic by Brian De Palma's film adaptation. "*Todo es calma en La Maravillosa.... Sin embargo ... la mano de Carrie atraviesa la tierra y sale de su tumba*" (All is calm in La Maravillosa ... yet ... Carrie's hand shoots through the earth, out of the grave) (107–8; 96), writes Nurit in her first report for *El Tribuno* from La Maravillosa. In her ironic repetition of the much-parodied graveyard scene, Nurit juxtaposes the supposed paradisiacal atmosphere suggested by the community's humorously hyperbolic name to the chilling wake of a murder rampage. This reference to *Carrie*, a story that treats the hypocrisy underlying modern middle-class American values, is highly suggestive in the context of a wealthy community in greater Buenos Aires. Additionally, it is significant that Carrie's killing spree is also about revenge for humiliation, another connection between the texts, which foretells the reason behind the serial murders. At the same time, the evocation of *Carrie* to describe the mood in La Maravillosa can be seen as a tongue-in-cheek spoof of Nurit's writing, in particular her best-seller status, because she is not above exploiting the lurid and campy "teen-shlocker" to appeal to readers.[22] Piñeiro's allusions to both a story considered "high art" as well as to an iconic work of popular culture enacts the breakdown of barriers between "high" and "low" culture, emblematic of postmodernity and perhaps a performance of Piñeiro's conception of her own art. Indeed, this mingling of diverse literary traditions characterizes *Betibú*: as I will discuss in the next section, it combines elements of the detective genre, traditionally considered popular or "low" art, with sophisticated narrative techniques.

As a form of ironic self-mockery, Nurit's literary career replays aspects of Piñeiro's. The autobiographical references in *Betibú* seem to be plentiful, and two salient and easily documentable examples are the fact that Nurit is referred to as "la dama negra de la literatura argentina" and the first question in an interview is "¿Te molesta ser un *best seller*?" (Do you mind being known as an author of bestsellers?) (60; 54). This is an obvious parody of Piñeiro's life but is repeated with ironic distance because Nurit is a fictional character—this is not an autobiography!—and, unlike Piñeiro, Nurit has lost her nerve to write after she tried her hand at a sentimental novel that was panned by the critics. Piñeiro has stated that in this novel she is laughing at herself and exorcising her fears.[23]

Taking Hold of the Telling: Fiction about Fiction

The narrator frequently intrudes in the narration of the story, marking its presence and violating diegetic levels. The most frequent narratorial intrusion creates the illusion of simultaneity or a cinematographic split screen and is usually introduced by the words "en el mismo momento en que" (at that very moment). This device makes its first appearance in the opening of chapter 2, to introduce Nurit: "En el mismo momento en que Gladys Varela está gritando en una calle sin salida del Club de Campo la Maravillosa, Nurit Iscar intenta ordenar su casa" (At the very moment Gladys Varela is screaming in a cul-de-sac at the Maravillosa Country Club, Nurit Iscar is trying to restore order to her house) (19; 17). The simultaneity effect occurs at least six more times in the course of the novel, and all subsequent references have to do with what Nurit, Jaime Brena, and *el pibe de Policiales* are doing. For instance, we learn that while Jaime Brena and *el pibe* are driving to the ranch of Emilio Casabets (the last man in the photo who is still alive), Nurit is taking a walk in La Maravillosa and, since she has forgotten her cell phone, they are unable to contact her. In a later chapter we learn that the moment Nurit's taxi exits La Maravillosa en route to her climactic meeting with Roberto Gandolfini, *el pibe* is departing from his home, on his way to the press room. These split screen views usually show that one person was carrying out an important mission or making an important discovery while the other was ignorant of it, involved in a more routine or mundane activity. This technique also functions on an ontological level insofar as it creates the illusion that the characters have lives of their own, existing independently of the narrator's telling of them.

The other frequent metalepic recourse is the narrator's disclosure of what a character or characters do not know yet but will soon know—always a vital piece of information—sometimes telling what they would have done, had they known it at that moment.[24] For instance, in the continuation of the aforementioned passage that depicts Nurit tidying up her apartment while Gladys is screaming in the street, the narrator tells us, "Todavía no sabe que Pedro Chazarreta está muerto" (She doesn't know yet that Pedro Chazarreta is dead). The narrator then proceeds to tell us that if she had known, she would have turned on the TV and the radio or she would have gone to the internet to read online news portals. "Pero Nurit Iscar no lo sabe. Aún. Lo va a saber unas horas después" (But Nurit Iscar doesn't know. Not yet. She won't find out for a few more hours) (19; 17). Once more, the narrator jumps a diegetic level, outside the cognition of the characters, looking at them from a superior level of knowledge, and reminding us that the text is the artifice of its narrator. This overt manipulation calls attention to the existence of a narrator who knows all and controls what the characters know and do not know and when they find it out. By saying what they would do if they did know it, the text creates possible worlds, other ways in which events could have unfolded had they had this knowledge. Additionally, this technique creates suspense as the reader anticipates when and how they will become aware of a dramatic discovery and how they will react. Surely the most noteworthy of these instances occurs toward the story's conclusion while Nurit and Brena, thinking that they have cracked the mystery and finished their work, are on their "first date"—dining together at a neighborhood restaurant. Playing on the television above their heads is a news story that pertains directly to their investigation and that they would find shocking, totally upending their understanding of the case: the news reports that businessman Roberto Gandolfini has been assassinated in a settling of scores. But they do not look up and thus do not see it. If they had, they would also have seen Venturini hovering in the background of the crime scene. Once again, the narrator teases the reader, making us wait to see how they will react when they eventually turn on the news. The delay of their discovery is crucial for plot development because their all-important love scene takes place after dinner and this "earth-shattering" news story surely would have thrown this plan off track. What is more, the juxtaposition of the scene of the romantic dinner to the report of this troubling news anticipates the dual ending—happy for the couple but disturbing from a sociopolitical standpoint. Thus the narrator continues to remind us that it (the narrator)[25] is in control, manipulating the text for maximum reader involvement and coherency of the message.

Key metaleptic intrusions occur when Nurit imagines herself as a character in a novel that she could write or might write someday. But if she were including this incident in *her* novel, the narrator tells us, she would change some of the details. In these passages, the character is not moving between textual levels because this happens at the same level as the surrounding narration—in Nurit's mind. But Nurit's imagination creates an ontological meta-level by projecting herself mentally into a fictional text of her own authorship, turning her "real" life into a novel in her mind. The three passages where this occurs have the opposite effect of the preceding device—rather than pointing to the narrator's control of *fictional* characters, Nurit, the character, indicates her "reality" (in the created world). If she can imagine herself as fictionalized in another text, it is because in this "incarnation"—in the text we are reading—she is *not* fiction. These three scenes are pivotal moments in the plot. One is Nurit's meeting with the powerful entrepreneur Roberto Gandolfini, the man she suspects is the mastermind behind the serial murders, in his office in a high-rise. The "real-life" setting (that is, the real life of the novel) is not right, according to Nurit. The huge picture window behind Gandolfini's desk from which she has a stunning view of the river is too attractive a backdrop for the dark tone of the conversation that is about to take place: "Si ésta fuera una novela de Nurit Iscar, sacaría esa ventana" (If this were a Nurit Iscar novel, she'd lose the window) (310; 281).

The other two scenes are climactic points in Nurit's budding romance with Jaime Brena. The first is immediately after they view Luis Collazo (one of Chazarreta's school buddies in the photo) hanging from a tree and Jaime explains to her the difference between "ahorcados blancos" and "ahorcados azules" (white hanging victims and blue hanging victims)—this is the forensic detail that explains why Collazo's white face means he did not commit suicide but was murdered. Nurit shudders, and Jaime, noticing it, puts his arm around her. Since this embrace is a highly emotional moment for Nurit, she puts quite a bit of thought into how she would write the scene.

> Entonces él le pasa una mano por detrás de la espalda, la toma del hombro y la acerca a él. Así, con esas palabras prefiere pensarlo ella.... Así lo escribiría si estuviera trabajando en su propia novela. Porque si escribiera "Jaime Brena me abraza" o "Jaime Brena la abraza," el personaje abrazado,

o sea Betibú, ella, se estremecería aún más. Y mucho menos escribiría: "Por fin un hombre la abraza después de tres años." Ella, Nurit Iscar, no le haría algo así a uno de sus personajes. (254)

[So Jaime Brena puts his arm around her, takes her shoulder and brings her close to him. That's how Nurit likes to think of it, anyway. Those are the words she would use to describe the gesture if she were working on her own novel, because if she wrote "Jaime Brena embraces me" or "Jaime Brena holds her," the held person—that is her, Betty Boo—would shiver even more. And she certainly wouldn't write: "Finally, for the first time in three years, a man holds her." Nurit Iscar would never put one of her own characters through something like that.] (228–29)

Here Nurit, the recipient of this arousing embrace, instead of being "in the moment" reverts to imagining the scene in her hypothetical novel. Her vacillation in regard to the use of first person or third person as she tries out different narrativizing strategies demonstrates the artistic choices that the novelist mulls over. When she clarifies who is the recipient of this action, she uses the terms "el personaje abrazado, o sea Betibú, ella," but when she refers to herself writing the novel, she calls herself "Nurit Iscar." In this passage, Nurit creates multiple versions of herself: the "real" person (within the universe of the novel we are reading), the character in the novel she would write, and the author who would sign the book, signaling her modes of existence, all with different levels of fictionality.

Again, as the final love scene unfolds, Nurit imagines how this would be told in her novel. As they walk together, Jaime Brena puts his arm around Nurit, but this time it is around her waist, which, according to Nurit, has much more "punto G" than her shoulder. What happens next? "Si esto fuera una novela de Nurit Iscar," the narrator tells us, "ella no contaría qué pasa un rato después" (If this were a Nurit Iscar novel, she wouldn't describe what happens soon after that) (344; 312). She would just tell about the kiss, "pero no contaría el recorrido en el ascensor, donde las manos ya se sienten libres. Y mucho menos lo que sucede cuando los dos entran en su departamento. No, definitivamente ella no incluiría nada de eso en una novela suya" (but she wouldn't describe the rush to the lift, and the liberation of their hands in its confines. And much less what happens when the two of them enter her apartment. No, she definitely wouldn't put any of that in one of her novels) (344; 312). Once again, Nurit is separated into the character experiencing the love scene and the character mapping out how she would narrate it in her novel. The narrator of *Betibú* also refrains from narrating what happened next; instead it focalizes Nurit, telling us what Nurit would *not* recount in her novel.

Thus when reality is not quite right—the atmosphere of Roberto Gandolfini's office is too beautiful for the sinister mood she would create in her novel—Nurit, as novelist, has the ability to alter it. Also important is to treat her character—the character that is a projection of her (fictional) life—with dignity, intentionally excluding the fact that she, or her character, is desperate to receive a man's embrace after three fallow years and leaving out the description of erotic moments. These procedures create universes that are "other" than the life of the characters, and also relate how Nurit's hypothetical novel would recount a certain episode, thematicizing the composition of a literary work.

Without a doubt, the most conspicuous metaleptic and metatextual passage appears in Nurit's final essay for *El Tribuno* when she says she will write a novel about a housekeeper who waits in line to enter a "country" and then finds her employer with his throat slit. This passage takes us aback because we realize we are reading that very novel. But if we take the preceding observations into account—that Nurit would carefully redact certain scenes—we must come to the conclusion that *Betibú* is *not* that novel written by Nurit because she has told us that some of the passages would be written differently from how she experiences them in the novel.

The case of Nurit—a character who is herself a novelist—creates "a perfect example of *pure* mise en abyme" (Cohn, "Metalepsis" 109). When Nurit says she will write a novel about a housekeeper, and so forth, this projected novel could have within it a novelist who says she is going to write a novel about a housekeeper who comes across her deceased employer, and so on, projecting an infinitive series of Nurits writing novels. In his essay "Partial Enchantments of the Quixote," Borges suggests "if the characters in a story can be readers or spectators, then we, their readers or spectators, can be fictitious" (234–35). Similarly, if the novel we are reading is a speculation or a projection of a fictional character, then we, the readers, can also be fictitious—a thought that produces a sensation of vertigo. As Dorrit Cohn explains, both metalepsis and mise en abyme, as intrusions in our reality, project human anxieties ("Metalepsis" 210). The celebrated example of this phenomenon—the very story that *Betibú* evokes—is Cortázar's "Continuidad de los parques" because it conjures up the danger to the reader when the barrier separating the world of fiction from the "real" world collapses.

A salient characteristic of *Betibú*, then, is its metafictionality as it constantly draws attention to its storytelling process. This is done by violating diegetic levels, usually by means of narrative splitting: the extradiegetic narrator distances itself from the narrative to comment on it, and Nurit splits herself into the "real" Nurit in this novel and the fictional Nurit in the novel she could write or might write someday. The procedure expresses the ironic superiority of the narrator who steps out of the text to comment on it, reminding us that the narrator of the story does not inhabit the universe of the novel; rather it inhabits a different universe in which it possesses superior knowledge compared to the characters of the novel. Referring to the unhinged or "mind warp" effect of mise en abyme, Cohn points out that in a humorous novel, the anxiety experienced by readers when they find themselves at the same level as fictional characters gives way to amusement ("Metalepsis" 111). But *Betibú* is a humorous novel with a dark message.

## The Social Critique

Similar to the other novels studied in this chapter, by means of the "country club" setting, *Betibú* examines consequences of neoliberal structural changes, one of which is the exacerbation of class differentiation and separation. In *Betibú*, this is evidenced in the elaborate security measures of the fortified country, as well as the attitude of the country dwellers toward others. The fact that Chazarreta's murder takes place in a gated community and the investigators and their guests are outsiders gives Piñeiro the opportunity to describe the excessive and humiliating security procedures to which they must submit each time they enter. While all nonresidents are subjected to some form of security screening, there is differential treatment and there are different reactions depending on the social status of the individual being screened.

When Nurit attempts to enter La Maravillosa for the first time, the contrast between her reaction and that of her taxi driver to the security routine is a mark of their social divide. Undoubtedly considering herself an equal to the country dwellers, she is indignant about the measures to which she is subjected. The guard informs her driver that they cannot park at the entrance to the "country" while they are waiting for authorization to enter. Nurit becomes angry and gets into an argument with the guard, but the taxi driver, who apparently is used to this kind of humiliation, takes it more stoically, telling Nurit, "Hay causas perdidas" (There are some lost causes) (101; 90).

Those who are invited by residents are differentiated from the "help," who pass through a separate gate where they are subjected to more extensive and more invasive screening. In the novel's opening sentences we are immediately introduced to the inspection that the employees must endure: "Los lunes son los días que lleva más tiempo entrar en el Club de Campo La Maravillosa. La cola de empleadas domésticas, jardineros, albañiles, plomeros, carpinteros, electricistas, gasistas y demás obreros de la construcción parece no terminar nunca" (Mondays are the days it takes longest to get into the Maravillosa Country Club. The line of domestic staff, gardeners, builders, plumbers, carpenters, electricians, gasmen and other assorted labourers seems to go on forever) (11; 9). We experience the tedious and time-consuming ritual from the perspective of Chazarreta's housekeeper, Gladys Varela, as she waits in line at the gate labeled "Personal y proveedores" (Personnel and suppliers). Guests enter through a gate marked "Visitas" (Visitors), thus the separation between the groups is also marked physically by distinct entrances. Norms are made stricter from one day to the next—the increased security reflects the uptick in violence as the economic downturn results in more poverty. However, despite the extensive and costly security measures, total security is impossible. When the action begins, two murders have occurred within the gates.

As is characteristic of the *novela negra*, this text critiques official corruption. The journalists point to embezzlement of government officials: for instance, the cover story of *El Tribuno* will be the suspicious growth in net worth of a high-ranking Ministry of Finance employee. Criticism of the president is voiced by Rinaldi, the director of the paper, who complains about the president's murky business dealings and the disastrous state of the country. Most importantly, the conclusion of the novel reveals complicity of the police with organized crime when police superintendent Venturini is discovered to be the ultimate mastermind behind the murders.

Still another area of critical scrutiny is the practice of journalism. A central issue is the clash between old and new journalistic practices. Brena practices "old school" journalism (contacts and "mucha calle" [a lot of shoe leather]), while *el pibe* depends on the internet (Twitter, Google, and Facebook) for his information gathering. He is "Generación Google: sin calle ... todo Internet" (The boy's all Google ... no street) (33; 31). Brena repeatedly tells the rookie he needs to exercise his shoe leather, but eventually each will recognize the benefits of each other's methods when Brena uses internet searches and *el pibe* hits the street. The novel incorporates a running commentary on the ethics of journalism, as well as on the limits of journalism when compared to fictional writing, a topic I will discuss in this section.

The writers also address the ethics involved in true crime writing. Chazarreta was preceded in death by his wife, Gloria Echagüe, who also died in their country club home in suspicious circumstances. This fictional murder has many similarities to the real-life case of María Marta García Belsunce. Like the actual crime, the fictional woman's death is a homicide, and certain individuals took great pains to try to make it look like an accident. In addition, the husband is the prime suspect and his last name, Chazarreta, sounds like Carrascosa, the real person's name. Significantly, the "true crime" link—the killing of the wife—is only referred to as the event that will precipitate the serial murders. Our heroine will not investigate this crime but rather the purely fictional "spin-off" events—the murder of the husband and his schoolmates. On the occasion of Gloria Echagüe's death, Nurit was called upon by Lorenzo Rinaldi to write a series of articles for the paper, "*non fiction* ... como Truman Capote" (62). When Nurit protests that it is not clear what happened in the case, Rinaldi tells her to "inventar, imaginar, ficcionalizar" (invent, imagine, fictionalize). "Me parece poco serio," Nurit replies, "que salga en un diario algo inventado por mí sobre un caso real, la gente se puede confundir.... No me quiero sentir responsable de eso" (It would be cavalier ... for a newspaper to publish something invented about a real case. People get confused.... I don't want to be responsible for their confusion) (62; 56). Here, Nurit serves as Piñeiro's alter ego, voicing her stand in relation to cases of true crime, and Piñeiro is replying to those who expected her to write about the García Belsunce case. Piñeiro explains her stance as follows: "I like to invent stories and not look for news.... The journalist cannot invent but the writer has that license, although I believe that it must be exercised responsibly. In the case of a homicide, I think you cannot point out who you think the culprit is" (Piñeiro, "Los crímenes"). Thus, while Piñeiro has no qualms about inserting details from and referring to actual crimes in *Betibú*, she delineates her ethical boundaries. Obviously, her refusal to signal whom she thinks is the killer is at odds with Argemí's novel based on the García Belsunce crime since it identifies the husband as the killer.

The journalists also discuss whether Rodolfo Walsh's revolutionary journalism is still a viable model for contemporary journalists.[26] In Brena's opinion it is not, because times have changed: "Hoy en este país no hay quien se pueda parecer a Rodolfo Walsh ... [porque] era un revolucionario, y el periodismo ya nada tiene que ver con la revolución. Nos aburguesamos, pibe" (Nobody, not me nor anyone else in this country today, can come close to Rodolfo Walsh ... [because he] was a revolutionary, and journalism has nothing to do with the revolution anymore. We turned bourgeois, kid) (153; 138). However, Walsh's principles are still relevant: "Como dijo Walsh, si no hay justicia, por lo menos que haya verdad" (As Walsh said, if there is no justice, at least let there be truth) (220; 198), says Brena. Another issue is whether journalists should silence the truth when publishing it could harm others. When the trio discovers that Nurit and her family and friends could be in danger if the author or authors of the crime are named, they decide they must be satisfied with the fact that they discovered the truth, even if they cannot publish it. After all, they point out, they are journalists; it is not their job to administer justice. But maybe they can relate the truth in code, like they did during the dictatorship. This is exactly what Nurit's final article does; however, Rinaldi refuses to publish it. *El pibe*, who believes that this is Nurit's best article and is angered by having to silence what they have discovered, will post it on blogs and on Facebook. He resigns from his job at *El Tribuno* with the intention of setting up an online news portal. In this way, the rookie ends up modeling a bold and ethical pose. Nurit has her own way of dealing with the situation—she will return to fiction writing. When Roberto Gandolfini tells her she cannot write about the murders because she has no sources, she replies, "Yo no soy periodista, soy escritora, puedo contar sin citar fuentes, puedo dar por hecho algo que sólo está en mi imaginación" (I'm not a journalist, I'm a writer: I can tell a story without quoting sources, I can take as given something that is only in my imagination) (317; 287). In her final report for *El Tribuno*, she writes that she will return to her world of ficiton, "*porque en ese lugar no tengo miedo, porque en ese lugar puedo inventar otra realidad, una aún más cierta*" (because it is a place where I'm not frightened, a place where I can invent another reality, an even truer one) (332; 302). Here, once again, Nurit is expressing Piñeiro's view, as the author has stated: "In this mess we are in, I have the feeling that today it is better not to do journalism, but to turn to fiction" (Aguirre, "Los temas están en el aire").

Thus at the end of the novel, Nurit will abandon an assignment that requires her to write nonfiction and return to her "safe" world of fiction, pointing to the capacity of fiction to treat certain themes that cannot be handled by nonfiction. Osvaldo Aguirre spells out how Piñeiro's novel reverses the traditional opposition between fiction and journalism, as it proposes "the inversion of Rodolfo Walsh's well-known formula (according to which fiction was the bourgeois form and journalism was a revolutionary possibility)" ("Los temas están en el aire"). This marks a defeat insofar as it acknowledges that the wrongdoers are too powerful to name and will go unpunished, at least by legal means, but it is a gain insofar as it reveals truth by another method.

Celebrating the Powers of Fiction

Why does Nurit love her fictional world so much, ultimately abandoning her journalistic assignment to return to that world? What kind of knowledge is imparted by fiction and what are the benefits of fiction as opposed to nonfiction? We might say that Piñeiro's novel demonstrates the responses to these questions—the capacities of fiction as opposed to nonfiction. Indeed, *Betibú* can be considered a celebration of fiction and what it can do, as elucidated by certain theorists.

Kalle Pihlainen points out that while both fictional and nonfictional narratives partake in the production of knowledge, they have different means of producing it. He notes that the "human truth" of historical texts is more specific—they "represent *particular real people*" (56), the implication being that fictional texts represent more "universal" truths, or in other terms, we receive metaphorical insights from literature (40). Fiction enjoys a privileged status: it is not bound to referentiality as is nonfiction, thus giving its writer creative liberty. Nonfiction or historical fiction's commitment to referentiality, Pihlainen suggests, means that "historical narratives generally [produce] less compelling metaphors ... due to the way that the commitment to referentiality disrupts the uniformity among what Riffaterre terms 'indices of fictionality'—the elements which create coherency in the narrative, thus generating its metaphoric dimension" (43). The writer of fiction, not being bound to referentiality, is free to create a moral closure that produces aesthetic pleasure. This difference in referentiality is also reflected in the narrative form, as narrativizing implies selection and foregrounding (42). Ultimately, then, what makes the difference is not the "fictionality but the resulting complexity in form" (43), and this is another component of our aesthetic pleasure.

A "signpost of fictionality," according to Cohn, is the separation between the biographical author and the narrator of the story, which allows for narrativizing techniques and focalization, bringing in the imaginative and creative level. What is more, an imaginary character and his inner life can be known to his narrator as no real person can be known to a real speaker ("Signposts" 785). Fiction also elicits greater emotional involvement of the reader—Marie-Laure Ryan observes that nonfiction's allegiance to objectivity and verifiability dulls the narration and hampers the reader's emotional involvement in the narrated events. According to this theorist, "Readers feel more at home, textually speaking, in the worlds of fiction than in the world of nonfiction" (171). Finally, because "real world facts are turned into fictional truths," fiction can aim at two referents—the real world and the fictional world—at the same time (171).

Returning to *Betibú*, its constant play with diegetic levels exemplifies how narrative can be artistically manipulated to achieve different effects such as suspense, humor, or an emotive identification with the character. Importantly, *Betibú* calls attention to its nature as fiction, its artifice: it is a construction, not an unmediated picture of real life. Ultimately, metafiction serves to thematicize fictionality and celebrate its creative capacity, demonstrating why Nurit loves her world of fiction.

### THE GATED COMMUNITY: A DISTURBING MESSAGE

To conclude, these three novels use murders disguised as accidents or suicides in an exclusive gated community as a point of departure to cast a critical eye on contemporary society. "A police case—the process of investigating and understanding a violent death," Daniel Link tells us, "is a discursive phenomenon" (6, 10), and the form of the crime reveals certain truths about the society that produces it. Both *Retrato* and *Las viudas* show the extremes to which individuals will go to retain their status. Argemí's novel, a fictional re-creation of the García Belsunce murder, dramatizes the stunning erosion of family solidarity, as well as the accomplices' belief in their impunity. *Las viudas de los jueves* presents a panoramic view of the lifestyle of the residents of a fictional "country," winners of neoliberal structural changes and members of a consumer society in which a person's worth is based on his or her ability to consume. The crime reveals anxiety about the social identity of these nouveau riche when they fear loss of their status and lifestyle. *Betibú*, moving between the exurbs and Buenos Aires, looks at the "country" from the perspective of outsiders, focusing on the humiliation caused by the excessive security measures. The novels all critique the exclusionary and discriminatory practices of this social group.

All three novels employ metafictional strategies. In *Retrato* and *Las viudas*, the play with temporal and diegetic levels creates a type of "narrative surround" that we may conceive as analogous to the country clubs' walls. That is, the narrators position themselves at a vantage point outside the gated community to provide a perspective for their critique of what goes on within. In *Betibú*, on the other hand, the extensive use of parody, intertextuality, and self-referentiality speaks to the very nature of fiction—its process of composition and mode of comprehension of reality.

Comparing the motives of the crimes, in *Retrato* and *Las viudas* the *ostensible* motive is fiscal, the retention of wealth, but since the plot reveals an addiction to a consumer lifestyle as a mark of success, behind the economic motive we can perceive deep-seated psychological disturbances. Here we turn to the words of Ross MacDonald's detective, Lew Archer: "You can't blame money for what it does to people. The evil is in people, and money is the peg they hang it on. They go wild for money when they've lost their other values" (*The Moving Target* 166 [*El blanco móvil* 173], cited by Giardinelli, *El género negro* 248). In *Betibú*, the initial solution shows the crimes were motivated by primordial emotions: revenge for sexual abuse. However, the suggestion of an "empresa sicaria" and the complicity of the police imply that these were not exclusively crimes of passion but part of a complex network of murder-for-hire protected by the police. All three novels take an ethical stance, critiquing unethical behavior and practices. To this end, Dussere points out the seeming contradiction surrounding the existence of noir films and novels—they are "both an indictment and artifact of capitalism, a populist invention and a popular entertainment" (23). I agree with his judgment that this paradox should not lead us to dismiss their political potential (45).

In regard to justice, it is nonexistent in *Retrato* due to the suspects' connections and their successful manipulation of their surroundings. *Las viudas* suggests the possibility of justice when the Guevara family, due to the pressure of their adolescent son, decides to leave the "country" to report the crime to the police. Thus expulsion or self-exile from the "country" is the only way for truth to prevail in the valley of lies, and hope for change is deposited in the youth. In *Betibú*, despite its lighter tone, humor, and "happy ending," the sociopolitical message of the novel is grim, as the conclusion suggests that the "tailored" serial murders were pulled off thanks to the conspiracy of big business and the police. The fact that the "detectives" are ultimately too terrified to disclose their discovery and the criminals will remain unpunished is indeed a dark and disturbing message.

Finally, the authors of these novels, while perceiving the country club as a contemporary version of the country house / locked room template popular during the golden age of detective fiction, use it with the opposite message in regard to justice. During the interwar period, this setting featured the English countryside and the landed gentry of the upper bourgeoisie class in the final years of the caste system. In its contemporary Argentine reincarnation, the exurban venue depicts a relatively new phenomenon in urban development, made possible by a class recently enriched by economic restructuring. While the golden age plots served to reassure their audience and preserve the status quo via a neat resolution of the crime and punishment of the wrongdoers, Argemí's and Piñeiro's novels depict the gated community as a place where murderers can potentially remain unpunished due to corruption and insularity, thus communicating an unsettling portrait of contemporary society.

Chapter Five

# THE "OTHER SIDE"
## The Urban Poor and the Crime Novel

> Argentina ha intentado alimentar el mito de que es un país de clase media, pero es mentira.
> —Sergio Olguín, "El mito de la Argentina de clase media es mentira"

PUERTO MADERO, BUENOS AIRES' REFURBISHED PORT AREA FEATURING luxury restaurants and apartment buildings, is a showcase of the modernization and privatization push of the Menem years. It is adjacent to the Reserva Ecológica, a natural area formed by reclaimed land from the river. *Puerto Apache* (2002) by Juan Martini portrays the efforts of a group of marginalized people to establish a squatter settlement in the reserve, a stone's throw away from this paragon of Argentina's market-based economic reform. By situating these two disparate environments side by side, the novel highlights not only the contrast but also the interrelatedness of the two phenomena—how urban impoverishment was part and parcel of Argentina's neoliberalization. *La fragilidad de los cuerpos* (2012) by Sergio Olguín—through the investigation of deaths on the railroad tracks—explores the condition of marginal social sectors in Buenos Aires and, in particular, scrutinizes the complex relationships that can develop between individuals from different social groups. While in the previous chapter I considered novels set in the gated neighborhoods of the wealthy, in this chapter I turn to novels that deal with the plight of those on the other side—the urban poor.

### NO LONGER A MIDDLE-CLASS SOCIETY

"The mass of the Argentine poor are a casualty of turning the nation into an early neoliberal experimental field," according to sociologist Guillermina

Seri (67). María del Carmen Feijoó speaks of a new social structure, calling it "a new country, a new poverty, a mutation of the historical social actors" (8). In this section, I will look at the causes of the exponential rise in the number of Argentines living in poverty, the impact of this change on Argentine society, and the mapping of the neighborhoods of the rich and poor in Buenos Aires, phenomena that are explored in the novels by Martini and Olguín.

In contrast to the majority of other Latin American countries, Argentina traditionally prided itself in being a middle-class nation. As Graciela Silvestri and Adrián Gorelik explain, "Beginning in the first decade of the twentieth century, the popular sectors embarked on the path of social ascent that would create one of the differential aspects of Buenos Aires in the Latin American context: the *porteña* middle class" (462). By 1930 Argentina was a middle-class society and Buenos Aires was the capital of this middle-class lifestyle (Mora y Araujo 247). Feijoó discusses the characteristics of the "viejo país": The central values were personal effort and sacrifice, solidarity and charity. The *barrio* was a place of security and identity. Social mobility was a group phenomenon and the rules of the game were clear in regard to how and when the move was legitimate—individuals did not try to "*zafarse*" (get ahead by dubious means) (18–22).

The "new scenario" began in the mid-1970s, explains Feijoó, intensified in the "lost decade" of the 1980s, and was completed in the early 1990s with the reimplantation of neoliberalism (55). While sectors in the most dynamic areas of the economy grew richer, these policies also led to widespread unemployment and impoverishment. Import deregulation eroded domestic industry: industrial areas in and around Buenos Aires that could not compete in the global marketplace due to obsolescence were abandoned, leaving many workers unemployed (Seri 62; Silvestri and Gorelik 462). Between 1988 and 2000, greater Buenos Aires, the industrial heartland of Argentina, lost 5,508 industrial plants, experiencing a 22 percent decrease in nine years (Auyero, "The Hyper-Shantytown" 100). Privatizations of government holdings also resulted in large-scale job loss, and the retrenchment of the welfare state, part of the austerity plan, left these individuals without a safety net, resulting in a dramatic increase in the number of people living in poverty. Many of the unemployed have become service workers for the rich—maids, nannies, gardeners, chauffeurs—outside the protection of labor legislation, while others resort to marginal activities: the drug trade, prostitution, delinquency (Auyero, *Poor People's Politics* 38–39; Feijoó 37). "The passage of thousands of workers from factory work to informal and precarious jobs is the most significant economic phenomenon of the last fifteen years," states Javier Auyero (*Poor People's Politics* 31). Seri sums up the process as follows: "Decades of deindustrialization, recessive cycles, structural adjustment and thin social policies led to the pauperization of millions and threw hundreds of thousands more into villas while worsening their already precarious conditions of living" (65).

Feijoó explains that the new poverty changed Argentina's self-image as a largely homogeneous society, creating two different societies, juxtaposed but still closely linked. There has been a loss of sociability as class differences between neighborhoods has intensified, turning them into two coexisting but different worlds separated by only a few blocks. Poor and rich alike have become afraid, each with their own set of problems. Initially there was compassion and solidarity toward the poor, but as it became a long-term phenomenon, this has changed and people blame the poor for the growth of social evils, such as delinquency, drug addiction, and social disorganization, considering them dangerous classes (Feijoó 51–56). Seri remarks that shantytown dwellers are stigmatized as criminal, seen as security threats, and "treated as less than civilized or properly human." The "young, the homeless, and the poor are harassed and turned into *delincuentes* while the wealthier, perceived as in need of protection, are turned into decent citizens, *la gente*" (67, 60).

As Buenos Aires expands, it is increasingly marked by strong social and spatial inequalities. Its northern zone—including the neighborhoods of Barrio Norte, Recoleta, Palermo, and Belgrano—is home to the affluent, while the southern and southwestern areas became a zone of factories and working-class neighborhoods. The movement of the wealthy to higher grounds in the northern sector of the city began in the second half of the nineteenth century, provoked by the yellow fever epidemic of 1871, which spawned in the low-lying areas in the south in the vicinity of the Riachuelo River. Other factors contributing to the northward flight included increased industrial activity on both sides of the Riachuelo, the expansion of the Italian immigrant community in La Boca (in the southern sector), and the greater attraction of the Delta (Troncoso 95–96).[1] The big houses in the central and southern sections of the city that the rich abandoned in their exodus to the north were subdivided or rented by room, becoming the *conventillos* or tenements of generations of immigrants (Yujnovsky 436). By the turn of the century, luxurious French-style mansions were constructed in the prestigious Barrio Norte—home to those who benefited from Argentina's expansion in agriculture and commerce. At the same time, working-class neighborhoods began to develop along the Riachuelo and in the southern sector of the city. The Riachuelo was an ideal location for meatpacking plants because wastes were eliminated in the river, which was also an economical mode of transport. Other industries established near the Riachuelo included meat-salting plants, tanneries, metallurgical plants, shipyards, and soap factories. This industrial activity left the Riachuelo permanently contaminated. Industries that did not require a nearby water source were established in the southern sector of Buenos Aires and extensive neighborhoods housing workers grew up around them, lending the southern zone a distinctive working-class identity. At the same time, industries began to be established in the peripheral zones of Buenos Aires, to the west and the north (Schvarzer 210–12). With the industries, *villas* sprang up in the periphery, the same areas where gated communities for the wealthy mushroomed beginning in the late 1980s.

According to Eileen Stillwaggon, "Over ten million Argentines live in shanties or tenements, in houses without sanitary facilities, in mud houses, lean-tos, or caves, or crowded three or more to a room" (54, quoted in Auyero, *Poor People's Politics* 39). While, as noted in chapter 4, the "countries" are emblematic of the concentration of wealth and privatization of the new rich, on the other extreme are the *villas miseria*. The *villas miseria*, or shantytowns, are not a new phenomenon. Between 1930 and 1943, they began to grow in neighborhoods in the southern sector of Buenos Aires and in outlying areas where small industries were installed. Lands were occupied illegally and precarious homes multiplied, constructed out of cardboard, tin cans, and old automotive parts, and without public services (Romero 202, 206). José Luis Romero speaks of the social composition of these early *villas*: "There were undoubtedly some criminals and many people with irregular lifestyles; but the society of the *villeros* was generally composed of honest and hardworking people whose fundamental problem was the impossibility of getting another kind of housing" (206). The problem became more acute with the outbreak of World War II, which made it necessary to produce domestically what European markets could no longer supply. The new job market in Buenos Aires attracted huge waves of workers from the interior of Argentina and bordering countries, and availability of housing could not keep up with the influx of people. The result was a chaotic mix of already established residential zones with industrial districts, working-class neighborhoods, and *villas de emergencia* (Chiozza 417). By the end of the 1960s, the growth of *villas* had transformed 13 percent of Buenos Aires' surface. Although big housing projects replaced many *villas* that were eradicated or dispersed, the lack of adequate housing programs for low-income people made the *villas* an endemic problem for Buenos Aires (Chiozza 421). While *villas miseria* originally served as sites of passage toward stable working-class jobs and neighborhoods, years of crisis and recessive policies made the shantytowns of the neoliberal era permanent places to stay, with no way out. The fictional Puerto Apache is such a place.

## COLLATERAL DAMAGE OF CONSUMER SOCIETY:
### *PUERTO APACHE* BY JUAN MARTINI

The Reserva Ecológica Costanera Sur is a two-kilometer-long tract of reclaimed land alongside the Costanera, a wide avenue originally built as a riverside promenade. Plants took root in the silt and animals found homes, and today the area is covered with vegetation and teeming with wildlife. The government declared it a nature reserve, and it has become a popular place to escape the city for hiking, biking, bird watching, picnicking, and simply enjoying its natural beauty. It is in this natural reserve, just across from Puerto Madero, that the fictional squatter settlement called Puerto Apache is founded.[2] Its name combines Puerto Madero and Fuerte Apache, the popular name of the Barrio Ejército de los Andes, a poor neighborhood known for poverty and delinquency that came to represent the failure of state housing policies (Jajamovich).[3] In the juxtaposition of Puerto Madero, a neighborhood emblematic of Argentina's market-orientated privatization policy, and Puerto Apache, refuge of the homeless, Juan Martini constructs a critique of the deleterious effects of the economic policy embraced by the Menem administration and how those excluded from consumer society became "un problema del siglo XXI," as the inhabitants of Puerto Apache call themselves.[4]

My analysis focuses on how the novel serves to critique and denounce the impact of market forces and the allure of consumerism, especially in the lives of the poor who cannot participate in consumer society. In particular, I discuss the role of the novel's narrator, la Rata, a marginal person who is caught between two worlds: while he champions the cause of the utopian squatter settlement that characterizes itself as apart from market forces, at the same time he is mesmerized by the life of luxury provided by consumerism. Since he and his peers can only access this lifestyle with money from the illegal drug trade, it is inextricably linked to violence and corruption. I will also consider the depiction of Buenos Aires, seen as fragmented and deteriorating due, at least in part, to the new approach to urban planning.

### A New Model of Urban Planning and Its Collateral Effects

Puerto Madero, the vanguard of the new urban configuration of the 1990s, is a prime example of the use of sizeable sums of private capital in initiatives that affect large tracts of the city. It represents the policy of the urban fragment, which focuses on the development of those sectors of the city with most promise for private businesses. Gated communities, discussed in chapter 4, also exemplify this model. Previously, this type of project had been publicly decided, and only the state carried out large-scale interventions (Silvestri and Gorelik 489–90). The reconversion of Puerto Madero, overseen by a team of Catalonian city planners, quickly became a showcase for Buenos Aires' modernization. The adjacent natural area formed by reclaimed land from the river, the Reserva Ecológica, was left intact and the old port's brick warehouses were repurposed to create a hypermodern and sophisticated place for business, leisure, and habitation. Thus the abandoned wharf area was transformed into a highly successful real estate venture with upscale restaurants and cafés, luxury apartments, businesses, banks, and a private university, giving this sector of the city a facelift in tune with the new global age.

However, the development of Puerto Madero has not had a trickle-down effect on the most deteriorated zones of the city, such as the center and the south. These grand private undertakings, Silvestri and Gorelik tell us, do not function as "exceptions within a context of urban decay (to whose eradication they would, therefore, contribute), but as its necessary counterpart." "In Buenos Aires," they explain, "the conceptual turn of urban planning ended up being the alibi of the neoconservative ideology that inaugurated the 1990s" (491). According to these urban sociologists, the growing impoverishment of large sectors of urban society is accelerated by the new role of the state as a promoter of large-scale privatization and private development, a phenomenon that is evidenced in the decay of public infrastructure, the deterioration of institutions that lend to social cohesion, and a host of other problems.

The view of the escalation of poverty as an inevitable consequence of neoliberal policy produces what sociologist Zygmunt Bauman calls "collateral damage." Borrowing this term from the war chest, Bauman explains that "casualties are dubbed 'collateral' in so far as they are dismissed as not important enough to justify the costs of their prevention, or simply 'unexpected' because the planners did not consider them worthy of inclusion among the objects of preparatory reconnoitering" (*Collateral Damage* 8). Bauman uses the situation of young delinquents in Bradford (an area of London) to illustrate this concept: "They lie in a combination of the consumerist life philosophy propagated and instilled under the pressure of a consumer-oriented economy and politics, the fast shrinking of life chances available to the poor, and the absence for a steadily widening segment of the population of realistic prospects of escaping poverty in a way that is socially approved and assured.... The situation of the youth in Bradford is a *collateral casualty* of profit-driven, uncoordinated and uncontrolled globalization" (*Collateral Damage* 4). This characterization—conceiving individuals as collateral casualties of market-driven economic policy—could also apply to the fictional inhabitants of Puerto Apache who attempt to make their home in the Reserva Ecológica.

## An Unlikely Detective Seeking an Identity

The characterization of la Rata (the Rat), in particular his confusion regarding his identity, is central to *Puerto Apache*'s portrayal of the alienating effects of a consumerist society. He carries out the detective function in the narrative as he strives to unravel a mystery involving revenge among drug traffickers. The key to la Rata's character is his "hybridity," meaning that he participates in two worlds. On the one hand, la Rata forms part of the "utopian" resistance settlement with other marginalized people, literal outcasts who vindicate their right to establish their own self-regulated community. A resident of Puerto Apache and the son of one of its founders, la Rata expresses pride in its progressive principles. On the other hand, he participates in and benefits from a consumer society financed by the illegal drug trade. His income source is drug trafficking, and he enjoys having access to material luxuries via his girlfriend, Maru, a kept woman of a drug dealer known as el Pájaro. Principles may be noble, but consumerism is seductive, and few can escape its lure. As other critics have pointed out, la Rata constantly traverses urban boundaries, mediating between two symbolic universes: the space of resistance to neoliberal society and the space of co-optation (Close, *Contemporary Hispanic Crime Fiction* 134; Jacovkis).

A detective plot serves as the narrative frame of the novel: it opens with la Rata receiving a beating from three hired thugs, and his subsequent movements are dictated by his investigation into who ordered his beating and why. La Rata's probe leads him to the discovery of a violent turf war within the local drug trade. In the meantime, through flashbacks, he recounts the establishment of the squatter settlement, Puerto Apache, and describes its ongoing struggle to survive. We also meet the main people in his life—his parents; his common-law wife, Jenifer; his girlfriend, Maru; his friends Cúper and el Toti; and his employer, el Pájaro—as well as others in the settlement.

The novel incorporates two narrative threads—the story of la Rata and his investigation into the drug intrigue, and the creation and demise of Puerto Apache. While these seem to be separate stories linked only by la Rata's involvement in both, there is a hidden link, something that la Rata is only vaguely conscious of: "me pregunto si es posible que el quilombo que hay con el Pájaro y con sus negocios no tenga nada que ver con el quilombo que se está armando en el Puerto" (I wonder if it is possible that the mess with el Párajo's business has to do with the mess that is being stirred up in el Puerto) (113). It turns out that the key to this connection is the slippery figure of "el negro Sosa," who is a participant in both the drug war and the takeover of Puerto Apache with the aim of establishing a drug network there.

A marginal individual with a low echelon role in the illegal drug trade, la Rata is an unlikely detective figure.[5] His job is to memorize a string of numbers provided by el Pájaro, the distributor, and recite them back to Barragán, the supplier. La Rata knows that the numbers are coded drug orders, but he does not know what they mean, nor is it in his interest to know them.

La Rata narrates his story in the present of his investigation, but the time of narration is an unspecified moment in the future, revealed, for example, when he jumps forward in time and says, "Lo que no puedo saber es que ésta es la última vez que veo a Maru" (What I don't know is that this is the last time that I see Maru) (119). The order of his narration is basically chronological except for two chapters that backtrack to provide a more detailed account of events mentioned in the preceding chapter. Mockingly called a "villero ilustrado" by his friends because he uses multisyllable words such as "osteoporosis," la Rata shows a keen sense of language and incorporates *lunfardo*, using words such as "yugar" (to work) and "boleta" (dead), as well as a handful of words in English. These two linguistic registers are another manifestation of his hybrid social reality.

This self-fashioned detective has a wry and sometimes scatological or self-deprecating sense of humor that serves to temper undesirable or unpleasant realities. A prime factor affecting la Rata's narration of the intrigue is that, as a marginal figure, he has only a partial understanding of what is going on and slowly unravels things, a fact that he acknowledges in his typical self-deprecating style. Poking fun at his investigative skills, he says, "¿Encontré o no encontré una noche al Ombú y un mediodía al Pájaro? Muertos, pero los encontré" (Did I or didn't I find el Ombú one night and el Pájaro one afternoon? Dead, but I found them) (167). On other occasions, he shows his scatological inclination. After he escapes the beating, la Rata is amused to come across one of his pursuers having a bowel movement in a vacant lot and describes with genuine delight the moment a stray dog runs up and sticks its snout into the fellow's rear end. Also, when la Rata has to cross a police line to get to Puerto Apache, he comes up with a credible lie in order to gain access, telling the police guard that he works as a cleaning assistant at the nearby yacht club. The police officer asks if he cleans the "mierda seca de los ricos" (dry shit of the rich) (162), to which he replies that he does. Later, when la Rata realizes that the police have to protect the bastions of the wealthy, he comments that the police also have to keep their toilets clean. La Rata's dry humor is a constant. Mocking the showy attire of a minion of a politician turned drug dealer, he says, "No le miro los zapatos. Tengo miedo que el brillo me deje ciego" (I don't look at his shoes. I fear that their shine will blind me) (168).

A leitmotif running through la Rata's narration is his attempt to figure out who he is. "Yo soy la Rata" (I am la Rata) (9) are his first words, thus he begins by identifying himself with what is apparently his tough-guy moniker. Feijoó helps us understand the connection between this identity confusion and the new social order—*the new poverty*—by pointing out that the question "Who are you?" was historically answered with the name of the company one works for and the job one has as well as one's neighborhood (8). The loss of these leads to "the anguish of defining who I am" (81). This explains, at least in part, la Rata's dilemma. His employment does not provide a sense of identity as he has only done odd jobs and now works for a drug dealer. While he mentions his childhood in Pompeya, one of the poorest neighborhoods in the southern part of Buenos Aires, he no longer lives there and does not seem to identify with any neighborhood other than the newly established Puerto Apache. Indeed, his nickname could also allude to his lack of rootedness. In the conclusion of the novel, when he has to exit quickly from Puerto Apache to avoid being killed, he says, "Hay que saltar. Como saltan las ratas, los desesperados, los que quieren seguir viviendo" (One must jump. Like the rats jump, like the desperate people, those who want to stay alive) (178). Thus the rat can also be associated with la Rata's need to displace himself frequently in order to survive.

Another part of his identity problem may originate in the fact that his parents do not provide role models worthy of emulation or identification. His father was a pimp who exploited four fifteen-year-old girls. One of them was his mother, who became pregnant with him at age seventeen. La Rata expresses a desire to understand his father, clearly an effort to know himself. Now retired from the pimping business, la Rata's father has mellowed considerably and is a community organizer of Puerto Apache. When his father dies, after being viciously attacked by invaders of Puerto Apache, la Rata no longer feels the visceral hatred he held for him; he only feels sadness. Ultimately, there is a moment of identification with his father: for the funeral la Rata dresses in a white shirt, jacket, and tie. Looking in the mirror, he recalls the words of his mother: " 'Vos sos un compadrito,' me decía mi vieja, 'como tu padre' " ("You are a *compadrito*," my mother told me, "like your father") (150). Finally, he acknowledges a kinship with his father through the figure of the *compadrito*, variously translated as "dandy," "amiable scoundrel," "macho," and "ruffian." As Close has pointed out, la Rata is closer to a *pícaro* than a Chandleresque private eye (*Contemporary Hispanic Crime Fiction* 134).

Undoubtedly, another source of identity confusion is his sporadic access to the global "high life" through Maru and his role in the drug trade. Maru brings him a T-shirt from Miami with "Versace" stamped on it. He puts it on and looks at himself in the mirror, musing, "¿Quién soy?" (Who am I?) (66). This boy from a poor Buenos Aires neighborhood sports a T-shirt bearing the name of the flashy Italian designer acclaimed by the Menem circle and purchased in Miami. La Rata's inability to recognize himself illustrates what Gorelik describes as "the search for self-knowledge impeded by the masks of metropolitan society" (*Miradas sobre Buenos Aires* 169). Partaking of globalized consumer culture distances la Rata from his roots and makes him wonder about his place in society. He is not sure if he or Maru have a legitimate right to the luxuries of consumer society: "A veces pienso que soy un ladrón. Y a veces pienso que la chorra es ella. No tengo clara esta cuestión" (Sometimes I think that I am a thief. And sometimes I think that she is the crook. I'm not clear about this matter) (24). Ultimately, he proclaims himself a hybrid along with Maru and el Pájaro: "Yo ... soy un híbrido. Maru también. El Pájaro es el más híbrido" (I am a hybrid. So is Maru. El Pájaro is the most hybrid) (24). "The social universe that the novel constructs shows the complexity of the globalized reality in Argentina at the end of the century," explains Liliana Tozzi in her analysis of *Puerto Apache*, and the concept of "hybrid" conveys a particular iteration of the division between global and local (247). La Rata, Maru, and el Pájaro are all individuals who have been raised in poor Buenos Aires neighborhoods and aspire via the drug trade to the trappings of wealth and globalization that were dangled before the public as objects of desire by the discourse of marketing and modeled by Menem and his coterie, and capitalist society in general. Ultimately, la Rata's lack of identity stems from the fact that he is caught between two worlds: his background identifies him as marginal, but he aspires to the life of the globalized high rollers who have access to consumer society. La Rata exposes his envy of the affluent when he and his friend Cúper vandalize an ultraluxurious apartment in the building where Maru lives, a scene I discuss in the section "In Thrall of Consumer Society."

### A Power Struggle among Traffickers

*Puerto Apache* describes a society penetrated by organized and petty crime. The main crime network is that of the drug trade and the plot intrigue is propelled by a struggle for control among dealers and those linked to political power. Other shady activities include purse snatching and organized rings of beggars and prostitution. El Pájaro's lucrative career in crime took off when he became a hit man for politicians. With his earnings, he opened bars and restaurants that were frequented by the elites of Argentine neoliberal society and served as fronts for his narcotrafficking business. He acquired a house in Las Cañitas, two cars, a motorcycle, and a yacht.[6] He also lured the gorgeous Maru away from la Rata and got her an upscale apartment in Puerto Madero. But el Pájaro's stint as head of the local network is short-lived. As la Rata learns later, Walter Monti, an "ex diputado de la provincia," conspired with the supplier Barragán to take over el Pájaro's business. El Pájaro's assistants, Tony and el Ombú, betrayed their boss to go with Monti.

After coming across the corpses of el Ombú and el Pájaro, la Rata knows that he must get to the bottom of things if he wants to survive. Finally, la Rata tracks down Monti's secretary, who explains the intrigue: When el Pájaro found out that el Ombú and Tony had betrayed him to join Monti, he ordered el Ombú's killing. Monti then used this as an excuse to order el Pájaro's killing. Although Monti supposedly has no issue with la Rata, la Rata discovers that Tony has planted cocaine in his house and has notified the police. Therefore, la Rata has to disappear before the police arrive.

As is invariably the case in the *novela negra*, politicians are involved in the criminal activity. While Monti is no longer in politics, he is still considered a politician by those who benefit from his influence. When Tony and el Ombú betray el Pájaro, Tony's girlfriend tells Cúper that they joined up with a politician. Apparently Tony explained the lay of the land to her in the following terms: " 'hoy la política está en todas partes, así que para no quedarse afuera hay que entrar en la política' " (nowadays politics is everywhere, so if you don't want to be left out you have to get involved in politics) (144). In other words, political corruption is the source of big money.

The drug trade is shown in all its violence. A gruesome and eerie moment is created when la Rata comes across el Ombú's cadaver sitting on a chair on la Rata's porch, and la Rata's discovery of el Pájaro's body is undoubtedly the most gory and macabre scene of the novel. El Pájaro's corpse is in the fountain situated in the patio of his house, the water red with his blood and a bloody hand protruding from the water. "Fue una ametralladora. O dos. Casi seguro dos.... El hombre cocido a balazos, liquidado ... fue mi patrón y fue el novio de mi novia" (It was a machine gun. Or two. Almost certainly two.... The man who was cooked by bullets, liquidated ... was my boss and was my girlfriend's boyfriend) (160), says la Rata, who is obviously in shock.

Other forms of criminality are depicted in the novel. La Rata and Cúper steal from the purses of girls in the bars along Corrientes Street, and Cúper's girlfriend works with her nephew, who oversees bands of youngsters who beg on the fanciest streets of the Recoleta neighborhood. He is also in the prostitution business, managing a dozen young girls who offer tricks in the famous Recoleta cemetery, by Sarmiento's mausoleum, the tomb of Rosas, and the Duarte family pantheon housing Evita Perón. "Imaginate. Sexo en la necrópolis más concheta del país" (Just imagine. Sex in the classiest necropolis in the country) (129), says el Toti. Close unpacks the message projected by this image: "Such a business speaks eloquently of the fate of nationalist ideals in a hedonistic neoliberal economy of commodified pleasures" (*Contemporary Hispanic Crime Fiction* 137).

## Disposal People

Through the tale of the creation of Puerto Apache, Martini provides a snapshot of the new poor: people who have been excluded from the system and need a place to live. As Tozzi notes, Puerto Apache reflects the growth of poverty and social exclusion along with new forms of work characterized by informality and social and economic decline of middle-class members who joined the ranks of the poor and destitute (245). Martini considers the novel's engagement with the poverty that resulted from the economic restructuring of the 1990s to be a necessary and crucial social commitment for him as a writer: "It's been four or five years since poverty has made people into trash pickers.... I think that what a lot of people of good will cannot accept is how we have been reduced to this. I found it interesting to focus on that settlement installed right across from Puerto Madero, one of the places that is emblematic of Buenos Aires' reconversion in the 90s. At such a critical, devastating moment, we writers cannot bury our heads in the sand" (Guerriero).

La Rata recounts the story of the establishment of Puerto Apache in flashbacks while he is being beaten. But this chronicle is actually being told to his friend Cúper: "Yo estoy acá desde la primera noche, le cuento a Cúper. Éramos 15, 20 ... 25 los que entramos primero. Mi viejo era el que mandaba. Reventamos los cerrojos y los candados de las puertas y entramos" (I've been here since the first night, I tell Cúper. There were 15, 20 ... 25 of us who entered first. My old man was the one in charge. We busted the locks on the doors and entered) (13). He provides an exact location to this fictional settlement, using real parameters: Puerto Apache extends along the Costanera from the Yacht Club to Corrientes Street, facing the old dikes of the port of Buenos Aires. Puerto Apache has a utopian quality, according to la Rata's description of its principles and its civic organization. He defends it as a responsible and ecologically sound use of the land, a positive alternative to profit-driven real estate developers who wanted to burn it, destroying nature in order to exploit land for profit. Tozzi points out that the concept of "legality" put forward by the Puerto Apache squatters is based on ecological principles—they do not burn anything nor do they harm wildlife (248). "Acá ... nadie mata un mosquito" (Here, no one kills a fly), insists la Rata (17). Puerto Apache did not grow in a haphazard way, as is typically the case with *villas*: la Rata stresses the thought and effort put into the process of marking off the streets, assigning lots, and establishing a governing body.

In an interview for a TV spot about Puerto Apache, el Chueco, another founder, defines who the residents are and, especially, who they are not: "Se dice que esto es una cueva de delincuentes, un nido de malandras, borrachos y drogados, se dice que somos zurdos, vagos y pendencieros. Y no es así." He insists that they are decent people who do honest labor: "Puerto Apache ... está lleno de peones, albañiles, obreros del riel, empleados municipales, tacheros, mozos, vendedores" (They say that this is a cave of delinquents, a nest of criminals, drunkards and drug addicts, they say that we are leftists, lazy and quarrelsome. And it is not like that. Puerto Apache ... is full of laborers, masons, railroad workers, municipal employees, taxi drivers, waiters, peddlers) (62). La Rata also belabors these points, insisting that Puerto Apache is a settlement and not a *villa*, and that it has many good people who are there because they cannot find another place to live, not because they do not deserve to be somewhere else. Both el Chueco and la Rata attempt to establish an identity by differentiating themselves from traditional *villeros* insofar as they are an organized collectivity. Their insistence that they are decent people and not wrongdoers is clearly a response to society's stigmatization and criminalization of the poor.

The stories of several individuals serve as examples of those who find themselves in the ranks of the marginal. La Rata's friend Cúper was a soccer player recruited by a team in Spain, but they discovered he had a heart murmur and sent him back to Argentina. Now he gets by distributing vegetables and stealing purses from inattentive girls. Garmendia is an example of a middle-class entrepreneur who fell out of the system. "Yo en 1971 era dueño de un taller mecánico" (In 1971 I owned an automobile repair shop), he explains to the television interviewer (67). He says that he was doing well until the military takeover in 1976, and he blames José Alfredo Martínez de Hoz for ruining him. As Natalia Jacovkis points out, "The breaking point [for Garmendia] is the beginning of the dictatorship and the beginning of the implementation of neoliberal economic policies during the period when Martínez de Hoz was Minister of Economy." Garmendia had to sell everything at a loss and move in with his son. In the 1980s, his son lost everything and they became street people, then entered a *villa*, and finally arrived at Puerto Apache. " 'Hoy nadie tiene trabajo' " (Nowadays everyone is out work), Garmendia concludes (69). Puerto Apache is also home to others who are not part of the formal labor market: for instance, reformed pickpockets converted into painters and a stripper.

"Somos un problema del siglo XXI" (We are a problem of the twenty-first century) (173), reads the banner that occupants of Puerto Apache put up as the new century dawned. What are they communicating with their ironic epithet? Bauman explains that poor people are not useful to capitalist society, which has shifted its sources of profit from exploitation of factory laborers to exploitation of consumers: "Poor people, stripped of the resources needed to respond to the seductions of consumer markets, need currency and credit accounts (not the kinds of services provided by the 'welfare state') to be of any use in consumer capital's understanding of 'usefulness'" (*Collateral Damage* 16). As such, these people correspond to Bauman's definition of the underclass: "a congregation of individuals who, unlike the rest of the population, do not belong to any class—and so in fact do not belong to society.... It does not contribute anything the society needs for its survival and well-being; in fact, society would do better without it" (3). The *villeros* are aware of this phenomenon—that market society has worked to expulse them and has no place for them.

Under siege from developers who want to use the land for real estate ventures as well as environmentalists who want the area to remain a nature reserve, Puerto Apache is engaged in a struggle for its survival. Gangs have come in and beaten up the residents, including la Rata's father. The final blow comes when el negro Sosa takes over, announcing on TV that he is the spokesman for Puerto Apache and is ready to dialogue about its future, implying that he will pact with business interests. In so doing, he will betray the principles of the community. He is also in with the drug dealers and wants to establish a trafficking network there. Thus the reach of organized crime threatens to sully a settlement that prided itself as being apart from the vicissitudes of market-driven society. This is the destiny of the "ciudad de los negocios": in the battle of interests, the most powerful triumph, not the most just or the most reasonable (Gorelik, *Miradas sobre Buenos Aires* 203–4).

## In Thrall of Consumer Society

The novel stresses the central role of the market economy, globalization, and consumerism in the lives of those who live in their thrall. Juxtaposed to the occupants of Puerto Apache are the "winners" of the new order. Maru's rise in society is based on marketing—she began her career in advertising at age seventeen doing promos for *alfajores* (shortbread cookies), Marlboro cigarettes, and cell phones. Thus, not only did she work for the marketing industry; she herself became a commodity. Thanks to her relationship with el Pájaro, Maru lives a life of luxury, at least according to la Rata's standards, in a duplex in Puerto Madero. It is fitted with luxurious objects that dazzle la Rata: "La cama de Maru, arriba, es una King, o sea una especie de sueño interminable con sábanas de lino.... Hay luces con pantallas de tela y cuadros por todos lados, hasta en el baño" (Maru's bed, upstairs, is a King, a kind of unending dream with linen sheets.... There are lamps with cloth shades and pictures everywhere, even in the bathroom) (23). After visiting Maru's condominium, la Rata and Cúper break into another condo in the building. If they were impressed by Maru's place, they find this sumptuous apartment mind-boggling: it has four bedrooms, lots of bathrooms, and quarters for two maids. La Rata digs his fingernail into one of the paintings and is ticked off to find that it is real. He and Cúper make a shambles of the apartment, pulling clothes and food out of drawers and cupboards, throwing everything onto the floor. But he insists that it could have been worse: they refrain from making a dirty mess by breaking eggs and defecating because "eso lo hacen los resentidos, los tipos con mala onda... Nosotros no. No tenemos motivo. Un poco de bronca.... Eso es todo" (that's what resentful people do, the guys with bad vibes.... Not us. We have no motive. A bit of anger.... That's all) (32). On the way out, they view the enormous living room with various seating groups; "several kilometers" away is a long table with seating for twelve, and much further are a library and an office. Antique Persian rugs adorn the vast open spaces on the floor. The two men raised in poverty seem to be fascinated and appalled by the thought of "la incontable cantidad de guita que tienen los dueños del palace" (the incredible amount of dough that the owners of the palace have) (32). Cúper urinates in the potted plants and the two exit, carefully shutting the door behind them. What can we make of this episode? Here are two shantytown fellows confronted with the trappings of opulence and excess. They are resentful and outraged by this inequality: while others wallow in overabundance, they have next to nothing. Rather than feeling guilty about rifling the possessions, they congratulate themselves for not doing worse damage. The indignation of la Rata and Cúper is a product of their reaction to the ever-present enticement of consumer society, which provides a constant display of images projecting a life that we are encouraged to strive for. This is a portrait of how it feels to be on the outside of the candy store looking in. In contrast to Piñeiro's *Las viudas de los jueves*, which portrays insiders who fear being expelled, the protagonist of *Puerto Apache* is an outsider despising those who have the luxury goods beyond his reach.

La Rata's role in the drug trade acquaints him with the cultural codes that confer status and distinction (Close, *Contemporary Hispanic Crime Fiction*

135). Appearance is everything for those who market themselves and those who want to pass as belonging to consumer society. When el Pájaro began to rise in society through his drug dealing, he cleaned up his act, cutting his hair and wearing expensive clothes. Maru, when she accompanied him to the United States, got a breast augmentation and fixed her teeth. La Rata dresses in his most chic clothes—a leather jacket, new jeans that look old, shoes stolen from an upscale store in the Alto Palermo shopping center—when he goes to work for el Pájaro because, when you show up in el Pájaro's clubs, you have to look presentable. If you look like a *villero*, he gets nervous and kicks you out.

La Rata describes the "winners" of the neoliberal economy, characterizing them as people from the political establishment, addicts and scoundrels living high on the hog with profits gained from plundering the common people. When he and Cúper pass by an establishment in Puerto Madero that is managed by a friend of Cúper's, la Rata comments: "Es un boliche lleno de caretas, ex funcionarios, algunos productores de la TV, tipos enriquecidos a costillas de todos nosotros, merqueros y vividores de calañas diversas y estirpes múltiples. O sea, un paraíso argentino" (It's a bar full of fakes, former officials, TV producers, guys who have become rich on the backs of the rest of us, drug dealers and all types of swindlers. In other words, an Argentine paradise) (97). La Rata continues to decry the high-flying fauna of the night: stylish, rolling in money, and shamelessly corrupt, they make a nightclub prosperous if they decide to grace it with their presence. He scornfully details what they consider glamour, and the ostentation of their consumer habits and appearance: "Corre el champán, el pescado crudo, las mezclas de cordero patagónico con yuyitos de Indonesia. Hay ... pieles bronceadas en soles de otro lado, remeras negras, camisas blancas, relojes macizos, hombres de pelo en pecho con las mechas teñidas o pintadas, ruido a celulares" (Champagne runs freely, raw fish, Patagonian lamb with Indonesian herbs. There are ... skins tanned in distant suns, black T-shirts, white shirts, massive wristwatches, men with dyed chest hair, the sound of cellular phones) (101).

Finally, la Rata paints a bleak picture of the future of the Argentine nation in hands of the rich and corrupt.

> [Los bacanes] se van a ir. Los que ya estén hechos se van a ir a Miami. Y los que todavía tengan cuentas para cobrar, laburos negros, estafas pendientes, se van a ir a barrios privados, a ciudades privadas, a palacios con murallas, ejércitos de seguridad rodeando las murallas, cuidándoles las

casas, los autos, los colegios, las canchas de golf.... Cuando terminen de afanar, cuando ya no quede nada, nada de nada, entonces ellos también se van a ir.... Entonces todo se va a llenar de mendigos, de ladrones, de putas, y de putos. (122)

[The rich are going to leave. Those who've already made it will go to Miami. And those who still have accounts to collect, dirty business, unfinished swindles, will go to gated communities, private cities, walled palaces with armies of security guards surrounding the walls, protecting their houses, their cars, their schools, their golf courses.... When they've finished robbing, when nothing's left, nothing at all, then they will leave too.... Then the place will fill with beggars, thieves, hookers, and queens.]

In sum, la Rata has no doubt that the country is going down the drain.

Another sign of Argentina's changing society is its consumption of US culture, reflected in la Rata's fascination with American movies and the stars of the silver screen. For instance, when he is being beaten, la Rata alludes to the gangster movie *Chinatown*, saying that he wants to slice the nose of one of his attackers, like what happened to Jack Nicholson. He talks about repelling the thugs as if he were Bruce Willis, and says that in the upscale restaurants, patrons are treated as if they were Brad Pitt. When la Rata enters the casino to look for Monti, he recalls Maverick movies in which the cowboys played poker with Maverick in floating casinos on the Mississippi. This reflection inspires him to recite a string of male leads that his father likes: John Wayne, Gary Cooper, Glenn Ford, Henry Fonda, Kirk Douglas, Burt Lancaster, Randolph Scott, and Alan Ladd. Another manifestation of US influence is la Rata's abundant sprinkling of English-language words related to drug trafficking and trappings of contemporary culture: "los business son los business," "Western," "reality-show," "palace," "personal trainers," and "dílers" (dealers). All these references speak to a globalized Argentina, but as opposed to Argentine society of the late nineteenth and early twentieth centuries that looked to France as its model to emulate, la Rata and his pack find their role models in US popular culture.

### A Deteriorated Buenos Aires

As in many of the other novels I have discussed, the city of Buenos Aires is an integral element of the plot action in *Puerto Apache*. The city is relentlessly mapped, pinpointing streets and plazas that the characters frequent or traverse. The novel presents a particular urban configuration: in this case it is of a fragmented and deteriorated city with pockets of wealth contrasting with zones that have fallen into decay. One of the areas mapped is the disposition of the fictional Puerto Apache in relation to the city—it is close and yet "other." The proximity of Puerto Apache and Puerto Madero is apparent when la Rata sees the lights of Puerto Apache from Maru's apartment in Puerto Madero and vice versa. When a television report is done about Puerto Apache, the splicing of frames presents Buenos Aires as if it were apart from Puerto Apache. The picturesque traditional neighborhood of San Telmo is also depicted as near yet far: "Parece mentira que entre la placita Dorrego y Puerto Apache haya apenas veinte cuadras de distancia" (It seems incredible that there are only twenty blocks separating Plaza Dorrego and Puerto Apache) (86), remarks la Rata when he meets with Cúper at a San Telmo bar. His subsequent reference to the lagoon that is part of the ecological reserve and the open sky—"como si estuviéramos en el campo o en una isla" (as if we were in the countryside or on an island) (86)—highlights the contrast between the urbanized city and the nature surrounding Puerto Apache. In his study of the novel, Guillermo Jajamovich points out that while Puerto Apache is presented as outside the city, la Rata frequently travels over spaces that signal the links between the two areas. La Rata describes his trajectories, traversing Córdoba or Corrientes—wide avenues running from Puerto Madero into the heart of Buenos Aires—and entering the city. Thus while the *villa miseria* may appear to be distant and "other," it is intimately linked to the rest of the city.

A critical mark of the divide between Puerto Apache residents and the wealthy areas of the city is unequal policing. When la Rata tries to enter Puerto Apache, he finds federal policemen controlling the passage to Costanera. His first thought is that the police are protecting the residents of Puerto Apache from intruders, but he immediately realizes that this is not the case and that they are actually controlling the security of Puerto Madero. Thus the poor people are cast as dangerous, and the wealthy are in need of protection from them when the *villeros* begin a campaign to try to save their community.

Other images point to the deterioration of traditional Buenos Aires neighborhoods. An example is Lavalle, a pedestrian street where many popular movie houses are located: "Camino por Lavalle. La calle está llena de coreanos y kosovares, de putas, tramposos, dílers y pibes fisurados. La calle está llena de bolsas de basura, de restos de comida, latas, mugre. Un valle de lágrimas, Lavalle" (I walk along Lavalle. The street is full of Koreans, Kosovars, whores, cheats, dealers, wasted kids. The street is full of bags of garbage, leftover food, cans, filth. A valley of tears, Lavalle) (71). La Rata is not exempt from the contempt some *porteños* feel toward immigrants who have changed the city's face—his list implicitly equates immigrants from Korea and Kosovar to criminals and garbage. Other deteriorated areas are mentioned. For instance, el Ombú lives in a dilapidated pension in Plaza Italia (in Palermo), and when la Rata is escaping pursuers, he ducks into a shabby hotel on Paseo Colón. Even the upper-class Recoleta has gone to seed, as indicated in dialogue between la Rata and el Toti.

> —¿Vos pensás que Puerto Madero va a terminar como la Recoleta?— le pregunto al Toti.
> —¿Cómo terminó la Recoleta?
> —Llena de mendigos, chorros y putas . . .
> —Si. . . . Va a terminar igual. Todo en este país va a terminar igual. O peor. (121–22)

> [Do you think that Puerto Madero is going to end up like Recoleta? I ask el Toti.
> How did Recoleta end up?
> Full of beggars, thieves and whores . . .
> Yes. . . . It's going to end up just like that. Everything in this country is going to end up like that. Or worse.]

La Rata and his friend Cúper trace a contrasting trajectory of the city when, in search of Monti, they visit the three top hotels in Buenos Aires. La Rata characterizes them as pockets of affluence: "El Sheraton es un hotel para ejecutivos de empresas de otro mundo. El Plaza cambió los dandys y las chicas glamorosas por turistas ricos. El Alvear es otra cosa. Tiene la pinta de un palacio con barandas de oro, arañas de cristal y escaleras de mármol" (The Sheraton is a hotel for corporate executives from another world. The Plaza traded its dandies and glamorous girls for wealthy tourists. The Alvear is something else. It looks like a palace with gold railings, glass chandeliers and marble staircases) (166).

### Maru: A Marketable Woman

Female characters play supporting roles in *Puerto Apache*. As in the traditional hard-boiled detective stories, an upward-bound femme fatale complicates the relationship between the male characters. Despite her ambition,

Maru appears to have a good heart, as seen in her kindness to la Rata. Maru was la Rata's girlfriend when they were teenagers, but she always aspired to more and took up with el Pájaro, who was on the rise thanks to his role in the drug trade. Even though el Pájaro is Maru's official boyfriend, she continues seeing la Rata, who is still crazy about her and enjoys hanging out in her luxurious apartment and having sex with her. While Maru treats him sweetly when he comes to her with his injuries from the beating, la Rata later discovers that she falsely implicated him as having stolen some of the *merca*, using him as a decoy to divert el Pájaro from her planned betrayal of el Pájaro with Walter Monti. Always in need of something new, Maru set her sights on Monti, the richest and most powerful man she knew. Maru's extraordinary beauty is a leitmotiv of la Rata's narrative, as he repeatedly praises her looks.

> Maru es una diosa. [Maru is a goddess.] (23)

> Flaca, alta, impresionante, Maru siempre tuvo impacto. [Skinny, tall, impressive, Maru always made an impact.] (28)

> Las piernas de Maru, con tacos altos, son de campeonato. [Maru's legs, with high heels, are championship category.] (67)

> Vestida como una diosa. Más linda que nunca. [Dressed like a goddess. More beautiful than ever.] (93)

> Los tipos no pueden dejar de mirarla. Siempre es así. [The guys can't stop looking at her. It's always like that.] (118)

Maru's looks turn her into a prize, a commodity that gravitates to the wealthiest man who can provide her the life of luxury she craves. Maru's beauty stands in contrast to Monti's repulsive nature, as described by la Rata.

> Monti es un gordo de grasa fofa.... Tiene incrustado en todos los gestos, en el más evidente de la mirada y en cada milímetro de la piel, ese borde canalla que no se borra con nada. Es un turro, Monti, un cagador, un fascista.... Su ropa cara es guita tirada a la basura porque nada puede quedarle bien a un tipo así. (76)

> [Monti is a flabby fat man.... Imbedded in all his gestures, evident in his gaze and in every millimeter of his skin, is that coarse bastard that cannot be erased with anything. He's a motherfucker, Monti, a scoundrel, a fascist.... His expensive clothes are dough thrown into the trash because nothing can look good on a guy like that.]

Walter Monti. Un tipo sudoroso, de saliva espesa y manos húmedas. Tiene el pelo teñido, Monti. Poco pelo, engrasado y teñido. (138)

[Walter Monti. A sweaty guy with thick saliva and clammy hands. Monti has dyed hair. Thinning, greasy and dyed.]

This makes the marriage of the mismatched pair much more unstomachable. Having sold herself to the highest bidder, marrying a revolting scoundrel for his wealth and power, Maru embodies unethical market-driven values.

Other female characters, such as Jenifer and Guada, demonstrate nobility and redeeming qualities despite their station in life. Jenifer is a good homemaker who puts up with la Rata's infidelity but finally gets fed up and leaves him, taking their two children with her. Guada is a stripper who sleeps with la Rata's father. She lives with her mother, who works as a maid for families in Palermo y Barrio Norte. To his surprise, la Rata discovers that he likes Guada; she is a wise and decent girl with a sense of style. Other female characters are seen as pathetic but kindly, such as la Rata's mother, who is still pretty but dying of cancer, and her cousin Angela, an unmarried schoolteacher and a woman without a future, according to la Rata. Both enjoy la Rata's company when he travels to Rosario, where they live. His mother is elated just to spend time with him, and Angela hastens to prepare dinner for him and agrees to sleep with him. La Rata definitely has a way with women—they like him and he likes them, resulting in an ostensibly sympathetic portrayal of the female characters in his narrative. However, Maru is ultimately both a villain—having betrayed la Rata—as well as a victim of her ambition.

The novel concludes after la Rata discovers cocaine planted in his home. La Rata represents a threat to the plans of Sosa, who now works for Monti, to build a drug empire in Puerto Apache. Since Sosa's group is in control, la Rata is no longer safe in Puerto Apache; he must "saltar," or start anew in another place. Puerto Apache was conceived as an alternative community set apart from market values, but ultimately drug lords overrun it.[7] La Rata's story demonstrates that there is no outside, no alternative to market forces. The market, the media, and consumerism are everything in the world that he inhabits, and these are permeated by corruption. As is the case in nearly all the novels discussed in this book, corruption prevails at the end.[8] While in the other works, the investigators try to expose wrongdoing, establish justice, or bring about accountability for wrongdoers, in *Puerto Apache* la Rata sets out to determine the reason for his beating, and in so doing finds the underlying cause in a power struggle between drug lords. He is able to save himself, but he is powerless to prevent Puerto Apache's takeover by an organized crime syndicate.

La Rata takes off alone into the clear night but suddenly spots his friend Cúper running to catch up. Together they exit to an uncertain future. "¿Qué pasó?—me pregunta Cúper. A él le gusta que yo le cuente historias" (What's up? Cúper asks me. He likes me to tell him stories) (183). Here the story goes full circle, returning to the opening scene, where la Rata begins relating his saga to Cúper. In his analysis of the film *Mala época*, Gorelik notes that it paints a portrait of a cruel and inhospitable Buenos Aires without a "redemptive counterpart [*contrafigura salvadora*] to the moral and social misery of the city" (*Miradas sobre Buenos Aires* 168). As opposed to *Mala época*, *Puerto Apache* does have a "contrafigura salvadora" to the consumer society and market-driven interests: these are the bonds of friendship and the power of telling one's story. Similar to *Los hombres te han hecho mal*, *Ciudad Santa*, and *Betibú*, this novel has a sentimental ending. La Rata's friendship with Cúper celebrates nourishing human ties that serve as an antidote to a society based on market value and personal gain.

### FATAL ATTRACTION: *LA FRAGILIDAD DE LOS CUERPOS* BY SERGIO OLGUÍN

In the midnineties Sergio Olguín watched a program on Argentine public television hosted by journalist Fabián Polosecki and titled *El otro lado*. With his characteristic deep engagement with human issues, Polosecki reported on people who commit suicide by throwing themselves under trains. His moving program included interviews with railroad engineers, witnesses, and others. Shortly afterward, Polosecki committed suicide by flinging himself under a train. This chilling sequence of events would become the seed for Olguín's thriller *La fragilidad de los cuerpos* ("Sergio Olguín: 'Mi libro' ").

Olguín grew up in Lanús, a working-class neighborhood in the southern sector of greater Buenos Aires, and his fiction is often set in peripheral areas of the city. Frequent themes in Olguín's novels are class difference as well as the degradation of life in the neighborhoods of the *zona sur* of Buenos Aires, including the violence caused by both local mafias and the Bonaerense police (Friera, "Siempre caigo"). *Lanús* (2008)—a novel named after his old *barrio* containing autobiographical material—depicts both the "gatillo fácil" of police as well as the breakdown of social fabric due to mafia presence. The protagonist, who now lives in downtown Buenos Aires, returns to the *barrio* to investigate the death of a childhood friend who was shot by the police; however, his efforts are blocked by his old band of friends, who are involved with the mafia.

*Oscura monótona sangre* (2010), Olguín's subsequent novel, is infused with spellbinding action, eroticism, and a tone of despair. It also deals with an individual who revisits his old *barrio* but for a much different reason. Expressing irritation with the media's unequal treatment of victims based on where they live—"It is much more terrible if they rob you in Palermo or Recoleta than if they kill you if you live in a *villa*" (Friera, "Estamos viviendo")—Olguín changed the dynamics in *Oscura monótona sangre*. "I liked the idea of inverting the roles: a well-to-do middle-class person could become a dangerous individual for the people of a *villa* based on a fortuitous circumstance," he states (Friera, "Estamos viviendo"). The protagonist of this novel, a wealthy self-made businessman who has risen from humble origins, leads a double life. In search of intense passions, he returns to the *villa*, where he becomes obsessed with a teenage prostitute and ends up killing a young boy. As a reviewer states, "In . . . *Oscura monótona sangre*, Olguín links those distant worlds (that of the middle classes and that of extreme poverty, that when they connect, it is usually through violence)" (Morán).

Class connections steeped in violence are also key to *La fragilidad de los cuerpos*, which introduces investigative reporter Verónica Rosenthal. Verónica continues her investigative work, coupled with her headstrong pursuit of emotional intensity, in Olguín's subsequent novels, *Las extranjeras* (2014) and *No hay amores felices* (2016). *La fragilidad* revisits the issue of class difference via the explosive affair between the middle-class reporter and a railroad engineer. An intertwined plotline deals with the vulnerability of poor youth who are exploited by a local mafia to play a dangerous game of "chicken" on the railroad tracks: the game involves betting on which boy will be the last to jump out of the way of the oncoming locomotive. The winning boy receives one hundred pesos, unless of course he does not jump in time and is run over by the train. Due to the indifference of local authorities who are in cahoots with the mafia, Verónica becomes the champion of the exploited youths. The plotline relating Verónica's investigation into deaths on the tracks develops simultaneously with the story of Peque and Dientes, two boys who live in a marginal neighborhood and who are induced to play the game. The threads merge when Verónica's inquiries lead her to the boys.

In addition to considering the issue of class difference, my analysis of the novel addresses the ethical complexity of Verónica. The female reporter cum detective presents an all-too-human mix of good intentions and reckless behavior, strength and frailty. Also of concern are the social conditions that allow for the exploitation of youth and others in the poor neighborhoods, the same mechanisms that provoke a journalist to carry out the work that should be done by the police and the justice system. The precarious situation of the inhabitants of the marginal neighborhoods clearly demonstrates the perils to which the economically disadvantaged are exposed. Much more subtle and insidious are the deleterious effects of the ill-fated affair between the journalist and the railroad engineer. The pleasure/danger formula that drives their sexual relationship, along with their morbid fascination with the train's potential to crush a human being, invite a reflection on the thriller's production of viewer pleasure by means of shock and terror.

The topic of railroad accidents touches a raw nerve for Argentines. The Sarmiento railroad, the line featured in the novel, has had a series of accidents involving fatalities, the most tragic one in February 2012 when a brake failure caused a train to crash into the Once station, leaving fifty-one dead and over seven hundred wounded. The author describes real-life references that factor in his novel: "the precariousness of railway services, the connections between the political and business worlds and the mafias … journalism that tries to expose and denounce what should have been investigated by the police and the justice system" (Mavrakis). While most of the novels treated in this book critique corruption and social breakdown linked to Menem's neoliberal policies, a central factor in these railroad crashes was the criminal mismanagement of antineoliberal Peronist officials in the Fernández de Kirchner government. Twenty-one individuals, including two former transportation secretaries and other Fernández de Kirchner government officials, have been sentenced for their responsibility in the Once accident.[9]

In the case of *La fragilidad*'s depiction of a reporter who takes the investigation of a criminal network into her own hands, Olguín is tapping into a trend in the Argentine *novela negra* that I have discussed in previous chapters. In addition, as in *El vuelo de la reina*, *Asalto al paraíso*, and *Betibú*, Olguín's female investigator breaks with the tradition of casting a male as sleuth. However, while challenging some aspects of the traditional representation of femininity, the text upholds others. What is more, the novelist appears to be caught up in the "masculinity" of the detective figure, portraying Verónica as a female version of the hard-boiled private eye, as I will discuss in the next section. And while Verónica embodies the sexually uninhibited and empowered woman who resists gender norms, her independence and sexual freedom come with certain consequences.

Verónica's investigation into deaths on the tracks brings her into contact with Lucio Valrossa, a married locomotive engineer with whom she develops a torrid, sadomasochistic affair. Their affair will bring to bear deep-seated fears and anxieties related to the lethal power of the locomotive as well as issues of class, gender, and identity. The "fragilidad de los cuerpos" ends up referring both to the physical destruction of bodies by the locomotive as well as the emotional devastation that can result from a "fatal" attraction. It is not only the poor youth who expose themselves to danger; so too do Lucio and Verónica in their fierce, passionate affair spurred by their mutual fascination with the violent deaths.

### Another Strong-Willed and Sexual Female Journalist

When Verónica Rosenthal, a reporter for the weekly magazine *Nuestro Tiempo*, hears about a suicide in which the victim—a railroad employee named Alfredo Carranza—left a note asking forgiveness for the four people he killed, one of them a young boy, she is intrigued and latches onto the story. An unusual variation from the typical detective plot that opens with a murder, the genesis of the action is a suicide. Verónica believes that Carranza may have been a repentant serial killer. Instead, she will find out that he was a railroad engineer and the deaths that haunt him were accidents on the tracks—or at least they were all believed to be accidents.

Verónica is portrayed as a dedicated and highly competent journalist and a fighter for justice. The polar opposite of a shrinking violet, she is a take-charge and hard-living type of person: she smokes heavily, likes her Jim Beam, and engages freely in sex with numerous partners. Olguín concedes that he consciously created an Argentine female version of the North American hard-boiled private eye: "Verónica is an absolute transposition of the classic investigator but in a feminine version. I wanted her to have the same characteristics as the men: that she could get drunk, sleep with whomever she wanted without having moral problems and consider it totally natural. That she could be quite masculine despite being very feminine" (Cordeu). Philippa Gates, in her study of female detectives in the Hollywood film industry, points out that reconciling "traditional notions of femininity with the perceived masculine demands of the detective plot" has been a problem since the first female detectives appeared in narratives in the late nineteenth century and continues to plague contemporary film (14). As we have seen, Martínez, Aguinis, and Piñeiro have taken differing approaches to the representation of their female investigators. Olguín, for his part, confronts the issue in this novel by "masculinizing" his female investigator. It turns out that he is in good company, as Gates notes that the female criminalist of the new millennium tends to be presented as a masculinized woman who is sexually aggressive (284). (Of course, this perspective presupposes fixed gender traits associated with men and women, an issue that has been taken up by feminist theorists such as Judith Butler.) Olguín counters Verónica's "masculine" qualities by making her a very attractive and sexual young woman and focusing the male gaze (and touch) on her shapely body.

While Verónica does not intentionally exploit her sexuality, as does Cristina in *Asalto al paraíso*, she is a liberated woman who claims her sexual desire. Her sexuality is a central aspect of her characterization, and it is mentioned from various narrative viewpoints. In chapter 1, we learn that Verónica tells friends who call her before 10:00 a.m.: "Las putas y los periodistas nos levantamos tarde" (We whores and journalists get up late) (17). By indirectly equating herself to a prostitute, she seems to be "owning" her sexuality. She enters the shower, and the extradiegetic narrator's description of her sensations emphasizes her condition as a sexual body: "dejó que el agua caliente recorriera su cuerpo como una caricia demorada y varonil" (she let the warm water run over her body like slow, masculine caress) (17). The narrator continues to sexualize Verónica, mentioning her need for a tampon and detailing her mismatched underwear. From the perspective of various characters, the narrator frequently describes her tall, slender, elegant, and smartly dressed figure. Even her female boss enviously takes note of "su ajustado culo" (her tight ass) (98), and her good looks come in helpful at times on the job. For instance, the slimy Rivero, a subordinate to the mafia boss who fronts as a soccer coach, would normally have shunned a reporter, but he cannot resist meeting with this attractive young woman: "La minita estaba muy bien" (The girl was very good-looking), he reflects (228).

Through conversations with her girlfriends, we learn of Verónica's affairs and her attitude toward the men in her life. She and her friends give her lovers creative names that ridicule them: the most recent love interest is "El Marinero Bengalí" because he has a boat, and Lucio becomes "El Maquinista Degenerado." Her friend Paula was witness to "la época más promiscua de Verónica" (Verónica's most promiscuous period) (102) after she broke off a six-year relationship and sometimes slept with two different men during a weekend, or three if it was a long weekend. In one scene, after an argument with Lucio, she beds a stranger she meets in a bar and the confused young man leaves money for her on the hotel room nightstand, an indication that, at least in his mind, women normally do not have sex with random men for free. Verónica's curiosity leads her to visit pornographic websites, and she has dabbled in pornographic writing under a pseudonym. Verónica shares her liberal attitude with like-minded girlfriends who revel in their feminism; for instance, they hold get-togethers to eat succulent steaks, celebrating their bonding over meat-eating as an assault on the last bastion of masculinity. In a sense, Verónica remains a male fantasy—her "liberation" is not achieved by refusing to be defined by her sexuality but rather by refusing to assume the passive role.

Another defining characteristic of Verónica is her professionalism, which is bolstered by her self-confidence and poise. The thoughts of her boss, Patricia, highlight her skills and commitment.

> Verónica quería estar en la calle, investigando, en contacto con la gente, encontrando explicaciones a los problemas y mandando al frente a los responsables. Era minuciosa, obsesiva, lúcida y escribía muy bien.... Además tenía olfato.... Donde alguien veía un hecho ordinario, Verónica era capaz de descubrir una serie de sucesos espeluznantes. (98)
>
> [Verónica wanted to be on the street, investigating, in contact with people, finding explanations to the problems and calling out the responsible parties. She was meticulous, obsessive, lucid and she wrote very well.... Besides she had a nose for a good story.... Where someone saw an ordinary matter, Verónica was able to discover a series of hair-raising events.]

She makes a conscious effort to dominate challenging people and situations. The above-mentioned Rivero, who salivates over meeting with such a good-looking woman, finds her self-assurance annoying, and once she mentions Juan García, the mafia kingpin, Rivero realizes that she is dangerous. Although she is not able to control García, he is also irritated by her tone. Men feel threated by Verónica's drive to control every situation, as her behavior blurs gender boundaries.

From the perspective of her father, we learn that Verónica is a crusader for justice, a trait that is also crucial in her role investigating the exploitation of children: "Le gustaba defender a todos los débiles con los que se había cruzado en la vida.... Odiaba la injusticia y no se callaba nunca" (She liked to defend all the defenseless people she came across.... She hated injustice and never was silenced) (95). Evidence of her sense of justice is the fact that she is not satisfied merely to have obtained enough information to write a breaking story about the betting ring. She wants to right the wrongs by punishing the criminals and ending the game on the tracks that puts children in danger. But Verónica's elevated sense of ethics is at times tempered by pragmatism—she is not above using her father's name and influence to her benefit. Aaron Rosenthal is a respected high-profile attorney with powerful connections, and Verónica's last name wins her differential treatment and protection when she is working with judges.

Verónica is a nuanced and complex character, and her volatile combination of traits leads to mixed results in her personal and professional life. While her passion for justice propels her to help victims of oppression, her occasional rash behavior and her active libido sometimes result in harm to others. We learn of her less admirable qualities: she can be arrogant, disdainful, exploitative, and irresponsibly headstrong. A prime example of this behavior is her relationship with Federico, a young man who works in her father's law office. They grew up together and he is like a brother to her, despite the fact that they had a one-night stand and he has a huge crush on her. She takes advantage of his devotion to her in order to obtain his assistance in her investigation with all the muscle and logistics that a major legal firm can offer. At the same time, she is demeaning and flippant with him. For instance, when he answers the phone, she is amused by his voice, which she considers "falsamente profesional" (falsely professional), and when he asks what he will get in return for all the free legal assistance that he is lending her investigation, she replies, "Mi amor eterno y el de mi papá" (My eternal love and that of my father) (206). Another trait that comes to the fore is her devil-may-care attitude in her relations with men. For instance, as Lucio watches the elegant movements of her nude body, he reflects, "Mostraba cierta indiferencia por lo que despertaba" (She showed a certain indifference for what she aroused) (244). At times, this behavior can be characterized as reckless: she has sex with Father Pedro, a troubled priest, fully realizing that this encounter is far more conflictive for him than it is for her.

To her credit, Verónica is equally headstrong in her drive to help the defenseless. She comes to the aid of Rafael, a barman at the soccer club who denounced the gambling ring and exploitation of children to the police and was promptly beaten up by thugs. When he calls Verónica asking for help, without a second thought, she goes to his distant neighborhood to fetch him and shelters him in her apartment. By doing so, she puts herself and others in danger because the hit men are sent to her home. As the thugs are chasing Rafael and the doorman outside her apartment building, she runs over them with a car and then crashes through the plate-glass entrance. In this case, Verónica's behavior was impulsive and destructive but effective, and her vehicular homicide is declared accidental thanks to the judge's diffidence toward her influential father. Verónica's unwavering commitment to protecting Peque and Dientes and to catching and punishing the culprits who are exploiting them and other children earns her the boys' admiration and respect; they nickname her "Superchica."

While Verónica's outward appearance is that of self-sufficiency and independence, she harbors an inner conflict: ultimately, she longs for domestic partnership, a man who will never leave her. For instance, when Rafael tells her that he still loves his ex-wife, Andrea, and all he wants is to get back together with her, Verónica feels envy for Andrea. Another revealing moment is when Nina Simone's rendition of "The Other Woman" happens to be playing on Verónica's stereo while she is thinking about her relationship with Lucio. A glimpse at the song's lyrics explains Verónica's feelings of melancholy: they describe a mistress who pampers herself and lives an unencumbered life of luxury but who ultimately ends up alone, crying herself to sleep. And in one of the final scenes, Verónica imagines being together with Lucio listening to music or watching a movie: "Al final, la felicidad era eso. El momento en que alguien decidía no dejarte. Quedarse con vos" (In the end, happiness was that. The moment someone decided not to leave you. To stay with you) (316). This depiction seems consonant with Susan Faludi's description of the feminist backlash—the idea that women may be free and equal but they are unhappy because they are free (x), suggesting that the novel falls short of a wholesale commitment to a feminist agenda.

There is no doubt, however, regarding the novel's denunciation of official corruption. Verónica's investigation reveals that children are being exploited because the police are protecting the criminals. As noted above, Rafael reported to the police the responsibility of the sports trainer in the deaths of youths on the railroad tracks. The police commissary thanked him for his bravery, but hours later he was beaten up by three men who taunted him: "—Andá a denunciar esto a la policía, hijo de puta" (Go denounce this to the police, son of a bitch) (236). This makes it clear that police are in on the racket. Verónica also discovers that the mothers of the children who are killed on the tracks are offered houses in the interior of Argentina along with generous moving expenses by the government office of Social Development, thus further confirming government involvement with the gambling ring.

When Verónica becomes aware of the extent of the official complicity, she resolves to catch the culprits herself. The confusion in roles is evident in Verónica's exchange with the boys when she tells them that she wants to bring Rivero and his cronies to justice: "—¿Usted es policía?—No, soy periodista" (Are you a police officer? No, I am a journalist) (267). The boys' question drives home the fact that journalists are doing the work of police.

In chapter 1, I addressed novels that portray politicians who are deeply involved in mafia dealings but are untouchable. This pattern of criminality is similar in *La fragilidad*. Juan García was a local mayor in the province of Misiones and had to leave town when it was revealed in the national news that he was involved in human trafficking. "'Lo denunció un periodista de Buenos Aires. El tipo salió airoso de la causa que le siguió la justicia misionera'" (It was reported by a journalist from Buenos Aires. The guy got off scot-free in the case tried by the Misiones regional justice system), Verónica informs Federico (206). Here we see the repetition of a troublesome pattern: wrongdoing is brought to light by the press, but the justice system does not touch powerful figures. García then moved his operations to Buenos Aires, where he controls an empire of illegal activities. One of Verónica's colleagues gives her a detailed report: "'Juan García ... era algo así como un mayorista en el mundo del delito. Tenía la ilegalidad que quisieras: trata de mujeres, tráfico de bebés, mano de obra esclava para los latifundistas. También manejaba el mercado de las apuestas y seguro que andaba con la droga'" (Juan García ... was something like a wholesaler in the world of crime. He was involved in all the illegal dealings you could imagine: trafficking in women, trafficking in babies, slave labor for landowners. He also managed the betting market and I'm sure he was involved in drugs) (149). Due to García's control of local politics, Verónica finds herself forced to negotiate with him: he provides evidence to convict his accomplices in exchange for his impunity. In this way, Verónica achieves partial success—while she succeeds in stopping the games on the tracks, this is but a small portion of García's empire. The mafia kingpin will go unpunished, continuing his illegal activities in other spheres.

### Mapping Social Class: *Zona sur* and *zona norte*

In a divided society, Fredric Jameson notes, the detective provides a force of linkage, traversing neighborhoods of the city in search of clues (131), and, for better or for worse, Verónica creates this connection in the novel. *La fragilidad* maps out streets, parks, and neighborhoods of Buenos Aires, providing place-names that enable the reader to identify precise locations on a map. Verónica discovers the geographical pattern pertaining to the origin of the boys who died on the tracks: "las víctimas eran chicos pobres, la mayoría provenientes de barrios carenciados o villas" (the victims were poor children, mostly from poor neighborhoods or *villas*) (141). Mapping out the residences of the young victims, she finds that they come from a three-kilometer radius. The mapping goes as far as to pinpoint "el centro geográfico" (the geographic center) of the victims, on the corner of Larrazábal and Zelarrayán—a point between Villa Lugano and Villa Soldati (166). These neighborhoods are within the *comuna* 8, the southernmost district of the city and described by the narrator as "la más pobre de Buenos Aires, la que tiene la tasa más alta de mortandad infantil, de desocupación y de analfabetismo" (the poorest in Buenos Aires, which has the highest rate of infant mortality, unemployment and illiteracy) (152).[10] As discussed in the first section of this chapter, the *zona norte* of Buenos Aires is largely the domain of the upper and middle classes, while the poor neighborhoods are in the *zona sur*. Peque and Dientes live in Villa Lugano, and Vicen, a boy who is killed on the tracks, lives in Ciudad Oculta, a *villa miseria* within Villa Lugano.

The exploited boys live in crowded conditions; four families occupy the tenement house where both Peque and Dientes live with their mothers and siblings. Peque's mother, who barely gets by with the money she earns cleaning houses, has two rooms and shares the bathroom with two other renters. Vicen's mother also works cleaning houses; thus both hold informal jobs in the service sector with no benefits or security. Neither Peque nor Dientes knows much about his father: Dientes's father was slain and Peque's father abandoned the family. The boys are desperate to get ahold of money, and Rivero, an experienced predator, learns of their vulnerability and exploits it. When Peque shows up at the club alone, he makes a "generous" exception to the rule that a parent should accompany minors. Verónica calls Rivero's victims "'chicos abandonados de la mano de Dios, que tal vez no van a la escuela o no tienen padres que les den una alimentación adecuada'" (children abandoned by God, who perhaps do not go to school or have parents who give them adequate alimentation) (225).

The trope of the game serves as an ironic metaphor for the situation of poor children. At first it is thought that the children are playing on the tracks of their own volition for fun, but Verónica learns that they are actually pawns of a gambling racket. Thus this game is not idle play; it is high-stakes and potentially deadly, controlled by a ruthless mafia. The children's desperation for money is seen in the horrible fate of those who stay on the tracks too long. It does not seem to be random that Vicen—whose eagerness to win another 100-peso bill resulted in his death under the locomotive—comes from Ciudad Oculta. A *villa miseria* where the inhabitants live in a situation of extreme poverty, it was so named because in 1978, upon the occasion of the World Cup, the military dictatorship constructed a wall to hide it from the view of foreign tourists ("Villas Argentinas").

While Peque, Dientes, Vicen, and Rafael represent the vulnerable *zona sur* residents, Verónica represents the middle-class people who live in the northern part of the city. She is a self-described "chica de Recoleta" (118), the most exclusive district of Buenos Aires. The "chica de Recoleta" serves as a physical, corporeal link between the wealthy enclaves and the poor neighborhoods; between affluent, powerful groups and humble, disadvantaged groups. Connections between the upper and lower social classes are traced as Verónica launches her investigation into the reasons behind Carranza's suicide. Her research leads to Carranza's friend and coworker Lucio and to the youths who are exploited by the mafia to serve as pawns for the gambling racket. Verónica's lack of familiarity with the *zona sur* is evidence of the strongly delineated geographical class divisions and the fact that a middle-class person typically does not set foot in poor neighborhoods. A lifetime resident of Buenos Aires, she does not remember ever having been in that sector of the city, and she confuses the districts—Mataderos with Lugano, Soldati with Pompeya, Ciudad Oculta with la Villa 1-14-21.

Through Verónica's trips to the *zona sur* to gather information, we learn additional details about the living conditions in these areas. "Entrar en la villa no iba a ser fácil.... No había calles, y las casas tenían números caóticos" (Going into the *villa* was not going to be easy.... There were no streets and the numbering of the houses was haphazard) (189), she notes. The second time, however, the *zona sur* neighborhood seems friendlier, consistent with the author's qualms about the *villas* being depicted by the media as dangerous places: "Verónica veía pasar gente, madres con chicos, adolescentes con guardapolvos, como en cualquier barrio de Buenos Aires" (Verónica saw people going by, mothers with children, teenagers in school uniforms, like in any neighborhood of Buenos Aires) (192). Nevertheless, while talking to Vicen's sister, her thoughts paint a bleak picture of the girl's circumstances.

> Verónica no se animó a preguntarle qué hacía. No quería ponerse en el papel de un adulto dando consejo a una adolescente que tal vez se drogaba o se prostituía, o esperaba que algo ocurriera en su vida que la sacara de la villa.... En pocos años esa chica iba a parecer de treinta y cuando llegara

a los treinta iba a parecer de cincuenta. Se llenaría de hijos en el mejor de los casos, si es que no moría joven por culpa del paco, o en manos de un marido borracho y golpeador. (197)

[Verónica did not dare ask her what she did. She did not want to put herself in the position of an adult giving advice to a teenager who might use drugs or prostitute herself, or who hoped that something would happen in her life that would take her out of the *villa*.... In a few years that girl was going to look like she was thirty and when she was thirty she would look like fifty. She would have a lot of children in the best of cases, if she did not die young because of crack, or at the hands of a drunk and abusive husband.]

Using Verónica as his vehicle, the author expounds on the dim prospects for the youth of the *villas*. Indeed, Seri states: "To be born in the *villa* becomes an automatic stigma that narrows life possibilities and pushes one into a horizon of crime, drugs, alcohol and violence" (72).

While the social conditions of the marginal groups are not developed in as much detail as in *Puerto Apache*, it is apparent why these boys become victims of exploitation. They are helpless to change their situation and, according to the plot of *La fragilidad*, in need of assistance from the educated middle class: Verónica, the "chica de Recoleta" with a drive for justice, "swoops in" to save the day. Indeed, her nickname, "Superchica," makes her a female version of Superman. At the same time, her actions put others, such as Rafael, Father Pedro, and Lucio, in precarious situations.

### "La chica de Recoleta" and the Railroad Engineer: Does Class Matter?

The volatile "other" class connection is developed via Verónica's steamy relationship with Lucio, a working-class man. Their relationship is problematic for several reasons: Lucio is married, they come from different social classes, and the sadomasochistic nature of their interaction is clearly a displacement of their anxieties about the horrible accidents on the tracks, as I will discuss in the next section.

The unlikelihood of such a relationship is established in a conversation among the railroad engineers. After Verónica has accompanied Lucio on a nocturnal run, his coworkers ask him if he bedded her. Lucio lies and says "no way." A companion expresses the impossibility of working-class men like them having a relationship with a girl like Verónica: "—Mirá si le va a dar bola ... a una grasa como este. A esas minas, como mucho, les olés el perfume. No son para nosotros" (Imagine if she is going to pay attention to a working-class guy like him. With these girls, at the most you smell their perfume. They aren't for us) (119). The class difference, however, is part of the appeal for both of them—Verónica feels attracted to this rugged indocile man who is so different from the buttoned-up professional men that she is used to dating. Lucio, for his part, thinks that it is too good to be true that she could be interested in him.

The subsequent references to class difference between Verónica and Lucio are subtle and refer to a cultural, not an economic, gap. For instance, when Verónica argues with Lucio, she belittles his wife with class-based insults, assuming that his wife has a lower cultural level than she does: "—Tu esposa ... habla de la telenovela de la noche. Tu esposa no escucha a Mike Harvey. Se emociona con Arjona" (Your wife ... talks about the soap opera. She doesn't listen to Mike Harvey. She gets excited about Arjona) (245).[11] When Lucio says he used to be a voracious reader, Verónica says she thought that railroad engineers did not read. In addition, the fact that Verónica likes sushi and Lucio does not points to her more sophisticated palate. There is a reference to skin color when their intertwined bodies are reflected in the mirror on the ceiling of the hotel room—"Su cuerpo más oscuro que el de ella" (His body darker than hers) (112). We never learn where Lucio lives, but the fact that he helps Verónica find her way around the *villas* when she goes to interview the families of the victims indicates his familiarity with these areas. Compared to these families, Lucio's economic situation seems comfortable: he has steady work and an income that is adequate to support his family.

The contrast between Lucio's and Verónica's outlooks on fate and free will, however, reveals deeper and more significant implications of how they are determined by their upbringing, their line of work, and their social class. The railroad engineers are depicted as a fatalistic bunch. For instance, in his suicide note Carranza wrote, "'Yo sabía que ese día lo iba a matar.... Que me iba a tocar a mí hacerlo'" (I knew that that day I was going to kill him.... That it was going to be my fate to do it) (33). It is no wonder that they are fatalistic—they operate in a world where they are powerless to prevent imminent tragedy that could occur at any moment. Even a light rail train requires about six hundred feet to stop—the length of two football fields. If a person appears on the tracks, the driver will not be able to stop the train in time and he will be helpless to prevent the horrific sensation of human bones being crushed under the locomotive. The engineers regard this certain and imminent traumatic experience as "un destino inmodificable" (an unmodifiable destiny) (73). Lucio is no exception—he is deeply fatalistic. He knows that experiencing moments of horror driving the night shift is a destiny he cannot escape because he has no agency over his fate. He accepts working the night shifts of the train, believing in the inevitability of the fact that sooner or later the locomotive he is driving will crush a human body. Verónica, on the other hand, has a firm conviction in the efficacy of her actions. She believes she can determine not only her own future but that of others. She is an activist—her career as an investigative reporter is a direct consequence of her relentless drive to bring about a more just society by uncovering and denouncing wrongdoing and corruption wherever she sees it.

What is more, their relationship tests gender boundaries because Verónica, as an independent-minded, sexually aggressive, and willful professional woman who is used to calling the shots, challenges Lucio's masculinity. Their different concepts of gender behavior cause an argument when, after their first tryst, Verónica insists that she wants to pay for half of the hotel bill: "Que era una mujer independiente y que nadie le pagaba su placer. Lucio no estaba dispuesto a someterse a la humillación de compartir el pago. Era ferroviario, tal vez ganaba menos que una periodista, pero el hotel lo pagaba él" (She was an independent woman and nobody paid for her pleasure. Lucio was not willing to submit to the humiliation of sharing the cost. He was a railroad worker, maybe he earned less than a journalist, but he paid for the hotel) (112). Sometimes Verónica will play at being the submissive female; for instance, when she serves sushi, she tells him, "—Hoy soy tu geisha" (Today I am your geisha) (202). The fact that she playfully assumes subservience as part of their sex play underlines the fact that this is not her customary role—it is mere posture that she can turn on and off. She induces him to tolerate the pain she causes when she sinks her fingers into his wounds: "—No seas maricón" (Don't be a sissy) (169), she chides him, thus calling into question his manhood. Although the fact that Lucio is married means that he determines when they can meet, in many ways Verónica has the upper hand in the relationship because of her higher social status. She decides how she will depict Lucio in her articles on railroad accidents or whether she will refer to him at all, thus rendering him powerless in this regard. As we have seen in the cases of Rivero and García, Verónica makes men anxious by her insistence on being in control, threatening their manhood as she constantly blurs the gender boundary; her relationship with Lucio is no exception.

Another issue is that the affair contains an element of guilt for Lucio, but it does not for Verónica. While Verónica is unattached and has had many sexual partners, Lucio married young and has never been unfaithful to his wife. And while Lucio feels that he can confide in no one about the affair, Verónica does not need to keep it secret—she discusses it with Paula and is unconcerned that the doorman sees Lucio's comings and goings to her apartment. *La fragilidad* thus taps into a component of noir malaise—the sexually aggressive female who is in control. Indeed, Kelly Oliver and Benigno Trigo maintain that the threat of lost boundaries is an inherent anxiety represented in film noir (xiv). However—as I will discuss in the subsequent section—the most unsettling aspect of their sexual relationship is its violent, sadomasochistic nature.

"No nos une el amor sino el espanto":
Looking Awry at a Doomed Relationship

In *Looking Awry*, Slavoj Žižek uses popular culture to understand Jacques Lacan, or vice versa: he uses Lacan to understand popular culture.[12] He reads some of Lacan's theoretical motifs with and through exemplary cases of contemporary mass culture, including Alfred Hitchcock, film noir, detective fiction, and other popular genres. Žižek's reading of noir texts with Lacan helps us unravel the psychoanalytic reading of *La fragilidad* that beckons to us beneath the surface of Lucio and Verónica's ill-omened affair.

According to Žižek's reading of the Lacanian structure of the psyche, "the Real" is our psychic reality, the truth of our desire, and "Reality" is our daily reality, which we enter with the emergence of language and our acceptance of the rules of society, also known as the symbolic order. The barrier separating these two realms—our desires and our daily reality—prevents us from sliding into psychosis, but the frontier is maintained by a fragile equilibrium that can be destroyed when trauma erupts. When this occurs, psychic reality takes over, resulting in psychosis. These motifs launch my reading of how Verónica incites Lucio's path of self-destruction. Roughly analogous to the two realms cited by Žižek, Lucio conceives himself as existing in two parallel dimensions—his day-to-day routine life with his wife and children, and a secret, unspoken universe consisting of the mystery and horror of the night trains. Lucio's fantasy of duality, his sense of existing in two parallel realms that will not cross and cannot comfortably coexist, is a recourse characteristic of the noir thriller. Similar to Lucio's fantasy, in Žižek's reading of a work of science fiction, he perceives that the characters exist in two separate discontinuous realities, one of which is fundamentally unreal, constituting another mode. The "horrifying effect" of the text is produced when the characters become aware of the frontier separating the two realms and experience their outside reality as fictional (15).

Verónica functions to heighten Lucio's fascination with the violent realm of the death trains. The first time she rides the train with him, he alludes to the "cosas terribles" that happen (68). She seizes this remark and wants to know more, but he does not want to talk about them. Then she tells him that they have the same name—Valrossa and Rosenthal. His is Italian, hers is Jewish, and they both mean valley of roses. In effect they are doubles. As if their common name has established an intimate bond, he now replies to her questioning, admitting that he has six "muertos" and describing how it feels to crush a human body with the locomotive.

> "Primero un golpe seco, como un disparo, y después, pegado a ese disparo, sentís cómo se revienta el cuerpo, los gritos de terror que no los cubrís con la bocina y que siguen oyéndose después de que el cuerpo se destrozó. Sentís cómo los huesos se quiebran debajo de tus pies." (70–71)
>
> [First a sharp impact, like a shot, and then, immediately following that shot, you feel how the body explodes, the screams of terror that you cannot drown out with the horn and that continue to be heard after the body is destroyed. You feel how the bones are crushed under your feet.]

This excruciatingly horrific sensation—of feeling a human body reduced to "ruido" (noise) or "polvo" (dust) under one's feet—invades their senses and tinges their relationship with a sadomasochistic hue.

Knowing that Verónica is transfixed by the horror of the deaths on the tracks and wanting to see her again, Lucio asks to change shifts with a coworker so he can drive the night run with her aboard. The fact that driving the "death train" means an encounter with Verónica infuses the dreaded moment with a new thrill: "Invitar a Verónica le permitía esperar ese instante fatal con la esperanza de volver a verla, una expectativa que nunca había sentido antes" (Inviting Verónica allowed him to anticipate that fatal moment with the hope of seeing her again, an expectation he had never felt before) (73). It is because of her fascination with the deaths on the track that they met in the first place, and it is also for this reason that he requests the night run, fully aware that these trips force him to confront the horror—the horror that Verónica is drawn to. Thus his relationship with her is inextricably connected to the other universe, that of the "death trains."

Verónica stimulates him to probe this other realm. She perceives the violence in his eyes, and tells her friend Paula, " 'Hay algo violento en él.... Está inmerso en un universo de dolor' " (There is something violent in him.... He is immersed in a universe of sorrow) (105). Her intuitive nature senses his psychic reality and she is intent on plumbing it. Lucio realizes that Verónica has made him confront this secret hidden sphere: "Y Verónica había aparecido para enfrentarlo con lo que llevaba encerrado en su interior" (And Verónica had appeared to confront him with what he had locked inside himself) (74). Lucio perceives Verónica as forming part of this "other," parallel realm marked by the mystery and horror of the trains and apart from his routine family life.

> Quizá [Verónica] formaba parte de esa vida irreal que llevaba arriba del tren. Porque si algo tenían en común las muertes en las vías y su relación con Verónica era que no las podía compartir con nadie. Participaban de una dimensión paralela a la vida de su familia, de sus compañeros de trabajo, de la rutina... que solo se rompía ante un accidente de su tren y ahora con la presencia de Verónica. (120)
>
> [Maybe [Verónica] was part of that unreal life that he experienced riding on the train. Because if the deaths on the tracks and his relationship with Verónica had something in common, it was that he could not share them with anyone. They were part of a dimension that was parallel to the life of his family, of his coworkers, of his routine... that was only broken when there was an accident on his train and now with Verónica's presence.]

Their mutual horror and awe in face of the terrifying power of the locomotive to decimate a human body is played out in their violent, sadomasochistic sex. Verónica accompanies Lucio on the nocturnal train run and experiences sheer terror when the train's headlights illuminate two young boys on the track staring at the oncoming locomotive. The boys jump off to the side just in time, and Verónica is trembling and crying. Verónica and Lucio kiss—or bite—each other until they taste blood. Their relationship originates in the instant of mutual terror in the engine room on that fateful night, and they play out their panic and anguish on each other. Both of their bodies bear the marks of their rough sex play. Lucio must live with the fact that he has run over and crushed human bodies and the certainty that it will happen again, and Verónica's morbid curiosity results in her passage into his secret world as she experiences a transference of his anxiety. They enact a "pleasurable" version of the involuntary sadomasochistic conflict between the engineer and his victim, displacing and projecting their fear of or fascination with the train's crushing potency into their rough sexual practices.[13]

A pleasure/danger formula drives their violent sex play. Verónica plays at being crushed by the murderous engineer: "Dale, asesino, cógeme así" (Come on, assassin, fuck me like that), she commands Lucio. Lucio fulfills her wishes and registers her pleasure: "Él golpeó todavía con más fuerza mientras la palabra asesino lo cubría como una saliva pegajosa. . . . Verónica lo miró con una sonrisa indescifrable" (He thrust even harder while the word assassin covered him like a sticky saliva. . . . Verónica looked at him with an indecipherable smile) (170). Lucio admits to himself that he enjoys hurting her: "¿Reconocer que él también disfrutaba cuando ella sufría, que no estaba dispuesto a ser generoso con ella?" (Recognize that he also experienced pleasure when she suffered, that he was not willing to be generous with her?) (256–57). The pleasure that Lucio and Verónica derive from hurting each other corresponds to Lacan's notion of surplus enjoyment (*plus-de-jouir*), which has the power to convert pleasure objects into their opposite, rendering "inexplicably attractive what is usually considered a loathsome act," for instance, "torturing a beloved person" (Žižek 13).

If Verónica and Lucio indulge in their surplus enjoyment to its ultimate consequences, they will annihilate one another, and indeed, they both dream of destroying each other. Verónica, at some level, is aware of the harm she is causing Lucio; she dreams that she is tattooing a love letter on his bleeding body. In Lucio's nightmare, he is driving a train. Suddenly day turns to night and a flowered dress flies against his windshield. He realizes it is Verónica's dress and thinks she must have been run over by the train. Žižek explains that our dreams are the psychic reality of our desires and awake we are nothing but the consciousness of our dreams. Our everyday, social reality is but "a fragile equilibrium" that rests on the repression of the real of our desire and "that can at any moment be torn aside by an intrusion of the real" (16–17).

Lucio, sensing the destructive nature of their relationship, becomes aware that they must end it. Verónica exists in the other universe that is marked by the mystery and the horror of the trains; she was the one who brought death and pain into their sex play by calling him "asesino" and sinking her fingers into his wounds. This sphere becomes distant, unsavory, and unreal to him, like a pornographic movie he is a part of and must exit. He is certain that he must not see Verónica again.

The narrator sets up an atmosphere of suspense for Lucio's climactic final night run. It is a moonless night and the train's headlights provide the only illumination. Lucio knows it is inevitable there will be boys on the track, but suddenly it occurs to him that Verónica, wearing the flowered dress from his dream, may appear on the tracks instead of them. Does he fear/desire to crush her body with the train? As if his thoughts had conjured her up, Verónica calls his cell phone to tell him that today the boys are competing on the tracks. At this moment Lucio realizes he cannot relinquish his desire for her: "Verónica, Verónica, Verónica, Verónica, Verónica. La nombraba y volvía a aparecer el deseo. La escuchaba y lo único que quería era tenerla entre los brazos" (He named her and the desire returned. He heard her voice and all he wanted was to hold her in his arms) (311). When he realizes this—that he is trapped in the realm inhabited by his desire for Verónica, which is fused to the fascination of crushing or being crushed by the locomotive—he experiences a psychotic breakdown. The barrier between the realms is torn down, and the "real," or his psychic reality, his unspoken desire, overflows into his daily life and takes over.

> Los trenes de la muerte y Verónica volvían a juntarse. Esa vida secreta donde convivían el cuerpo de Verónica y los cuerpos aplastados en las vías volvía a presentarse como lo que era: la realidad. El sueño era lo otro ... su esposa, sus hijos, las rutinas que amaba. ... El sueño era creer que la vida le podía ofrecer tranquilidad. (311)
>
> [Once again the death trains and Verónica came together. That secret life where Verónica's body coexisted with the bodies crushed on the tracks presented itself once again for what it was: reality. The dream was the other ... his wife, his children, the routines he loved. ... The dream was to believe that life could offer him peace of mind.]

In his mind, the spheres become transposed: his tranquil routine life with his family seems to him a dream and the only reality is his desire for Verónica, the continued runs of the death train, and the unending accidents.

Suddenly the boys appear on the track. Lucio brakes and the boys jump in time. Beside himself with rage, Lucio emerges from the locomotive and chases them, grabbing one of the boys, who begs Lucio not to kill him. Desperately attempting to recover his everyday reality, Lucio recalls his own children and wishes he were playing with them, but that existence seems unreal to him, as if he were awakening from a pleasant dream that he cannot recapture. Two men appear and tell Lucio to release the boy. Lucio realizes the men are part of the mafia exploiting the boys, and confronts them. This is a suicidal gesture, but for Lucio there is no return: "Sabía que no iba a retroceder hasta el tren, que ya no iba a conducirlo" (He knew that he was not going back to the train, that he would no longer drive it) (313). One of the men gives the order to liquidate Lucio and the other shoots him in the face.

Žižek's analysis of the path of the paintings produced by abstract expressionist Mark Rothko provides a parallel of sorts to Lucio's psychic collapse. In these images, Žižek witnesses the process of the breakdown of the barrier separating our everyday life from the real of our desire. Rothko's paintings present a set of color variations of the relationship between the real (desire) and reality (everyday life). He depicts the tension between these spaces as a central black spot spreading menacingly against a gray background. In his final canvasses, Žižek tells us, this "minimal tension between black and gray changes for the last time into the burning conflict between voracious red and yellow, witnessing the last desperate attempt at redemption and at the same time confirming unmistakably that the end is imminent." Rothko was found dead in his New York loft in a pool of blood—he had cut his wrists. "He preferred death," Žižek says, "to being swallowed by the Thing" (19). The barrier separating the real (psychic reality) from reality (everyday life) is the condition of a minimum of normalcy. Madness is when the barrier is torn down and the psychic reality takes over.

My detour, reading Olguín with Žižek reading noir with Lacan, teases out the psychic essence of the novel. The violence that Verónica perceived in Lucio's eyes was the call of "surplus enjoyment," the unthinkable desire to experience in his own flesh what it felt like to have his bones crushed by the oncoming locomotive, a desire that he projected onto Verónica, his double and his accomplice who sensed and shared this urge. Verónica's horrified fascination with the pulverizing power of the locomotive and her violent sex play served as catalysts to activate the real of his psychic desire, which he had been repressing in his everyday life, represented by his routine and his family. When Lucio realized he had become trapped in the parallel realm of his psychic reality, like Rothko (and unlike Fabián Polosecki), he carried out a suicidal gesture to avoid the inevitability of being swallowed by the void of his desire. Reading *La fragilidad de los cuerpos* with Žižek, we uncover the underlying story of the process of hystericization of Lucio via his fateful relationship with Verónica.

The novel's tragic conclusion brings to a head the ethical complexity of the character of Verónica. On the one hand, she has championed the cause of exploited youth; on the other hand, she has indulged her pursuit of pleasure regardless of possible ethical implications or physical danger and emotional damage. Does Verónica deserve the horrible outcome—Lucio's untimely death—that she has to live with? Might we read the conclusion as feminist backlash or a moral message—the consequence of Verónica's liberated attitude or "out-of-bounds" sexuality? Is she actually guilty of anything, or is following one's desire intrinsic to the nature of free, desiring human beings? Ultimately, Verónica is a tragic figure, and obviously, there are no clear-cut answers to these questions, reflecting the ambiguity of the human condition.

## The Workings of Noir

Lucio's was a death foretold, and the narrator hooks us from the beginning of this noir-tinged tale, maintaining our rapt attention with suspense, premonition, and foreshadowing. For example, when Verónica hears about the suicide of a railroad employee, she speculates, "—Se habrá matado por amor" (He might have killed himself for love) (22), unwittingly foreshadowing the connection between love and death that will play out in her relationship with Lucio. The first time Verónica hears Lucio's name from the sister of the dead engineer, she has a premonition and repeats, "Lucio" "en un susurro sin saber que repetiría su nombre tantas veces, de tantas maneras" (in a whisper without knowing that she would repeat his name so many times, in so many ways) (42–43).

Moments of high anticipation and suspense occur during the nocturnal train runs. "Vos me preguntabas por las cosas terribles de este trabajo," Lucio says to Verónica in their nocturnal ride. "Vas a ver una" (You asked me about the terrible things about this job.... You are going to see one) (76). The suspense of these episodes is built on the tension between the image of the children positioned on the track and the image of the oncoming locomotive. A climatic moment is the death of Vicen, Peque's opponent, on the tracks. Rivero takes bets and suspense mounts as the boys hold their position while the train approaches, each waiting for the other to jump first. Peque finally jumps, and "el sonido del tren lo cubrió como si cayera sobre él la pierna de un monstruo. Pero solo eran ruidos, gritos.... Su ojo o su cuerpo había registrado ... a Vicen quieto en la vía. Quieto cuando él saltaba y el tren pasaba entre rechinos y una bocina aterradora.... Y por encima de su cabeza, gritos. Más gritos" (the sound of the train covered him as if a monster's leg had fallen on him. But it was just noises, screams.... His eye or his body had registered ... Vicen laying still on the track. Silent when he jumped and the train went by with the shrill sound of the brakes and a terrifying horn.... And overhead were screams. More screams) (135). The scene conveys the heart-stopping moment when the shrill braking noise and deep train horn is answered with the silence of death.

Other scenes project the noir technique of high contrast between dark and light. *Claroscuro* imagery is created when Verónica accompanies Lucio on the night train and they peer out to view "las vías iluminados por la luz del tren, que rompía la densa oscuridad de la noche" (the tracks illuminated by the light of the train, which broke the dense darkness of the night) (76). In this moment, the faces of the boys appear. This is the same atmosphere of suspense that is set up for Lucio's final nocturnal run, as he drives "sumido en la oscuridad solo iluminada por la luz del tren.... A Lucio no le gustaban las noches sin luna" (plunged into darkness only illuminated by the light of the train.... Lucio did not like moonless nights) (288). Macabre and horrific images fill out the noir repertoire; for instance, when Verónica talks to the doorman of the tall building where the railroad engineer committed suicide, he can only offer "una descripción de película de terror sobre el cadáver estrellado contra el pavimento" (a description from a horror movie of the crushed body on the pavement) (27). In sum, Olguín achieves a spellbinding tale by creating anticipation and terror linked to the nocturnal train trips and the deadly game, the peril-filled investigation, and the doomed love affair. Indeed, sections of the novel read like the script for a noir thriller. Besides creating film noir type scenarios, the turns of the plot exude the fatalism of film noir in which ordinary people meet terrible destinies due to fate beyond their control (Oliver and Trigo 88–89).

Horsley points out that "the noir sensibility may come to the fore at any time of discontent and anxiety, of disillusionment with institutional structures and loss of confidence in the possibility of effective agency" (*Twentieth-Century Crime Fiction* 116–17). In keeping with Horsley's observation, *La fragilidad de los cuerpos* reflects a troubling socioeconomic reality. Like *Puerto Apache*, this novel depicts economic and institutional determinants that imperil marginalized groups. But at the same time, it operates on a deeper level, portraying existential anguish linked to anxieties related to gender, class, and bodily integrity, and reflecting our primal drives and anxieties. It uses artistic devices to build suspense and arouse fear as the reader becomes engaged with the dangers and ethical dilemmas of the characters.

As mentioned in the beginning of my discussion of *La fragilidad*, its depictions and artistry open to a consideration of the thriller's production of pleasure via its generation of shock and terror. Bringing to mind Ana María Amar Sánchez's explanation of popular fiction's seduction of the reader, Olguín's novel may seduce us into complicity with the characters' morbid curiosity. As Hitchcock maintained, all of us harbor the dark recesses of violence and horror; we want to be shocked. In effect, we could say that, like Lucio and Verónica's fascination with the bone-crushing potency of the locomotive, *La fragilidad* and similarly well-executed thrillers beckon us to the call of "surplus enjoyment." Indeed, the relationship between the writers of *novelas negras* and their readers can be likened to Verónica and Lucio's sadomasochistic sex play imitating the locomotive's pulverization of a human body: the masters of suspense employ their artistic skills to terrify us and we "pleasurably" submit to being frightened out of our wits. Our entertainment—in this case in the form of horrified fascination—is integral to our ability to appreciate noir's probing insights into our reality.

Conclusion
# SOCIAL COLLAPSE AND HUMAN CONNECTIONS

IN HIS 2016 ESSAY "REPENSAR EL POLICIAL HOY EN LA ARGENTINA" (REthinking the detective genre in Argentina today), Jorge Lafforgue reviews the history of the genre in his country, assessing the high and low points of its trajectory. He lists four periods: "I) formative, II) classic, III) of transition, and IV) *negro*," and points to the dilemma of theorization and categorization of current production when he leaves the next period as an open question, asking, "Could one speculate about a fifth period?" (47). Continuing to reflect on how to characterize the continuity of the genre in Argentina, he suggests that for answers we look toward the totality of Hispanic letters and beyond, noting the surge of a universal and heterogeneous literary movement at the end of the twentieth century. Paradoxically, says Lafforgue, this is when certain critics lamented (or welcomed) the decline and stagnation of the *policial* in Argentina, predicting its demise (49). Lafforgue admits he was among those who did not see evidence that Argentine writers could go beyond the "período negro"—using this term to refer to the variant modeled on the hard-boiled ethos—until the appearance, in 1997, of Piglia's *Plata quemada*, which marked new directions. He concludes by pointing to the many signs of the continued life of the genre in Argentina: festivals, congresses, contests, collections, researchers, and writers who are identified with the genre but at the same time open new paths (53).

In full agreement with Lafforgue's observations, the present book has sought to demonstrate the vitality and diversity of the genre in Argentina. I have chosen to address the much-debated issue of categorization by using the concept of *novela negra* in its most comprehensive definition—"a broad generic category encompassing both detective-centered and criminal-centered subgenres" (Close, *Contemporary Hispanic Crime Fiction* 62). This admittedly amorphous category sidesteps the need for the texts to meet specific thematic or technical requirements—for instance, the presence of a detective or the investigation of an enigma—while it inserts Argentine letters into a transatlantic context. Since literary trends are most accurately defined in retrospect, a more specific reply to Lafforgue's query regarding a possible fifth period for the Argentine *policial* may emerge in the not-too-distant future. In this conclusion, I venture some considerations toward that effort.

Brigitte Adriaensen and Valeria Grinberg Pla, in the introduction to their edited volume, *Narrativas del crimen en América Latina: Transformaciones y transculturaciones del policial*, flesh out the theoretical foundation of their approach to contemporary Latin American crime fiction. Using "policial" as a term that encompasses the multiple variants of the genre, they posit that the genre's survival and expansion in Latin America is due to its transformation enabled by transculturation. Indeed, the concept of transculturation can be considered "key to understanding Latin American civilization, cultural production, and creative originality" (Lund 179). Ángel Rama, in 1982, was the first to systematically theorize transculturation in relation to Latin American literary studies. He characterized "the current culture of the Latin American community" as "a product of long-term transculturation and in constant evolution," emphasizing transculturation's "capacity for creative originality" that is propelled by the "criteria of selection and inventiveness" (19–22). In relation to the evolution of crime fiction, Adriaensen and Grinberg Pla define transculturation as "a process of multiple exchanges, borrowings and fusions between the different cultural areas in which crime fiction circulates on both sides of the ocean, and not as a one-way street" (16). They note that both North American and European crime fiction receive this transfer, giving as examples of European reception of Argentine influences Umberto Eco's references to Borges in *The Name of the Rose* and novels such as Vázquez Montalbán's *Quinteto de Buenos Aires*. Rather than reproduce European or US models, Adriaensen and Grinberg Pla explain, Latin American authors have appropriated them and adapted them to their narrative necessities and local problematics, and it is precisely this process of territorialization that makes possible the transformations and transculturations (13). There can be no doubt that Argentine crime fiction participates, along with the rest of Latin America, in this process of transculturation, transformation, and territorialization, as it plays with the conventions of the genre and employs techniques that go beyond the limits of what is traditionally considered detective fiction. We may consider this tripart process as fundamental to the current "boomlet" in the Argentine *novela negra* and a leading clue in the investigation of how to characterize the continuity of the genre.

The novels discussed in this book demonstrate how Argentine crime fiction adapts certain literary techniques to address national problematics. Insofar as they were chosen for their engagement with determined sociopolitical issues—and not their degree of experimentation or conformity to the cannon—these novels may be considered a "random sample" of the process of transformation, as theorized by Adriaensen and Grinberg Pla, that functions to "territorialize" the problematics they treat. Next I consider how they participate in the processes of territorialization and transformation.

## TERRITORIALIZATION AND TRANSFORMATION

The eleven novels selected for this book treat prominent issues within Argentine society. Foremost are the profound social and economic repercussions of the market-oriented restructuring of Argentine economic and political policy that culminated in the 1990s. Another leading concern is the corruption of the police and the political class, a phenomenon that is depicted in all the featured novels. Linked to that problem is the impact of organized crime, specifically narcotrafficking and, to a lesser degree, human trafficking. While these concerns are shared across Latin America and many other regions of the world, the novels deal with how they are manifested in Argentina. A problem specific to Argentine culture and politics that is broached in two of the novels are the lasting repercussions of the mishandled investigation of the bombing of Jewish institutions in Buenos Aires in the 1990s.

Regarding literary style, this book has addressed how the novels—in their critique of these local and national concerns—rework the tenets of the genre and employ a wide variety of schemes and techniques from other literary traditions. In particular, the authors make use of the following "transformations" or variations: the reworking of generic formulas, the choice of the detective figure and the setting, the depiction of female characters, the incorporation of real-life events and individuals, and the use of generic hybridity and metafictional recourses. This final category includes strategies such as intertextuality and self-reflexivity, the play with diegetic levels, framing, and mise en abyme.

A procedure common to many *novelas negras* is the incorporation and manipulation of the formulas dear to the classic enigma-based subgenre—this is a fundamental way in which the genre is renovated and reformulated.[1] In my study of how *El vuelo de la reina* and *El muerto indiscreto* convey a critique of the Menem administration, I have discussed, drawing from Amar Sánchez, their manipulation of the triad "crime, truth, and justice," marked by the inevitable absence of the final term. Several novels, for instance *Las viudas de los jueves*, *Betibú*, and *El muerto indiscreto*, open with the requisite corpse of the classical enigma mystery—though with a twist in the last case—yet there is a lack of the classic genre's final solution or restoration of justice. The frustration of justice, while often linked to the choice of the detective figure, is repeated in a variety of forms in all the novels under study, conveying a pattern of systemic corruption. Also incorporated and altered in several novels is the character triangle—criminal, victim, and detective—when, for instance, the detective becomes the criminal or the victim. In the case of *El vuelo de la reina*, the transformation of the "detectives"—Camargo and Reina—into criminal and victim when Camargo stalks and kills Reina serves to configure Camargo as a metaphor of the atmosphere of corruption and arrogance of the country under Menem's rule, while Reina can be read as an allegory of the nation.

The urban setting is characteristic of the hard-boiled genre, while the country house is a favorite recourse of the classical model. The choice of setting in the featured novels often serves to address and interrogate the cherished notion of Argentina as a middle-class society. By means of their setting in ex-urban gated communities, or "countries," *Retrato de familia con muerta*, *Las viudas de los jueves*, and *Betibú* focus on the nouveau riche who have chosen to live in luxurious enclaves separated and walled off from the perceived unsafe and unhealthy environment of the city. Depicting how these islands of wealth share the urban periphery with *villas* and working-class areas, the novels further highlight inequality. The portrayal of Buenos Aires, often seen as fragmented or deteriorating, is essential to the message of many of the novels. *Puerto Apache* and *La fragilidad de los cuerpos*, for instance, focus on class division within the city by juxtaposing urban spaces. Martini's novel juxtaposes a fictional squatter settlement to upscale Puerto Madero in order to depict urban impoverishment as a consequence of Buenos Aires' neoliberal push to privatization and modernization. *La fragilidad de los cuerpos* uses the detective figure, a middle-class reporter, to link the more prosperous *zona norte* to the working-class *zona sur*, but the plot functions to call attention to their problematic interaction. In *Los hombres te han hecho mal*, the *villa* where the victimized Lindaura lives stands in contrast to the luxurious Recoleta neighborhood where the wealthy Sofía lives: here, the areas of the city serve to reinforce the novel's message regarding the culpability of the frivolous rich in the reigning national disorder that enables corruption. Orsi's novel *Ciudad Santa* interrogates stereotypical representations of Buenos Aires. Teeming with corrupt officials and violent warring drug traffickers, its juxtaposition to the Tierra Santa theme park suggests a city in need of redemption. By depicting tourists who encounter squalid neighborhoods that make them recall the slums of Bombay and who are kidnapped and executed, Orsi ridicules the official propaganda that seeks to promote Buenos Aires as the Paris of South America. Germane to Orsi's depiction of Buenos Aires is Adriaensen and Grinberg Pla's discussion of the concept of the "exoticization of violence," seen particularly in the Mexican and Colombian *narconovelas* that contribute to the reaffirmation of "the stereotype of the violent essence of Latin America" (17). However, as Adriaensen and Grinberg Pla point out, the *novela negra* does not contribute "sin más" (simply) to this exoticization of violence due its critical vision of violence (17–18). In my analysis of Orsi's novel, I have focused on this writer's extensive use of irony, black humor, and parody, as well as the running commentary of the acerbic extradiegetic narrator. These techniques serve as a means to examine and deconstruct stereotypical representations of Buenos Aires, both the overly adulatory and the excessively bleak.

*Asalto al paraíso* portrays Jewish Buenos Aires, envisioning its thriving Jewish community as the reason why the Argentine capital ended up in the crosshairs of global terrorism. *Asalto* also presents an unexpected comparator city for Buenos Aires: Beirut. The Hezbollah terrorist compares Buenos Aires to the beauty of stately prewar Beirut, while the journalist walking among the rubble of the bombed Israeli embassy compares it to the demolished Beirut.

Through their innovative representations of Buenos Aires, the novels explore sociopolitical problems and engage with the issue of Argentine national identity, questioning traditional representations. All the novels reference actual places in Buenos Aires and its surroundings; while the three novels set in "countries" give them fictional names, their characteristics are based on actual features, and the Buenos Aires settings repeatedly name real streets, plazas, and neighborhoods, demonstrating a strong "territorialization" of their fictional plots.[2]

A central point of transformation of the genre is the figure of the detective and the outcome of his or her efforts. Most of the novels in this book adhere to this defining characteristic of detective fiction by including an investigator of some sort who attempts to solve an enigma, expose official wrongdoing, or bring criminals to justice. A striking feature is the repeated use of an investigative journalist in the role of sleuth, either solely or as part of a team. This is the case in five of the eleven novels: *El vuelo de la reina, El muerto indiscreto, Asalto al paraíso, Betibú,* and *La fragilidad de los cuerpos.* While some of these reporters succeed in exposing crime or solving a small portion of the problem, some of them fail completely and none of them enjoy full success in eradicating crime or bringing the wrongdoers to justice.

The use of reporters as protagonists thus reinforces the image of systemic corruption and impunity of corrupt officials and the powerful criminals they protect. Sometimes these characterizations serve to pay tribute to the role of Argentina's watchdog journalism in exposing corruption during the 1990s, as in the case of *El vuelo de la reina, El muerto indiscreto,* and *Asalto al paraíso.* At the same time, certain novels cast a critical eye on journalistic ethics; for instance, Cristina in *Asalto al paraíso* admits that she uses dubious means for a noble cause, and the three reporters in *Betibú* engage in an ongoing discussion of the role of journalism and whether Rodolfo Walsh's model of the politically committed reporter is still viable. In both *El muerto indiscreto* and *Betibú* the newspaper editors refuse to publish the investigators' findings that point to the criminality of government officials or the police. Other novels deride journalists for their lack of ethics, portraying them as motivated by profit rather than the search for the truth—doing superficial coverage instead of in-depth investigation and favoring sensationalist stories that pander to the public's desire to consume gore and scandal. This critique is proffered in *El fiscal* and is also implied in *Betibú.* In *La fragilidad de los cuerpos,* the "do-good" reporter is so determined to bring about justice for the exploited children that she takes matters into her own hands, resorting to a type of vigilantism that she is only able to carry out thanks to her powerful and connected father and the logistical help she gets from his law firm. Worst of all, her impulsive behavior wreaks havoc in the lives of others.

We see unique solutions to the issue of who will do the detecting work in *Retrato de familia con muerta* and *Puerto Apache,* the first using a judge who considers himself a social misfit and the second a picaresque figure who lives in a *villa* and is a minor player in a narcotrafficking ring. The judge's efforts, of course, end in utter failure to bring about justice or even to discover the truth, but he does "judge" and condemn what he considers the shameless behavior of the conspirators who tried to cover up the murder of their family member / neighbor. In *Puerto Apache*, la Rata does solve the initial mystery—who ordered his beating—and while his sleuthing enables him to save his own life, it does nothing toward stopping the violence of the drug war or preventing the expansion of the drug trade. The use of this marginal figure who is confused about his identity due to his exposure to the "high life" through his connection to the drug trade serves to critique the alienating effect of consumer culture. Two of the novels lack a detective figure—*El fiscal*, a spy thriller, and *Las viudas de los jueves*—unless we consider the teenagers in *Las viudas* who film the crime in their neighborhood to be the detectives.

Finally, *Los hombres te han hecho mal* and *Ciudad Santa* go against the grain of the current Latin American *novela negra* by using the classic—and anachronistic—figure of the honest policeman. Daniel Noemi Voionmaa, in his study of Heredia and Belascoarán Shayne, the fictional detectives of Chilean writer Ramón Díaz Eterovic and Mexican writer Paco Ignacio Taibo II, argues that these characters are instances of a distancing from or resistance to reality, constituting states of exception (199). Since Mallo's and Orsi's works feature honest *police*, as opposed to private eyes, we might posit that they demonstrate an even further remove from reality. Consider, for example, Gamerro's number one precept for Argentine detective fiction: the police commit the crime. But, on the other hand, we may ask, what do Mallo's and Orsi's "relatively honest" policemen accomplish? The answer is not much. "El Perro" Lascano is diverted from his police work when he agrees to do a shady side job for a bank for personal gain, and once he becomes a private eye, he does make a small, albeit temporary, contribution to fighting human trafficking in Mar del Plata. Walter Carroza, for his part, is assigned to assist in the recovery of hostages, which is an absolute debacle since they are all assassinated by his corrupt colleague, but at this point Carroza is much more preoccupied with dealing with the troublesome women in his life. In sum, the detective figure in these novels seems to be employed mainly to illustrate that crime, being systemic and endemic, has no solution.

Casting a woman in the detective role is a major international trend in crime fiction, as writers challenge and break down the male-centeredness of the genre at the same time that they reflect women's expanded opportunities in the workplace. But this characterization is problematic—and not just in Hispanic or Argentine letters—because, as Philippa Gates notes, "discontinuity ... arises when a female protagonist is placed in the central position of a male genre" (32). Four of our writers join in on this trend, all using a female journalist in the detective function: Reina Remis in *El vuelo de la reina*, Cristina Tíbori in *Asalto al paraíso*, Nurit Iscar in *Betibú*, and Verónica Rosenthal in *La fragilidad de los cuerpos*. Reina, Cristina, and Verónica are all self-confident, skilled, independent, and savvy investigators who prove that women are capable of carrying out what was considered to be a man's job. At the same time, however, they are sexualized as their shapely bodies are described in tantalizing detail, usually filtered through the male gaze. What is more, all three, due to their sexuality, become a threat to men with whom they interact. Camargo, tormented by Reina's rejection, becomes a crazed murderer, and Cristina Tíbori intentionally uses her body to extract information from two sources, both of whom suffer a cruel fate due to their vulnerability to her charms. Verónica's unbridled passion combined with her morbid curiosity serves as a catalyst to her lover's psychotic breakdown, resulting in his suicidal gesture. In contrast to the sexualization and frequent demonization of the female detective by these male writers, Piñeiro portrays her female detective in a more realistic and nonsexualized manner. Nurit is a capable investigator but suffers from a lack of self-confidence due to her recent literary failure and her perception that her body is aging, and she deals with issues presented by everyday life with which many women can identify.

Other female characters also suffer the vicissitudes of the misogyny of hard-boiled fiction, as our writers engage with this tradition in different ways: imitating it, ignoring it, or countering it. *Ciudad Santa*, *El muerto indiscreto*, *El vuelo de la reina*, and *Asalto al paraíso* all perpetuate the image of the dangerously alluring sexual woman who ensnares men in her web. The first three novels portray binary categories of women: the ugly wife or female cop juxtaposed to a gorgeous seductress, or the plain home-making wife set in contrast to a sensual and shrewd mistress. As is typical of classic detective fiction, in several of the novels—for instance, *Los hombres te han hecho mal*, *El vuelo de la reina*, and *Retrato de familia con muerta*—women are the victims of violence. It is noteworthy that Argemí seeks to reconstruct the subjectivity of the murdered woman by using another female character and a female Greek chorus to identify with or represent her. Piñeiro, for her part, intentionally reverses this trend by creating only male victims, both in *Las viudas de los jueves* and *Betibú*. What is more, her characters call attention to the problem of violence against women by recounting the story of Olive Thomas, the actress who first embodied Betty Boop and was suspected to have been poisoned by her husband, and by bringing up actual cases of unsolved murders of women in Argentina. These issues are set forth by means of Piñeiro's ample use of digressions. As far as *Puerto Apache* is concerned, male and female characters alike succumb to the allure of consumer society, but it is "marketable Maru" who shamelessly uses her body to attain a life of luxury, ultimately selling herself to a repulsive scoundrel who is the highest bidder. *El fiscal* has a fairly neutral portrayal of women. The two protagonists, both negatively portrayed as self-serving and seriously flawed, are males, and women play secondary roles, such as ex-wife and helper. It is true that Paula, the high-class prostitute whom Lerman comes to appreciate, is actually working for Trusso and thus betraying Lerman. But this is also the case of Castagnino, Lerman's most trusted assistant, who is bought out by Trusso.

A much-utilized procedure that I have discussed extensively in relation to these novels is the incorporation of historical events and figures, most frequently unsolved crimes and individuals connected to crime and corruption. Invariably, the insertion of historical elements is a feature of the text's *denuncia social*, but the modes of mingling fact and fiction vary, as does how this impacts our reading of the texts that contain them. For instance, *Los hombres te han hecho mal* incorporates details from the real-life case of the slaying of María Esther Amaro but never names the case. Apparently, the author perceived it as a model to inspire his critique of human trafficking, while finding it unnecessary, or a detraction from the text's fictionality, to point to the factual references of certain portrayals. In *Betibú*, Piñeiro takes details from the unsolved García Belsunce case to develop the plot but pointedly avoids speculating in regard to who was her killer. The characters mention other unsolved killings of women as part of the novel's feminist agenda; however, these do not figure in the plot action. *Retrato de familia con muerta*, on the other hand, is explicit about the novel's fictionalization of a real crime, modeling the concept of the "policial palimpséstico," as identified and analyzed by Osvaldo Di Paolo. Using the structure of the framed story, the novel takes advantage of the interstice between official reports about the García Belsunce crime (the hypotext) and its fictional re-creation (the hypertext) to criticize negative effects of neoliberalism, which, according to this narrative, have broken down the social fabric. *El vuelo de la reina* and *El muerto indiscreto* also deliver a critique of the neoliberal era by means of incorporating a slightly altered version of President Menem and by portraying corrupt actors in his administration, many of whom took advantage of the structural changes to enrich themselves via bribes and kickbacks.

*Asalto al paraíso* and *El fiscal*, also with plots based on actual events, illustrate crime fiction's use of generic hybridity, in this case to intervene on sensitive national issues. Each constitutes a fusion of genres that serve to "emplot" the events according to the authors' ideological stance regarding the terrorist attacks carried out in Buenos Aires during the 1990s along with the repercussions of their failed investigation. Aguinis's novel, by inserting the pseudo-*testimonio* of a Hezbollah militant, portrays the attacks as an extension of the Arab-Israeli conflict, while the anticonspiracy thriller serves to denounce the complicity of Argentine officials with the bombings and the failure to solve them. Pratt's spy thriller, combined with the roman à clef, serves a politically partisan function, backing the claim of the Fernández de Kirchner administration that Alberto Nisman's death was the work of a rogue spy. An example of more limited generic hybridization is the fairy-tale ending of *Los hombres te han hecho mal*, a recourse that attenuates an otherwise grimly realistic portrayal of organized crime and corruption.

Finally, a creative and productive way in which crime fiction writers renovate the genre is by means of metafictional recourses. In their articles in the Adriaensen and Grinberg Pla collection, Hartmut Nonnenmacher and Rosa Pellicer explore the manifestation and function of metafictional devices in Latin American crime fiction. Nonnenmacher, who focuses on the thematization of literary works within detective fiction, presents this self-referential process as a way that works of "popular" culture seek greater literariness and aspire to "high" culture. He points to the duality of "lo popular y lo intelectual" that is seen in the alternating references to popular or mass culture and to "high art" as characteristic of a considerable portion of Latin American detective literature. Nonnenmacher notes that "this hybridization between high and popular art in the Spanish American detective novel is at the same time a reflection and a consequence of the 'incorporation into cultural modernity' of the Latin American countries" (235). Pellicer, on the other hand, considers metafiction a way to renovate an exhausted genre, as the text questions its own nature and process of composition. Citing Borges and Walsh among others, Pellicer points out that the parodic character has been present from the origins of the genre in Argentina, but since the 1990s, the metaliterary component has become more widespread and more complex. The novels studied in this book participate in this revitalization of the genre with recourses that include intertextuality and self-referentiality, and various forms of metalepsis or play with diegetic levels, such as the framed story, the use of disembodied choral voices, and mise en abyme.

Various critics have taken note of the intertextuality or self-consciousness of Latin American crime fiction, as it signals its belonging to the genre. The references of Argemí's narrator to Agatha Christie, Edgar Allan Poe, and Serpico illustrate transculturation, transformation, and territorialization, as he ironically compares the details of the murder in the Argentine gated community to these classics. Several novels, while lacking overt references to Raymond Chandler, feature detective figures who take on traits reminiscent of Philip Marlowe, his iconic hard-boiled private eye—for instance, Mallo's Lascano, Orsi's Carroza, and Correa's Dargas. Orsi parodies the Che Guevara "text" through ironic comparisons of the Marxist revolutionary to Pacogoya, the Che look-alike tour guide / drug dealer / male prostitute, in a running commentary on the loss of idealistic values in the "ciudad santa." In *Las viudas de los jueves*, the repeating embossed titles of literary classics on the empty book shells—*La vida es sueño*, *Fausto*, *Crimen y castigo*—speak to the false life in the country club along with its residents' aspiration to "possess" culture as yet another commodity.

*El vuelo de la reina* and *Betibú* are the most technically complex novels of the group, each employing numerous recourses that are considered characteristic of "high" literature. At the same time, intertextuality and references to manifestations of popular culture play an important role in these texts, serving to break down the division between "high" and "low" literature. It is Camargo's and Reina's common fascination with the actor Robert Mitchum that brings about their fateful encounter, and references to iconic noir films—*The Rear Window* and *Night of the Hunter*—serve to create mental images and help set up a noir atmosphere. Rodolfo Walsh's watchdog journalism is a model for Camargo, and Reina is a magnet for intertextuality. Her in-depth knowledge of the Bible enables her to explain why the president's "mystic vision" is a hoax and her fascination with the Gnostic gospels is a key element in the novel's development of the double and the extended metaphor of the good and evil twins. We also learn that Reina's prose is as insidious as that of Patricia Highsmith, and that she has read all of Julio Cortázar's stories. The Cortázar tribute is more prominent in *Betibú*: the discovery of Chazarreta's corpse in a green velvet chair with his throat slit plays with the Cortázar story "Continuidad de los parques," a parody that is reinforced when the characters themselves take note of the similarity. This reference to a canonical author is followed up by allusions to popular culture: Nurit's reference to the graveyard scene in Stephen King's *Carrie* and, of course, the cartoon character Betty Boop, who provides Nurit's nickname and the novel's title. The references to Betty Boop, a figure associated with both women's liberation and victimization, develop the feminist themes. All these intertextual references enliven and help "flesh out" the stories at the same time that they thematicize and problematize the division between "high" and "low" art.

Another metafictional strategy used by our authors is metalepsis, or the play with diegetic levels. An example mentioned above is the narrative frame of *Retrato de familia con muerta* that turns the real-life crime into a story within a story, setting it at a remove that allows the fictional narrator of the frame story to turn it into an indictment of the shameless behavior of the perpetrators of the cover-up. In *Las viudas de los jueves*, on the other hand, it is the disembodied choral voice speaking from an unspecified future time that allows the characters themselves to reflect on their misguided assumptions that led to the untimely deaths of their neighbors. This voice-over effect also lends the story an aura of tragedy and otherworldliness. Once again, the topic of critique is the nouveau riche and their obsession with social status and a lifestyle of luxury.

Finally, both *El muerto indiscreto* and *Betibú* evoke the figure of the mise en abyme when the journalists who take on the detective function, Dargas and Nurit, respectively, tell us that their discoveries are too dangerous or too explosive to publish, and therefore they will resort to fiction to speak the truth. Thus the reader realizes that he or she is actually reading that novel, placing us within the world of the novel and, in the case of *Betibú*, conjuring up the image of an infinite series of stories repeating themselves. By using this recourse, these narratives speak to the power of fiction, setting forth the idea that, in certain circumstances, fiction is better suited to telling the truth than nonfiction. While Dargas's projected novel is only mentioned in passing, Nurit's repeated references to her hypothetical novel provide an extended commentary on the powers of fiction.

In sum, metafictional devices, while serving to dissolve the perceived barrier between high and popular literature and to proffer a philosophical reflection about human endeavors and existence, are an important way in which Argentine crime fiction, along with its counterparts in other regions of the world, renovates and rejuvenates itself. At first blush, the concept of the text as artistic gesture—implied in the metafictional musings—seems to be at odds with the concept of the text as political gesture, which is a basic tenet of the present book. While the perception of the text's social or political role implies its reference to an outside world, the metafictional components call attention to its artificial or constructed nature. However, this paradox—the text's dual existence as both mirror to reality and as artifice—is intrinsic to fictional discourse. The entities (peoples, places, actions, ideas) in a literary work are characterized as being products of *invention*, and the text as political gesture critiques an actual world by presenting a *version* of that world from a critical stance and by a fictional narrator (Meyer-Minnermann 49). The metafictional recourses remind us of the texts' essence, highlighting the fact that transparent realism is a naïve concept and these are constructed versions of reality. Ultimately, the metafictional components of these novels allow the text to question its mode of comprehension of reality, its process of composition, and its own nature.

## THE SENTIMENTAL SUBTEXT

Finally, this book has discussed the surprisingly sentimental ending to several of these dark and violent tales. As I have noted repeatedly, all narratives depict the persistence of crime and corruption despite the investigators' determined efforts to expose and denounce it, and the wrongdoers invariably go unpunished. The city is chaotic, fragmented, and deteriorating. But we have seen that some writers temper this gloomy picture with a sentimental subtext. Both *Los hombres te han hecho mal* and *Ciudad Santa*, which portray in crude and vivid detail the heartless and violent world of human- and narcotrafficking, are deeply invested in sentimentality. Each ends with the coupling of the noble but weary police detective with the woman of his dreams, providing a happy ending that attenuates the text's grim realism in its depiction of crime. What is more, each text gestures to family unity, Mallo's novel doing so by repeatedly portraying failed or dysfunctional families and Orsi's by the final union of Ana, the lethal Bolivian beauty queen, with her long-lost policeman father. *Betibú* joins the novels that conclude on a romantic note as all three of the "detectives" find romantic partners. Some of *Betibú*'s digressions also deal with human ties; for instance, we see Nurit's interaction with her sons and her supportive female friends. Argemí's novel, in its very title—*Retrato de familia con muerta*—evokes family unity, precisely to lament what is lacking in this family that colludes to cover up the murder of one of its members. *Puerto Apache*, while showing a fractured society and broken or hideously mismatched couples, ends by depicting male bonding. As la Rata flees from Puerto Apache during the night, certain that the drug mafia has framed him, his friend Cúper runs to catch up with him and accompanies him to an uncertain future. *Las viudas de los jueves* also closes with a flight from home; this time it is the Guevara family that departs from the protective gated community in order to report the truth about the murder-suicide that took place in el Tano's swimming pool. Like la Rata, they have no place to go and there will be no return, but parents and son have united in their decision to expose the fraud perpetrated in the "country." The most ironic of the sentimental endings is that of *El vuelo de la reina*. Camargo, who railed out against his mother and his lover because they abandoned him, ends up partially paralyzed and obliged to spend his final years in the unctuous care of his devoted wife, Brenda, who secretly delights in his dependence on her. Even *La fragilidad de los cuerpos*, with its potentially home-wrecking protagonist and disturbing climax, has its sentimental side. Verónica's apparent rejection of domesticity and her seduction of a priest and a family man make her an edgy, antisentimental character, but, as noted, she secretly craves a domestic partner who will never leave her. After Lucio's heart-wrenching death, the novel concludes on an upbeat note with the boys Peque and Dientes walking with little Martina and putting together their coins to buy her a Coke. This conclusion suggests that the coupling that evaded Verónica will be carried out by the next generation, via the children she has fought to protect.

These novels demonstrate that criminality does not cancel out sentimentality. Far from it, the plots gesture toward nurturing ties of romantic love, family, and friendship in an unsympathetic world. It is up to the reader to decide whether the affective dimension of the novels means that the characters have retreated into their own private world, turning their back to the seemingly insurmountable social disarray and political corruption, or if it is a suggestion that healing and change must begin with individual human connections.

This book has only scratched the surface of the burgeoning field of the contemporary Argentine *novela negra*, but it is my hope that it has contributed to our understanding of how novels published since the turn of the century engage and explore Argentine reality as they participate in the processes of transculturation, transformation, and territorialization. There is no reason to believe that the production of Argentine *novela negras* will abate any time soon, as unfolding events continue to supply scandals and intrigue. In 1995, the son of Carlos Menem and Zulema Yoma was killed in a helicopter crash. Some insisted that his death was not accidental but rather the third strike of a Syrian mafia angry with Menem for forgoing campaign promises (the first two strikes being the bombing of the Israeli Embassy and the AMIA). Now, over two decades later, the conspiracy theory has gained new fuel, with both Menem and Yoma making public declarations—Menem blames Hezbollah for the death of his son, while the boy's mother connects it to narco-terrorism (Ruiz). The case of the sabotaged AMIA investigation continues: Carlos Menem has been called to testify and a federal judge has requested that Cristina Fernández de Kirchner be charged with treason for allegedly taking part in a cover-up of the investigation of Iran's role in the attack. After Kirchner's presidential term ended in December 2015, the government of her successor, Mario Macri, has not hesitated to unleash a list of indictments against her and her family and associates; they have been accused of embezzling, bribe-taking, misappropriating public funds, and money laundering. Bizarre cases have been in the public spotlight: Argentine television showed earthmovers digging up a Patagonian farm where a vast Kirchner fortune is rumored to be buried (Goñi). August 2018 brought dramatic breaking news: a judge obtained notebooks with the detailed records kept by the former driver of an official in the Planning Ministry who delivered bags of cash around the city. This resulted in the arrest of powerful figures in business and government implicated in the scandal, and was quickly followed by the cooperation of at least seventeen of them in the inquiry into a vast system of kickbacks under the Kirchners, amounting to an estimated $36 billion between 2003 and 2015 (Politi). We can await with baited breath the next round of *novelas negras* from Argentina.

# NOTES

## INTRODUCTION

1. Unless otherwise noted, all translations are my own. Sources for De Santis quote: "¿Qué define al policial argentino?"; for the Olguín quotes: Enríquez.

2. Indeed, David Frank Schmid has observed, "No genre is better equipped in critique of neoliberalism than crime fiction."

3. The "Washington Consensus" is described by Paul Blustein in the following terms: "a sort of economic Ten Commandments prescribed by the IMF, the World Bank, and the US government. Among the main elements of this recipe are the eradication of inflation, the privatization of industry, the deregulation of the economy, and the removal of trade barriers" (4).

4. For a comprehensive study of how the Latin American detective genre evolved from its British and US roots as well as a discussion of terminology relating to variations of the genre, see Braham i–xv and 1–17.

5. As an example of alternative terminology, Sergio Olguín refers to "ficción policial" or "policial"—for instance in his interview with Silvina Friera, "Siempre caigo en el policial"—in the sense that I am using "novela negra." Another commonly used term is "neopolicial" or "neopoliciaco," coined by Cuban writer Leonardo Padura Fuentes and described by Braham as "loosely based on the hard-boiled genre" but "more overtly political and leftist," "primarily urban," and representing "an irrational, violent world" (xiii).

6. Lee Horsley states that she uses the term "crime fiction" in her study for the genre as a whole, as well as for the large subgenre of detective-less, generally transgressor-centered crime novels. She warns against labeling of subgenres due to fluidity of the genre (*Twentieth-Century Crime Fiction* 2–3).

7. See Gerardo Pignatiello's article for a study of how the role of the police changes in *Luna caliente* when the state becomes the criminal.

8. "Proceso" is short for Proceso de Reorganización Nacional (National Reorganization Process), a name given to the military dictatorship in Argentina that lasted from 1976 to 1983.

9. See Swanson's articles for his reading of the ambiguities posed by this postmodern detective novel.

10. For a study of the memory narrative in *Lo que nosotras sabíamos*, see my article.

11. In the original Spanish: "No escribo novela policial."

12. Studies of *Plata quemada* that I have found particularly helpful are those by Joanna Page, Michelle Clayton, Edgardo H. Berg, Adriana Rodríguez Pérsico, Julio Premat, and Valeria Grinberg Pla ("*Plata quemada*").

13. Transcribed by author from "Guillermo Orsi nos habla sobre presencia de la dictadura en la literatura: 'Medellín Negro' 2012," www.youtube.com/watch?v=VSFWE1A6hfk.

14. Jameson makes this observation in respect to the role of Chandler's detective, Philip Marlowe, in Los Angeles.

15. Close's article "The Detective Is Dead: Long Live the *Novela Negra*!" spells out this change. Close's analysis demonstrates that, with the trend of "criminal ascendency" reflecting regional crises (147), the old-style private eye has practically disappeared from Latin American "detective" fiction. Close discusses the decision of Colombian novelist Santiago Gamboa to reject "the private investigator in favor of a journalist protagonist who would provide . . . a more credible approximation to the immediate reality of Bogotá" (*Contemporary Hispanic Crime Fiction* 151).

16. See Godsland, *Killing Carmens* 7; Plain 41 and 48; and Worthington 167.

17. This situation is changing: Mallo's detective, "el Perro" Lascano, has appeared in six novels, while Sergio Olguín's female investigator, Verónica Rosenthal, has taken the lead in three novels. Remil, Jorge Fernández Díaz's spy, has appeared in two novels and promises to return.

## CHAPTER 1

1. Horsley identifies the origins of crime fiction in the gothic: dark secrets of an oppressive nature, for example the criminally guilty father figure. Crime fiction, she asserts, is linked "from its inception to the gothic representation of excess, violence, and transgressions of the boundaries of reason and law" (*Twentieth-Century Crime Fiction* 4).

2. Data on Argentina's human trafficking status come from the "Country Narratives" and "Tier Placement" reports of the US Department of State's

Office to Monitor and Combat Trafficking in Persons and the article by Suárez. To put the case of Argentina in context, three recent book-length studies of human trafficking that look at the issue from a global perspective—by Dalla et al., Jonsson, and Kara—do not mention Argentina at all. Only Louise Shelley mentions Argentina and it is in reference to the defunct Zwi Migdal, a notorious Jewish organization of white slave traders that operated from the 1860s to 1939 and was centered in Buenos Aires. Perhaps a more objective measure is the Department of State's tier system used to indicate the level of governmental cooperation in combating trafficking in persons. Tier 1 countries are those whose governments are fully compliant with the Trafficking Victims Protection Act's minimum standards, Tier 2 countries do not fully comply but are making significant efforts to bring themselves into compliance, and Tier 3 countries are not fully complying and not making significant efforts to do so. Argentina is ranked as a Tier 2 country, along with the majority of other Latin American countries (US Department of State, *Trafficking in Persons Report: Tier Placements*).

3. To maintain a perspective on the situation in Argentina, it is important to note that problems with police corruption are widespread across Latin America and are more severe in other countries, for example in Brazil (Hinton 12).

4. *La aguja en el pajar* and *Delincuente argentino* are the original names for the novels, which were first published in Argentina. Upon their publication in Spain, they were renamed *Crimen en el Barrio del Once* and *El policía descalzo de la Plaza San Martín*, respectively. Mallo said that these name changes were the decision of the Spanish publisher and that he did not allow a title change for his third Lascano novel, *Los hombres te han hecho mal* (unpublished interview by author, August 4, 2013). *Aguja* and *Delincuente* have been published in English as *Needle in a Haystack* and *Sweet Money*, respectively. In 2015 the trilogy was published in a single volume titled *El comisario Lascano*.

5. Mallo currently lives in Barcelona, and inserts an amusing autobiographic wink, giving Lascano an encounter "de la cuarta dimensión." Lascano exchanges glances and a half smile with a familiar-looking man in a bar. Upon inquiry, the waiter tells Lascano that the man is the famous writer "Ernesto Rayo" (*El hilo de sangre* 180).

6. Ejército Revolucionario del Pueblo was an urban guerrilla group that opposed the dictatorship and fused with Montoneros. Mallo has admitted that some readers thought a militant falling in love with a federal policeman

strained credibility since the police were deeply involved with the military in the repressive campaign against urban guerrillas and others that they deemed "subversivos" (Berlanga).

7. As noted in the introduction to this chapter, the critique of Menem's "criminal frivolity" is the topic of Mallo's novel *Me verás caer*.

8. The setting of *Los hombres te han hecho mal* in Mar del Plata reflects the beach town's reputation as a sex playground. A *Página/12* article on the killing of prostitutes in the region reports, "All year long, but especially during summer, the sex for sale in Mar del Plata offers more varieties of quality, quantity and price than its gastronomy or theater shows" (Rodríguez). A 2009–10 investigation revealed that in Mar del Plata approximately four thousand women are sexually exploited in four hundred brothels (Lag).

9. All italicization in quotations is in original unless indicated otherwise.

10. Fabiana Túñez, of the Argentine NGO Casa del Encuentro, explains how trafficked women are treated: "Once they are in the hands of the mafia, women are subjected for twenty days to what in the jargon is called 'softening,' which includes rape, torture, threats to their families, and also drugs, to break down them psychologically and to be able to make their 'transfer' to the brothels." (Suárez).

11. Extradiegetic narration refers to "narration that comes from outside the story world" (A. H. Porter 75).

12. The complicity of police officers in human trafficking is a major problem, as documented in the US Department of State's narrative on Argentina. According to NGOs, international organizations, and officials, the trafficking-related complicity of some government officials was a serious concern. Some police officers reportedly condoned human trafficking activity or tipped off brothel owners about impending raids, and some judges reportedly did not adequately investigate signs of official complicity in trafficking cases (US Department of State, *Trafficking in Persons Report: Country Narratives*). Another report informed that officials delayed raids or arbitrarily threw out possible cases of human trafficking that security forces brought before the justice system ("Nuevos métodos para eludir la ley").

13. *Delincuente argentino* presents yet another case of a broken family: Eva's sister is taken away by the military because they mistake her for Eva, a militant of the ERP. Their parents never recover from the grief. There is also the case of Giribaldi's family in *La aguja en el pajar*: this plot line addresses the kidnapping of babies born to captive women during the dictatorship. Since his wife was not able to bear a child, Giribaldi obtained a baby born to

a woman in captivity, but his wife, insisting that the baby despised her, was not able to bond with the child.

14. English translations for quotes from *Ciudad Santa* are from the Kindle edition, and the cited locations refer to part and chapter, that is, 2.8 means part 2, chapter 8. Further citations of quotes are to the Spanish-edition pages followed by those of the English edition. "Merca" is the slang generally used for cocaine.

15. I have inserted "their comrades" to correct this omission in the translated edition.

16. Puerto Madero will be discussed in conjunction with the analysis of *Puerto Apache* in chapter 5, and the Riachuelo River and its process of contamination will be discussed in the section of chapter 5 titled "No Longer a Middle-Class Society."

17. "Bolita" is a pejorative term for Bolivian.

18. I am indebted to Aníbal González's *Love and Politics* for this concept.

## CHAPTER 2

1. Not all critics are in full agreement that *El vuelo de la reina* is a *novela negra*. For instance, Godsland writes, "Although generic classification of *El vuelo de la reina* is ... not straightforward, [its] foundation in overt and extreme manifestations of brutality, characterization of female victims and male aggressors ..., solidly political overtone, and gradual revelation of what happened ... might suggest a tentative categorization within a broad crime genre" ("Allegory, Gender and Aggression" 191). However, following Close's criteria for the *novela negra* that I cited in the introduction as my standard, *El vuelo* fits the definition due to the central role of criminality and the investigation of wrongdoing in the plot development.

2. For a detailed account of the labyrinthine negotiations and questionable handling behind the privatization process, see Verbitsky's *Robo para la corona*.

3. Several biographies of Menem have been published. For an account of his flashy lifestyle, see Walger's *Pizza con champán*. The biographies by Cerruti, Vázquez, and Wornat also include accounts of his life and political career, as well as his temperament and idiosyncrasies.

4. Waisbord reports that *Página/12* "has become synonymous with watchdog journalism in contemporary Argentina," adding that "one of its main contributions has been to put watchdog journalism at the center of

the Argentine media and to push other dailies to produce investigations" (*Watchdog Journalism in South America* 77).

5. For an analysis of the HIV/AIDS metaphor and Camargo's revenge, see the article by Jodi Parys.

6. The crime that Camargo will imitate—the murder of Sandra Gomide by Pimenta Neves, director of the *Gazeta Mercantil* in São Paulo—actually happened. Martínez said that when his project for the novel was all but abandoned, this true crime story revived it: " 'The story coincided in the smallest details with the scheme for the novel that I had sketched months ago,' [Martínez] explained. That strange coincidence returned him to his writing, and marked the novel's fortune" (Denoy). Martínez wrote an article about the crime, titled "Pasiones brasileñas," which was published in *La Nación* on 2 September 2000. *El vuelo de la reina* includes a crime report with nearly the same title, "Una pasión brasileña," and the same date, published in the fictional *El Diario* (50). The article in the novel is a slightly edited version of what Martínez wrote for *La Nación*; it incorporates some additional details, such as Neves's character traits of "altivez" (arrogance) and "orgullo" (pride), the fact that his wife is from the US, and that he asked other directors not to hire Sandra because she received bribes.

7. I am indebted to Shelley Godsland's 2014 article, "Allegory, Gender and Aggression," for this observation in regard to *El vuelo de la reina*. In *The Fatal Woman*, James F. Maxfield draws a distinction between the terms "femme fatale" and "fatal woman": while the femme fatale "deliberately tries to lead men to their destruction," the fatal woman's destructive effects are not necessarily intentional (9). From this perspective, we can consider Reina to be a fatal woman and Belle a femme fatale.

8. See Myriam Osorio's study for an analysis of the regimes of power in *El vuelo* and the social and political implications of Camargo's attempt to subject Reina.

9. Another notorious example in Argentine crime fiction of the mother being blamed for the adult male's perversion is the character of Morvan in *La pesquisa* by Juan José Saer.

10. Citing *Double Indemnity* and *Vertigo* as examples, Maxfield notes that the threat of loss of male control is a major issue in all noir films. And manhood, in this case, is chiefly defined in terms of dominance—not only over the seductive female but also over competing males (10).

11. For analysis of how ostensibly nonfictional investigative journalism makes use of fictional techniques to explain the 1990s in Argentina and the

"fenómemo menemista," see the 2003 studies by Hugo Hortiguera: "De la investigación periodística al potín" and "El folletín delictuoso argentino."

12. Cerruti uses the nickname to title her biography *El Jefe: Vida y obra de Carlos Saúl Menem*. Vázquez points out that "the term [el Jefe] shows commonalities with the behavior of a mafia, a kind of club of men united by illicit affairs and quasi-blood fidelities. The appellative is a sign and password for those in the know, those who belong, who, at the most extreme, are the sycophants, obedient/obsequious willing to give their lives for the boss/godfather" (195).

13. These aspects of Menem's life are chronicled in the biographies by Cerruti, Walger, and Wornat.

14. In *Pizza con champán*, Sylvina Walger's account of the *farándula menemista*, she relates events involving these men that Correa attributes to the fictional Kunny. These incidents are reported in greater detail in other sources.

15. Sources for information on Rubén Cardozo include "Embajadas del escándalo"; "Falleció ayer Rubén Cardozo"; "Los casos que conmovieron al Servicio"; and Walger 268–70.

16. The author explains: "The real thing with Cardozo is that he supposedly died from a heart attack by late March 1997; I was in New York at the time and got the news through the Internet.... And then, more than a year later, that unexpected encounter at El Mirasol. I remember that unconsciously I said 'look, here comes the dead man.' And after a casual, irrelevant five minutes talk, he and the man I renamed Del Morral left. Never heard of Cardozo again since that night and never looked for him." Email correspondence with Rubén Correa, 8 April 2008.

17. For details, see Martorell; Quilodrán; "Revés de Spinoza [sic] Melo en la Corte"; "Spinosa Melo desmiente"; and Sanz, "El embajador del miedo." Spinosa Melo's account of his diplomatic career, *Sobre el volcán*, refutes many of the charges of wrongdoing.

18. This bizarre behavior is related in "Despiden a un embajador."

19. There are many mentions of Ramón Hernández in Wornat's biography that describe his closeness with the president.

20. For information about the investigation into Hernández's overseas accounts, see the articles by Alconada Mon and Rodríguez Yebra.

21. Hernández has been implicated in the death of Poli Armentano, a nightclub owner who allegedly refused to cooperate with the trafficking of "a huge amount of drugs that had entered the country as part of payment for arms smuggling to Ecuador and Croatia" (Sanz, "El caso Armentano").

22. The fascinating saga of the kidnapping of the Born brothers and the mystery of what happened to the millions composing the largest ransom in history is chronicled by María O'Donnell in her book *Born* (2015). After decades of silence, Jorge Born agreed to be interviewed by O'Donnell, and, not surprisingly, since this is Born's version of events, he comes out as the hero of this episode of Argentine history.

23. Wornat reports, "In 1995 a party was thrown ... where Carlos Menem, surrounded by his close friends and associates, celebrated the dimension his fortune had reached: 1.5 billion dollars" (147). By the time *El muerto indiscreto* was published in 2003, Menem had been under investigation for two years for alleged cases of corruption during his presidency. By March 2004, Menem faced a complicated judicial situation, with a series of cases initiated against him by Argentine courts. The charges included (1) maliciously omitting a Swiss bank account from his sworn declaration of properties as head of state—money possibly received from illegal arms trafficking, which would constitute crimes of ideological falseness and money laundering; (2) "bribery and fraud against the State in the construction of two jailhouses during his mandate"; and (3) abuse of power ("The Menem Case"). However, Menem, then married to a Chilean citizen and former Miss Universe, Cecilia Bolocco, was residing in Chile with his wife and their son and refused to return to Argentina to face the charges. In December 2004, he finally returned to Argentina. The trial was long and drawn-out. On 4 June 2009, Menem, along with eight of his ex-functionaries, was indicted for embezzlement and a freeze was imposed on $100 million of his assets. Evidence connected to the case indicated up to $400 million in embezzled funds (Fernández Moores; "Sobresueldos"; "Un sobresalto por los sobres").

24. A 1998 *New York Times* article by Clifford Krauss reported on the suspicious deaths and allegations of hired killers.

25. Estrada had been maintaining silence about allegations related to illegal arms sales, but it was believed that he was about to talk. His death was read as a warning to Diego Pallares, another person involved in arms trafficking, who had declared that he received a bribe to facilitate arms trafficking to Croatia and had hinted that he was ready to provide telling details. See Calv; Gutma; Krauss; and Santoro, "Los mensajes cifrados."

26. The death of fictional senator Valenti also borrows details from the death of Miguel Roig. Roig, appointed by Menem to the post of Minister of Economy, died in his apartment one week after his appointment. Those close to him were sure that it was suicide, but the death was officially declared a

heart attack (Cerruti 307–8). Although Roig's death was prior to and unrelated to the arms scandal, the official report altered the cause of death for political purposes, like that of the fictional Valenti.

27. The episode about the fictional president's son is not based on reality, as Menem's son Carlitos was killed in a helicopter accident in 1995.

28. For a description of the charges, see note 23 of this chapter.

29. Menem has been accused of authorizing illegal weapons sales between 1991 and 1995 to Croatia and Ecuador, in defiance of UN embargoes. In 2001 he spent five months under house arrest while authorities looked into these charges, but they were dismissed for lack of merit. The case was filed again after President Néstor Kirchner replaced all the judges, and in 2008 Menem was formally charged with involvement in arms trafficking. In 2011 a court dismissed the charges, only for another court to revoke the dismissal in 2013 and sentence him to seven years of prison time for the illegal weapons sale. As of June 2018, he is still at liberty because the charges are pending appeal. Even if the charges are confirmed, Menem enjoys immunity as a senator representing his home province of La Rioja, and the Supreme Court would have to ask the Senate to revoke his immunity ("Carlos Menem fue condenado"; "En marzo podrían ordenar detener a Carlos Menem"; Fernández Moores, "Menem debió sentarse"; "Menem Arms Charges Dropped"; "Menem Charged with Arms-Smuggling").

30. Outside the space of the novel, Martínez has acknowledged its historical allusions, for instance, in this quote: " 'I did not want to give names to the presidents of the republic because none of the acts that the presidents do in the novel is strictly true, but I cannot deny the obvious allusions' " (Denoy). "Presidents" refers to Fernando de la Rúa, who is also depicted in the novel.

31. Vázquez comments on Zulemita's 1993 trip to Rome: "Zulemita spends money in the shops of Via Frattina and Via Condotti.... Such extravagance speaks of a fruition practiced without limits. Loaded with dollars, Zulemita prepares to spend them.... She [Zulemita] is one of the few Argentines who has a Rolex limited edition decorated with diamonds on her wrist, valued at around 80 thousand dollars" (83). Getting to the crux of the issue, Vázquez later remarks, "Zulemita spends fortunes, the origin of which raises doubts" (121).

32. Cerruti explains the sense in which José Luis Manzano said this: "When José Luis Manzano uttered his famous phrase 'I steal for the Crown' he was, finally, making a delimitation of legitimacies. With the same logic as his Italian Socialist friends, Manzano believed that any method to get money

to do politics and have power was justified. What was not allowed was to do it outside the circuit and only for personal enrichment" (363). Verbitsky used the phrase for the title of his detailed investigation and denunciation of corruption in the Menem administration's privatization process.

33. In an interview, Martínez compares Camargo's fear of abandonment to Argentina. To the inquiry as to whether Camargo's "gran soberbia" (great arrogance) and the abandonment he is incapable of assimilating can serve as a metaphor for Argentina, Martínez replies, "I think so. Argentina has been punished for its arrogance by an unforeseen form of humiliation, which is that of abandonment.... Argentina has finally discovered that it means very little in the world" (Bracho). Thus, while Reina can be considered an allegory for Argentina, the novelist envisions Camargo as a representation of his country.

34. Waisbord explains the sense of failure felt by journalists with the following facts: "In Argentina none of the seventy-one officials of the Menem administration legally accused of corruption between 1990 and mid-1995 have been convicted.... All individuals charged in the Yomagate (the investigations about the involvement of aides to President Menem in drug-money laundering) were cleared and the cause was annulled. Judge María Servini de Cubria was accused of mishandling the process and received a sixty-dollar penalty from the Supreme Court. Two associates of President Menem charged with selling rotten milk to a government children's program were absolved." Waisbord concludes that there is no convincing sign that corruption has been eradicated in Argentina (*Watchdog Journalism in South America* 212–14).

## CHAPTER 3

1. Nisman's death was initially ruled a suicide, but in September 2017, a team of forensic experts issued a new report presenting evidence that Nisman was murdered, and in December 2017, a federal judge ruled his death a murder ("Argentina Prosecutor"). As of this writing, the perpetrators remain unknown.

2. It should be noted that there does not exist universal agreement that a car bomb delivered the explosives that destroyed the AMIA. Some allege that the explosion came from within the building and that the pieces of a Renault Traffic van found at the bombsite were actually brought from a junk yard and planted at the site as part of a conspiracy. As my discussion of the novel indicates, this theory is cited in Pratt's *El fiscal*.

3. The investigation into the attacker also suffered reverses. In 2003 Ibrahim Hussein Berro, a Lebanese citizen and Hezbollah militant, was identified as the suicide bomber by the SIDE, FBI, and Mossad; it was also reported that he entered Argentina via the Triple Frontera. However, when Berro's brothers were located by the CIA in Michigan, they declared that they could not envision Ibrahim being a suicide bomber because he wanted to get married and have a family. What is more, all were convinced that he died in Lebanon (Kollmann, "Una causa").

4. Sheinin further states that those who accuse Nisman of being a US stooge do so based on a gross misreading of certain documents that have turned up on WikiLeaks, and this comes from a fallacious view shared by many Argentines who "cannot accept that high-ranking Argentine officials worked cooperatively with the United States on Iran policy" ("The Death of Alberto Nisman" 36).

5. In December 2017, a federal judge charged Fernández de Kirchner with treason for her role in the cover-up of the investigation of Iranian involvement in the AMIA bombing and sought her arrest. She enjoys immunity due to her role as a senator, but this can be revoked by a two-thirds vote of the senate ("Argentine Judge Seeks Arrest").

6. For the investigation into Nisman's death, see note 1 of this chapter.

7. For a focus on Aguinis's role as a public intellectual who advocates for reform and healing, along with an analysis of *Asalto* in this context, see Wassner's *Harbinger of Modernity*.

8. For a discussion of this heterogeneous body of works, see Sadow's "Lamentations for the AMIA."

9. The Triple A was a clandestine paramilitary ultra-right wing organization active during the 1970s. Also known as the Death Squad, it kidnapped and murdered hundreds of individuals whom they considered to be enemies of the government.

10. With "focalizer" I am using Gérard Genette's terminology and conceptualization in regard to narrative discourse. He breaks down the question "Who is the narrator?" into the questions "Who speaks?" and "Who sees?" He calls the person who perceives or sees "the focalizer" (*Narrative Discourse* 185–94).

11. See, for instance, Francescato's description of the response of Jewish readers to Aguinis's novel *Refugiados: crónica de un palestino* in her article "Marcos Aguinis: A Controversial Argentine Jewish Writer."

12. Another Argentine crime novelist who depicts Jewish culture in Buenos Aires is María Inés Krimer. Her works are discussed in the introduction.

13. Aguinis leaves no doubt that he considers the AMIA attack a prelude to 9/11. In an interview he replies to the question about how the novel was conceived: "When September 11, 2001, occurred, and the United States believed that for the first time the American continent had been desecrated, that was too much for me. I started writing. In my opinion, September 11 had already been rehearsed in Argentina" (Izaguirre 569).

14. Le Carré, *A Most Wanted Man*, 317, quoted in Pepper 411.

15. See, for instance, Kollmann's 2015 article "La relación de Nisman" and the article "La denuncia de Nisman contra Cristina la hizo Stiuso." Gerardo "Tato" Young's *Código Stiuso* deals with the SIDE and Stiuso's role in it.

16. Castagnino is based on Diego Lagomarsino, Nisman's assistant.

17. This characterization of Trusso as the driving force behind Lerman's accusation is in accord with Young's description of the relation between Nisman and Stiuso: "Without Stiuso, Nisman had nothing. The complaint against Cristina is a complaint by Stiuso and Nisman. Nisman gives legal form to what Stiuso says" ("Exespía argentino").

18. In the novel, the ex-head of Interpol is named Ronald Jackson. In reality, his name is Ronald Noble.

19. When Stiuso finally testified regarding Nisman's death, it came as no surprise that his testimony supported the first theory, with the caveat that he stressed the ex-president's intentionality. See, for instance, "La declaración de Antonio Stiuso."

20. See, for instance, Calero; S. O'Donnell; and Sheinin, "The Death of Alberto Nisman."

21. Jorge Lanata is an influential broadcast journalist and an outspoken Fernández de Kirchner critic. The day after Nisman was found dead, a *Clarín* headline read: "Las dudas de Lanata: '¿El tipo antes de declarar se mata? Vamos, chicos'" (Lanata's doubts: "The guy kills himself before declaring? Come on, guys…").

22. Ignacio Iraola, head of the Planeta publishing group, says that the cover is an homage to *The Next Day*, David Bowie's latest album, in which Bowie's face is obscured by a white box ("El misterioso autor").

23. As a veiled political exposé, *El fiscal* is in good company. For instance, in 1976 John Ehrlichman published a roman à clef about his experience in the Nixon administration. It is titled *The Company* after an insider term for the CIA, and Ehrlichman specifies that all the characters in the novel are fictional. However, no one in their right mind would believe this. The novel features a president who is paranoid, weird, and hypersensitive to criticism, and

depicts a burglary of a Democratic headquarters. "Is it fiction?" writes author and columnist Richard Reeves: "Simon and Schuster [its publisher] certainly hopes no one will think so—Simon and Schuster is not in the habit of printing 50,000 copies of ordinary first novels" (40). Indeed, roman à clef political fictions and exposés depicting endemic corruption, criminal conspiracies, and renegade agents in the CIA are a genre in US fiction; some examples are James Ellroy's *An American Tabloid* and *Harlot's Ghost* by Norman Mailer.

24. "La Côte Basque, 1965," a story *à clef*, is set in a Manhattan restaurant of the same name and relates the lunch date of Jonesy (Truman Capote) and Lady Ina Coolbirth (Capote's good friend Slim Keith). Consisting mainly of a succession of stories told by Lady Ina, it deals with gossip of New York society insiders, relating "a series of painful, shockingly personal anecdotes, all, apparently, true to a degree, and all about named or barely disguised friends and enemies of Truman Capote" (Marsh 218). Many of those who appear in the stories shunned Capote for life (Marsh 221).

25. Quoted by Francisco Peregil in his review of *El puñal* by José Fernández Díaz. Eerily, this statement was published on 7 January 2015, eleven days before Nisman was found dead.

## CHAPTER 4

1. Antonio Berni (1905–81) was an Argentine artist associated with the movement called *nuevo realismo*. His later works were known for their incorporation of discarded material in order to depict poverty and the effect of industrialization.

2. In 2015, after he turned seventy, Carrascosa was released from prison and was allowed to live in a friend's house under house arrest (Carabajal).

3. The names and alleged roles of those accused of involvement in the cover-up—the individuals who will inspire the characters in Argemí's novel—are as follows:

- Guillermo Bártoli, the brother-in-law of the victim. Among the first to arrive at the house, he obtained a falsified death certificate saying she died of a nontraumatic heart attack and made the arrangements with the funeral home.
- Horacio García Belsunce, brother of the victim and a lawyer and journalist. He called the police three times to ask them not to come to investigate. He threw the sixth bullet, which bounced off

the victim's head, into the toilet; this action was a key element in the accusation of a cover-up on the part of the family.
- John Hurtig, stepbrother of the victim. He found the sixth bullet and participated in the decision to throw it into the toilet. He lifted the body from the bathroom floor and carried it to the bed. Despite his doubts about what had happened to her, he did not call the police.
- Juan Gauvry Gordon, the first medic to arrive on the scene and examine the body. Accused of endorsing the theory of accidental death and overlooking the five bullet holes in the victim's skull, he insisted that the family had tricked him into thinking it was an accident.
- Sergio Binello, a neighbor. He called the president of the country club to tell him to prevent the police from entering. "If you have to pay out money to bribe them, do it," he is attributed to have said ("Quién es quién").
- Beatriz Michelini, the victim's masseuse. She had the bad fortune to have an appointment to give the victim a massage on the afternoon of her death. The first nonfamily member to arrive on the scene, she gave mouth-to-mouth resuscitation to the victim and followed her employer's orders to clean up the blood.
- Nora Taylor, a friend of the victim. She is said to have prevented an autopsy and tried to accuse a neighbor of the crime.
- Juan Carlos March, the doctor who signed the death certificate.

4. Those receiving sentences were Guillermo Bártoli, Horacio García Belsunce, John Hurtig, Juan Gauvry Gordon, and Sergio Binello. Beatriz Michelini, the masseuse, was absolved for lack of evidence and because she tried to revive the victim (Caruso).

5. The sentences of Horacio García Belsunce, John Hurtig, and Sergio Binello were confirmed while the sentence against the doctor, Juan Gauvry Gordon, was revoked. The fifth defendant, Guillermo Bártoli, died in 2014 (Carabajal).

6. "Carrascosa pide una insólita audiencia"; Kollmann, "La sombra del Cartel de Juárez."

7. Those whose blood was extracted for a possible DNA match with blood found at the crime scene include Nicolás Pachelo, who had been accused of robberies in the area; his ex-wife, Inés Dávalos Cornejo; five former guards

of the country club; a neighbor, Sergio Binello; and four family members: Carracosa, Horacio García Belsunce, and John and Irene Hurtig (Balonga).

8. Argemí lived in Barcelona from 2000 to 2013, thus the reference to the fact that he was visiting Argentina when the crime was brought to light.

9. For a fascinating study of the eroticization of the female corpse in crime fiction, see Close's "Desnudarse y morir."

10. See Close's aforementioned article for a discussion of the role of the female corpse in this Poe mystery.

11. In this context, "servicios" refers to the "servicios de seguridad" of the military regime, which carried out acts of state terrorism.

12. I am indebted to Di Paolo's study *Cadáveres en el armario* for his identification of the "creative interstice" as well as his analysis of its function.

13. English translations of *Las viudas* and *Betibú* are taken from the print versions, *Thursday Night Widows* and *Betty Boo*. Further citations of quotes are to the Spanish-edition pages followed by those of the English edition.

14. Here, the English translation slightly alters the original version, eliminating "la nuestra"—*our* death.

15. Interestingly, the film based on *Las viudas* does not use the voice-over, perhaps because this technique is considered dated and does not appeal to today's audiences.

16. For a study that focuses on *Las viudas* as a post-McOndo literary expression, see the article by Lígia Bezerra. McOndo is a literary movement that questions the image of Latin America projected by magic realism as a place "where exotic people living in the middle of the jungle can fly." Instead, this writing, typified by realism, represents "a Latin America inhabited by individuals immersed in a world of mass culture and consumerism" (Bezerra 19). Among other issues, Bezerra examines *Las viudas*' emphasis on the banalities of its characters' lives as well as their obsession with consumer culture.

17. As is often the case, reality echoes fiction. An article by Drew Reed tells of the plight of the working-class community Las Tunas situated thirty-five kilometers from Buenos Aires. In 2013 it was flooded by a creek due to blockage caused by a ten-foot-tall concrete structure built to wall off Nordelta, a wealthy gated community. Reed's report highlights the ecological disruption caused by the hydrological engineering involved in constructing "countries" on top of wetlands.

18. See chapter 2 for information about these suspicious suicides.

19. See Carolina Rocha's article for a detailed analysis of the teenagers' role in seeing and exposing the systemic violence at the base of the community's lifestyle.

20. French novelist Eugène Sue (1804–57) established the genre of the serial novel with his popular and melodramatic series, *Les Mystères de Paris*.

21. See Jennifer Byron's article for a discussion of Claudia Piñeiro as postfeminist.

22. I am in debt to Joseph Aisenberg's study for the discussion of *Carrie*'s themes and reputation.

23. For instance, an article written by Argentine writer Raúl Argemí about Piñeiro is titled "Una dama negra en Barcelona," and writer Gabriela Cabezón Cámara cites this remark of Piñeiro in regard to *Betibú*: "What I was exorcising in this novel is the prejudice of 'since you are a best-seller, I do not read you.'" In an interview with Juan Carrá, Piñeiro further discusses the self-parody: "It seems to me that one of the things you have to laugh at is yourself, so in the novel [*Betibú*] I laugh at many things that happened to me as a writer since *Las viudas de los jueves*. That's why the writer returns to the country, that's also why she cannot write because they criticized her work.... There are a lot of things, which are subtle, but they were things that happened to me and I wanted to laugh at them."

24. For a brief explanation of metalepsis, see the section about the choral voices in *Las viudas de los jueves* on page 146.

25. I am using the neutral "it" to refer to the narrator since "its" gender is unspecified, and the use of "they" could cause confusion with the characters.

26. See my discussions of Rodolfo Walsh in the introduction and chapter 2.

## CHAPTER 5

1. The Delta, also known as the Tigre Delta, is a northern suburb of Buenos Aires. Formed by the conjunction of the rivers Paraná and Plate, it consists of waterways among many islands and became a retreat of the leisure class.

2. There is actually a *villa* that was established in the Reserva Ecológica, but not in the same area as the fictional Puerto Apache. Villa Rodrigo Bueno, as it is called, was created in 1986; its existence has been threatened by pressure from the local government, private enterprise, and an NGO. In 2011 a judge ordered that the *villa* be urbanized, but the city appealed this

judgment. According to the 2010 census it had a thousand families, and for the time being at least, it appears that Villa Rodrigo Bueno is not going anywhere (Lladós; L. Rocha).

3. Barrio Ejército de los Andes is an extensive housing complex created in 1970 on the outskirts of Buenos Aires as part of a plan to eradicate *villas miseria* from the city center. Known for crime and narcotrafficking, it has been occupied by the National Guard since 2003 and became notorious due to the assassination of a guardsman in the neighborhood. Auyero cites excerpts from chronicles illustrating that a factor in the killing was retaliation for violence exerted by state agents who forcefully control the behavior of the urban poor ("The Hyper-Shantytown," 10–11).

4. Juan Martini is a major Argentine writer who has published over a dozen novels and two collections of short stories. His 1973 novel, *El agua en los pulmones*, garners him a place among the initiators of the hard-boiled novel in Argentina. Continuing to work with the genre, he served as director of Bruguera's Serie Novela Negra while exiled in Barcelona during the Argentine dictatorship. *El agua en los pulmones*, along with two subsequent novels, *Los asesinos prefieren las rubias* (1974) and *El cerco* (1977), were later published together as *Tres novelas policiales* (1985). The novels in this detective trilogy depict a world of violence and paranoia, developing intrigues involving Argentine politics, corruption, betrayal, and mafias.

5. While la Rata is unlike the other detective figures I have discussed in this book, Close points out that an investigation carried out by a criminal protagonist occurs in other post-*neopoliciaco* works (*Contemporary Hispanic Crime Fiction* 134).

6. Las Cañitas district, a small neighborhood wedged between Palermo and Belgrano, is described in touristic literature as a modern and lively gastronomical area.

7. Auyero notes that the invasion of drugs is one of the dominant concerns in shantytowns ("The Hyper-Shantytown" 96).

8. The open end to *Las viudas de los jueves* presents a possible exception.

9. Their crimes included embezzlement, taking kickbacks from businesses they were supposed to regulate, and benefiting from the purchase of trains in poor condition from Spain and Portugal. In 2016 former Federal Planning Minister Julio De Vido was called to stand trial over his alleged criminal responsibility in the 2012 crash, including gross criminal mismanagement and fraud ("De Vido to Stand First Trial"; "El ranking de los embargos contra ex funcionarios K"; "Tragedy Had Strong Political Reverberations").

10. The City of Buenos Aires is divided into fifteen administrative districts called *comunas*. According to a report prepared by the government of the City of Buenos Aires using 2007 data, the *comunas* with the highest levels of poverty and unemployment are *comunas* 4 and 8, the two southernmost districts of the city ("Informe sobre distribución presupuestaria").

11. The Mike Harvey show is a syndicated radio show featuring golden oldies; Ricardo Arjona is a Latino pop star known to be one of the most successful Latin American artists of all time.

12. The quote in this section's title is from Jorge Luis Borges's poem "Buenos Aires," in the collection *El otro, el mismo*. The full phrase is "No nos une el amor sino el espanto; será por eso que la quiero tanto" (It is not love that unites but horror / maybe that is why I love her so much [translation by Peter Henderson]).

13. While the novel's steamy sex scenes may justify making a case for considering *La fragilidad* to be an erotic thriller, Linda Ruth Williams's distinction would exclude its full-fledged membership in that category: "[whereas] *noir* used sex to make a political point, the erotic thriller uses *noir* to contextualise its pornographic tableaux" (35).

## CONCLUSION

1. See Grinberg Pla's essay "Subversiones genéricas."

2. An interesting point brought out by Adriaensen and Grinberg Pla is that many authors have begun to position themselves in European or international markets, a phenomenon that contributes to their territorialization (16). This process is patent in the transformation of the titles of Mallo's novels: as mentioned in note 4 to chapter 1 (p. 239), his Spanish publishers changed *La aguja en el pajar* to *Crimen en el Barrio del Once* and *Delincuente argentino* to *El policía descalzo de la Plaza San Martín*, thus marketing his novels for a Spanish public by identifying them with specific Buenos Aires neighborhoods.

# WORKS CITED

Abdala, Verónica. "¿Qué no es traducción . . . ?" Interview with Pablo De Santis. *Página/12*, 15 Sept. 1998.
Adriaensen, Brigitte, and Valeria Grinberg Pla. "Introducción a cuatro manos." *Narrativas del crimen en América Latina: Transformaciones y transculturaciones del policial*, edited by Brigitte Adriaensen and Valeria Grinberg Pla, Lit Verlag, 2012, pp. 9–24.
Aguinis, Marcos. *Asalto al paraíso*. Planeta, 2002.
——. *La gesta del marrano*. Planeta, 1993.
——. *La matriz del infierno*. 1997. Planeta, 2004.
——. "Los creadores somos aves de rapiña." *Revista Cambio*, 8 Nov. 2003.
——. *Refugiados, crónica de un palestino*. 1969. Sudamericana, 1995.
Aguirre, Osvaldo. *El novato*. Aquilina, 2011,
——. *Enemigos públicos*. Aguilar, 2003.
——. *Historias de la mafia en la Argentina*. Aguilar, 2003.
——. *Los indeseables*. Aquilina, 2008.
——. "Los temas están en el aire y uno los baja." Interview with Claudia Piñeiro. *Diario La Capital*, 10 July 2011.
——. *Todos mienten*. Aquilina, 2009.
Aisenberg, Joseph. *Studies in the Horror Film: Brian De Palma's* Carrie. Centipede Press, 2011.
Alcoba, Laura. *La casa de los conejos*. Edhasa, 2008.
Alconada Mon, Hugo. "Suiza investiga a más de 200 argentinos." *La Nación*, 29 Jan. 2004.
Almada, Selva. *Chicas muertas*. Random House, 2014.
——. *Ladrilleros*. Mardulce, 2013.
Almeida, Eugenia. *La tensión del umbral*. Edhasa, 2015.
Alter, Alexandra. "Fiction's Global Crime Wave." *Wall Street Journal*, 2 July 2010, pp. 1–5.
Álvarez Plá, Bárbara. "Las mil caras del crimen: Arranca la semana de la novela policial." *Clarín*, 2 Aug. 2013.
Amar Sánchez, Ana María. *Juegos de seducción y traición: Literatura y cultura de masas*. Beatriz Viterbo, 2000.

Andahazi, Federico. *El libro de los placeres prohibidos*. Planeta, 2012.
Antolín Almirón, Hugo. "Organized Crime: A Perspective from Argentina." *Organized Crime: World Perspectives*, edited by Jay S. Albanese, Dilip K. Das, and Arvid Verma, Prentice Hall, 2003, pp. 317–29.
Aranguren, Miguel. "Alberto Nisman, la historia de una novela negra." *Teinteresa.es*, 26 Jan. 2015, www.teinteresa.es/autores/miguel_arangu ren/Alberto-Nisman-historia-novela-negra_0_1292271209.html.
Argemí, Raul. *A tumba abierta*. Navona, 2015.
———. *Penúltimo nombre de guerra*. Algaida, 2004.
———. *Retrato de familia con muerta*. Roca, 2008.
———. *Siempre la misma música*. Algaida, 2006.
———. "Una dama negra en Barcelona." *Sigueleyendo*, 7 Mar. 2012.
"Argentina Prosecutor Alberto Nisman Was Killed, Judge Rules." *BBC News*, 27 Dec. 2017.
"Argentine Judge Seeks Arrest of Ex-President Fernandez." *New York Times*, 7 Dec. 2017.
"Asís sobre la muerte de Nisman: 'Esto fue desde o en contra del Gobierno.'" *Perfil*, 19 Jan. 2015.
Auerbach, Jonathan. *Dark Borders: Film Noir and American Citizenship*. Duke University Press, 2011.
Auyero, Javier. "The Hyper-Shantytown: Neo-Liberal Violence(s) in the Argentine Slum." *Ethnography*, vol. 1, no. 1, 2000, pp. 93–116.
———. *Poor People's Politics: Peronist Survival Networks and the Legacy of Evita*. Duke University Press, 2001.
Balmaceda, Carlos. *Manual del caníbal*. Roca, 2005.
Balonga, María Laura. "Cotejo de ADN por el crimen de María Marta: demoras, enojos y un sospechoso en patrullero." *Clarín*, 14 May 2018.
Barbano, Rolando. "A dos años, ya nadie investiga el asesinato de María Marta." *Clarín*, 27 Oct. 2004.
———. "Carrascosa, otra vez en la mira por el crimen de María Marta." *Clarín*, 17 Nov. 2004.
Barón, Ana. "En la CIA creen que Nisman murió por una interna de la SIDE." *Clarín*, 1 Jan. 2015.
Battista, Vicente. *Cuaderno del ausente*. El Ateneo, 2019.
———. *La huella del crimen*. Cántaro, 2007.
———. *Ojos que no ven*. El Ateneo, 2012.
———. *Siroco*. 1985. Emecé, 1994.
———. *Sucesos argentinos*. Planeta, 1995.

Baudrillard, Jean. "From *The Precession of Simulacra.*" *The Norton Anthology of Theory and Criticism*, edited by Vincent B. Leitch, Norton, 2001, pp. 1732–41.

Bauman, Zygmunt. *Collateral Damage: Social Inequities in a Global Age.* Polity Press, 2011.

———. *Consuming Life.* Polity Press, 2007.

Bellmann, Elisa. *Asfixia.* Homo Sapiens, 2011.

Berg, Edgardo H. "La novela que vendrá: Apuntes sobre Ricardo Piglia." *Ricardo Piglia: La escritura y el arte nuevo de la sospecha*, edited by Daniel Mes Gancedo, Secretariado de Publicaciones, Universidad de Sevilla, 2006, pp. 23–53.

Berlanga, Ángel. "Momento shakespeareano." Interview with Ernesto Mallo. *Página/12*, 28 Mar. 2006.

Bernas, Frederick. "Argentine Prosecutor's Ex-Wife Says She Was Given Magazine with 'Bullet Mark' Photo the Day before His Death." *Vice News*, 4 Feb. 2015.

Beverley, John, and Marc Zimmerman. *Literature and Politics in the Central American Revolutions.* University of Texas Press, 1990.

Bezerra, Lígia. "Everyday Life in the McOndo World: Consumption and Politics in Claudia Piñeiro's *Las viudas de los jueves.*" *Chasqui*, vol. 41, no. 2, 2012, pp. 19–32.

Biron, Rebecca E. "Introduction. City/Art: Setting the Scene." *City/Art: The Urban Scene in Latin America*, edited by Rebecca E. Biron, Duke University Press, 2009, pp. 1–34.

Blustein, Paul. *And the Money Kept Rolling In (and Out).* Public Affairs, 2006.

Bogado, Fernando. "Panorama desde el muelle." Interview with Guillermo Saccomanno. *Página/12*, 2 Sept. 2012.

Bonasso, Miguel. "A manera de prólogo." *Análisis de la Actualidad* (Paraná, Argentina), Dec. 2001.

Borges, Jorge Luis. "Buenos Aires." *El otro, el mismo. Poesía completa.* Vintage, 1995.

———. "El jardín de senderos que se bifurcan." *Ficciones*, Emecé, 1956, pp. 87–102.

———. "La muerte y la brújula." *Ficciones*, Emecé, 1956, pp.133–48.

———. "Partial Enchantments of the Quixote," translated by Ruth L. C. Sims. *Borges, a Reader*, edited by Emir Rodríguez Monegal and Alastair Reid, Dutton, 1981, pp. 232–35.

Bracho, Edmundo. "Argentina ha descubierto que significa muy poco." Interview with Tomás Eloy Martínez. *Tal Cual*, 18 June 2002.

Braham, Persephone. *Crimes against the State, Crimes against Persons: Detective Fiction in Cuba and Mexico.* University of Minnesota Press, 2004.

Brecht, Bertolt. "The Threepenny Opera," translated by Ralph Manheim and John Willett. *Collected Plays*, vol. 2, Random House, 1977, pp. 145–226.

Brizuela, Leopoldo. *Una misma noche.* Alfaguara, 2012.

Browder, Laura. "True Crime." *The Cambridge Companion to American Crime Fiction*, edited by Catherine Ross Nickerson, Cambridge University Press, 2010, pp. 121–34.

Bulla, David W., and David B. Sachsman. "Introduction." *Sensationalism: Murder, Mayhem, Mudslinging, Scandals, and Disasters in 19th-Century Reporting*, edited by David B. Sachsman and David W. Bulla, Transaction, 2013, pp. xvii–xxxiv.

Byron, Jennifer. "Challenging the Male Paradigm: A Comparative Analysis of the Protagonists V. I. Warshawski and Nurit Iscar as Models of Postfeminism in Crime Literature." *Out of Deadlock: Female Emancipation in Sara Paretsky's V. I. Warshawski Novels, and Her Influence on Contemporary Crime Fiction*, edited by Enrico Minardi, Cambridge Scholars, pp. 135–53.

Cabaleiro, Juan Ángel. *El secreto de la Quebradita.* Reino de Cordelia, 2017.

Caballero, Juan. "Ricardo Piglia's *Blanco nocturno* (2010): A Paranoid History of Neoliberalism." *Polifonía*, vol. 3, no. 1, 2013, pp. 120–31.

Cabezón Cámara, Gabriela. "El capitalismo está cerca del fracaso, en algún momento tiene que caer." Interview with Claudia Piñeiro. *Clarín*, 3 Apr. 2011.

——. *La Virgen Cabeza.* Eterna Cadencia, 2009.

——. *Le vista la cara a Dios.* La Isla de la Luna, 2011.

——. *Romance de la negra rubia.* Eterna Cadencia, 2014.

Calero, César G. "EEUU dirigía la investigación de Nisman sobre el caso AMIA." *El Mundo*, 4 Feb. 2015.

Calv, Pedro. "Creen que Estrada iba a hablar." *Clarín*, 27 Aug. 1998.

Camauër, Solange. *Sabiduría elemental.* Edaf, 2014.

Campos Hernández, Yunnuen. "El 'Asalto al Paraíso.'" *Es más*, 2 Apr. 2003.

Caplán, Raúl, and Erich Fisbach. "Violencia policial, violencia política en la narrativa de Ernesto Mallo." *Les armes et les lettres: La violence politique dans la culture du Rio de la Plata dès années '60 à nos jours*, edited by Cecilia González, Dardo Scavino, and Antoine Ventura, Presses Universitaires de Bordeaux "Collection de la Maison des Pays Ibériques," 2010, pp. 153–67.

Capote, Truman. *In Cold Blood*. Random House, 1966.
Carabajal, Gustavo. "Caso García Belsunce: Ratifican las condenas por encubrimiento a dos de sus familiares." *La Nación*, 24 Oct. 2015.
"Carlos Menem fue condenado a siete años de prisión en la causa armas." *Clarín*, 1 June 2013.
Carrá, Juan. "Claudia Piñeiro, el policial desde una mirada femenina." *Criminis Causa*, 13 June 2011, criminiscausa.blogspot.com/2011/06/clauidia-pineiro-el-policial-desde-una.html. Accessed 8 Oct. 2013.
"Carrascosa pide una insólita audiencia pública ante la Corte." *Clarín*, 22 Feb. 2011.
Caruso, Liliana. "Belsunce: Piden 6 años de cárcel para el cuñado y el hermano." *Clarín*, 20 Sept. 2011.
"Caso Belsunce: Absolvieron a Carlos Carrascosa por el crimen de su mujer y queda en libertad." *Clarín*, 20 Dec. 2016.
"Caso Belsunce: Los condenados por encubrimiento apelaron ante Casación." *Clarín*, 25 Nov. 2011.
"Caso García Belsunce: Un nuevo informe criminalístico retoma las hipótesis que acusan o a Carrascosa o a Nicolás Pachelo." *La Nación*, 27 Oct. 2015.
Cassuto, Leonard. *Hard-Boiled Sentimentality: The Secret History of American Crime Stories*. Columbia University Press, 2008.
Cavanagh, Gaston. "Antonio Stiuso, the Feared Ex Spy Chief Making Argentina's Government Tremble." *Vice News*, 6 Feb. 2015.
———. "One Year Later, Alberto Nisman's Death Is Still a Troubling Mystery for Argentina." *Vice News*, 18 Jan. 2016.
Cawley, Marguerite. "Argentina's Ports 'Free Zones' for Drug Trafficking: Inspector General." *InSight Crime*, 11 July 2013, www.insightcrime.org/news/brief/argentine-ports-lack-adequate-controls-comptroller/.
Cerruti, Gabriela. *El Jefe: Vida y obra de Carlos Saúl Menem*. Planeta, 1993.
Chevigny, Paul. *Edge of the Knife: Police Violence in the Americas*. New Press, 1995.
Chandler, Raymond. "The Simple Art of Murder." *Rex Stout Mystery Quarterly* no. 2, 1945, pp. 94–97.
Christie, Agatha. *The Murder of Roger Ackroid*. Dodd, Mead and Co., 1926
———. *The Mysterious Affair at Styles*. 1920. Dodd, Mead and Co., 1958.
Chiozza, Elena M. "La integración del Gran Buenos Aires." *Buenos Aires: Historia de Cuatro Siglos*, edited by José Luis Romero and Luis Alberto Romero, vol. 2, Altamira, 2000, pp. 411–34.

Clavé, Montse. "Federico Levin: Ceviche y ceviches." *Gastronomía negra y criminal* (blog), 1 Apr. 2012, www.gastronomianegraycriminal.word press.com/2012/04/01/ceviche-y-ceviches/.

Clayton, Michelle. "Ricardo Piglia: *Plata quemada*." *Ricardo Piglia: Conversation in Princeton*, PLAS Cuadernos, no. 2, 1990, pp. 45–52.

Close, Glen S. *Contemporary Hispanic Crime Fiction: A Transatlantic Discourse on Urban Violence*. Palgrave Macmillan, 2008.

———. "Desnudarse y morir: La erotización del cadáver femenino en el género negro." *Narrativas del crimen en América Latina: Transformaciones y transculturaciones del policial*, edited by Brigitte Adriaensen and Valeria Grinberg Pla, Lit Verlag, 2012, pp. 89–107.

———. "The Detective Is Dead: Long Live the *Novela Negra*!" *Hispanic and Luso-Brazilian Detective Fiction: Essays on the* Género Negro *Tradition*, edited by Renée Craig-Odders, Jacky Collins, and Glen S. Close, McFarland, 2006, pp. 143–61.

———. "Translators Slain at Seaside." *Latin American Detective Fiction: New Readings*, edited by Shelley Godsland and Jacky Collins, Manchester Metropolitan University Press, 2004, pp. 11–22.

Cohen, Harley. "Argentina: The New Narco State." *Foreign Policy*, 19 Apr. 2012.

Cohn, Dorrit. "Metalepsis and Mise en Abyme." *Narrative*, vol. 20, no. 1, 2012, pp. 105–14.

———. "Signposts of Fictionality: A Narratological Perspective." *Poetics Today*, vol. 11, no. 4, 1990, pp. 775–804.

Colmeiro, José F. *La novela policiaca española: Teoría e historia crítica*. Anthropos, 1994.

Convertini, Horacio. *El último milagro*. Del Nuevo Extremo, 2013.

———. *La soledad del mal*. Eduvim, 2012.

Cordeu, Mora. "El periodismo de investigación mueve los hilos de un policial." *El Tribuno*, 7 Nov. 2012.

Correa, Rubén. *El muerto indiscreto*. Algaida, 2003.

———. *Interrupción del olvido*. vonDargas, 2009.

Cortázar, Julio. "Continuidad de los parques." *Cuentos completos*, vol. 1, Alfaguara, 1994, pp. 291–92.

"Cronología de la investigación." *Clarín*, 23 Dec. 2002.

Cué, Carlos E. "Nisman, el gran misterio argentino se complica dos años después." *El País*, 9 Jan. 2017.

Dalla, Rochelle L., Lynda M. Baker, John DeFrain, and Celia Williamson, eds. *Global Perspectives on Prostitution and Sex Trafficking: Europe, Latin America, North America, and Global*. Lexington Books, 2011.

Denoy, Marina. "Tomás Eloy Martínez cuenta el secreto del éxito de su última obra." *LosAndes*, 25 May 2002.
De Santis, Pablo. *Crímenes y jardines*. Planeta, 2013.
———. *El enigma de París*. Planeta, 2007.
———. *Filosofía y letras*. Seix Barral, 2002.
———. *La traducción*. Planeta, 1998.
"Despiden a un embajador." *Microsemanario*, no. 111, 21–27 June 1993.
"Despouy: 'El Estado renunció a ejercer el control de tráfico de drogas.'" *La Nación*, 10 July 2013.
"De Vido to Stand First Trial." *Buenos Aires Herald*, 6 Sept. 2016.
Diez, Rolo. *Papel picado*. Umbriel, 2003.
"Dijeron que murió en un accidente doméstico, pero la mataron a tiros." *Clarín*, 12 Dec. 2002.
Di Paolo, Osvaldo. *Cadáveres en el armario: El policial palimpséstico en la literatura argentina contemporánea*. Teseo, 2011.
———. "El poshumanismo apocalíptico en la novela negra argentina contemporánea: *Ciudad santa* y *77*." *Literatura y Lingüística de la Universidad Católica de Chile*, vol. 25, 2012, pp. 39–59.
Doane, Mary Ann. *Femmes Fatales: Feminism, Film Theory, Psychoanalysis*. Routledge, 1991.
Drucaroff, Elsa. *El último caso de Rodolfo Walsh*. Norma, 2010.
Duchini, Alejandro. "Beatriz Sarlo: 'El Gobierno hace política en el absoluto presente.'" *La Gaceta*, 26 Apr. 2015.
Dussere, Erik. *America Is Elsewhere: The Noir Tradition in the Age of Consumer Culture*. Oxford University Press, 2013.
Dutil, Carlos, and Ricardo Ragendorfer. *La Bonaerense: Historia criminal de la policía de la provincia de Buenos Aires*. Planeta, 1997.
Eaton, Kent. "Paradoxes of Police Reform: Federalism, Parties, and Civil Society in Argentina's Public Security Crisis." *Latin American Research Review*, vol. 43, no. 3, 2008, pp. 5–32.
Eco, Umberto. "Narrative Structures in Fleming." *The James Bond Phenomenon: A Critical Reader*, edited by Christoph Lindner, Manchester University Press, 2003, pp. 34–55.
Ehrlichman, John. *The Company*. Simon & Schuster, 1976.
Ellroy, James. *The Black Dahlia*. Mysterious Press, 1987.
"El misterioso autor detrás de la primera novela del caso Nisman." *Infobae.com*, 14 Apr. 2015, www.infobae.com/2015/04/14/1722152-el-misterioso-autor-detras-la-primera-novela-del-caso-nisman/.
"El ranking de los embargos contra ex funcionarios K." *Clarín*, 7 July 2017.

"Embajadas del escándalo." *Microsemanario*, no. 107, 17–23 May 1993.

"En marzo podrían ordenar detener a Carlos Menem por el contrabando de armas a Croacia y Ecuador." *Clarín*, 15 Dec. 2017.

Enríquez, Mariana. "De la gorra: Policía y ficción." *Página/12*, 3 Nov. 2003.

Ernesto Mallo desea concienciar sobre la trata de personas." *El Universal*, 26 Oct. 2012.

Etcheves, Florencia. *Cornelia*. Planeta, 2016.

———. *La hija del campeón*. Planeta, 2014.

———. *La Virgen en tus ojos*. Planeta, 2012.

"Exespía argentino es convocado a declarar en caso Nisman." *El Universo*, 5 Feb. 2015.

"Falleció ayer Rubén Cardozo." *La Nación*, 17 Mar. 1997.

Faludi, Susan. *Backlash: The Undeclared War against American Women*. Crown, 1991.

"Fantasía, ficción y espías en el jardín de Casa de América." *Casa de América archivo*, n.d., www.casamerica.es/contenidoweb/fantasia-ficcion-y-espias-en-el-jardin-de-casa-de-america. Accessed 14 June 2018.

Feijóo, Cristina. *La casa operativa*. Planeta, 2006.

———. *Los puntos ciegos de Emilia*. Tusquets, 2011.

Feijoó, María del Carmen. *Nuevo país, nueva pobreza*. Fondo de Cultura Económica, 2001.

Feinmann, José Pablo. "Estado policial y novela negra argentina." *Los heroes "difíciles": Literatura policial en la Argentina y en Italia*, edited by Giuseppe Petronio, Jorge B. Rivera, and Luigi Volta, Corregidor, 1991, pp. 141–53.

———. *Últimos días de la víctima*. 1979. Seix Barral, 2006.

Fernández Díaz, Jorge. *El puñal*. Planeta, 2014.

———. *La herida*. Planeta, 2017.

Fernández Moores, Lucio. "Carlos Menem debió sentarse por quinta vez en el banquillo de los acusados." *Clarín*, 6 June 2018.

———. "Sobresueldos: Procesan a Menem y lo embargan en $100 millones." *Clarín*, 4 June 2009.

Ferrari, Kike. *Que de lejos parecen moscas*. 2011. Alfaguara, 2018.

Fields, Liz. "Argentina Wants Americans to Think Alberto Nisman Was Full of Shit." *Vice News*, 8 Mar. 2015.

Figueiras, Mauricio Montiel. "De la tragedia a la conspiración: Entrevista con Ricardo Piglia." *La Nación*, 18 May 2003.

Filkins, Dexter. "Death of a Prosecutor." *New Yorker*, 20 July 2015, pp. 38–54.

Foster, David William. *Violence in Argentine Literature: Cultural Responses to Tyranny*. University of Missouri Press, 1995.
Francescato, Martha Paley. "Marcos Aguinis: A Controversial Argentine Jewish Writer." *Folio: Essays on Foreign Languages and Literatures*, vol. 17, 1987, pp. 57–63.
Friera, Silvina. "Estamos viviendo en una sociedad dividida en zonas." Interview with Sergio Olguín. *Página/12*, 1 Mar. 2010.
———. "La ficción permite meterse donde el periodismo no puede." Interview with Claudia Piñeiro. *Página/12*, 30 May 2011.
———. "Siempre caigo en el policial." Interview with Sergio Olguín. *Página/12*, 27 Aug. 2008.
———. "Yo no rechazo escribir con odio." Interview with José Pablo Feinmann. *Página/12*, 9 June 2007.
Furst, Alan. Introduction to *The Book of Spies: An Anthology of Literary Espionage*, edited by Alan Furst, Modern Library, 2003, pp. vii–xi.
Gallego-Díaz, Soledad. "Personajes al límite." Interview with Claudia Piñeiro. *El País*, 25 Sept. 2010.
Gallo, Daniel. "Los escáneres de los puertos no detectan drogas." *La Nación*, 10 July 2013.
Gamerro, Carlos. *El secreto y las voces*. Norma, 2002.
———. "Notas para una redefinición del género policial argentino." *El nacimiento de la literatura argentina y otros ensayos*, Norma, 2006, pp. 56–65.
García Canclini, Néstor. *Consumers and Citizens: Globalization and Multicultural Conflicts*. Translated by George Yúdice, University of Minnesota Press, 2001.
Gates, Philippa. *Detecting Women: Gender and the Hollywood Detective Film*. State University of New York Press, 2011.
Geherin, David. *Scene of the Crime: The Importance of Place in Crime and Mystery Fiction*. McFarland, 2008.
Genette, Gérard. *Narrative Discourse: An Essay in Method*. Translated by Jane E. Lewin, Cornell University Press, 1980.
———. *Palimpsests: Literature in the Second Degree*. Translated by Channa Newman and Claude Doubinsky, University of Nebraska Press, 1997.
Giardinelli, Mempo. *Cuestiones interiores*. Página/12, 2013.
———. *El décimo infierno*. Colibrí, 1999.
———. *El género negro: Ensayos sobre literatura policial*, 2nd ed. Op Oloop, 1996.

———. *Luna caliente*. 1983. Seix Barral, 1999.
———. "Mi libro refleja la corrupción absoluta del menemismo." Interview by Óscar Enrique Ornelas. *El Broli Argentino*, 27 Apr. 1999.
———. *Qué solos se quedan los muertos*. 1983. Página/12, 2011.
Gigena, Daniel. "Marcelo Luján ganó el premio Hammett de Novela Negra." *La Nación*, 15 July 2016.
Girona Fibla, Nuria. "Locos que dicen la verdad en *Respiración artificial* de Ricardo Piglia." *Locos, excéntricos y marginales en las literaturas latinoamericanas*, edited by Joaquín Manzi, Centre de Recherches Latino-Américaines, Université de Poitiers, 1999, pp. 521–31.
Giuffré, Mercedes. *Deuda de sangre*. Suma de Letras, 2008.
———. *El carro de la muerte*. Suma de Letras, 2011.
———. *El peso de la verdad*. Edebe, 2010.
Godsland, Shelley. "Allegory, Gender and Aggression in Some Recent Argentine Novels of Violence." *Trece formas de entender la novela negra*, edited by Gustavo Forero Quintero, Laboratorio de Medellín, 2014, pp. 189–212.
———. *Killing Carmens: Women's Crime Fiction from Spain*. University of Wales Press, 2007.
Goñi, Uki. "The Corrupt Zigzag, an Argentine Dance." *New York Times*, 13 June 2016.
González, Aníbal. *Love and Politics in the Contemporary Spanish American Novel*. University of Texas Press, 2010.
González, Cecilia. *Narcosur: La sombra del narcotráfico mexicano en la Argentina*. Marea, 2013.
González, Gail. "La evolución de la novela policial argentina en la posdictadura." *Hispania*, vol. 90, no. 2, 2007, pp. 253–63.
González, Horacio. "The Journalist as the People's Detective." *The Argentina Reader*, edited by Gabriella Nouzeilles and Graciela Montaldo, Duke University Press, 2002, pp. 495–99.
Goransky, Tatiana. *Los impecables*. Comba, 2016.
———. *¿Quién mató a la cantante de jazz?* 2008. Letra Sudaca, 2014.
Gorelik, Adrián. "Buenos Aires Is (Latin) America, Too." *City/Art: The Urban Scene in Latin America*, edited by Rebecca E. Biron, Duke University Press, 2009, pp. 61–84.
———. *Miradas sobre Buenos Aires: Historia cultural y crítica urbana*. Siglo Veintiuno Editores, 2004.
Greenberg, Nathaniel. "War in Pieces: AMIA and the Triple Frontier in Argentine and American Discourse on Terrorism." *A Contracorriente*, vol. 8, no. 1, 2010, pp. 61–93.

Grenville, J. A. S. *A History of the World in the Twentieth Century.* Belknap Press of Harvard University Press, 1994.

Griesse, James M. "Economic Crisis and Identity in Neoliberal Argentina: Claudia Piñeiro's *Las viudas de los jueves.*" *Latin Americanist*, vol. 57, no. 4, 2013, pp. 57–72.

Grillo Trubba, Diego. *Crímenes coloniales: Los asesinatos de las invasiones inglesas.* Del Nuevo Extremo, 2010.

———. *La mafia política: Renacerás de tus cenizas.* Planeta, 2013.

Grimson, Alejandro, and Gabriel Kessler. *On Argentina and the Southern Cone: Neoliberalism and National Imaginations.* Routledge, 2005.

Grinberg Pla, Valeria. "*Plata quemada*: Ensayo sobre capitalismo y violencia en la tradición de la novela negra latinoamericana." *Badebec*, vol. 4, no. 8, 2015, pp. 407–32.

———. "Subversiones genéricas: Una vuelta de tuerca latinoamericana a la clásica novela de enigma." *Narrativas del crimen en América Latina: Transformaciones y transculturaciones del policial*, edited by Brigitte Adriaensen and Valeria Grinberg Pla, Lit Verlag, 2012, pp. 39–57.

Guerriero, Leila. "Problemas del siglo XXI." Interview with Juan Martini. *La Nación*, 22 Sept. 2002.

Gutma, Daniel. "Misteriosa muerte de un oficial naval vinculado a la venta de las armas." *Clarín*, 26 Aug. 1998.

Heyne, Eric. "Where Fiction Meets Nonfiction: Mapping a Rough Terrain." *Narrative*, vol. 9, no. 3, 2001, pp. 322–33.

Hinton, Mercedes S. *The State on the Street: Police and Politics in Argentina and Brazil.* Lynne Rienner, 2007.

Horsley, Lee. "A Life Spent Lying: The Identity Crises of Post-9/11 Spy Fiction." *Paradoxa*, vol. 24, 2012, pp. 161–76.

———. *The Noir Thriller.* Palgrave Macmillan, 2001.

———. *Twentieth-Century Crime Fiction.* Oxford University Press, 2005.

Hortiguera, Hugo. "De la investigación periodística al potín: El relato documental argentino de fin de siglo." *CiberLetras*, vol. 9, July 2003.

———. "El folletín delictuoso argentino: Discurso periodístico y géneros populares en los umbrales del nuevo milenio." *Delaware Review of Latin American Studies*, vol. 4, no. 2, 2003.

Hutcheon, Linda. *Narcissistic Narrative: The Metafictional Paradox.* Methuen, 1984.

———. *A Theory of Parody: The Teachings of Twentieth-Century Art Forms.* 1985. University of Illinois Press, 2001.

———. *Irony's Edge: The Theory and Politics of Irony.* Routledge, 1994.

"Informe sobre distribución presupuestaria y prestaciones de los programas sociales de la subsecretaría de fortalecimiento familiar y comunitario." Gobierno de la Ciudad de Buenos Aires, n.d., www.buenosaires.gob.ar/areas/des_social/familia_comunidad/pdf/programas_sociales_ssfort alecimiento.pdf. Accessed 10 Sept. 2014.

Islas, Alejandro, and Daniel Míguez. *Heridas urbanas: Violencia delictiva y transformaciones sociales en los noventa*. Editorial de Las Ciencias, 2003.

Izaguirre, Ester de. "Introducción a *Asalto al paraíso*: Entrevista a Marcos Aguinis." *Alba de América: Revista de Literatura*, vol. 22, nos. 41–42, 2003, pp. 567–74.

Jacovkis, Natalia. "La ciudad neoliberal en la novela negra argentina: *Puerto Apache*, de Juan Martini." *CiberLetras*, vol. 15, July 2006.

Jajamovich, Guillermo. "La ciudad del *business*: Literatura y ciudad en 'Puerto Apache' de Juan Martini." *Questión*, vol. 1, no. 18, 2008.

James, P. D. *An Unsuitable Job for a Woman*. Scribner, 1972.

Jameson, Fredric. "On Raymond Chandler." *The Poetics of Murder: Detective Fiction and Literary Theory*, edited by Glenn M. Most and William W. Stowe, Harcourt Brace Jovanovich, [1970] 1983, pp. 112–48.

Jeanmaire, Federico. *Fernández mata a Fernández*. Alfaguara, 2011.

Jonsson, Anna, ed. *Human Trafficking and Human Security*. Routledge, 2009.

Kaminsky, Amy. "The Jew in the City: Buenos Aires in Jewish Fiction." *City/Art: The Urban Scene in Latin America*, edited by Rebecca E. Biron, Duke University Press, 2009, pp. 165–82.

Kara, Siddharth. *Sex Trafficking: Inside the Business of Modern Slavery*. Columbia University Press, 2009.

Kershner, Isabel. "Israel Rebukes Argentina for Deal with Iran to Investigate '94 Attack." *New York Times*, 29 Jan. 2013.

Knight, Stephen. *Crime Fiction since 1800: Detection, Death, Diversity*, 2nd ed. Palgrave Macmillan, 2010.

Kohan, Martín. "Ricardo Piglia: 'Veía esta novela ligada a la revolución.'" *Clarín*, 13 Aug. 2013.

Kohut, Karl, ed. *Un universo cargado de violencia: Presentación, aproximación y documentación de la obra de Mempo Giardinelli*. Vervuert Verlag, 1990.

Kokotovic, Misha. "Neoliberal Noir: Contemporary Central American Crime Fiction as Social Criticism." *Clues*, vol. 24, no. 3, 2006, pp. 15–29.

Kollmann, Raúl. "La relación de Nisman con Stiuso, la DAIA y la embajada de EE.UU.: El avance de la causa; Los mitos y verdades del caso." *Página/12*, 1 Feb. 2015.

———. "La sombra del Cartel de Juárez en el caso Belsunce." *Página/12*, 17 Feb. 2004.

———. "Una causa que no puede salir de los escombros." *Página/12*, 18 July 2009.

Krause, Krystin. "From *Guerra Sucia* to *Gatillo Fácil*: Violence and the Argentine Federal Police." Annual meeting of the Southwestern Political Science Association, 23 Mar. 2005, Fairmont Hotel, New Orleans, LA, www.allacademic.com/meta/p88939_index.html. Accessed 30 Sept. 2013.

Krauss, Clifford. "Deaths in Argentina Feed a Taste for Conspiracy." *New York Times*, 25 Oct. 1998.

Krimer, María Inés. *La inauguración*. El Ateneo, 2011.

———. *Lo que nosotras sabíamos*. Emecé, 2009.

———. *Noxa*. Revólver, 2016.

———. *Sangre fashion*. Aquilina, 2015.

———. *Sangre kosher*. Aquilina, 2010.

———. *Siliconas express*. Aquilina, 2013.

Kristeva, Julia. *Powers of Horror: An Essay on Abjection*. Columbia University Press, 1982.

"La declaración de Antonio Stiuso: 'A Nisman lo mató un grupo vinculado al Gobierno de Cristina Kirchner.'" *Diarioveloz.com*, 1 Mar. 2016, www.diarioveloz.com/notas/157489-la-declaracion-antonio-stiuso-a-nisman-lo-mato-un-grupo-vinculado-al-gobierno-cristina-kirchner.

"La denuncia de Nisman contra Cristina la hizo Stiuso." *Diarioveloz.com*, 5 Feb. 2015, www.diarioveloz.com/notas/138875-la-denuncia-nisman-contra-cristina-la-hizo-stiuso.

Lafforgue, Jorge. "Repensar el policial hoy en la Argentina." *Crimen y pesquisa: El género policial en la Argentina (1870–2015); Literatura, cine, televisión, historieta y testimonio*, edited by Román Setton and Gerardo Pignatiello, Título, 2016, pp. 45–56.

Lafforgue, Jorge, and Jorge B. Rivera. *Asesinos de papel: Ensayos sobre narrativa policial*. Colihue, 1996.

Lag, Nahuel. "El lado de Mar del Plata que no es feliz." *Página/12*, 25 Jan. 2010.

"Las dudas de Lanata: '¿El tipo antes de declarar se mata? Vamos, chicos...'" *Clarín*, 19 Jan. 2015.

Latham, Sean. *The Art of Scandal: Modernism, Libel Law, and the Roman à Clef.* Oxford University Press, 2009.
le Carré, John. *A Most Wanted Man.* London: Hodder, 2009.
Lehman, Daniel W. *Matters of Fact: Reading Nonfiction over the Edge.* Ohio State University Press, 1997.
Levín, Federico. *Bolsillo de cerdo.* Aquilina, 2011.
———. *Ceviche.* Aquilina, 2009.
———. *La lengua estofada.* Aquilina, 2013.
Lewis, Paul H. *The Agony of Argentine Capitalism: From Menem to the Kirchners.* Praeger, 2009.
Lezcano, Fabio Nahuel. *Crímenes apropiados.* JPM Ediciones, 2015.
Lindstrom, Naomi. *Jewish Issues in Argentine Literature: From Gerchunoff to Szichman.* University of Missouri Press, 1989.
Link, Daniel, ed. *El juego de los cautos: La literatura policia; De Poe al caso Giubileo.* La Marca, 1992.
Lladós, José Ignacio. "Una villa en plena Reserva." *La Nación,* 18 Jan. 2005.
López-Calvo, Ignacio. "*Refugiados* y *Asalto al Paraíso* de Marcos Aguinis: Apropiaciones y reapropiaciones del discurso palestino." *A Contracorriente,* vol. 11, no. 1, 2013, pp. 170–90.
"Los casos que conmovieron al Servicio." *Clarín,* 13 Sept. 1998.
Ludmer, Josefina. *The Corpus Delicti: A Manual of Argentine Fictions.* Translated by Glen S. Close, University of Pittsburgh Press, 1999.
Luján, Marcelo. *Subsuelo.* Salto de Página, 2015.
Lund, Joshua. "Magic Socialism." *Cultural Critique,* vol. 92, 2016, pp. 179–89.
MacCannell. Dean. "Staged Authenticity: Arrangements of Social Space in Tourist Settings." *American Journal of Sociology,* vol. 79, no. 3, 1973, pp. 589–603.
MacDonald, Ross. *The Moving Target. Archer in Hollywood,* Alfred A. Knopf, 1967, pp. 3–169. Spanish edition: *El blanco móvil.* Alfa, 1974.
Mallo, Ernesto. *Delincuente argentino.* Planeta, 2007. Madrid edition: *Policía descalzo de la Plaza San Martín.* Siruela, 2011. English translation: *Sweet Money.* Translated by Katherine Silver. Bitter Lemon Press, 2011.
———. *El hilo de sangre.* Siruela, 2017.
———. *La aguja en el pajar.* Planeta, 2006. Madrid edition: *Crimen en el Barrio del Once.* Siruela, 2011. English translation: *Needle in a Haystack.* Translated by Jethro Soutar. Bitter Lemon Press, 2010.
———. *La conspiración de los mediocres.* Siruela, 2015.
———. *Los hombres te han hecho mal.* Siruela, 2012.

———. *Me verás caer*. Del Nuevo Extremo, 2013.
"Mallo desnuda el negocio de la violencia en la saga del 'Perro Lascano.'" *El Comercio*, 9 Aug. 2013.
Marcos, Carlos, and José María. *Muerde muertos (quién alimenta a quién . . .)*. Muerde Muertos, 2012.
Maristany, José Javier. *Narraciones peligrosas: Resistencia y adhesión en las novelas del Proceso*. Biblos, 1999.
Marsh, Kelly A. "Empathy, Authority, and the Narrative Ethics in Capote's 'La Côte Basque, 1965.'" *Journal of Narrative Theory*, vol. 43, no. 2, 2013, pp. 218–44.
Martelli, Juan Carlos. *Los tigres de la memoria*. Sudamericana, 1973.
Martínez, Guillermo. *La muerte lenta de Luciana B*. Planeta, 2007.
———. *Los crímenes de Oxford*. Ocho y Medio, 2008. Originally published as *Crímenes imperceptibles*, Planeta, 2003.
Martínez, Tomás Eloy. *El cantor de tango*. Planeta, 2004.
———. *El vuelo de la reina*. Alfaguara, 2002.
———. *Ficciones verdaderas: Hechos reales que inspiraron grandes obras literarias*. Planeta, 2000.
———. *La novela de Perón*. 1985. Vintage Español, 1997.
———. "Pasiones brasileñas." *La Nación*, 2 Sept. 2000.
———. *Purgatorio*. Alfaguara, 2008.
———. *Santa Evita*. Alfredo A. Knopf, 1995.
Martini, Juan. *El agua en los pulmones*. 1973. Tantalia, 2007.
———. *El cerco*. 1977. Legasa, 1985.
———. *Los asesinos prefieren las rubias*. La Linea, 1974.
———. *Puerto Apache*. Sudamericana, 2002.
———. *Tres novelas policiales*. Legasa, 1985.
Martorell, Francisco. *Impunidad diplomática*. Planeta, 1993.
Mavrakis, Nicolás. "No conozco un periodista que sufra ante la página en blanco." Interview with Sergio Olguín. *Tiempo Argentino*, 23 Dec. 2012.
Maxfield, James F. *The Fatal Woman: Sources of Male Anxiety in American Film Noir, 1941–1991*. Fairleigh Dickinson University Press, 1996.
McCann, Sean. *Gumshoe America: Hard-Boiled Crime Fiction and the Rise and Fall of New Deal Liberalism*. Duke University Press, 2000.
McSherry, J. Patrice. *Incomplete Transition: Military Power and Democracy in Argentina*. St. Martin's, 1997.
"Menem Arms Charges Dropped." *BBC News*, 28 Aug. 2003.

"The Menem Case." *Santiago Times*, 31 Mar. 2004.
"Menem Charged with Arms-Smuggling." *BBC News*, 29 Nov. 2008.
Messi, Virginia, and Juan Manuel Bordón. *Narcolandia: Por qué la Argentina se convirtió en el paraíso de los narcos colombianos*. Sudamericana, 2014.
Meyer-Minnemann, Klaus. "Narración paradójica y ficción." *La narración paradójica: "Normas narrativas" y el principio de la "transgresión,"* edited by Nina Grabe, Sabine Lang, and Klaus Meyer-Minnemann, Iberoamericana Vervuert, 2006, pp. 49–68.
Miller, D. A. *The Novel and the Police*. University of California Press, 1988.
Morán, Carlos Roberto. " 'La fragilidad de los cuerpos,' de Sergio Olguín: Al filo de la muerte." *El País*, 21 Feb. 2013, archived at roberto253.rssing.com/chan-6346370/all_p1.html#item17.
Mora y Araujo, Manuel. "Las clases medias consolidadas." *Buenos Aires: Historia de Cuatro Siglos*, edited by José Luis Romero and Luis Alberto Romero, vol. 2, Altamira, 2000, pp. 247–57.
Molfino, Miguel Ángel. *Monstruos perfectos*. Visa Versa, 2010.
Moret, Natalia. *Un publicista en apuros*. Mondadori, 2012.
NancyO. "Holy City, by Guillermo Orsi." *Crimesegments.com*, 9 Apr. 2012, ww.crimesegments.com/2012/04/holy-city-by-guillermo-orsi.html.
Néspolo, Matías. *Con el sol en la boca*. Los Libros de la Lince, 2015.
——. *Siete maneras de matar a un gato*. Los Libros de la Lince, 2009.
Nonnenmacher, Hartmut. "La temática de la literatura y la cultura popular en la narración policíaca hispanoamericana." *Narrativas del crimen en América Latina: Transformaciones y transculturaciones del policial*, edited by Brigitte Adriaensen and Valeria Grinberg Pla, Lit Verlag, 2012, pp. 235–48.
Norden, Deborah L., and Roberto Russell. *The United States and Argentina: Changing Relations in a Changing World*. Routledge, 2002.
"Nuevos métodos para eludir la ley." *Página/12*, 9 Apr. 2012.
Núñez, Jorgelina. "Entrevista a Claudia Piñeiro, ganadora del Premio 'Clarín' de Novela." *Agenda de las Mujeres*, n.d., www.agendadelasmujeres.com.ar/notadesplegada.php?id=1637. Accessed 28 May 2009.
Núñez Jaime, Víctor. "Selva Almada, la escritora rural que sale al mundo." *El País*, 17 Sept. 2015.
O'Donnell, María. *Born*. Sudamericana, 2015.
O'Donnell, Santiago. "Nisman se había hecho muy dependiente de los EE.UU." *Página/12*, 23 Mar. 2015.
Olguín, Sergio. "El mito de la Argentina de clase media es mentira." *El Periódico*, 20 Mar. 2010.

———. *La fragilidad de los cuerpos*. Tusquets, 2012.
———. *Lanús*. Tusquets, 2008.
———. *Las extranjeras*. Suma de Letras, 2014.
———. *No hay amores felices*. Suma de Letras, 2017.
———. *Oscura monótona sangre*. Tusquets, 2010.
Oliver, Kelly, and Benigno Trigo. *Noir Anxiety*. University of Minnesota Press, 2003.
Orsi, Guillermo. *Ciudad Santa*. Almuzara, 2009. English translation: *Holy City*. Translated by Nick Caistor. MacLehose Press, 2013.
———. *Fantasmas del desierto*. Almuzara, 2014
———. *Nadie ama a un policía*. Almuzara, 2007.
———. *Segunda vida*. Norma, 2011.
———. *Siempre hay alguien a quien matar*. Editorial Revólver, 2015.
———. *Sueños de perro*. 2004. Umbriel, 2007.
———. *Tripulantes de un viejo bolero*. 1995. Almuzara, 2007.
Osorio, Elsa. *A veinte años, Luz*. Siruela, 2008.
———. *Doble fondo*. Tusquets, 2018.
Osorio, Myriam. "Subjection and Injury in *El vuelo de la reina* by Tomás Eloy Martínez." *Violence in Argentine Literature and Film (1989–2005)*, edited by Carolina Rocha and Elizabeth Montes Garcés, University of Calgary Press, 2010, pp. 23–46.
Oyola, Leonardo. *Sacrificio*. Aquilina, 2010.
———. *Santería*. Aquilina, 2008.
"Pablo De Santis: 'Me atrae el ambiente intelectual como escenario del crimen.'" Interview with Pablo De Santis. *Sudestada*, no. 5, Dec. 2001.
Page, Joanna. "Crime, Capitalism, and Storytelling in Ricardo Piglia's *Plata quemada*." *Hispanic Research Journal*, vol. 5, no. 1, 2004, pp. 27–42.
Parys, Jodi. "The Body as Weapon: HIV as Revenge." *CiberLetras*, vol. 14, Dec. 2005.
Paszkowski, Diego. *Tesis sobre un homicidio*. Sudamericana, 1999.
Pellicer, Rosa. "Estratégias metaficcionales en la narrativa policiaca hispanoamericana." *Narrativas del crimen en América Latina: Transformaciones y transculturaciones del policial*, edited by Brigitte Adriaensen and Valeria Grinberg Pla, Lit Verlag, 2012, pp. 249–64.
Pepper, Andrew. "Policing the Globe: State Sovereignty and the International in the Post-9/11 Crime Novel." *Modern Fiction Studies*, vol. 57, no. 3, pp. 401–24.
Peregil, Francisco. "La política argentina es una novela negra." *El País*, 7 Jan. 2015.

Pérez, Genaro J. *Ortodoxia y heterodoxia de la novela policíaca hispana: Variaciones sobre el género negro*. Juan de la Cuesta, 2002.

Piglia, Ricardo. *Blanco nocturno*. Anagrama, 2010.

——. *Crítica y ficción*, 2nd ed. Seix Barral, 2000.

——. *El camino de Ida*. Anagrama, 2013.

——. "La ficción paranoica." *Clarín*, 10 Oct. 1991.

——. "La loca y el relato del crimen." *Prisión perpetua*, Sudamericana, [1975] 1988.

——. *Plata quemada*. 1997. Anagrama, 2000.

——. *Respiración artificial*. 1980. Sudamericana, 1990.

Pignatiello, Gerardo. "Rol policial y estructura de género en la 'novela negra' de la dictadura: *Nadie nada nunca* y *Luna caliente*." *PhiN*, vol. 70, 2014, pp. 107–15.

Pihlainen, Kalle. "The Moral of the Historical Story: Textual Differences in Fact and Fiction." *New Literary History*, vol. 33, no. 1, 2002, pp. 39–60.

Piñeiro, Claudia. *Betibú*. Alfaguara, 2011. English translation: *Betty Boo*. Translated by Miranda France. Bitter Lemon Press, 2018.

——. *Elena sabe*. 2007. Alfaguara, 2011.

——. *Las grietas de Jara*. Alfaguara, 2009.

——. *Las maldiciones*. Alfaguara, 2017.

——. *Las viudas de los jueves*. Alfaguara, 2005. English translation: *Thursday Night Widows*. Translated by Miranda France. Bitter Lemon Press, 2009.

——. "Los crímenes dicen mucho sobre la sociedad en que se cometen." Interview with Claudia Piñeiro. *La Gaceta Literaria*, 5 June 2011.

——. *Tuya*. 2005. Alfaguara, 2008.

——. *Una suerte pequeña*. Alfaguara, 2015.

Plain, Gill. *Twentieth-Century Crime Fiction: Gender, Sexuality and the Body*. Edinburgh University Press, 2001.

Plante, Alicia. *Fuera de temporada*. Adriana Hidalgo, 2013.

——. *Una mancha más*. Adriana Hidalgo, 2011.

——. *Verde oscuro*. Adriana Hidalgo, 2014.

Politi, Daniel. "'Beats Watching Netflix': Graft Scandal Engrosses Argentina and Heralds Change." *New York Times*, 25 Aug. 2018.

Porretti, Eduardo. "Los usos de Feinmann." *La astucia de la pasión*, 2010, jpfeinmann.com/index.php?option=com_content&view=article&id=3&Itemid=2. Accessed 14 June 2018.

Porter, Abbott H. *The Cambridge Introduction to Narrative*. Cambridge University Press, 2008.

Porter, Dennis. *The Pursuit of Crime: Art and Ideology in Detective Fiction.* Yale University Press, 1981.
Pratt, Mary Louise. *Imperial Eyes: Travel Writing and Transculturation.* Routledge, 2007.
Pratt, R. S. *El fiscal.* Emecé, 2015.
Premat, Julio. "Los espejos y la cópula son abominables." *Ricardo Piglia: Una poética sin límites,* edited by Adriana Rodríguez Pérsico, Instituto Internacional de Literatura Iberoamericana, 2004, pp. 123–34.
Priestman, Martin. *Crime Fiction: From Poe to the Present.* Northcote House, 1998.
Puig, Manuel. *Buenos Aires Affair: Novela policial.* Seix Barral, 2000.
"¿Qué define al policial argentino?" *Clarín,* 15 June 2012.
"Quién es quién." *Clarín,* 17 Jan. 2003.
Quilodrán, Federico. "Spinosa y Vázquez, a los ojos de Chile." *La Nación,* 12 Jan. 1998.
Rama, Ángel. *La ciudad letrada.* Ediciones del Norte, 1984.
———. *Writing across Cultures: Narrative Transculturation in Latin America.* Edited and translated by David Frye, Duke University Press, 2012.
Reddy, Maureen T. "Women Detectives." *The Cambridge Companion to Crime Fiction,* edited by Martin Priestman, Cambridge University Press, 2003, pp. 191–207.
Reed, Drew. "Story of Cities #46: The Gated Buenos Aires Community Which Left Its Poor Neighbours under Water." *The Guardian,* 19 May 2016.
Reeves, Richard. "What Ehrlichman Really Thought of Nixon." *New York Magazine,* 10 May 1976, pp. 40–48 and 53–56.
Reid, Michael. *Forgotten Continent: The Battle for Latin America's Soul.* Yale University Press, 2007.
"Revés de Spinoza [sic] Melo en la Corte." *La Nación,* 6 Sept. 2006.
Rocha, Carolina. "Systemic Violence in Claudia Piñeiro's 'Las viudas de los jueves.'" *Arizona Journal of Hispanic Cultural Studies,* vol. 15, 2011, pp. 123–29.
Rocha, Laura. "Un dejà vu de la villa Rodrigo Bueno." *La Nación,* 12 Mar. 2014.
Rodríguez, Carlos. "Una trama oscura." *Página/12,* 21 Jan. 2010.
Rodríguez Pérsico, Adriana. "*Plata quemada* o un mito para el policial argentino." *Ricardo Piglia: Una poética sin límites,* edited by Adriana Rodríguez Pérsico, Instituto Internacional de Literatura Iberoamericana, 2004, pp. 113–22.

Rodríguez Yebra, Martín. "Menem: 20 dudas que Suiza promete develar." *La Nación*, 1 Feb. 2004.

———. "Viajan a Suiza dos jueces que investigan causas sobre Menem." *La Nación*, 5 Feb. 2004.

Rolón, Gabriel. *Los padecientes*. Destino, 2010.

Romero, José Luis. "La ciudad de masas." *Buenos Aires: Historia de Cuatro Siglos*, edited by José Luis Romero and Luis Alberto Romero, vol. 2, Altamira, 2000, pp. 201–8.

Romero, Ricardo. *El síndrome de Rasputín*. Negro Absoluto, 2008.

———. *El spleen de los muertos*. Aquilina, 2011.

———. *Los bailarines del fin del mundo*. Aquilina, 2009.

Rosende, Mercedes. *La muerte tendrá tus ojos*. Sudamericana, 2008.

———. *Mujer equivocada*. Mondadori, 2011.

Roth, Marty. *Foul & Fair Play: Reading Genre in Classic Detective Fiction*. University of Georgia Press, 1995.

"Rousselot en trance." *Microsemanario*, no. 107, 17–23 May 1993.

Ruiz, Iván. "Menem atribuyó al grupo Hezbollah la muerte de su hijo." *La Nación*, 14 May 2016.

Ryan, Marie-Laure. "Postmodernism and the Doctrine of Panfictionality." *Narrative*, vol. 5, no. 2, 1997, pp. 165–87.

Rzepka, Charles J. *Detective Fiction*. Polity, 2005.

Saccomanno, Guillermo. *77*. Planeta, 2008.

———. "De género y popular." *La Nación*, 26 Aug. 2011.

———. *Cámara Gessell*. Planeta, 2012.

Sacheri, Eduardo. *El secreto de sus ojos*. Alfaguara, 2009.

Sadow, Stephen A. "Lamentations for the AMIA: Literary Responses to Communal Trauma." *Memory, Oblivion, and Jewish Culture in Latin America*, edited by Marjorie Agosín, University of Texas Press, 2005, pp. 149–62.

Saer, Juan José. *La pesquisa*. 1994. Muchnik, 2000.

Saldo, Ana. "Una entrevista con Paco Ignacio Taibo II." *ABC Cultural*, 1 July 2000, www.negraycriminal.com/index.php?view=temas.

Salem, Carlos. *Camino de ida*. Salto de Página, 2007.

"Sangre y cirugías estéticas en un policial trepidante." *El Patagónico*, 20 Aug. 2013.

Santoro, Daniel. "Los mensajes cifrados de la muerte de Estrada." *Clarín*, 30 Aug. 1998.

Sanz, Christian. "El caso Armentano y la injusticia: Reflexiones en torno a la muerte de la madre de Poli." *Tribuna de Periodistas*, 18 Sept. 2004.

———. "El embajador del miedo: Oscar Spinosa Melo y su extorsión al menemismo." *Tribuna de Periodistas*, 29 May 2006.
Sarlo, Beatriz. *Instantáneas: Medios, ciudad y costumbres en el fin del siglo*. Ariel, 1996.
———. *La ciudad vista: Mercancías y cultura urbana*. Siglo Veintiuno, 2009.
———. "Sarlo: 'La muerte de Nisman es un magnicidio.'" *TN.com.ar*, 12 Mar. 2015, www.tn.com.ar/politica/sarlo-la-muerte-de-nisman-es-un-magnicidio_576531.
———. "Violencia en las ciudades: Una reflexión sobre el caso argentino." *Espacio urbano, comunicación y violencia en América Latina*, edited by Mabel Moraña, Instituto Internacional de Literatura Iberoamericana, 2002, pp. 205–14.
Sassone, Martín, and Virginia Messi. "Un anónimo inició la pista del lavado como móvil del crimen." *Clarín*, 22 Feb. 2007.
Sasturain, Juan. *Arena en los zapatos*. Verlag, 1989.
———. *Manual de perdedores*, vol. 1. 1985. Sudamericana, 2008.
———. *Manual de perdedores*, vol. 2. Legasa, 1987.
———. *Los sentidos del agua*. 1992. La Página, 2007.
———. *Pagaría por no verte*. Sudamericana, 2008.
Scaggs, John. *Crime Fiction*. Routledge, 2005.
Schmid, David Frank. "Neoliberal Amnesia in Martín Solares's *The Black Minutes*." Paper read in absentia at the Modern Languages Association Convention, Vancouver, 8–11 Jan. 2015.
Schmidt-Cruz, Cynthia. "Complicitous Housewives during the Argentine Dictatorship: Reconstructing a Tenebrous Past in *Lo que nosotras sabíamos* by María Inés Krimer." *Bulletin of Spanish Studies*, vol. 94, no. 1, 2016, pp. 127–48.
Schvarzer, Jorge. "La implantación industrial." *Buenos Aires: Historia de Cuatro Siglos*, edited by José Luis Romero and Luis Alberto Romero, vol. 2, Altamira, 2000, pp. 209–26.
Seed, David. "Spy Fiction." *The Cambridge Companion to Crime Fiction*, edited by Martin Priestman, Cambridge University Press, 2003, pp. 115–34.
"Sergio Olguín: 'Mi libro es una novela negra y una historia de amor.'" *Sigueleyendo*, 6 Mar. 2013.
Seri, Guillermina. *Seguridad: Crime, Police Power, and Democracy in Argentina*. Continuum, 2012.
Setton, Román. *Los orígenes de la narrativa policial en la Argentina: Recepción y transformación de modelos genéricos alemanes, franceses e ingleses*. Iberoamericana/Vervuet, 2012.

Sheinin, David M. K. *Argentina and the United States: An Alliance Contained.* University of Georgia Press, 2006.

———. "The Death of Alberto Nisman, the Argentine Presidency Unhinged, and the Secret History of the Shared United States-Argentine Strategy in the Middle East." *LASAFORUM*, vol. 67, no. 1, 2016, pp. 34–38.

Shelley, Louise. *Human Trafficking. A Global Perspective.* Cambridge University Press, 2010.

Sietecase, Reynaldo. *A cuántos hay que matar.* Alfaguara, 2010.

———. *Pendejos.* Alfaguara, 2007.

———. *Un crimen argentino.* Alfaguara, 2002.

Silver, Alice. "Presentación *El policía descalzo de la Plaza San Martín* de Ernesto Mallo en Estudio en Escarlata." *Mis detectives favorit@s* (blog), 20 Nov. 2011, www.detectivesdelibro.blogspot.com/2011/11/presentacion-el-policia-descalzo-de-la.html.

Silvestri, Graciela, and Adrián Gorelik. "Ciudad y cultura urbana, 1976–1999: El fin de la expansión." *Buenos Aires: Historia de Cuatro Siglos*, edited by José Luis Romero and Luis Alberto Romero, vol. 2, Altamira, 2000, pp. 461–99.

Sinay, Javier. *Sangre joven: Matar y morir antes de la adultez.* Tusquets, 2009.

Sinay, Sergio. *Ni un dólar partido por la mitad.* 1975. Navona, 2013.

"Solange Camaüer, ganadora del XVIII Premio de Novela Negra 'Ciudad de Getafe' con 'Sabiduría elemental.'" *Getafe.es*, 24 July 2014, www.getafe.es/solange-camauer-ganadora-del-xviii-premio-de-novela-negra-ciudad-de-getafe-con-sabiduria-elemental/.

Soriano, Osvaldo. *Triste, solitario y final.* Seix Barral, 2003.

Soto, Máximo. "Para Olguín, en la Argentina el policial reemplazó a la novela política." *Ciudadanoweb.com*, 21 Nov. 2012, www.elciudadanoweb.com/para-olguin-en-la-argentina-el-policial-reemplazo-a-la-novela-politica/.

Spinosa Melo, Oscar. *Sobre el volcán: Memorias de un diplomático.* Urraca, 1993.

"Spinosa Melo desmiente." *La Nación*, 26 May 1999.

Stallard, Ronald Michael. "Entrevistamos al escritor argentino Raúl Argemí." *Blogcindario*, 10 Nov. 2008, thrillernegro.blogcindario.com/2008/11/00006-entrevistamos-al-escritor-argentino-raul-argemi.html.

"Stall Stories." *The Economist*, 25 Jan. 2014, 28 and 30.

Stillwaggon, Eileen. *Stunted Lives, Stagnant Economies: Poverty, Disease, and Underdevelopment.* Rutgers University Press, 1998.

Stougaard-Nielsen, Jakob. *Scandinavian Crime Fiction*. Bloomsbury Academic, 2017.
Suárez, Josefa. "ONG advierte que crece exponencialmente los secuestros de mujeres para trata." *Nortecorrientes.com*, 25 Feb. 2014, www.norteco rrientes.com/article/27813/ong-advierte-que-crece-exponencialmen te-los-secuestros-de-mujeres-para-trata.
Svampa, Maristella. *La brecha urbana: Countries y barrios privados*. Capital Intelectual, 2004.
———. *La sociedad excluyente: La Argentina bajo el signo del neoliberalismo*. Taurus, 2005.
———. *Los que ganaron: La vida en los countries y barrios privados*. Biblos, 2001.
Swanson, Philip. "The Detective and the Disappeared: Memory, Forgetting and Other Confusions in Juan José Saer's *La pesquisa*." *Investigating Identities: Questions of Identity in Contemporary International Crime Fiction*, edited by Marieke Krajenbrink and Kate M. Quinn, Rodopi, 2009, pp. 277–94.
———. "Don Quijote y el detective postmoderno en la narrativa hispano-americana." *Foro hispánico*, vol. 40, 2010, pp. 263–79.
Terranova, Juan. "El pálido género negro." *Revista Paco*, 29 July 2015.
———. *El vampiro argentino*. Lengua de Trapo, 2011.
———. *Lejos de Berlín*. Aquilina, 2009.
Thuillier, Guy. "Gated Communities in the Metropolitan Area of Buenos Aires, Argentina: A Challenge for Town Planning." *Housing Studies*, vol. 20, no. 2, 2005, 255–71.
Tizziani, Rubén. *Noches sin luna ni soles*. Siglo Veintiuno, 1975.
Todorov, Tzvetan. "The Typology of Detective Fiction." *Modern Criticism and Theory: A Reader*, edited by David Lodge and Nigel Wood, 2nd ed., Pearson, 2000, pp. 137–44.
Tozzi, Liliana. " 'Un problema del siglo XXI': Los nuevos grupos sociales en *Puerto Apache*, de Juan Martini." *Cuadernos de Aleph*, vol. 3, 2011, pp. 243–56.
"Tragedy Had Strong Political Reverberations." *Buenos Aires Herald*, 30 Dec. 2015.
Troncoso, Oscar A. "Las formas del ocio." *Buenos Aires: Historia de Cuatro Siglos*, edited by José Luis Romero and Luis Alberto Romero, vol. 2, Altamira, 2000, pp. 93–102.
"Un sobresalto por los sobres." *Página/12*, 4 June 2009.

US Department of State. *Trafficking in Persons Report: Country Narratives: A–C*, 2013. www.state.gov/documents/organization/210738.pdf.
———. *Trafficking in Persons Report: Tier Placements*, 2013. www.state.gov/j/tip/rls/tiprpt/2013/210548.htm.
Valle, Amir. "Vicente Battista, el negro-criminal." *Otro Lunes: Revista Hispanoamericana de Cultura*, vol. 24, 2012.
Vázquez, Luciana. *La novela de Menem: Ensayo sobre la década incorregible*. Sudamericana, 2000.
Vázquez-Rial, Horacio. *La capital del olvido*. Alianza, 2004.
Velasco Oliaga, Javier. "Tal vez me mude, solo para estar más cerca de Gijón." Interview with Guillermo Orsi. *Todo Literatura*, 28 July 2010.
Verbitsky, Horacio. *Robo para la corona: Los frutos prohibidos del árbol de la corrupción*. Planeta, 1991.
Viau, Susana. "Alberto Kohan, el misterioso: De armas llevar." *Página/12*, 8 Feb. 2004.
Vidal, Hernán, and René Jara, eds. *Testimonio y literatura*. Institute for the Study of Ideologies and Literature, 1986.
Vilalta, Lídia. "Las mujeres hacen justicia en sus novelas negras." *Ameco Press*, 20 Feb. 2012.
"Villas Argentinas: Ciudad Oculta—Villa 15." *Taringa!*, n.d., www.taringa.net/posts/info/14838746/Villas-argentinas-Ciudad-Oculta--Villa-15.html. Accessed 14 June 2018.
Voionmaa, Daniel Noemi. "Literatura y estado de excepción desde Heredia y Belascoarán Shayne." *Narrativas del crimen en América Latina: Transformaciones y transculturaciones del policial*, edited by Brigitte Adriaensen and Valeria Grinberg Pla, Lit Verlag, 2012, pp. 187–202.
Waisbord, Silvio. "Reading Scandals: Scandals, Media, and Citizenship in Contemporary Argentina." *Enforcing the Rule of Law: Social Accountability in the New Latin American Democracies*, edited by Enrique Peruzzotti and Catalina Smulovitz, University of Pittsburgh Press, 2006, pp. 272–303.
———. *Watchdog Journalism in South America: News, Accountability, and Democracy*. Columbia University Press, 2000.
Walger, Sylvina. *Pizza con champán: Crónicas de la fiesta menemista*. Espasa Calpe Argentina, 1994.
Walsh, Rodolfo. "Cuento para tahúres." *Cuento para tahúres y otros relatos policiales*, Ediciones de la Flor, 2005, pp. 7–15.
———. *Diez cuentos policiales argentinos*. Hachette, 1953.
———. *Operación masacre*. 1957. Ediciones de la Flor, 2007.

Wassner, Dalia. *Harbinger of Modernity: Marcos Aguinis and the Democratization of Argentina*. Brill, 2014.

White, Hayden. "The Historical Text as Literary Artifact." *Tropics of Discourse: Essays in Cultural Criticism*, Johns Hopkins University Press, 1987, pp. 81–100.

Willett, Ralph. *The Naked City: Urban Crime Fiction in the USA*. Manchester University Press, 1996.

Williams, Linda Ruth. *The Erotic Thriller in Contemporary Cinema*. Edinburgh University Press, 2005.

Wornat, Olga. *Menem: La vida privada*. Planeta, 1999.

Worthington, Heather. *Key Concepts in Crime Fiction*. Palgrave Macmillan, 2011.

"Ya salió una novela sobre el caso Nisman y ocultan quién la escribió." *Clarín*, 17 Apr. 2015.

Young, Gerardo "Tato." *Código Stiuso: La SIDE, la política desde las cloacas y la muerte de Nisman*. Planeta, 2015.

Yujnovsky, Oscar. "Del conventillo a la 'villa miseria.'" *Buenos Aires: Historia de Cuatro Siglos*, edited by José Luis Romero and Luis Alberto Romero, vol. 2, Altamira, 2000, pp. 435–47.

Zambrano, Guillermo. "El tono de la novela." *La Ventana*, 27 Nov. 2002.

Zina, Alejandra. "No me quiero defender del prejuicios [sic] del otro, ni pedir disculpas por lo que escribo." Interview with Claudio Piñeiro. *Revista Calibre*, vol. 38, 26 July 2011.

Žižek, Slavoj. *Looking Awry: An Introduction to Jacques Lacan through Popular Culture*. MIT Press, 1991.

# INDEX

abject, the, 11, 16, 27–28, 45, 46, 47
Adriaensen, Brigitte, 222–23, 225, 230, 254n1
Aguinis, Marcos, xliv, 201, 247n7, 247n11, 248n8
  *Asalto al paraíso*, xlv, 85, 90–108, 120, 199, 201, 225, 226, 228, 230, 248n13
Aguirre, Osvaldo, ix, xxxvi, 159, 170–71
Alcoba, Laura, xxiii
Allegory, xx, xxxviii, 21, 25, 55, 63, 64, 224, 246n33
Almada, Selva, xxix, xxx
Almeida, Eugenia, xxix, xxx
Amar Sánchez, Ana María, xvii, 56, 58, 219, 224
AMIA (Asociación Mutual Israel-Argentina), attack on, 85–95, 100–102, 108–16, 120, 235, 246n2, 247n5, 248n13
Andahazi, Federico, xxxvi–xxxvii
apocalypse, postapocalypse, xxxvii, 41, 47. *See also* urban collapse subgenre
Arab–Israeli conflict, 90–92, 108, 230
archetypical characters, xl, 13, 24
Argemí, Raúl, xxiii, xxxi, xxxix, xliv, xlv, 122, 142, 169
  *Retrato de familia con muerta*, xlv, 121–22, 123–42, 172–74, 224, 226, 228, 229, 231, 232, 233, 249–50n3, 250n4, 250n5, 250–51n7

Argentina:
  allegories of, xxxviii, 21, 55, 63–64, 81, 246n33
  crisis of 2001 in, xii, 27, 156
  *See also* Buenos Aires; dictatorship in Argentina, 1976–1983; Menemism
Auyero, Javier, 176–77, 178, 253n3

Balmaceda, Carlos, xxviii, 55
Battista, Vicente, xxiii, xxxi, xxxii
Baudrillard, Jean, 46–47
Bauman, Zygmunt, xlii, 143, 152, 155, 181, 189
Bellman, Elisa, xxix
Berg, Edgardo H., xxvi, 238n12
Beverley, John, 100–101
Bezerra, Lígia, 251n16
Bioy Casares, Adolfo, xiv, xviii–xix
Biron, Rebecca E., xli
Bolivia:
  immigration from, 40, 42, 107
  racism directed toward people from, 32, 37, 44–45, 241n17
Bond, James, 110
Borges, Jorge Luis, xiv, xviii–xix, xxxvii, 69, 70, 83, 166, 211, 222, 230, 254n12
Braham, Persephone, xvii, 237n4
Brazil, x, 8, 9, 59, 69, 239n3
Brizuela, Leopoldo, xxii
Browder, Laura, 142
Buenos Aires:
  comparator cities of, xiii, 41, 103–6, 225

See also identity, Argentine; *villas miseria*
  perceived deterioration of, xli, xlii, 2, 26–49, 64, 70, 180, 192–94, 224
  grandeur of, 41, 106, 225
  history of, xxxi, xxxvi, 70, 176–79
  image in literature of, 103
  imaginaries of, xli–xlii, 27–28, 37, 41, 45, 69, 92, 105–6
  Jewishness of, Jewish community in, xiii, 85–86, 92, 95, 102, 103–8, 223, 225, 225, 247n12
  "latinamericanization" of, xiii, xlii, 85–86, 102, 103, 125, 223, 225
  mapping of, xxxii, xli, xlii, 92, 106, 176, 205–7
  neighborhoods or districts of, xxxv, 43–44, 70, 106–7, 175–78, 183, 185, 187, 193–94, 197–98, 205–8, 224–25, 252n1, 254n10, 254n2
  Recoleta, xli, 106–7, 117, 186, 194, 198, 207–8, 224
  "northamericanization" of, xlii
Butler, Judith, 201
Byron, Jennifer, 252n21

Cabaleiro, Juan Ángel, xxxvi
Caballero, Juan, xxiv, xxv
Cabezón Cámara, Gabriela, xxx–xxxi, xxxv, 252n23
Camauër, Solange, xxix–xxx
Caplán, Raúl, 9
Capote, Truman, xxxiii, 119, 129, 169, 249n24
  *In Cold Blood*, xix, xxxvi, 142
*cartoneros* (trash pickers), xxxviii, 187
Cassuto, Leonard, xliv, 7, 23, 48
censorship, xx, 17
Central Intelligence Agency (CIA), 114–15, 247n3, 248–49n23

Cerruti, Gabriela, 77, 241n3, 243n12, 243n13, 244–45n26
Chandler, Raymond, xv, xx, xxiv, xxxii, xliii–xliv, 10, 12, 20–22, 36, 51, 56–58, 63, 82, 159, 161, 184, 231, 238n14. *See also* Marlowe, Philip
Che Guevara, parody of, 28, 32, 39–40, 231
Chile, 62, 64, 68, 69, 71, 73, 78, 122, 227, 244n23
Christ figure, 45–48. *See also* Jesus Christ
Christie, Agatha, xiv, xxxviii, 124, 139, 231
cinematographic techniques, 15, 162, 218, 251n15
class difference, xi, 126, 127, 139, 149, 177, 197–99, 209
Clayton, Michelle, xxvi–xxvii, 238n12
Close, Glen, xv, xviii, xx, xxxii, xxxviii, xli, 40, 126, 136, 182, 184, 186, 190, 221, 238n15, 241n1, 251n9, 251n10, 253n5
closed room mystery. *See* locked room mystery
Cohn, Dorrit, 166–67, 171–72
Colmeiro, José F., xvi, 158–59
Colombia, drug cartels of, 1, 3, 9, 15, 28–30, 37–38, 225
colonial heritage, of Latin America, 28, 44–45, 48, 91–92
Conan Doyle, Arthur, xiv
conclusion, 25, 48, 114, 158, 163, 173, 184, 233–34
  dual, 25–26, 57, 83, 163–64, 173, 233–34
  fairy tale, xxxix, 2, 10, 25–26, 230
  grim, 25, 168, 173–74, 216–17
  happy, xvi, 11, 25–26, 36, 48, 158, 164, 173, 197, 233–34
consumerism, xi, xli, 81, 143–44, 173, 179–97, 251n16

and the authenticity effect, 46–47, 143–44, 146–50, 152–53
consumer society, xlii–xliii, 46–47, 81, 142, 143–44, 149, 151, 155, 172, 173, 179–97, 227, 229, 251n16
noir as a response to, xlii–xliii, 143–44, 148, 155
"Continuidad de los parques" by Julio Cortázar, 161, 166, 167, 231
Convertini, Horacio, xxviii, xxxvii, xl
corpse, xxxiii, 56–57, 224, 231
  dehumanized, 15, 37, 47
  gory or macabre, 16, 132, 186
  treatment of female corpse, 136–37, 139, 251n9, 251n10
Correa, Rubén, xliv, 55
  *El muerto indiscreto*, xlv, 52, 55–83, 223–24, 226, 228, 229, 230, 231–32, 243n16
Cortázar, Julio, 161, 166, 231
country club or "country." *See* gated community
country house mystery, 123–24, 174

Dal Masetto, Antonio, xxiii
De Santis, Pablo, x, xxxvii–xxxviii
death:
  fascination with, 197, 199–200, 212, 214–16, 219
  and love, 133, 212, 213, 214–15, 217, 218, 228
*desaparecidos*. *See* disappeared, the
detective:
  absence of, xi, xl, 11, 238n15
  amateur, xv, xix
  ethics of, xv, xxxii, xliii, 9, 11–12, 22, 34–36, 63, 65, 97, 100, 135, 199, 158, 203, 216–17, 218
  hard-boiled, xv, xvii, xix–xx, xxliii, 22–23, 39, 51, 64, 200, 231
  as journalist, xi, xix, xxxii, xl, xlii, xlv, 51–84, 91–108, 157, 198–205, 226, 228, 232, 238n15

  as questing knight, xliii, 12, 23, 82
  as linkage between urban areas, xlii, 205–6
  and love interest, 21–22, 36–39, 48–49, 58–59, 65–66, 158, 233
  masculinity of, xliii, 63, 99, 199–201
  as misfit, 132–33
  police, xxx, xl, 1–2, 7–8, 11–12, 22, 34–36, 48, 227, 233
  private eye, 2, 10, 57, 58, 62–63, 184, 200, 227, 231, 238n15
  repeating figure or series, xxix, xxxvi, xliv, 198, 238n17
  as sentimental hero, 7, 22, 35
  *See also* female detective; Philip Marlowe
detective fiction:
  classic, xvi
  conventions of, xlii, xliii–xliv, 21–22, 38, 56–61, 67, 93, 114, 138, 157, 224, 238n1
  development of in Argentina, xiv, xviii, xxviii
  golden age of, 139, 174
  periodization of in Argentina, 221–22
  reworking or adaptation of, xvi–xvii, xviii, 56–57, 199–200, 223–33
  *See also* Christie, Agatha; country house
Di Paolo, Osvaldo, 41, 47, 129–30, 229, 251n12
dictatorship in Argentina, 1976–1983, xii, xiii, xx–xxiii, xxvii, xxix, xl, 4, 8, 12, 22, 28–29, 32–33, 35, 53, 122, 170, 188, 207, 237n8, 239n6, 253n4
  babies born in captivity during, xxi, xxxiv, 240n13
  legacy of, xxix, xl, 28, 33, 93–94, 127, 140
  memory of, xxi–xxiii, 8, 22, 29, 31, 55

transition to democracy, xxxiv, 8, 53
Diez, Rolo, xxiii
digressions, xxxv, 156, 158–59, 229, 233
disappeared, the, xxii–xxiii, xxxiv, 7, 56
Doane, Mary Ann, 69
Drucaroff, Elsa, xxiii, xxix
Duhalde, Eduardo, 87
Dussere, Erik, 143, 148, 151, 173
dystopia. *See* urban collapse subgenre

Eaton, Kent, xxxiii, 4, 6
Eco, Umberto, 110, 222
Ellroy, James, 40, 248–49n23
entertainment, detective fiction as, x, 82, 173, 219
erotic literature, xxxvi, 123, 198, 251n9, 254n10
Etcheves, Florencia, xxix–xxx
Europe, xxvii, xxxvii, 3, 25, 42–43, 48, 71, 107, 117, 178, 222
exile, xxiii, 55, 122, 173, 253n4

Faludi, Susan, 204
family, xxv, xxxviii, xxix, 13, 16, 20, 21–26, 37, 48–49, 72, 101, 123, 149, 234
  bourgeois, 24–26, 123, 152
  disintegration of ties, 127–42
  dysfunctional, 23–25, 123, 155, 206, 233, 240–41n13
  secrets, xxxix, 10, 16
  solidarity, xliv, 172, 233
farce, xxxvii, 123
fatal woman, 61, 82, 242n7. *See also* femme fatale
fatalism, 197–200, 209–10, 218
father:
  as character in novel, xxi, xxii, xxxiii, xxxix, 13, 20, 23, 48, 49, 66–67, 101, 184, 189, 192, 196, 202–4, 206, 226, 233, 238n1

and patriarchal power structure, 48, 69
evil stepfather, 21, 24–25, 48
FBI, xiii, xxv, 247n3
Feijóo, Cristina, xxiii, xxix
Feijoó, María del Carmen, 176–77, 183
Feinmann, José Pablo, xviii, xx, xxxi, xxxii
female characters:
  as absent, 8, 21–22, 38, 66–67
  as beast or mad, 38–39, 63, 66, 98, 99–100
  in binary categories, 38, 61–62, 64, 67–68, 228
  as catalysts to male self-destruction, xliii, 99, 216, 228
  as nuanced and realistic, 159–60, 203–4, 216–17, 228
  *See also* female detective
female detective, x–xi, xxx, xliii, 59, 64, 91–100, 108, 156–57, 159, 199–205, 227–28, 238n16
  as savvy, xliii, 61, 65, 96, 156, 202, 228
  masculinization of, 61, 199–202, 210
  sexualization of, 65–66, 95–100, 201–5
feminism, backlash against, 204, 217
femme fatale, xv, xxxv, xliii, 28, 36–39, 58, 61–62, 108, 160, 194–97, 242n7
  as detective, 95–100
  *See also* fatal woman
Fernández de Kirchner, Cristina, xiii, 85, 88–89, 108, 109, 116, 117, 119, 120, 199, 230, 234–35, 247n5, 248n17, 248n21
Fernández Díaz, Jorge, xxxiv, 54, 120, 238n17, 249n25
Ferrari, Kike, xxxiii
fiction:
  as artifice, 138–39, 156, 163, 172, 232–33

narrativizing as part of fictional process, 130, 133, 165, 171–72
as opposed to nonfiction, x, 51–52, 71–80, 129, 169, 170–73, 232, 242–43n11
powers of, 84, 171–72, 173
signposts of, 171–72
*See also* writing
film adaptations, of novels, xxviii, 161
film noir, xiii, xvii, 60–61, 145, 173, 211, 218, 231, 242n10
Fisbach, Erich, 9
Foster, David William, xxi
frame story, 82, 130–32, 133, 141, 182, 229, 231, 232
Francescato, Martha Paley, 247n11
friendship, 142, 234
 among men, 71, 153, 197
 among women, 160
 as support network, xxxv–xxxvi, 147, 160, 197, 234
fundamentalist terrorism, xi, 96, 104, 115, 225
Furst, Alan, 109

Gamerro, Carlos, xxii, xl, 227
Garcia Canclini, Néstor, 151
gated community or "country," xiii, xli–xlii, xlv, 121–74, 178, 180–81, 192, 224, 231, 234, 251n17
 as a contemporary version of the country house template, 123–25, 174
 as emblematic of the neoliberal era, 123–27
 as idyllic or utopic, 126, 127, 149
 as seen by outsiders, 156, 167–68, 218
 as self-regulated, 126, 154
 security of, xliii, 125, 126, 127, 128, 138, 148, 149, 150, 156, 157, 167, 168, 172
Gates, Philippa, 200–201, 227

gender roles:
 perceived crossing of "boundaries," 156–60, 202, 210, 211
 stereotypes of, 13, 36, 38, 58, 61, 136, 137, 194
Genette, Gérard, 118, 130, 146, 247n10
Giardinelli, Mempo, xxi, xxvii–xviii, xxxiii, xxvii, 55, 121, 173
Girona Fibla, Nuria, xxv
Giuffré, Mercedes, xxxi
globalization, x, xii, xiii, xl, xli, 28, 53, 103, 105, 181, 185, 189
Godsland, Shelley, 64, 159, 238n16, 241n1, 242n7
González, Aníbal, xliv, 241n18
González, Gail, xxii
González, Horacio, 56–57
Goransky, Tatiana, xxix
Gorelik, Adrián, xli–xlii, 104–5, 176, 180, 184, 189, 197
gothic elements in crime fiction, xxvii, 1, 16, 21, 24, 27, 47, 138, 161, 238n1
Greenberg, Nathaniel, 90–91
Griesse, James M., 150–51
Grillo Trubba, Diego, xxxiv–xxxv, 54
Grinberg Pla, Valeria, 222, 223, 225, 230, 238n12, 254n1, 254n2
Guerriero, Leila, 187

Hammett, Dashiell, xv, xxiv, 133, 159
hard-boiled subgenre:
 conventions of, xv–xvii, xliii–xliv, 36, 38–39, 56–61, 63, 100, 133–34, 161, 199–200, 218, 224, 228
 development of, xv, xviii, 99, 237n4
 *See also* Chandler, Raymond; Hammett, Dashiell
hedonism, 40, 45, 54, 63, 80, 81, 186
Heyne, Eric, 80
Hezbollah, 86, 87, 91, 102, 107, 116, 225, 230, 235, 247n3

Highsmith, Patricia, 61, 144, 231
Hinton, Mercedes S., 4, 5, 6, 239n3
Hitchcock, Alfred, 61, 67, 211, 219
Horsley, Lee, xlii, 46, 63, 67, 81, 93, 99, 100, 114, 124, 218, 237n6, 238n1
Hortiguera, Hugo, 242–43n11
human rights, xxi, 4, 86
humor, xxi, xxxii, xxxiii, xxvi, xxxvii, 2, 40, 136, 157, 159, 161, 167, 171, 173, 183
humor, black, xxxiii, 17, 18–19, 133, 142, 167, 225
Hutcheon, Linda, 31, 39–40, 138, 160
hybridity, of crime fiction, x, xi, xxvii, 26, 91, 223, 230

identity, Argentine, xi, xxxi, xli–xlii, 25, 48, 105, 107, 147, 172, 225. *See also* Buenos Aires
immigration to Argentina, xiii, xxxv, 3, 40, 42, 44, 70, 104, 107, 177, 194
intertextuality, 138, 173, 223, 230–32
Iran, as presumed author of terrorist attacks, 85–91, 94–95, 103–4, 107, 108, 111–16, 120, 235, 247n4
irony, xv, xix, xxvii, 26–27, 31, 39–40, 42, 44–45, 60, 99, 121–22, 141, 160–62, 206, 225, 231, 234
Islam, 94, 102, 104, 107. *See also* Muslim
Israeli Embassy, bombing of, xiii, 86, 90, 93–94, 96, 105, 107, 225, 235

Jacovkis, Natalia, 182, 188
Jajamovich, Guillermo, 179, 193
James, P. D., xliii
Jameson, Fredric, xlii, 24, 161, 205, 238n14
Jeanmaire, Federico, xxxiii
Jesus Christ, 26, 45–49, 65, 77. *See also* Christ figure

Jewish Buenos Aires:
  anti-Semitism, 91, 94, 103, 104, 108, 149
  community in Buenos Aires, xiii, xxix, 85–92, 95, 102, 103–8, 225
  immigration to Argentina, 104
journalism:
  compared to nonfictional clash between old and new methods, 168–69
  compared to fictional writing, 169–71
  ethics of, xliii, 54, 83–84, 95–96, 117, 169–71, 200–205, 226
  sensationalism of, xliii, 77, 117, 118–19, 226
  watchdog, xlii, xlv, 51–84, 95, 199, 200–205, 226, 231, 241–42n4, 246n34
  *See also* media; Walsh, Rodolfo; writing, fictional
judiciary, corruption of, 5, 6, 7, 17–18, 28

Kaminsky, Amy, 103, 105
King, Stephen, 161, 232
Kirchner, Néstor, xii, 87–88, 108, 245n29
Knight, Stephen, 13, 40
Kohan, Martin, xxiii
Kokotovic, Misha, xiii
Krimer, María Inés, xxii, xxviii–xxix, 247n12
Kristeva, Julia, 46–47

labyrinth, images of, 69–70
Lacan, Jacques, 211, 214, 216
Lafforgue, Jorge, xviii–xix, xxiii, 221–22
Latham, Sean, 109, 118
le Carré, John, 109–10, 248n14
Lebanon, 101, 102, 104–6, 225
Lehman, Daniel W., 71
Levín, Federico, xxxv

Lezcano, Fabio Nahuel, xxxiv, 54
Lindstrom, Naomi, 91
Link, Daniel, 172
locked room mystery, 124, 139, 174
López, Fernando, xxviii, xxxvi
López-Calvo, Ignacio, 102, 104
love story, xxx, 2. *See also* death
Ludmer, Josefina, xvii
Luján, Marcelo, xxxvii

MacDonald, Ross, 173
mafias, xv, xxxiv, xxxvi, 9, 10, 16, 17, 22, 25–26, 34, 69, 74, 197–98, 199, 201, 202, 205–7, 215, 234, 235, 243n12. *See also* organized crime
male roles:
  bonding among men, 197, 243n12
  fear of loss of control or identity, 62–63, 69, 98–99, 242n10
Mallo, Ernesto, xxviii, xxxi, xliv, 2, 6, 8, 9, 11, 12, 22, 25, 34, 35, 48–49, 55, 227, 231, 238n17, 239n4, 239–40n6, 240n7, 240n8, 245n2
  *Delincuente argentino*, 8–9, 12, 17, 22
  *La aguja en el pajar*, xxiii, 8, 9, 11, 22, 24
  *Los hombres te han hecho mal*, xliv, 1–3, 6–25, 28, 48–49, 197, 224, 227, 228, 229, 230, 233
mapping, xli, 40, 107, 165, 205–8
  of city, xi, xli, 29, 176
  *See also* Buenos Aires
Mar del Plata:
  as vacation site, 6, 23–24
  prostitution trade of, 7, 10–13, 16, 23, 25–26, 227, 240n8
Marcos, Carlos and José María, xxxvi
Maristany, José Javier, xxi
Marlowe, Philip (character), xx, xxxii, xliii–xliv, 22, 34, 58, 63, 82, 231, 238n14

Marsh, Kelly A., 119, 249n24
Martelli, Juan Carlos, xx
Martínez, Guillermo, xxxvii
Martínez, Tomás Eloy, xliv, 55–56, 201, 242n6, 245n30, 246n6
  *El vuelo de la reina*, xliv–xlv, 52, 55–84, 158, 199, 223–24, 226, 228, 229, 231, 234, 241n1, 242n6, 242n8
  *Ficciones verdaderas: Hechos reales que inspiraron grandes obras literarias*, 51–52, 55–56, 71, 80, 84
Martini, Juan Carlos, xx, xxxv, xliv, xlv, 253n4
  *Puerto Apache*, xlv, 175, 176, 179–97, 208, 218, 224, 226–27, 229, 233–34
masculinity:
  as challenged, xlii, 61, 63, 83, 202, 210–11, 228
  of detective genre, xliii, 156, 159–60, 199, 201, 227–28
masochism, 63, 100
Maxfield, James F., 68, 242n7
media, the, xi, xxiv, xxvi, xxx, xli, xliii, 4, 30, 51, 53, 83–84, 90, 92, 116–17, 129, 196, 241–42n4
  ethics of, xxvi–xxvii, xxx, 30, 83, 196, 198, 207
  sensationalization of violence, xxvi, 51, 121, 128
  *See also* journalism
Menem, Carlos Saúl, xi, xii, 2, 4, 241n3, 243n13, 245n29
  allegory of, xxvii–xxviii, 2, 10, 19–21, 25–26, 48
  corruption of, xi, xl, xlv, 10, 51–52, 54, 80–81, 83–84, 86–88, 92, 107, 150, 235, 240n7, 243n12, 244n23, 245n29, 245–46n32
  implementation of neoliberalism, xii, 4, 52–55, 117, 142, 155, 175, 179, 199

as portrayed in *El muerto indiscreto,* 51, 55–57, 71–75, 81, 83, 223–24, 229–30
as portrayed in *El vuelo de la reina,* 51, 55–57, 75–81, 83, 223–24, 229–30
Menemism, Menem era, xxxvii–xxxviii, 2, 10, 26, 51, 55, 80–82, 84, 121, 184, 185, 242–43n11
mestizaje, 27, 37, 44–45
metadetective fiction, xix
metafictional strategies, xi, 160–67, 172, 173, 223, 230–33. *See also* mise en abyme; metalepsis
metalepsis, 146, 166–67, 231, 232
metatextuality, 138–39, 166
Mexico:
  drug cartels from, 3, 11, 15, 129, 134, 225
  literature from, x, xvi, xliv, 225, 227
Miami:
  as place for the corrupt, 69, 191–92
  as setting, 62–63, 69, 73–74, 78, 152, 184
Miller, D. A., 111–12
mise en abyme, 60, 131, 166–67, 223, 231, 232
misogyny:
  defiance toward, 156
  of characters, 60, 61–69, 136
  of detective genre, 38, 67, 69, 83, 100, 136, 156, 228
Mitchum, Robert, 59, 60, 65, 83, 231
Molfino, Miguel Ángel, xxxvi
money laundering, 3, 54, 58, 69, 74, 129, 141, 235, 244n23, 246n34
Moret, Natalia, xxix
mother:
  as character in novel, xxxiv, 16, 37, 64, 70, 101, 157, 184, 196, 204, 206
  as "bad," 24, 25, 66–67, 68, 70, 83, 123, 234

as "good," 61, 67–68, 196
blaming of, 66–67, 242n9
Muslim, 96, 101, 103, 105, 107. *See also* Islam
mysticism, mystic visions, 76–77, 231

narcotrade. *See* trafficking; drugs
narratorial intrusion, 102, 162, 164, 166
Negro Absoluto collection, xxix, xxxi, xxxv, xxxvi
neoliberal noir, xiv, 133
neoliberalism, x, xi–xiv, xxiv, xxxviii, xxv, 52–55, 107, 117, 123–27, 150, 151, 176, 199, 237n2
  adoption of in Argentina, xi–xii, 52–54
  and deindustrialization, xii, 177
  and fragmentation, xli, 103, 180, 193, 224, 233
  and privatization, xii, xl, xli, xlii, 52, 54, 62, 125, 126, 157, 175, 176, 178, 179, 180, 224, 237n3, 241n2, 245–46n32
  critique of, xxvii, xl, 54–55, 103, 107, 155, 181–82, 186, 229, 237n2
  "winners" and "losers" of, 54, 122, 124, 125, 167, 172, 175–76, 179, 181, 185, 188, 191, 224
  *See also* Puerto Madero; Menem, Carlos
Néspolo, Matías, xxxiii–xxxiv
*Night of the Hunter,* 60, 83, 231
Nisman, Alberto, xlv, 85, 87–89, 118–19, 246n1, 247n4, 247n6, 248n15, 248n17, 248n18, 249n25
  as portrayed in *El fiscal,* 90, 108–20, 230, 248n17
  theories of death, 85, 89, 109, 110, 113–16, 230, 248n19
nonfiction, xxvi, xxxiv, 51–52, 57, 71, 80, 90, 129, 170–71, 232, 242–43n11

as opposed or compared to fiction, 51–52, 79–80, 169, 170–73, 232–33
  *See also* Capote, Truman; fiction; Walsh, Rodolfo
Nonnenmacher, Hartmut, 230
*novela negra*, defined, xv–xvi

Olguín, Sergio, x, xxxi, xxxv, xxxix, xliv, 175–76, 197–98, 238n17
  *La fragilidad de los cuerpos*, xlv, 175–76, 197–219, 224, 226, 228, 234, 254n13
Oliver, Kelly, 211, 218
organized crime, xv, xxxiv, xliv, 1–49, 54, 86, 168, 189, 197, 223, 230. *See also* trafficking
Orsi, Guillermo, xxiii, xxxi, xl, xliv, 1–2
  *Ciudad Santa*, xliv, 1–2, 3, 5, 6, 26–49, 197, 225, 227, 228, 231, 233, 241n14
Osorio, Elsa, xxiii, xxix
Osorio, Myriam, 66, 242n8
Oyola, Leonardo, xxxv

Padura Fuentes, Leonardo, 237n5
Page, Joanna, xxiv, xxvi, 238n12
*Página/12*, 57, 83, 117, 241–42n4
Palestine, 90, 91, 92, 94, 101–2, 105, 107
panoptic, 66, 111
parable or morality tale, xxviii, xxxviii, 47, 131, 141
Paraguay, 3, 62, 69, 73, 74, 107
paranoia, xxi, xxiv–xxv, 61, 109, 111, 253n4
paranoiac fiction, xxi, xxiv
parody, xiv, xix, xx, 39–40, 77, 160–62, 173, 225, 231, 252n23
  defined, 39
Parys, Jodi, 242n5
Paszkowski, Diego, xxxviii
Pellicer, Rosa, 230

Pérez, Genaro J., xvi
Perón, Juan Domingo, xix, 52, 55, 57, 199
Piglia, Ricardo, xv, xix, xx–xxi, xxiii, xxiv–xxvii, 10, 82, 133–34, 221, 238n12
Pignatiello, Gerardo, 237n7
Pihlainen, Kalle, 171
Piñeiro, Claudia, ix, xxv, xxviii, xliv, 122–23, 174, 201, 228–29, 252n23
  *Betibú*, xxv, xxviii, xlv, 122, 123, 141, 156–73, 197, 199, 224, 226, 228, 229, 231–32, 233, 251n13, 252n23
  *Las viudas de los jueves*, xxviii, xlv, 122, 123, 124–25, 142–56, 172, 173, 190, 224, 227–28, 231, 232, 233, 234, 251n13, 253n23
*pista iraní*, 86, 91, 107, 108, 115
*pista siria*, 86, 87, 91, 109, 115
Plante, Alicia, xxx
Poe, Edgar Allan, 139, 231, 251n10
police:
  Bonaerense, 4, 18, 32, 57–58, 87, 93–94, 129, 154, 197
  as complicit with organized crime, 1, 4–6, 7, 9, 10–12, 17–19, 25–26, 27, 87, 91, 93, 94–95, 158, 168, 173, 203, 204, 240n12
  role during dictatorship, 4, 8, 9, 28, 29, 31, 32–33, 237, 239–40n6
  esprit de corps of, 5, 32
  as ethical, 2, 7, 11–12, 22–23, 25–26, 28, 48, 223, 227, 233
  extrajudicial killings by, 5, 28, 32
  Federal Police (PFA), 2, 4, 7, 28, 29–30, 32–33, 34, 35, 48, 154, 193, 239–40n6
  rackets of, 5, 6, 18, 19, 28, 204
  reform of, 5–6
  as "trigger happy" (*gatillo fácil*), 4, 5, 30, 197–98

*policial palimpséstico*, viii, 129–30, 229
popular fiction, 26, 158, 219
pornography, xxxv, 202, 214, 254n13
Porter, Dennis, 159, 240n11
postcolonial critique, 28, 44
postmodernism, xxi, 28, 161
Pratt, Mary Louise, 44
Pratt, R. S. (pseudonym of undisclosed Argentine author), xliv, xlv, 86, 90–91, 120
*El fiscal*, xiv, 86, 90, 91, 108–20, 226, 227, 229, 230, 246n2, 248n23
Premat, Julio, xxvii, 238n12
Priestman, Martin, 93, 124
privatization. *See under* neoliberalism
*Proceso*. *See* dictatorship in Argentina, 1976–1983
prostitution, xxx, xli, 6, 7, 11–18, 23, 28, 111, 112, 113, 118, 176, 185, 186, 198, 201, 208, 229, 231, 240n8
psychoanalytic reading of text, 211–17
psychological thriller, xxix, xxxviii, 122
psychopath, 7, 46, 81, 82
Puerto Madero as symbol of urban renewal, 42, 43, 117–18, 175, 179, 180, 187, 190–91, 193, 224
Puig, Manuel, xx

racism, 28, 37, 41, 44–45, 149
Rama, Ángel, xli, 222
rape, xxii, 37, 44, 59, 64, 82, 101, 137
  of men, 158, 160
realism, xxxix, 1–2, 10–11, 233, 251n16
*Rear Window*, 61, 231
Reddy, Maureen T., xliii
redemption, 46, 47–48, 154–55, 216, 225, 196. *See also* salvation
Reserva Ecológica Costanera Sur, xxx, 175, 179–81, 189, 193, 252n2

Rivera, Jorge, xviii, xviii, xix, xxiii
Rocha, Carolina, 147, 155, 252n19
Rodríguez Pérsico, Adriana, 238n12
Rolón, Gabriel, xxxix
roman à clef, xxxiv, 71, 91, 109, 118–20, 230, 248–49n23, 249n24
Romero, Ricardo, xxxv–xxxvi
Rosende, Mercedes, xxxi
Roth, Marty, xliii, 21–22, 38, 98
Ryan, Marie-Laure, xxxix, 172
Rzepka, Charles J., xv

Saccomanno, Guillermo, xxi, xxxiii, 158
Sacheri, Eduardo, xxi–xxii
sadism, xix, 2, 14, 17, 31, 63
sadomasochism, 62, 200, 208, 211–17, 219
Sadow, Stephen A., 92, 95, 247n8
Saer, Juan José, xxii, 242n9
Salem, Carlos, xxxvii, xxxix
salvation, 46–48, 123
Sarlo, Beatriz, xli, xlii, 109, 118–19, 126, 141–42
Sasturain, Juan, xxi, xxix, xxxi–xxxii
satire, 26, 31, 34, 39, 40, 157
Scaggs, John, xv, 39, 40, 93, 124
scandals, political, xxxiv, xlii, 30, 52, 53–55, 56–60, 65, 71–72, 75–76, 77, 82, 83–84, 118, 226, 234, 245n26
Schmid, David Frank, 237n2
Secretaria de Inteligencia de Estado (SIDE), 87, 89, 94–98, 111–12, 114–16, 247n3, 248n15
seduction:
  of consumerism, 181, 189
  by female characters, 37, 46, 63, 94, 97, 98, 99, 106, 159, 228, 234, 242n10
  of the reader, xvii, 56, 58, 60, 219
Seed, David, 109, 114
self-reference, as trait of detective fiction, 160, 173, 230

INDEX    291

sensationalism, xxvii, 13–15, 17, 117, 122, 127, 226. See also media, the
sentimental action hero, 7, 22, 35
sentimentalism, xliii–xliv, 2, 6–10, 21–26, 48–49, 58, 159, 162, 233–35
Seri, Guillermina, 175–77, 208
Serpico, as model of honest policeman, 135, 139, 231
Setton, Román, xviii
sexuality, xxxvi, xliii, xlviii, 21, 22, 38, 63, 66, 136, 201–2, 217, 228
  exploitation of, 96–97, 100
shantytowns. See *villas miseria*
Sheinin, David M. K., 52–54, 88, 116, 247, 248n4
Sietecase, Reynaldo, xxi, xxxii, xl
Silvestri, Graciela, 176, 180
simulacra, 46, 76
Sinay, Javier, xxxiv
Sinay, Sergio, xx
Soriano, Osvaldo, xx
Spain, xxxvii, 2, 122
  literature from, ix, xxxiv, xxxvii, xliv, 55, 110, 122, 158, 236n4
spy novel, 109, 110, 113–14, 116, 119, 120
Stiuso, Antonio, 87, 88, 89, 248n15, 248n19
  as portrayed in *El fiscal*, 109–20, 248n17
storytelling, xxiv, xxvi–xxvii, 167
Sue, Eugène, 158, 252n20
suicide, 30, 69, 78, 123, 147, 153–54, 216, 234
  and the railroad, 197, 200, 207, 209, 215–16, 217, 218
  suspicious, 59, 76, 85, 89, 110, 113, 114, 116, 164, 244n26, 246n1
suicide bomber, 90, 92, 99, 100–102, 107, 247n3

supernatural, the, xxxv, xxxix, 2, 111, 251n16
surplus enjoyment (*plus-de-jouir*), 214, 216, 219
surveillance, 3, 66, 111–12. See also panoptic
suspense, ix, xv, xxiii, xxxvi, xxxix, 1, 7, 57, 58, 61, 93, 123, 153, 155, 163, 172, 214, 217–19
Svampa, Maristella, xlii, 121, 125, 126–27
Swanson, Philip, xxi, 238n9
Syria, 86, 87, 91, 101, 235. See also *pista siria*
Syrian origin of Menem, 72, 107

Taibo II, Paco Ignacio, xvi, xliv, 227
tango, 12, 27, 41, 43, 56
Terranova, Juan, xxxvii
territorialization, 222–33, 234
*testimonio*, defined, 100–101
thriller, defined, 93
Tizziani, Rubén, xx
Todorov, Tzvetan, xv
Tozzi, Liliana, 185, 187
trafficking, 1, 2–6
  of arms, 54, 58, 59, 75–76, 84, 87, 243n21, 244n23, 244n25, 244–45n26, 245n29
  of drugs, xxiii, xliv, 15, 27, 37–38, 39, 48, 92, 106, 110, 122, 129, 181, 185–86, 189, 192, 223, 225, 226, 233, 243n21, 253n3
  failings of enforcement against, x, xi, 2, 3, 9, 28–34
  human, xi, xxviii, xxx, xxxi, xliv, 2–3, 6–26, 205, 223, 227, 229, 233, 238–39n2, 240n10, 240n12. See also prostitution
  war among cartels, 1, 3, 29–31, 134
transculturation, 222, 231, 234
Trigo, Benigno, 211, 218
true crime, xix, 26, 121, 127, 129, 132, 142, 169, 242n6

United States:
  9/11 attacks on, 108, 114, 120, 150, 248n13
  influence on Argentine culture, 192
  crime fiction and film of, x, xv, xxiv, 54, 60, 222, 248–49n23
  influence in Argentine economic policy, xii, 53, 107, 237n3
  role in Argentine politics, 54, 88, 108, 114–16, 117, 247n4
urban collapse sub-genre, 40, 48. *See also* apocalypse
urban poor, xlv, 13, 19–21, 54, 125–27, 134, 149, 175–219, 253n3
  as "collateral damage," xlii, 179–97
  changing views toward, 177

Varela, Luis V., xviii
Vázquez Montalbán, Manuel, xliv, 159, 222
Vázquez, Luciana, 51, 80–81, 241n3, 243n12, 245n31
Vázquez-Rial, Horacio, xxii
Verbitsky, Horacio, 241n2, 245–46n32
verisimilitude, xxxiii, 18, 26, 104, 108
victim:
  blamed, 136–37
  female, xxii, xxx, xxxi, xliii, 12–13, 21, 23, 38, 64, 68, 82, 127–42, 159, 160, 196, 224, 249–50n3
Vidal, Hernán, 101
*villas miseria*, xiii, 177, 178–79, 252–53n2, 253n3
  as complementary to gated communities, 126, 140, 180
  as setting, xxxv, xli, 20, 39, 43–44, 107, 179–94, 198, 206–8, 209, 224, 226
*villero*:
  as resentful of gated community residents, 140
  as stigmatized, 140, 177, 188–89, 191, 193, 198
Voionmaa, Daniel Noemi, 227

Waisbord, Silvio, 54, 83–84, 241–42n4, 246n34
Walger, Sylvina, 73, 74, 80, 241n3, 243n13
Walsh, Rodolfo, xviii, xix, xxiii, 230, 252n26
  as model of investigative or revolutionary journalism, xix, xlii, 56–57, 71, 82–83, 169–71, 226, 231
Wassner, Dalia, 247n7
watchdog journalism. *See* journalism
welfare programs, xii, 4, 54, 176, 189
White, Hayden, xiv, 90
Willett, Ralph, 40
Wornat, Olga, 76, 77, 78, 241n3, 243n13, 243n19, 244n23
Worthington, Heather, xliii, 97, 124, 238n16
writing:
  as exorcism, 162, 252n23
  fictional compared to nonfictional, 51–52, 79–80, 169, 170–73, 232
  thematization of, xxvi, xxxviii, 130, 161, 162–67, 232–33
  *See also* fiction

youth:
  as hope for the future, 154, 173
  as juvenile delinquents, xxxiii–xxxiv, 7, 23, 32, 181
  true crime about, xxxiv, 102
  as victims, xxxiii–xxxiv, 23, 32, 181, 198, 200, 203–7, 216
  of *villas*, 206–8

Zimmerman, Mark, 101
Žižek, Slavoj, 211, 214, 216

www.ingramcontent.com/pod-product-compliance
Lightning Source LLC
Chambersburg PA
CBHW071827230426
43672CB00013B/2782